ADVENTURING IN HOME LIVING

BOOK 2

ADVENTURING IN

Book

2

Home Living

BY

HAZEL M. HATCHER

Professor, Home Economics Education and Home-Community Relations
The Pennsylvania State University

AND

MILDRED E. ANDREWS

Homemaker and Child Guidance Specialist

ILLUSTRATED BY ALICE FREEMAN

D. C. HEATH AND COMPANY
BOSTON

Library of Congress Catalog Card Number
54-8481

Preface

Adventuring in Home Living, Book 2 is a basal text for boys and girls in homemaking classes, similar in form and content to Book 1. One of its chief values to teachers lies in the easy transition which is made from the level of learning in Book 1 to that of a higher level in this book. This means that the students and the teacher who start out in Book 1 in the various areas, such as child development or foods, can progress easily and naturally, without undue repetition, to the more advanced study of these areas in Book 2. In fact, the material in the two books is so thoroughly integrated that no time need be spent trying to make one book fit in with the other.

It also seemed important to develop Book 2 in terms of the three goals used in Book 1 — to offer a basal text that students will enjoy, to exemplify teaching procedures that are educationally sound, and to write at an optimum reading level for young people.

In offering a book that students will enjoy, the authors adapted the material in so far as possible to the type of textbook that boys and girls in middle adolescence seem to prefer. It is hoped that the book will prove to be as stimulating and interesting to young people as Book 1 has been.

The cooperative teaching procedures developed in Book 1 are continued in this book. They involve student-teacher participation in planning, setting up, and carrying out class goals which are based on the students' personal and family problems. The students are encouraged to clarify these goals in terms of their own behavior — that is, how it is hoped they will think, feel, and act about the problems. This leads to the planning of school and home experiences that will help to achieve the desired results. Generalizations and information relating to the goals are assembled as the experiences are being carried out. Emphasis is placed on self-evaluation in attaining the goals through procedures developed cooperatively by the students and the teacher. The authors believe that whereas Book 1 has facilitated the work of teachers who do cooperative planning, or has encouraged other teachers to try this procedure, Book 2 will be equally helpful in increasing the quality of classroom teaching.

The reading level of the book is slightly higher than that of Book 1, and coincides with the anticipated development in knowledge and understanding of growing adolescents. The informal or personal approach, which implies the use of fairly short sentences that can be easily understood, has also been used in this book, though to a lesser degree than in Book 1. But all of the material is expressed in terms commensurate with the reading comprehension of young people at this stage of their development.

The authors wish to acknowledge the helpful suggestions given by faculty members and graduate students in the College of Home Economics at the Pennsylvania State University. We are especially grateful to Mrs. Christine F. Salmon for her excellent suggestions on the material in Chapter 4, and to Dr. Katherine H. Fisher and Dr. Mary P. Shelton — formerly on the staff — for checking the chart on Essential Food Nutrients, pages 96 to 99, and the Chart of Fiber Characteristics and Fabric Care, pages 372 to 373, respectively. The book has greatly benefited from the constructive help and inspiration they have given us.

HAZEL M. HATCHER
MILDRED E. ANDREWS

Acknowledgments

Grateful acknowledgment is made to the following sources for their kind permission to reproduce illustrations in *Adventuring in Home Living*, Book 2.

PAGE

7 *Practical Home Economics*, photograph by Dickey Meyer

15, 37 (lower), 43, 61 (upper), 453, 459 H. Armstrong Roberts

19 Louise B. Van der Meid

37 (upper) Household Finance Corporation

37 (center) *Practical Home Economics* and Institute of Life Insurance

60 (left), 73 (center) Lew Merrim from Monkmeyer Press Photograph Service

60 (right) Gouda Cheese

61 (center) Corn Products Refining Company

61 (lower), 162, 246 (upper left), 347, 436, 456 *Teen Times*

73 (upper) Carter Products, Inc.

73 (lower), 123 Campbell Soup Company

82, 100 Sealtest Kitchens

91 National Canners Association

114, 115, 116, 117, 170 National Live Stock and Meat Board

131, 132, 370, 374, 377, 378, 379, 380, 384 (right), 385, 386, 387 United States Department of Agriculture photographs

153 Bavinco Manufacturing Corporation

175 (left) Lawry's Products, Inc.

175 (right), 181 (lower), 184, 185 Corning Glass Works

176, 177 Birds Eye Frosted Foods

179 *What's New in Home Economics*

181 (upper) National Cranberry Association

188 Arvin Industries, Inc.

189, 376, 485 Gerber Baby Foods

191 (upper 3) General Foods Kitchens

191 (lower), 192 (right) Wesson Oil and Snowdrift Company

192 (left) Pillsbury Mills, Inc.

194 (upper 2), 261, 266, 267, 271, 275, 276 *Better Homes and Gardens* magazine

194 (lower) Poultry and Egg National Board

196 Standard Brands

246 (upper right) National Foundation for Infantile Paralysis

246 (center) Shellfoto

246 (lower left) Church and Dwight, photograph by Shigeta-Wright

246 (lower right) National Pressure Cooker Company

263 (upper), 272 Lightolier, Inc.

263 (lower) Lenox, Inc.

264 (upper), 264 (lower right) *American Fabrics*

PAGE

264 (lower left) Knoll Associates

302 *Forecast* and Evelyn Henshaw, Hedgesville High School, Hedgesville, West Virginia

327 *Forecast* and Wylma Cunningham, San Rafael High School, San Rafael, California

359 Curtis Publishing Company and Trumansburg Central School, Trumansburg, New York

384 (left) Cluett, Peabody, and Company

388, 389 Berkshire Knitting Mills

404, 426, 431 Simplicity Pattern Company

416 *Practical Home Economics* and Frances Tacionis, Florida State University, Tallahassee, Florida

439 Photograph by Harold M. Lambert

441, 445 Arizona Association, Future Homemakers of America

443 Orlando from Three Lions

452, 466 Don Knight

458 United States Office of Education

483 Fruit Dispatch Company

488 *Practical Home Economics* and Monrovia City Schools, Monrovia, California

Especially grateful acknowledgment is made to the following sources for their kind permission to reproduce illustrations appearing in the color inserts of this book.

Facing pages 86 and 87, between 166–167 (left) Campbell Soup Company

Facing page 118 Owens-Illinois

Facing page 119 St. Charles Manufacturing Company

Facing page 166 National Cranberry Association

Between pages 166–167 (upper right) Abbott Laboratories, (lower right) Cling Peach Advisory Board

Facing page 167 Pan-American Coffee Bureau

Facing page 262 Dow Chemical Company

Between pages 262–263 Imperial Paper and Color Corporation

Facing page 263 Pittsburgh Plate Glass Company

Facing page 454 Field Enterprises

Between pages 454–455 (left) Simoniz Company, (right) Consoweld Corporation

Facing page 455 Syracuse China Corporation

Contents

ADVENTURING IN HOME LIVING

BOOK 2

Accent on Families

Learning to understand myself and others

Getting along with my family

*Cooperating with the family
on money matters*

Having dates

Helping with family entertainment

Feeling at home when away from home

THE HOMEMAKING ROOM in the John Hunter High School was buzzing with excitement. Everyone seemed to be talking at the same time. Several students bent over a newspaper spread out on one of the tables. Another group with heads together was reading aloud from a clipping.

As Miss Corey, the homemaking teacher, waited for the final bell to ring, she realized that something unusual had happened. She guessed that it concerned Monica Fenton, a student who had been missing from Boydsville for several days. And she was right.

"They found Monica!" said Tom, waving the clipping excitedly. "She was wandering around the city, but she didn't know who or where she was. The newspaper said it was a case of amnesia, whatever that is."

"Oh, that's when you forget who you are," explained Ellen. "The report said that it was several days before the doctor found out her real name."

"I don't understand it," said Bruce. "What makes a person act that way? The newspaper said that Monica ran away from home because she was having trouble with her family. Could that make her forget who she was?"

"Yes, it might," replied Miss Corey. "Monica was probably very much disturbed. And when people become emotionally upset, they do strange things."

"What do you think was the matter?" asked Roy, looking toward Miss Corey.

"Well, it could have been any one of a number of things," she replied. 'The early- and mid-teen years is the period when young people are striving to become independent and to stand on their own two feet. The process of maturing — learning to become self-sufficient and to take on responsibility — gives rise to a number of problems, some more serious than others. Monica's situation is probably more unusual than are any of your problems."

"Such as making our parents realize that we're old enough to decide things for ourselves," suggested Grace.

"Or that it's time to ease up on rules and regulations that may have been necessary in our younger days," said John.

Miss Corey nodded. "It takes understanding on both sides to realize how necessary independence is, and to decide the degree to which it can be granted," she added.

GETTING STARTED ON THE CLASSWORK

"WE'VE already made plans to include understanding our families as part of our classwork for this year," said Ellen. "I'd like to get started on it and see what can be done."

"So would I," echoed others.

"I agree too," said Paul, "but I'd also like to know more about myself and why I do what I do. This might help me to understand why other people, like Monica, for example, behave as they do."

"Perhaps I'd find out why my brother and I have so much difficulty getting along," added Roy.

"You have two goals right there that would make a good beginning for this part of our classwork," said Miss Corey.

"Then we can start with *learning to understand myself and others?*" asked Paul.

"And the other goal could be *getting along with my family,*" said Roy.

There were affirmative nods from the rest of the class.

"It's going to take us quite a while to carry out our ideas on these two problems," said Michael. "Can't we decide on other important matters relating to the family as the classwork progresses?"

"I've been trying to think of an appropriate name for our classwork," said Mary. "What about 'Accent on Families'? That could cover everything we might want to include about our families."

Since Mary's suggestion was generally approved by the others, the name was accepted without further comment.

Before the closing bell rang, several students volunteered to help Miss Corey assemble books and pamphlets for the reference shelves. Other students were urged to bring in any material that might be helpful. From the interest that had already been shown, Miss Corey believed there would be some lively discussions as the classwork got under way.

UNDERSTANDING MYSELF AND OTHERS

WHEN the students began to discuss *understanding myself and others,* they decided to find out why people feel and behave as they do. In doing this, they would consider the good points which people have as well as their faults. And they would try to be frank and open-minded in all of their discussions.

What Makes Us as We Are

At this point Miss Corey reminded the class that "To Be or Not to Be" studied last year had some bearing on the subject. (See Book 1, pages 67–124.)

"Oh, yes," said Paul. "That was

on personality, wasn't it? I remember that we learned it's important for us to have friends. And we also learned some ways to make and keep friends."

"We learned a lot about manners and how to talk with people we meet," added Grace.

"The part on understanding ourselves helped me to overcome some of my clumsiness," said Roy.

"Yes, and we learned not to call unfavorable attention to ourselves," added Sarah, "but to have acceptable ways of expressing ourselves."

"We also talked about people who worry a lot, who lack self-

confidence, and who feel insecure," said Mark. "That helped me in more ways than one. But there's still a lot I don't understand about myself and others. I think we need to know what makes people feel secure or insecure, self-confident or not self-confident."

Raising questions about personality

"Then I think we'll have to learn more about personality," said Paul. "People use the word all the time, but if they are like myself, they don't really understand what it means."

"Some people seem to have lots of personality, while others don't appear to have any," said Carla.

"I don't believe that anybody is totally lacking in personality," explained Miss Corey. "Some people have more pleasing personalities than others, that's all."

These remarks, along with various questions, led to a decision to learn more about personality. The subject seemed to be so closely related to understanding oneself and others that it appeared important to find out the answers to the following questions:

- What is personality?
- When do we begin having it?
- How long does it continue?
- Can it be changed?
- Where do we get it from?
- What is the ideal personality?

Finding the answers to the questions on personality

The students consulted references, conferred with various people, and got information wherever they could on their questions dealing with personality. Finally, after a lively discussion and with the assistance of Miss Corey, they set up the answers to the questions as shown on page 8.

PERSONALITY Personality is the total person. It takes in all of us — how we look, how we feel, and how we act.

STARTS It begins to take shape soon after we are born.

CONTINUES It continues to develop as long as we live.

CHANGES By the time we reach the teen years, we have acquired certain personality traits. This is a good time to find out whether we want to keep these traits, or to change them. The older we become, the more difficult it is to change our personality.

FROM WHENCE Our personality is determined by many factors all related to one another. We are the result of the physical and mental capacities we inherit — which is called "heredity" — and the influences that surround us — which is called "environment."

We inherit physical characteristics, such as body build, our features, and the color of our eyes, hair, and skin. Our mental capacity, which is our ability to learn, is also part of our inheritance. But the important thing to remember is this. It isn't what we inherit that determines our personality. It is how we use what we have.

Our family, our friends, our school, and the community in which we live make up our environment. The most important influence on our personality is our family. It is while we live in the family group that we mold many of our personality traits.

PERSONALITY+ = Personality at its best is the ideal self each of us would like to be. It includes good health, the ability to get along with others, and being liked by them. Feeling self-confident and knowing that we can accomplish things is also part of the picture. All of these things build up security, which means feeling comfortable inside ourselves, with our family, our friends, and in our everyday life.

If we are this kind of person, it is largely because we have lived in a family that has made us feel that we are part of them, that we are loved and accepted for what we are. Through their guidance, we have learned to distinguish between what is considered "right" or "wrong." Feeling at ease with our family has helped us to make friends and to get along with other people. Having a sympathetic and understanding family has built up our self-confidence. We feel secure, able to meet our problems, and to resolve them in ways that are satisfactory to us and acceptable to our family and friends.

PERSONALITY— = At the other extreme, we may be a person who has grown up in a family that has not given us enough affection. If we feel unwanted at home, we are apt to be ill at ease in a group of people. We tend to think that they do not want us either. If members of our family do not get along well together, it may be difficult for us to learn how to be sociable and to make friends. Instead we become worried, down in the dumps, perhaps irritable and hostile. We feel unsure of ourselves and insecure.

PERSONALITY+ and — = Most of us fall between these two types. We are successful in attaining our ideal self in some things but not in others. With teen-agers, it is normal to feel insecure at times. Every age has its problems. We need to face them and try to resolve them satisfactorily if we hope to attain the ideal personality for ourselves.

CLASS MEMO:
What questions about personality would your class like to answer?

How People Meet Their Problems

As the students studied the answers to their questions, John offered a suggestion. "I think we need to find out how we can become the kind of person we want to be," he said. "But I don't quite know how to go about doing this."

"We could find out how various people act when they have problems," suggested Ellen. "Then perhaps we could see what will help us and what we need to avoid." Ellen looked toward Miss Corey.

"That would be a good plan," Miss Corey said. "In fact, last year a friend of mine was in an adult class that took much the same approach. They set up brief descriptions of undesirable and desirable behavior with illustrations of each. You might find it helpful to discuss some of the descriptions the adult class used. Then instead of taking

their examples, you could give some from your own experience."

This suggestion made an instant appeal to everyone in the class. Plans were made to put some of the descriptions of behavior on the blackboard for everyone to study. The students then gave illustrations which seemed to apply to the different situations. Since other classes may be interested in this same approach to the study of behavior, a summary of the classwork carried out by Miss Corey's group is given in the chart on pages 10 to 13.

CLASS MEMO:
What illustrations of desirable and undesirable behavior have you and members of your class observed?

UNDESIRABLE BEHAVIOR	ILLUSTRATIONS
Feeling sorry for yourself and telling your troubles to anyone who will listen	A boy I know is always getting into trouble. He keeps complaining that it's just his own hard luck. Whenever he's with a group of people, he begins talking about his difficulties. He takes it for granted that everyone is interested in them. And he acts hurt if you don't sympathize with him.
Letting yourself daydream too much and too often, so that it interferes with your daily work	Last quarter my older brother, who is a good student, failed in physics, a subject in which he has always been interested. My parents were disturbed and talked with his teacher. He said that Dick seemed to be losing interest in physics. During class he had a far-away look on his face and didn't take part in any of the discussions. He seemed to be living in a dream world.
Indulging in fantasies and building castles in the air that have nothing to do with real life as you live it	My brother Dick said that some of his daydreams were in the realm of fantasy. They included giving talks before the United Nations where he received overwhelming applause. At one time he fancied that he developed a cure for cancer, but his exposure to radioactivity resulted in his early death.
Losing control of your emotions when things go wrong or when you meet a difficult situation	I once saw a boy who was so mad when he learned he failed a test that he couldn't speak. He took his paper, tore it into shreds, and threw it into the wastebasket. He didn't even go over the questions to see which ones he missed.
	My sister wore a new dress to school one day, which made her look stunning. All of her friends admired it, but one of them remarked that another girl was wearing a dress just like it. My sister was so angry she couldn't reply. On the way upstairs, she stepped on the hem of the dress, which ripped the stitching at the waist. This gave her an excuse to go home and change her dress, which she never wore again. Now the dress is mine. That's how I happened to know about the incident.
Alibiing; using plausible but not real reasons to explain or justify what you are doing	One day my young brother forgot to pick up some groceries on his way home. He told my mother he was kept after school, and he thought she would want him to come home first. I think that was only an excuse for forgetting the groceries.

GROUP STUDIED BEHAVIOR

DESIRABLE BEHAVIOR	ILLUSTRATIONS
Discussing your troubles with someone who knows you well and has your interests at heart	A senior boy I know used to get himself into lots of trouble because of his quick temper. He talked over the problem with the school counselor who helped him work out some safeguards for blowing his top, as he calls it. He tells me it's now much easier for him to get along with himself and others.
Learning to snap out of it when dreaming interferes with your everyday activities	During an interview with the guidance counselor, Dick admitted that he had been daydreaming. As the work became more difficult, it seemed easier to imagine himself a great atomic scientist than to buckle down to learning how to become one. Dick agreed to snap out of it and to pay attention to what was going on in class.
Realizing that fantasies and castles in the air are generally a waste of time	After talking with his counselor, Dick realized that his fantasies about being a great scientist did not really inspire him. They were only a waste of time. In the future he's going to face hard work and keep his feet on the ground and his head out of the clouds.
Learning to control your emotions when things go wrong or you meet a difficult situation	For several weeks my oldest sister had been looking forward to a week-end house party. She bought some attractive clothes for the occasion and even had a new permanent. Then shortly before she was to leave, she sprained her ankle and couldn't go. I knew she was disappointed. Who wouldn't be? Most people would cry their eyes out. But my sister took it in her stride. She joked about being laid up, saying this was one way of getting an unexpected vacation from the office. And she even loaned her new sports coat to one of the girls going to the house party.
Admitting the real reasons for what you do; facing the music	The other day I was discussing a recent dance with one of my friends. I noticed that he had left the dance early; so I asked whether anything had been wrong. He hesitated before replying. Finally he said, "I could tell you that I was ill, but I'm not going to. The truth is that I'm a clumsy dancer and have trouble getting a partner. After three girls turned me down, I was too embarrassed to stay any longer."

UNDESIRABLE BEHAVIOR	ILLUSTRATIONS
Blaming another person or thing for your troubles or shortcomings	I know a girl who blames her teachers for her low marks. She is a slow reader and claims this is due to a poor teacher she had in the second grade. She also says that she never learned to understand fractions. That year her regular teacher was ill off and on, and the substitute teacher didn't explain things very well.
Resorting to childish behavior; doing things without stopping to think of the consequences	I read in the paper about several students who created a disturbance in class. They talked loudly, scuffed their feet, and threw spitballs. The teacher, who was inexperienced, sent the students to the principal's office. Later that afternoon, the teacher's car went out of control, and she was seriously hurt. It developed that a smoke bomb had been put in her car as a practical joke by these same students.
Feeling inferior or unworthy; worrying about not doing well; being afraid to face people; trying to cover up your real or imagined limitations	One Sunday at church, my chum and I were introduced to an attractive girl. We asked her to come to our Youth Group meetings, but she said she was too busy. Later on we learned that her mother was a widow, and the girl did not have as many of the things other girls had. She did not think she had suitable clothes to go out socially. She also refused to accept invitations to parties, because she felt that she couldn't entertain the same way her friends did.
Feeling superior; wanting to do something better than anyone else; always trying to be in the limelight	There's a very attractive girl living next door to my aunt. She's the center of attention wherever she goes. My aunt says that Gloria expects to be voted the most popular and best-looking girl in her class. Not long ago Gloria boasted that she could cut in on any date and get the boy more interested in her than in his girl friend.
Trying to overcome a physical or mental handicap in a way pleasing to you, but offering a small chance of success	My cousin knows a girl with a crippled foot who talks about becoming a great dancer. At college she studied physical education. One summer she supervised a children's playground. At the end of the summer she was very unhappy. She had not been able to keep up with the children. And they, in turn, had not seemed to adjust to her crippled foot.
Imagining that you have the same qualities as those of people you admire; adopting their mannerisms or style of dress without considering whether or not they fit your personality	There's a girl in the town where my cousin lives nicknamed Hollywood Jane. Right now she's trying to look and act like a certain well-known actress. She adopts the same hairdo and tries to make her voice low and husky. She even wears tight, slinky dresses. If Jane only realized how superficial these imitations are, she'd stop such a silly impersonation.

DESIRABLE BEHAVIOR	ILLUSTRATIONS
Placing the blame for your troubles or shortcomings where it belongs	My chum, who is interested in dramatics, has tried several times to get in school plays and failed each time. "I guess I'm simply not good enough yet," she says. "But I will be one of these days. You just watch and see."
Behaving like a mature person; showing consideration for others; thinking of the consequences before you act	Last winter my cousin's class won the championship in basketball. Some of the members were all for painting the school red to celebrate. But the class president did some fast thinking. He got the class together and gave them a wonderful talk about not doing anything childish or foolish. Then he arranged to have a party with refreshments then and there. The next day the principal congratulated the class for being such good sports and showing such mature behavior.
Turning your attention outward away from yourself; learning to build up self-confidence by constant effort	I used to be afraid to speak before an audience. Every time I tried to say something my knees shook, my mouth got dry, and I forgot what I wanted to say. Realizing that I needed to overcome this feeling or it would hamper me all my life, I began to speak every chance I got. I popped up in class meetings — without giving myself a chance to think — saying only a few words. Gradually my fears began to drop away.
Feeling that you can do something well without being conceited about it; getting pleasure by competing with your own record; being able to hold your own wherever you are	Last quarter, much to my surprise and delight, I got a high mark in English. But I wasn't at all sure that I deserved it. This next quarter I'm going to work hard on my English. And this time I'm going to feel sure that I earn what I get.
Overcoming a physical or mental handicap in a way which offers a good chance of success	One of the boys at the community center has a speech defect that cannot be corrected. He told us the other day that he plans to become a teacher for handicapped people who can't hear or talk.
Using successful and well-adjusted people as models; trying to develop in your own personality desirable traits which you admire in others	Last year in one of my brother's classes, each student selected a successful, well-adjusted person as a model. They studied these people to find out what traits they had which made them successful and caused people to admire them. Then the students made plans to develop these traits in their own personalities.

How Feelings and Emotions Affect Our Behavior

While the students were carrying out the classwork on behavior, they began to realize that feelings and emotions play an important part in the way people act. One day Michael suggested that it might be worth while to find out just how emotions affect one's behavior.

Miss Corey nodded, saying that emotions are the things which give color to our personalities, and make us become known as this or that sort of person. She then went on to explain that every emotion we have causes us to do or want to do something. Some emotions result in behavior which brings happiness to us and to those around us. Others make us miserable and lead to unhappy situations.

The class then decided to consult reference materials about different emotions, and to find out what ones are more desirable than others. The conclusions they reached follow:

Cultivate these

We need to cultivate pleasant feelings, such as joy, satisfaction, delight, happiness, and affection. These emotions cause us to relax and give us a glad-to-be-alive feeling. We acquire these emotions in different ways. We feel cheerful and good-natured when we get along smoothly with our family and our friends, and when we accomplish things. We feel satisfaction when we do things which make other people happy, and when we face and make a good adjustment to our problems. We may be made happy through such things as music, sports, hobbies, books, pictures, the theater, or the television.

Handle wisely

We need to learn to handle wisely unpleasant emotions, such as fear, anger, anxiety, worry, and jealousy. These are the emotions which often cause loss of sleep, bad dreams, or digestive disturbances. They may affect our ability to remember, or make it difficult for us to concentrate on what we are doing. Nearly everyone has unpleasant emotions at times. To handle them wisely, we need to learn to prevent them from becoming too intense or too overpowering. We can do this by channeling them into activities that will relieve our feelings and yet won't be harmful to us or to others. If we bottle them up and let them smolder, they will stand in our way of cultivating the more pleasant emotions.

Students' Experiences in Improving Their Behavior

By this time the students were eager to put into practice what they had learned about emotions and behavior. After a discussion, they decided to base the classwork on two questions growing out of the conclusions on emotions.

1. How many pleasant emotions do I have now, and how many can I cultivate?

2. How many unpleasant emotions do I need to learn to handle wisely?

The students would study themselves critically, using the chart on undesirable and desirable behavior. If there was any doubt about where improvement was needed, they

We need to cultivate pleasant feelings, such as joy, satisfaction, and delight, through such things as hobbies, appreciation of nature, and happy association with others.

were to consult one of their friends or a member of the family. Each student would then make a plan and carry it out for cultivating a pleasant emotion, or for handling wisely an unpleasant one. Reports were to be ready by the end of two weeks.

However, before the students started to work on their plans, Miss Corey brought out several points. She said that it is important to try to change your own emotions and behavior, but not that of others, unless they ask for your help. In fact, accepting people as they are is something everyone needs to learn.

She also added that improving yourself, doing away with undesirable habits and setting up new ones, is a slow process. For example, if you have not experienced much happiness, you cannot suddenly begin to be happy. It takes time to develop ways that bring satisfaction and contentment. Perhaps you have a tendency to want to get things done quickly. You do not like to think of keeping at a task, such as improving your personality, far into the future. However, you need to realize that you improve yourself by building up confidence, first in one way and then in another. There are bound to be discouraging situations. It is only through courage, persistence, and a determination to win that you can become your ideal self — the person you want to be.

The experiences which were planned and carried out by the class proved to be very interesting. Several examples are given to show how different students tried to make improvement in their behavior.

According to Grace

Grace decided that she was a little too critical and faultfinding. When things did not please her, she did not hesitate to say so. Her criticisms were usually accompanied by suggestions for improvement, such as "Why don't you do it this way?" Or "That's not right. Let me show you how to do it."

After studying the chart, Grace realized that this was a feeling of superior attitude of thinking she could do something better than anyone else. Her plan for improvement as she carried it out was as follows:

1. *To stop criticizing or finding fault.* Every time she criticized anyone or found fault with anything, she deprived herself of dessert at the next meal. She missed three desserts the first week, two the second.

2. *To offer suggestions only when asked.* Whenever she was on the verge of telling somebody how to do something, she contributed a nickel toward her young brother's fund for a pair of roller skates. During the first week the fund was considerably increased.

3. *To try to help other people feel important and happy by speaking well of them or of what they are doing.* This did not mean flattering people, but

trying to see the best in everyone. She chalked up two examples. One concerned a new blouse a classmate had made and asked Grace's opinion of. Grace liked the color but not the style or material, so she told the girl how well the color went with her eyes. She said nothing about the style or material. The other incident was a remark she made to a boy who was on the losing side of a debate. "You may have lost," she said, "but you really put up some good arguments."

4. *To be willing to accept criticisms from others.* She didn't get angry when her family criticized her new hairdo. They said it made her look years older. Grace admitted to herself that this was what she had hoped it would do. But after thinking it over, she decided it was childish to try to make herself look adultish when she really didn't feel that way.

According to Tom

Tom was anxious to be considered a jolly good fellow. He admitted he was shy and often felt inferior to other people. But he admired boys who were witty, full of fun, and knew how to make other people laugh.

His first attempt was at a church social where he circulated around the room, talking first to one person and then to another. It wasn't easy, because he didn't always know what to say. But he noticed that several people seemed to go out of their way to say good night to him. This encouraged him to greet and to talk to more people — at a class meeting, at a football game, and in the school cafeteria.

Another part of his plan was to develop a sense of humor. This included being able to tell jokes and amusing stories, and to laugh at his own mistakes and blunders, but never at those of other people. He tried out several stories on the family. Some fell flat or caused only a smile. It didn't seem to be the story itself, but the way he told it. He therefore tried to improve his technique, and at the end of two weeks he believed he was more successful. Another idea was to find games and stunts that groups of people would enjoy. He made a list, and had tried out two on the family. Tom realized that it was going to be slow work to become the kind of person he wanted to be. But this trial period had encouraged him to believe that eventually he would succeed.

According to Bruce

Bruce planned to release angry emotions instead of bottling them up. When he became angry, he usually went off by himself. Sometimes he didn't speak to anyone for several hours. He simply moped around, feeling sorry for himself as he mulled over the details of what happened to cause his anger.

During the two-week period, he became angry three times. The first time, he took a brisk walk with one of his chums. They discussed the incident causing the anger, and then talked about other things. When he returned home, he had forgotten about being angry. The second time, he worked off his feelings by washing the family car. Then one rainy day a passing truck splashed mud on his freshly pressed trousers. He went home at once, took a warm bath, and put on some lounging clothes. Then he tried to relax in a comfortable chair with a mystery story. When he finished the story, he had forgotten about being angry.

Bruce plans to try out other ways of relieving his anger and not letting it smoulder within him. He also hopes to learn to meet some situations without becoming angry, and to laugh them off instead.

In looking over their classwork, the students realized they could not cover all they needed to know about understanding oneself and others. However, they believed that what they had learned about personality, and about undesirable and desirable behavior would help each one to improve his or her own behavior. At the same time, it would contribute toward a better understanding of the rest of their classwork related to the family.

CLASS MEMO:
Your class may want to learn more about the effects of emotions upon one's behavior. If so, what can you suggest that will be helpful to members of your group?

GETTING ALONG WITH MY FAMILY

THE students were now eager to work out plans for their classwork on *getting along with my family*. Roy reminded the group that when they were setting up their goals, he had mentioned the difficulty he was having with his brother.

"My problem is with my grandmother," said Sarah. "I don't think we understand each other at all."

"We have a new stepparent in our family," added John, "and this is causing some difficulty."

These and similar remarks led to a spirited discussion on what would be the most helpful way of meeting the various needs of the students. As a first step, it was agreed that each student would look at his or her home situation very closely to determine just what problems there were in getting along with the family, and in each case which one seemed the most urgent. Surely, information was available on how to meet these problems.

Carrying Out a Problem-resolving Approach to Personal Problems

One day when books and pamphlets had been assembled on the reference shelf, Miss Corey pointed out that there was a scientific approach to analyzing problems. She went on to explain that a personal problem is seldom entirely solved. But by studying it carefully and trying out various procedures, a problem may be greatly reduced.

The students were very much interested in Miss Corey's remarks. They found the material she had referred to, and decided they could use the five steps presented for meeting their own problems. They called these steps the "problem-resolving approach to personal problems." In order to illustrate how each step could be used, they also decided to work out one problem as an example. Roy offered his — quarreling with his brother — and provided the necessary details. The class helped Roy with the first four steps, but he had to put his plan into action before he could complete Step 5.

Steps in the problem-resolving approach and Roy's problem are given in the chart on pages 20 to 21. Other classes may find them helpful in their work.

Learning how to get along with a younger brother or sister may be a desirable experience.

Assembling Information for Their Problems

Working through the steps of Roy's problem gave the students confidence that they too could meet their problems. However, other members of the class had different problems. As they studied their own situations, they decided that they needed information for Step 3 before it could be worked out. It therefore seemed advisable for the students to group themselves according to similarity of problem,

CHART SHOWING PROBLEM-RESOLVING

STEP 1. State your problem clearly as you see it.

How can I keep from quarreling with my younger brother Bob?

STEP 2. List the difficulties that make it a problem. These may involve other people — how they act, what they say, or how you think they feel toward you. They may also include your own attitude — the way you feel about things — and your behavior.

a. Bob keeps the room we share in a mess. He leaves his soiled clothes wherever he takes them off. He generally throws his trousers on the closet floor, saying there are never any hangers for him to use. His side of the bureau is a hodgepodge of everything from rock specimens to candy wrappers.

b. He borrows my things without asking, and usually forgets to return them. If he does bring them back, they are apt to be in a terrible condition.

c. He rummages through my desk, reading my personal letters.

d. He's always playing pranks whenever I have a date. He does such annoying things as taking out the light bulb in front of the mirror, or hiding some of the things I plan to wear. Sometimes I'm late for my date.

e. My own attitude toward Bob's behavior makes me quarrel with him.

STEP 3. List information which will help you with this type of problem. This can come from reading, talking with people, or from other sources.

a. It is natural for brothers and sisters to quarrel occasionally. Boys and girls of various ages have different interests, abilities, and personalities which often clash.

b. A limited amount of quarreling is valuable in learning the technique of give and take. But the difficulties need to be settled by the boys and girls themselves, and not by the parents.

c. In a useful quarrel, the participants treat each other as equals who have a right to air their grievances. They do not resort to name calling, bitter accusations, or any tactics which will cause hard feelings.

a. I can make arrangements for Bob to have a laundry bag for his soiled clothes. I can see that Bob has his share of hangers in the closet. By moving some of my things from the bookcase, I can make room for Bob's rock specimens. The wastebasket can be placed nearer to Bob's side of the bureau, so that he can dispose of his candy wrappers more easily.

b. Bob and I can practice the give-and-take technique. I can lend him some of my things, and I can ask to borrow some of his. This will probably please Bob in two ways. It will make him happy to use my things. And he will feel flattered that I'm asking to borrow his. Bob and I can also have an understanding that the things we borrow will not only be returned, but will be in the same condition as when taken.

STEP 4. List what you and others can do to help meet the problem, and indicate what you hope will result.

c. I can ask Mother to explain to Bob that it's not cricket to rummage through a person's desk or to read personal letters. This will help Bob to realize that people have certain things they want to keep to themselves.

d. Whenever I have a date, I can take Bob into my confidence. I think it will make him feel important and grown up to know where I'm going and what I plan to do.

e. I can avoid starting an argument when Bob does things that upset me. It takes two people to quarrel; so if I don't argue, there will be no argument.

STEP 5. Show what success you have in meeting your problem. Were the results satisfying to you? Did they meet with the approval of your parents?

Bob and I have practically stopped quarreling. When I began to show more kindness and interest toward Bob, his attitude toward me changed. He now seems to want to please me and tries to do his part in keeping our room more orderly. He's been very careful about returning things he borrowed. And now that he knows I am willing to lend him some of my things, he seems to have lost interest in wanting them. Mother's talk with Bob was helpful, because he no longer touches the things in my desk. Since I began telling him about my dating plans, he hangs on every word I say. There haven't been any pranks recently. He's too busy helping me keep my dates on time. My parents are pleased that Bob and I are learning to settle our difficulties in a friendly way. I'm very proud of the admiration Bob is giving me. I hope I can live up to it.

and then assemble the necessary information. The main points could be summarized, and made available for others interested in what was found.

The information which the students believed would be helpful in working on Step 3 for various problem situations follows:

Disagreement with parents about such matters as what you do, where you go, and what you wear

Most parents have the welfare of their sons and daughters at heart, and try to do what they think is best for them.

Sometimes parents do not know how to cope with present-day conditions. Changing customs, popular teen-age vocabularies, and new fads in dressing often confuse them. Some parents are unable to accept these changes; others are unwilling to.

When young people show a willingness to tell their parents about their activities, there is less misunderstanding all around.

Sometimes young people try to achieve their need for independence too quickly. They expect to have freedom without being ready or willing to assume the responsibilities which go with it.

Family favorites

Some parents prefer boys to girls or vice versa. This may cause them to show greater affection toward children of one sex than the other.

Sometimes a parent may get along better with one child than another, because they happen to have more interests in common. Or the child may have special traits which the parent admires.

When a child resembles an unpopular relative, a parent may turn to one of the other children more often.

A child who has been named after a parent or relative may receive more gifts and attention than the other children do.

A child who is successful in ways that parents consider important is often held up as an example to other children.

Having a stepparent in the home

It is difficult for a new parent to come into a ready-made family. It takes time for everyone to become adjusted.

The older children will need to assume some of the responsibility of making a new parent feel at home.

Children are not required to love a stepparent in the same way as the real parent. But they can learn to like a stepparent as an adult friend. It is not being disloyal to the real parent to enjoy such a friendship.

One-parent homes

The remaining parent has to adjust to a new role in the family — that of being both mother and father. It is not easy to be a breadwinner and a homemaker too.

Helping one another and sharing responsibilities will help to keep the household running smoothly.

A fatherless or motherless boy or girl needs the friendship of an adult to take the place of the missing parent.

An admired friend or a relative can help to fill this need.

It is more desirable to have two parents. But boys and girls in one-parent families sometimes become more self-reliant and meet responsibilities in life better than those with two parents.

Having grandparents in the home

If grandparents seem to interfere with the bringing up of boys and girls, it is because they are genuinely interested in their grandchildren's welfare.

Young people need to realize that elderly people like to talk about their younger days. They get great pleasure in having someone listen to them.

Grandparents like to feel important and useful in the home.

Getting to know older people can be a rewarding experience.

Having foreign-born parents

Parents from another country like to retain many of the customs they grew up with.

They usually find it easier to speak their native language.

Young people with foreign-born parents may believe that the American way of life is the best. But America is built on the customs and habits brought here from other countries. It is always interesting to find out what different countries have contributed.

Learning a foreign language directly from parents may be a great advantage in later life.

Nearly every national group has colorful costumes, unique ceremonies, and interesting foods. When these are shared with others outside the home, a better understanding of the parents is bound to result.

Foreign-born parents may not understand the social customs of this country, and may require their teen-age boys and girls to follow those of the old country. But parents often change their attitudes when they come in contact with other parents or with friends of their sons and daughters.

Living in a family where both parents spend much time outside the home

Everyone in the family needs to share in keeping the household running smoothly.

Older boys and girls may need to assume more responsibility for the care of their younger brothers and sisters if their parents are away during out-of-school hours.

It is important for young people without much parental supervision to learn to act in a way that will bring satisfaction to themselves and will be acceptable to others.

Living in a family that moves from one locality to another

It is usually difficult for boys and girls to make permanent friendships when they are in a place for a short time.

Changing schools often creates problems of adjustment to a different curriculum.

Parents need to give their children a sense of security and to make them feel that come what will, the family group will always stick together.

Moving from place to place tends to help boys and girls adjust easily to new situations.

Meeting different types of people and living in various localities tend to broaden one's viewpoint.

Using Role Playing to Report on a Problem

After each student had completed the five-step plan for the problem selected, the class decided to use the role-playing technique for reporting on some of the problems. Two examples are given to show how this technique was carried out:

Sarah's report

There were two scenes in Sarah's report. The first one showed why Sarah and her grandmother did not understand each other. The second scene indicated (1) what the grandmother might do to make the atmosphere of the home more pleasant, and (2) what Sarah could do to make her grandmother happier and more understanding of the younger generation. The scenes are given as follows:

SCENE 1 — *The Living Room*

The grandmother is knitting. Sarah, in dungarees and one of her father's shirts, is reading with her feet up over the arm of the chair.

GRANDMOTHER: Sarah, those clothes you're wearing are a disgrace. I think you ought to go upstairs and change them.

SARAH: Why, Grandmother, all the girls wear dungarees and shirts these days.

GRANDMOTHER: I can't help it. I disapprove all the same. Can't see why your mother lets you dress that way.

SARAH: Mother lets me do things the way other people my age do.

GRANDMOTHER: I don't approve of that either, and I will tell her so. I heard you come in last night and it was way after eleven o'clock.

SARAH: That was early, Grandmother. Most of the crowd stay out until after midnight.

GRANDMOTHER: Scandalous! My parents wouldn't have stood for such actions.

SARAH: But Grandmother, things are different now.

GRANDMOTHER: They certainly are. This generation is going to the dogs. It doesn't matter to me though. I'm no use to anyone anyway.

The scene ends with Sarah leaving the room, making a wry face at her grandmother.

SCENE 2 — *The Living Room*

GRANDMOTHER: You young people certainly do dress differently from the way we used to dress. In my day, shirts and dungarees were for boys, not for girls.

SARAH: Times have changed, Grandmother.

GRANDMOTHER: Yes, I dare say they have. It keeps a person busy trying to keep up with all the new-fangled ideas.

SARAH: I hope I didn't disturb you when I came in last night.

GRANDMOTHER: I heard you, but it didn't bother me. Eleven o'clock is pretty late to be coming in, isn't it?

SARAH: I don't think so, Grandmother. Most of my crowd stay out until after midnight. Mother lets me decide when to come home.

GRANDMOTHER: In my day, I was told what to do and when to do it. Discussing things with my parents was unheard of.

SARAH: I don't always like what I am supposed to do. But Mother is so sweet. She says, "We'll talk it over. I'm sure we can work it out." She discusses things with me and tells me what she thinks and why she thinks that way. And just because she seems so understanding about it, I end up by doing what she wants whether I like it or not.

GRANDMOTHER: I don't always approve of what your mother lets you do. But I don't say anything. I figure I've raised my family to the best of my ability, and your mother can do the same. It isn't good for an older generation to tell another generation what to do. Your parents are the ones to decide what is best for you.

SARAH: I think that's wise, Grandmother. It's fun to have you around. Tell me some of the things you used to do when you were my age.

GRANDMOTHER: I'll be glad to one of these days. But right now I'm busy. I have your socks to darn and a dress to mend for your mother. If there's time, I'm going to bake a batch of cookies before supper.

SARAH: You're wonderful, Grandmother. I don't know how we'd get along without you.

Sarah goes over to her grandmother and kisses her lightly on the forehead. They smile at one another as Sarah leaves the room.

John's report

John's problem concerned a new stepparent whom John and his twelve-year-old sister, Susan, had been hesitant about welcoming into the family group. The scene opens in the living room where the stepmother, John, and Susan are talking. It shows how older children can assume some of the responsibilities of making a new parent feel at home.

SCENE — *The Living Room*

STEPMOTHER: It's difficult for a new parent to come into a ready-made family. But I want you to know that I'll do my best to make things as pleasant for you as I can.

SUSAN: John and I will try to make you feel at home. Won't we, John?

JOHN: Of course we will. And if there's anything special you want me to do around the house, just name it. I always empty the trash baskets and keep the garage clean. But I'll do other things too if you need me.

STEPMOTHER: Thank you both. I know your father will be pleased to hear this.

JOHN: I'd like to bring Mr. and Mrs. Beekman, our next-door neighbors, in to meet you.

STEPMOTHER: I'll be only too glad to meet them.

SUSAN: Maybe you and I can arrange a tea some afternoon. We can ask some of the wives of Dad's friends and perhaps some of our teachers. I know they'll all want to meet you.

STEPMOTHER: That would be fun, I'm sure. I hope too that both you and John will feel free to bring your friends home any time you want to.

JOHN: And if you and Dad want to go away for a week end, Susan and I will look after things. We can both cook a little.

STEPMOTHER: That's very thoughtful of you both. I can see that my new home is going to be a pleasant one.

JOHN AND SUSAN: We hope so.

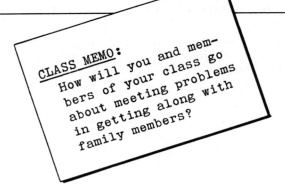

CLASS MEMO: How will you and members of your class go about meeting problems in getting along with family members?

MAKING PLANS FOR FURTHER CLASSWORK

DURING the classwork on *getting along with my family*, each student had selected and tried to resolve a problem that seemed most urgent. In many cases the choice was a difficult one to make. There were other problems which seemed equally important and which they wanted to know more about. Some of the most urgent ones involved money matters, dating, and entertainment. Further discussion on the subject led to an agreement of four

goals to complete the classwork in "Accent on Families." Bruce lined them up on the blackboard in the order shown below.

Miss Corey told the students that there was already considerable material on the reference shelves for their classwork. But she urged them to bring in newspaper clippings, magazine articles, and items from other sources which might be helpful. Everyone seemed eager to see the information.

Cooperating with the family on money matters
Having dates
Helping with family entertainment
Feeling at home when away from home

COOPERATING WITH THE FAMILY ON MONEY MATTERS

WHEN the class was ready to begin the classwork on *cooperating with the family on money matters*, Miss Corey offered a suggestion. She said she recently read an interesting short story that illustrated a money problem. She had brought the story to school and would read it at this time if the class thought it was a good idea.

Needless to say, everyone nodded in agreement and settled back

in pleasant anticipation of what was to come. The story as Miss Corey read it follows:

THE STORY

THE mailbox contained several bills and one large envelope with black lettering in the upper left-hand corner, and addressed to Mrs. Mary Elizabeth Jackson.

And because it was Saturday and dinner was due to be on the table within a short time, Mary Jackson put the bills on the hall table, folded the long envelope, and tucked it into her apron pocket.

"Must be something connected with Aunt Mary's death," said Mary Jackson to herself. A few weeks ago an elderly aunt for whom she was named had died out West. None of the family had seen her for several years, and except for an annual exchange of Christmas and birthday greetings, there had been little correspondence between her and the Jackson family. "Maybe Aunt Mary has left me a little remembrance," she thought as she made her way toward the kitchen.

Just then the front door slammed, and fifteen-year-old Carol hurried up the front stairs. Mary Jackson started to call to her. Carol was needed to help with the dinner. Six people were a lot to cook for, and a little assistance lightened some of the load which went with the preparation and serving for that many people. But when Carol's bedroom door slammed, Mary Jackson's face became thoughtful. She said nothing but continued toward the kitchen. Jane, her thirteen-year-old, would soon be returning from the store, and she would help.

In the kitchen the dinner was progressing satisfactorily. Mary Jackson glanced at the clock. Yes, there was plenty of time before John, her husband, would arrive from the printing office, which he insisted upon keeping open until noon Saturdays. Why, she never

could understand, except that John had been brought up on a six-day work week and was unwilling to change.

"People are always coming in from the country," John would say when his wife brought up the subject. "You'd be surprised how much business we do Saturday mornings." And since every penny counted in the Jackson household, there was no further argument. But Mary Jackson wished her husband would not work so hard. It would be nice if he could spend more time with his two sons — Bill, who was nearly eighteen, and young Bob going on eleven.

They were a happy family though. They owned their own home, and a very attractive one it was too, with a wide lawn and plenty of space for flower gardens. There was a large rumpus room in the basement and ample storage room on the third floor. Every summer John took a month's vacation, and the whole family piled into the car and went north to one of the many beautiful lakes where they swam and fished to their hearts' content. Yes, it was a pleasant life although a busy one.

Mary Jackson looked at the meat and vegetables and then sat down at the kitchen table to rest a moment. The room was warm, and as she reached for her handkerchief, her hand touched the folded letter in the apron pocket.

"Might as well take a look and see what it says," she thought, slit-

ting the envelope with one of the kitchen knives.

It was not a long letter, but very much to the point. Mary Jackson's face flushed with excitement as she read the contents. She, Mary Jackson, was the sole beneficiary of her late aunt's estate. The amount staggered her. She had no idea her aunt had been so wealthy. What would they do with all that money!

Just then thirteen-year-old Jane came in the back door, her arms loaded with packages. Mary Jackson crumpled the letter together and thrust it back into her apron pocket. She must have time to think before she could say anything to anyone.

Half an hour later the Jackson family was sitting around the dining table talking excitedly about the day's happenings. Meals were always pleasant affairs in the Jackson household.

Mr. Jackson was saying, "After dinner, Bill, we'd better take off the storm windows and put up the screens. I noticed several flies this morning."

If Bill had any other plans for the afternoon, he said nothing although his face looked slightly crestfallen as he said, "Yes, Dad."

His father glanced at him sharply and then added, "If Bob will help us wash the screens with the hose, I think we can finish the job in short order. Then we can go fishing at White Bear if you boys want to."

Two pairs of eyes sparkled instantly. Both Bill and Bob liked to go fishing with their father. They considered him an expert fisherman. He usually managed to catch fish when others failed.

"And can we take our supper?" asked Bob, looking toward his mother.

She nodded silently, seeming not to be aware of what was going on about her.

"Janie, over there," said her father, "can hook the screens from the inside and perhaps do a little window washing for some extra cash. How about it, Janie?"

Jane considered the proposition for a moment and then agreed that she could use some extra money.

"And you, Carol," added her father, "I suppose you'll be primping this afternoon. Isn't this the night for your class dance?"

Carol nodded, arching her eyebrows slightly and at the same time pushing back a curl with a hand well lacquered with red nail polish. Bob started to whistle but stopped abruptly as Jane kicked him under the table.

John Jackson then drew four envelopes from his pocket. Every Saturday his secretary made up the allowances for the four children. Saturday-afternoon work was always considered as extra, and each one who participated was paid on an hourly basis.

"Speaking of money," said Mary Jackson, who entered into the conversation for the first time, "what would you people do if we inherited half a million dollars?"

No one took her question seriously. She often asked hypothetical questions, and sometimes they seemed rather absurd. Mr. Jackson did not even appear to be listening but was handing out the allowance envelopes. Bill was finishing his last bite of pie and could not answer. Carol was the first to speak.

"I know what I'd do," she said somewhat vehemently. "I'd go down town and buy myself a whole new outfit — and end up with a mink coat. . . And then I'd apply for entrance to Bancroft Hall."

"Bancroft Hall?" said Jane. "What do you want to go to that snooty school for?"

"So that's the way it is," thought Mary Jackson, *"a mink coat for a fifteen-year-old girl. How ridiculous she would appear before her friends, most of whom wear sport coats the year around. And Bancroft Hall! All of the neighborhood girls attend public school. Could it be that my daughter is snobbish, and I haven't realized it before?*

Possibly I am not giving her the right kind of guidance. No, sudden wealth would not be good for Carol. She is not ready for so drastic a change."

Then young Bob spoke up. "Gee, Mom, if we had half a million dollars, think of all the things I could buy — a new bike, that airplane down at Clark's with the motor, a red canoe for the lake, a bobsled that will hold a dozen kids, a pair of fancy ice skates. . ." He paused for breath.

"Yes," thought Mary Jackson, *"you'd wear me down, teasing for this new gadget, longing for that,*

and never taking care of any of them. As soon as the newness wore off, it would be something just a little more expensive, something none

of the neighborhood boys would be able to afford. Yes, Bob, you would be the envy of your friends, and they would flock around you fawning for your favors. But you would soon tire of all these flashy playthings and eventually become bored with life. No, Bob, there is such a thing as having too much to play with. Better a few simple things and not many at a time. Too much money would not be good for Bob."

Then Jane spoke up. "I've been thinking, Mom, that if we had half a million dollars I could have a larger allowance. Then I could treat all the girls to those yummy fudge sundaes at Royal's and buy those expensive chocolates you won't let me have. We could even have ice cream every day too."

"Poor Jane, always thinking about her stomach. Jane, whose figure is far too plump now and whose blotchy complexion is anything but peaches and cream. No, a larger allowance would bring only

momentary happiness and would soon end in grief and despair for its recipient. Jane too is not prepared for money on a large scale," her mother concluded.

Bill had finished his pie by this time and had leaned back in his chair with a smile of satisfaction on his face. "Oh, boy," he said, "half a million bucks! That spells a new convertible for me — one of those snappy little numbers that roll along at eighty without a murmur. Wouldn't the girls go for me in a big way!"

"Yes, thought Mary Jackson, looking at her handsome son, "I guess they would. And what a temptation it would be to 'burn up' those long straight roads which run in all directions throughout the state. I can see him now in a shiny red convertible, a pretty girl at his side, ready to demonstrate what a man of the world he is. I

can feel the rush of wind on their faces as they speed along the highway, unaware perhaps that they are exceeding the speed limit. How easy it would be for the car to get out of control or a tire to blow without warning. Then unremitting sorrow and endless grief. No, Bill is not ready for a convertible. Better the old jalopy which bursts its seams if it goes over fifty."

By this time the head of the family appeared to be listening to the conversation. He was in an expansive mood as he settled back in his chair and surveyed his family.

"What's this about half a million dollars?" he said. "Let's see now. Your mother and I have always wanted to go on a cruise. Maybe we could even take a trip around the world."

"John," Mary thought, "leaving his printing shop to go around the world! It is hard enough to get him to go away for a month each summer. And what would we do with the children? Hired help isn't very satisfactory. Then too, something might happen while we were away. Bill is about ready to enter the university, but he would still be living at home. Carol is just at the age when she needs advice and guidance. Boys have become a disturbing factor in her life, and she hasn't been able to resolve some of her problems. And Jane — poor unattractive Jane needs close supervision until she develops better physical and mental balance. Bob, of course, is much too young to be left without his parents. Money would offer only a false security and would not compensate for the character influence which only parents can offer a growing boy. And John, himself, would be just as restless without the children as I would be. Of course we would enjoy seeing other countries and visiting exciting places. How romantic it would be to see the Taj Mahal or the Egyptian pyramids by moonlight! Perhaps we could take a luxury liner through the soft blue waters of the Mediterranean. I can picture myself walking on deck arm in arm with John — I the best-dressed woman on the

ship. . . . Goodness gracious, Mary Jackson, what are you thinking of! A soft easy life is not for me or John. Luxury might change our figures, for both of us love good food. Idleness might bring on complacency,

and tend to make us shirk responsibility. No, neither John nor I are ready for unexpected wealth."

She was conscious of the letter in her apron and pressed it deeper into the pocket. Why spoil such a happy family by offering them something they really didn't need and perhaps, in the long run, didn't want? Wealth might be glamorous at first, but how few people knew how to make it lead to happiness. No, she would suggest to John that

they put the legacy into trust funds for the children, to be used later on in life when they had learned to appreciate and evaluate material things. John would agree, she knew. He always thought well of her judgment.

And so the Jackson family rose from the table, each ready for an afternoon of work.

Studying Four Families with Money Problems

When Miss Corey finished reading the story, there wasn't a sound in the room. The students seemed to be reliving the events which happened in the Jackson family. Then suddenly as their thoughts and ideas crystallized, they began to comment about the story.

"I guess the Jackson family was not accustomed to talking over money matters together," said Michael. "If they had been, Mrs. Jackson wouldn't have worried about having too much money."

"Or she wouldn't have made the decision about the money without consulting all of the others," said Paul.

"In fact, Mrs. Jackson refused to face her problem, just as Monica Fenton did when she ran away to Chicago," commented Ellen.

"It doesn't seem to matter whether a family has a lot of money or only a little," added Roy. "There are problems just the same."

Deciding how to work

These and other comments led to a discussion in which the students decided to study some families with money problems. Miss Corey had showed them descriptions of four families — with one or more teen-agers — in which each family handled money differently. The students decided to study these descriptions, consult references, and summarize their ideas about the financial situation of each family.

At the same time, they would decide what the teen-agers needed to do to make their family's financial situation more satisfactory. The descriptions of the four families showing how the classwork was carried out follow:

THE BENSONS

When the children in the Benson family began to ask for spending money, their parents decided to hold family councils on money matters. Mr. Benson told the family what they had to live on after rent, taxes, social security, and insurance payments had been deducted. The family then set up a monthly budget plan for spending the income.

From time to time, various adjustments had to be made. There was a period when Mrs. Benson spent more money on food than the amount they had set aside. They hadn't expected that certain necessary items would jump in price. Mr. Benson offered to postpone getting a new topcoat and to let that amount go toward food expenses. Then there was the accident when Danny broke his arm. The insurance did not cover all of the expenses, and the emergency fund was earmarked for something else. The two teen-agers crossed off figure skates from their Christmas lists, and Mrs. Benson decided that she didn't need new accessories for her gray outfit. In this way the family met the expenses for Danny's accident.

Mr. and Mrs. Benson feel that the children are getting valuable experience through the family-council plan. However, Mrs. Benson has recently become a little worried about two matters. It seems that young Danny boasted to one of his friends about the family income. The boy's mother reported the incident to Mrs. Benson, who was quite embarrassed. The other matter concerns fifteen-year-old Helen. She seems to be trying to get more than her share of the clothing allotment. Helen has complained several times that she doesn't have as many school outfits as some of the other girls.

1. *What the class thinks about the Benson plan for handling money:*

a. The family-council plan provides an opportunity for children to understand and appreciate the financial problems of parents in maintaining a home.

b. Through the family council, the needs and wants of each member can be seen and planned for.

c. A family council is successful to the extent that each member is satisfied with the decisions that are made and does his or her share in abiding by them.

2. *What Danny and Helen need to do to make the family plan successful:*

a. Danny needs to learn to keep family affairs confidential and not make revealing statements to outsiders that might prove embarrassing to his parents.

b. Helen needs to recognize the difference between needs and wants.

c. Helen needs to learn to consider her wants in the light of the wants of others in the family.

d. Helen needs to be a good sport and to abide by the decisions she has helped to make.

e. Helen needs to accept the fact that more money will be spent on clothes in some families than in others.

THE MACDOUGALS

Mr. MacDougal believes that money matters belong entirely to the man in the family. Neither Mrs. MacDougal nor the three children have any idea what the family income is. They charge most of their groceries, which Mr. MacDougal pays for by check. Mrs. MacDougal is never given any spending money. But whenever she asks for anything for herself and the children, her husband usually gives her enough to cover the cost of what she needs. However, she often finds it difficult to know just how much they can afford to spend. Sometimes she feels they are living beyond their income.

Whenever the children want money for anything, they ask their father for it. Ten-year-old Enid has learned that when her father is in a happy mood or when guests are around, he often gives her more than she asks for. But most of the time they all receive much less than they want.

Now that Betty and Bob are in high school, they are constantly making requests for money. They never stop to consider what other members of the family may need or want. Instead they vie with one another to get as much as they can for themselves. Sometimes Bob feels that Betty gets more than her share. What he doesn't know is that Betty often buys some of her clothes with the money she receives. Both Betty and Bob are uncertain about setting up spending plans. They never know what they can count on.

1. *What the class thinks about the Mac-Dougal financial situation:*

a. Not knowing how much the family has to spend tends to cause feelings of insecurity among its members. They do not get a clear picture of the financial problem of maintaining a home.

b. The ask-as-you-want-it plan does not give children the experience they need in learning to use money. It also fails to provide an opportunity for them to see the needs and wants of others in the family.

c. The amount of money given to children should depend on what they are expected to do with it.

d. Young people do not like to ask for every nickel or dime they need. Nor do parents enjoy being constantly asked for this or that.

2. *What Betty and Bob need to do to make their financial situation more satisfactory:*

a. They need to understand that some fathers do not believe in sharing a knowledge of the family income with other members. Therefore in learning to appreciate the financial responsibility of maintaining a home, Betty and Bob need to look for clues that will give them an idea of how much the family can afford to spend.

b. They need to learn the differences between needs and wants.

c. They need to learn to consider the needs and wants of other members in the family in relation to their own.

d. They need to try to find out how much money their father is able to give them. If the amount seems insufficient for their personal expenses, they need to plan ways of cutting their expenses or of earning extra money.

THE LEONARDS

Doris Leonard, an only child, has been given an allowance since early childhood. As she grew older the allowance was increased, but there was very little said as to how it was to be spent. Doris often bought small items which caught her fancy, and treated the neighborhood children to ice cream and candy.

When Doris entered high school, her allowance was substantially increased. Although nothing much was said, her parents assumed there would be more than enough to cover her personal expenses. The first two times Doris asked for more money, her father advanced it from her next allowance. But the third time he refused to give another advance.

"Where does all your money go?" he asked. "You're getting all I can afford right now. If I give you any more, your mother and I will have to go without some of the things we need." Doris replied that the money just went. Last week it barely covered her expenses for movies, ice cream, cokes, and, oh, yes, a charm bracelet she simply couldn't resist. There was practically nothing left for her school lunches.

Right now things are at a standstill. Mr. and Mrs. Leonard told Doris that her allowance must go toward school needs first, and whatever was left could go for fun and foolishness. Doris isn't very happy about this and wonders how she is going to get along.

1. *What the class thinks about the allowance plan:*

a. Having an allowance provides an opportunity for children to learn to handle money. But there needs to be some guidance if the experience is to be valuable.

b. The rules for using an allowance should be understood by the children in advance. Then both children and

Talking over money matters with one's teacher is helpful.

parents are expected to stand by the rules.

c. Successful spending requires clear thinking and continuous planning.

2. *What Doris needs to do to make her spending plans more satisfactory*

a. She needs to learn the value of money in terms of what it costs her family to live.

b. She needs to take time to think about her purchases instead of buying on the

The family-council plan allows all members to understand family finances.

Doing odd jobs around the house may be one way of earning extra money.

impulse of the moment. This will help her to recognize the difference between needs and wants.

c. She needs to recognize the needs and wants of other members of the family in relation to her own.

d. She needs to discuss with her parents her personal expenses, and to evaluate them in terms of needs and wants.

e. She needs to know that one of the signs of growing up is having a greater understanding of her personal finances.

THE DESEAKS

The Deseaks live in a comfortable home well equipped with modern appliances. Mrs. Deseak does the housework and buys most of the food and clothing for the family. Mr. Deseak earns good wages, but he believes that boys should add to the family income as soon as they can do anything useful. Fifteen-year-old Gene has been earning money ever since he was nine years old. He always turns over everything he makes to his parents, but he understands that some of this money goes into a savings account.

Neither Mr. or Mrs. Deseak has ever heard of an allowance for children and the word "budget" is unfamiliar to them. Whenever Gene wants money, his parents give it to him. Gene seems to have everything he needs, but for some reason he isn't very happy. Recently he has been envying other boys who are allowed to keep the money they earn.

1. *What the class thinks about the Deseaks' financial situation:*

a. Some parents think that each wage earner should contribute to the family income whether the extra money is needed or not. Other parents allow their children to keep their earnings. Still other parents need the financial help of their children.

b. Whether or not children should contribute what they earn to their parents depends upon the financial circumstances of the family and the attitude of the parents.

c. There needs to be a purpose for saving money.

2. *What Gene needs to do to make his financial situation more satisfactory:*

a. He needs to discuss the situation with his parents. If the money is not needed, he can try to persuade his parents to let him keep his earnings.

b. He needs to learn the difference between needs and wants, so that he can assure his parents his money will be wisely spent.

c. He needs to find out from his parents for what purpose the money already in the bank is being saved. If there is no definite objective, he needs to plan for something which will be satisfactory to himself and to his parents. Then a part of his earnings can go into a savings account.

CLASS MEMO:
What other points that have not already been mentioned can you bring out regarding the financial situations of the four families?

Behind the Scenes at Home

After analyzing the four families, the students decided to put on a series of skits entitled "Behind the Scenes at Home." The class divided into four groups, each group taking one of the families as the basis for a skit. Using the points they had set up for making the financial situations more satisfactory, each group portrayed several scenes showing how the suggestions could be carried out. Some of the scenes from the various skits are shown in the illustration on the next two pages.

THE BENSON FAMILY

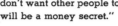

"Danny, when we talk about money here at home, let's keep it a family secret just among ourselves. Lots of families have things they don't want other people to know about. Ours will be a money secret."

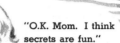

"O.K. Mom. I think secrets are fun."

"I'd like to have another skirt and sweater outfit for school, but I've used up all my clothing allowance for the next month. I know it isn't fair to ask for more, but isn't there some way I can have this outfit without upsetting the budget?"

"You can scout around the neighborhood, Helen, and try to earn some extra money. If you can earn enough to buy some yarn, I can show you how to knit a sweater. While you're knitting the sweater, we can reverse your red wool skirt, and it will be almost like new."

THE MACDOUGALS

"Dad, Bob and I would like to go over our expenses with you. We've figured out what we need each week. And we'd like to have your opinion on setting up a regular budget for school expenses and for some of our clothes."

"We realize, Dad, that it takes a lot of money to bring up a family these days. But I'm willing—and Betty is too—to try to earn something to add to the family income if you think it's necessary. We feel the best way to meet expenses is to know what we can count on regularly and then to make plans for earning anything extra."

"Doris, your mother and I think it would be a good plan for you to make a list of your weekly school expenses. This will give you a better idea of how much money will be left from your allowance for other things you may want."

"I'll get a notebook and try to keep track of all my school expenses for a week. And I'll think twice before I buy anything I really don't need."

THE DESEAKS

"I'd like to get more experience handling money. How about letting me manage what I earn if you don't need it for family expenses, Dad? I've made a list of what I need each week for school and what I usually spend outside of school. I'd also like to put some money in the savings bank for a vacation trip next summer to visit Cousin Jim in Wyoming."

"I never did think that children could handle money until they were out of school and on their own, Gene. But maybe this generation is different. You seem to know just where your money goes. And you don't appear to be spending it foolishly. We don't need your earnings; so you can try managing them yourself for a while. And it will be easier to save a little if you have something definite in mind."

Evaluating the Use of Money

At the time Miss Corey read the story of the Jackson family, the students believed that they were not well enough informed to analyze the situation critically. However, after using the reference materials and after discussing other families, they felt they were better prepared to evaluate what had happened in the Jackson family.

Now as they recalled the events of the story, they agreed that money itself need not necessarily be a problem. It is the attitudes and feelings which people have toward money that cause the difficulties. Miss Corey pointed out that families who have confused ideas about money and material things might have many problems if confronted with sudden wealth. Other families who have worked out a more balanced viewpoint on the value of money might be able to handle sudden wealth very satisfactorily. The question is: *what does a family need to know that will help its members develop satisfying values regarding money and its use?*

Taking this question as a basis for their classwork, the students with Miss Corey's assistance set up the following points:

1. Money isn't everything. Its value lies in securing the *needs* of life and some of the *wants* associated with happy living.

2. It takes time and experience to learn to handle money wisely. No one is born with an appreciation of the value of money or a ready-made ability to spend it wisely.

3. Education in handling money begins when parents give their children a small amount of money regularly as an allowance, and then guide the children in their spending experiences.

4. Family conferences, in which all members have a knowledge of the family income and a share in how it will be spent, develop a better understanding of money problems.

5. Successful spending requires continuous planning and clear thinking. Planning to meet fixed expenses, such as rent, taxes, and insurance premiums, helps the family to see what is available for other expenses. Keeping a record of these other expenses may aid the family in seeing how to spend more wisely.

6. People who have everything they want need to guard against losing their initiative and becoming bored with life.

7. The amount of money a family has is not necessarily the key to happiness. Being loved and feeling that you belong to the family group are more important than a dozen bank accounts.

Planning Individual Cooperation in Money Matters with One's Family

As the class began to make individual plans for home experiences, they realized that each family situation would be different. Some of the students had allowances. Others asked their parents for money whenever it was needed. Still others were accustomed to family councils in which money was discussed, but not always budgeted for individual needs and wants. And there were some families who did not talk about money matters at all.

The students therefore agreed that they would need to be guided by the customs and attitudes of their own family toward money matters. Those students who felt that they could handle their money better if they had a regular allowance would need to convince their parents that they would try to manage the money wisely. Other students who believed that they needed extra money, which the family could not supply, would seek satisfactory ways and means of earning this money. And if it meant living within a tight income that could not be easily stretched, they would try to make the most of what they had. But no matter what the situation, they would all make every effort to shape their spending habits to fit the needs and wants of the family group.

CLASS MEMO:
Your class may be interested in taking a different approach toward money matters from the one that Miss Corey's group took. If so, what plan for classwork can you suggest that will meet the needs of your group?

HAVING DATES

ONE of the most interesting topics selected for classwork was having dates. As the class began to consider how to approach the subject, Bruce opened the discussion.

"I don't understand why an activity as interesting as dating can cause so much concern," he remarked.

Several students smiled but made no comment. Instead they looked toward Miss Corey for an explanation.

"An important part of your personality development in the high school years," she said, "is the ability to get along with members of the opposite sex. This is the time when boys and girls become aware of each other as maturing young people. They begin to see the value of cultivating those qualities which make them popular and attractive to others. There is a feeling of warmth, affection, and happiness in being together and in sharing mutual interests. Making and keeping friends becomes more important now than at any other time.

"However, since having dates involves new experiences, problems are bound to occur. Most of these center around social etiquette, personal ideals, social needs, and family and home relationships."

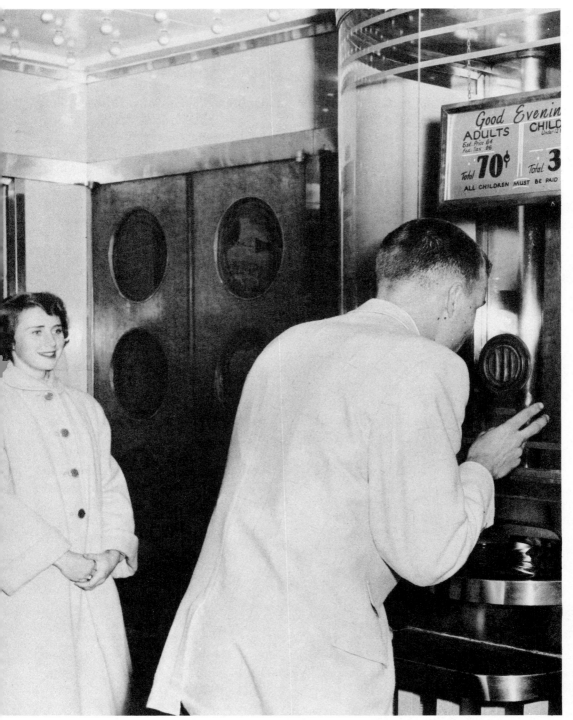

Feeling at ease, being yourself, entering enthusiastically into the entertainment planned, being courteous and well mannered—all of these contribute toward happy dating times.

Dating Problems

"Then I think the first thing we need to do is to learn what some of these dating difficulties are. After that we can see what can be done about them," said Michael. "What about each of us finding out from other boys and girls our own age, or older, what their dating problems are?"

Michael's suggestion appealed to everyone, and with Miss Corey's approval, it was soon put into operation. At the next meeting of the class each student turned in a report of the boys and girls who had been interviewed. There were so many responses that a committee was chosen to go over the papers very carefully. The committee, with Miss Corey's assistance, then selected the following general types of problems for class discussion: (1) parents and dating, (2) questions relating to dating behavior, and (3) going steady.

Planning a "Teen-Town Broadcast"

Now that the students had organized and classified problems on dating, they began to discuss ways of getting information. Various ideas were offered which eventually resulted in a plan they called a "Teen-Town Broadcast." The idea was to present a series of three broadcasts to cover the three types of problems as classified by the committee.

Several parents would be asked to participate in the broadcast concerning parents and dating. Four seniors — two boys and two girls — who were popular and respected would be invited to answer the questions relating to dating behavior. For the third broadcast, several students from their own group were to discuss going steady.

Various committees were appointed to secure the speakers, to work out the details of the material to be discussed on the broadcasts,

and to obtain helpful books and pamphlets on dating for the reference shelves. It was not long before all of these arrangements were carried out, and the eventful day of the first broadcast arrived.

Parents and Dating

All of the students' parents were invited to attend the first program, and a large number responded to the invitation. The speakers for the afternoon were three parents with teen-age sons and daughters. However, they were not the parents of any of Miss Corey's students. This was done to avoid embarrassment that might result from the discussion of personal experiences.

A reception committee greeted the guests as they arrived and found seats for them. Paul, who had been selected to serve as chairman of the three broadcasts, gave a brief outline of the topics to be discussed. He then introduced the speakers.

The role of parents in teen-age dating

The first speaker on the program was Mrs. Holmes. Her remarks were as follows:

"When boys and girls begin to think and talk about dating, parents realize as never before that their children are growing up. To some parents, dating is a normal and desirable part of this growing-up process. But to others, it comes as a shock, and they find it difficult to adjust to this new phase of development.

"These attitudes on the part of parents are quite understandable. Legally parents are responsible for the support of their children until they become of age. They are also held responsible by the community for the conduct, protection, and health of their children. Therefore it is reasonable to expect parents to be concerned over the activities of their boys and girls. It seems to me that the problem can be boiled down to one main question — how can parents protect the welfare of their children when it comes to dating?

"Not long ago this question was discussed at a regional conference on teen-age problems. I think you'll all be interested in the role recommended for parents."

1. Accept dating as a normal and natural part of a teen-ager's development.

2. Have an understanding with your sons and daughters about the number of dates they are to have a week, and the time they are to arrive home. Be guided by community customs, but only to the extent that they do not jeopardize the health of the young people.

3. Avoid being overly cautious and strict lest boys and girls sneak out on dates.

4. Encourage home entertaining occasionally for two or three couples. Arrange to meet the guests, but let the young people have the use of the living room without interference from other members of the family.

5. Show an interest in the social events in which your sons and daughters participate. But avoid taking a prying or snooping attitude.

6. Try to have an understanding that all members of the family will keep the others informed, in so far as possible, of their whereabouts. This will make young people more willing to report where they might go, whom they are with, and when they expect to return.

7. Make young people feel that you trust them and that you are counting on them to do what is socially acceptable.

8. Offer your assistance when difficulties arise. Give helpful suggestions rather than criticisms. Avoid showing concern or alarm over unfortunate situations in which your sons or daughters may have used poor judgment. Try to show them that they gain in experience if they profit by the mistakes they make.

The horn-tooting caller

Mrs. Dean, who was the second speaker on the broadcast, made her remarks as follows:

"Many parents have had personal experience with what I call the 'horn-tooting caller.' The visitor is usually a boy, alone or with a double date, parked in front of the house, sounding the horn for your daughter. The noise is loud and vibrant, setting your nerves on edge. You hope that the constant tooting is not going to annoy the neighbors, but you have your doubts. 'Why are young people so lazy and ill-mannered?' you ask yourself. 'Why don't they come to the front door and ring the bell?'

"Let me tell you what I think about these horn-tooting callers. They're not really lazy, and they don't mean to be rude and inconsiderate. They simply are too timid to come to the house. They are afraid that they may be faced with introductions or drawn into conversation with members of the family. It's a situation they don't know how to handle. They avoid it by staying away and announcing their presence by tooting the horn.

"This explanation may sound fantastic, but I believe that it's basically true. Many parents are unaware that teen-agers are often self-conscious and embarrassed about dating. They fail to realize that it's a new experience. It takes time for young people to develop poise and self-assurance in dating situations. If, at times, their behavior seems inconsiderate or ill-mannered, maybe we parents are somewhat at fault.

"For example, all too often the family teases teen-agers about their dates. This may be done in a spirit of fun, but it's anything but humorous to the young people, who consider dating a serious matter. Poking fun at them makes them feel ill at ease and insecure.

"Or take the example of a boy calling for his date. If the girl is not ready, he may be greeted at the door by one of her parents or by her kid brother with a supercilious grin on his face. The whole family is in the living room waiting to look him over, or so it seems. What will he say? How will he act? He fidgets around unable to carry on an intelligent conversation. The girl's parents make little or no effort to put him at his ease. In fact, they may do just the opposite by briefing him on how they expect their daughter to be treated and what time they want her home. 'Promptly too,' they add in an authoritative way. Small wonder that the boy is tongue-tied and does nothing but nod and nod. By the time the girl appears, beads of perspiration stand out on his forehead. He can't get away quickly enough. No, it's not surprising that he becomes a horn-tooting caller.

"Now let's see what might be done about the situation. First, I've asked Ellen to imagine that she's the girl receiving the caller. She will tell you how a teen-ager might handle the problem of a horn-tooting caller."

Mrs. Dean paused, and Ellen came forward.

ELLEN: "There are several things I might do. I could wait in the house until the caller gets tired of tooting and comes to the door. Or I might go out and cancel the date. Or I might keep the date, but tell the caller that I prefer to have him come to the house without announcing his arrival to the neighbors. I think this method would be the most satisfactory for all concerned."

MRS. DEAN: "How about your family? What would you do to make the caller feel at ease with them?"

ELLEN: "Well, in the first place, I would try to be ready and not keep my caller waiting. I could greet him

at the door, ask him in, and introduce him to the family if they hadn't already met him. We could make a few brief comments about the weather. I could say that I'd be home at whatever hour my parents and I had previously agreed on. Then we could leave."

Mrs. Dean thanked Ellen for her remarks. She then announced that Tom would present the caller's point of view.

TOM: "What Mrs. Dean has said about the horn-tooting caller is true. He is self-conscious about dating. He doesn't know how to handle the kid brother, and he's very apt to be ill at ease with the girl's parents. But this is what he needs to learn to do. I'll pretend that I'm the caller.

"I arrive on time with all the assurance and self-confidence I can muster up. If the kid brother meets me at the door, I look him straight in the eye and introduce myself. As I head toward the living room, I ask him what he thinks about the Dodgers or the Red Sox or some other team. Or if it's the football season, I mention a local game or a big college game coming up. The chances are he'll do all the talking for the moment.

"If one of the girl's parents meets me at the door, I follow the same procedure. After introducing myself, I comment on the weather. Then if I see that I'm in for a wait, I talk about something that interests adults. Usually whatever interests my own parents will serve as a good topic. In the meantime I try not to be fidgety. I realize that any show of embarrassment on my part may make the girl's parents feel ill at ease too. So I chat along easily and before I know it, my date has appeared. Before we leave,

I tell her parents that I'll bring her home on time. I figure that this will pay dividends when I meet her parents again. As I go out the door, I think to myself, 'Well, that wasn't so difficult after all.'"

Mrs. Dean thanked Tom, who then returned to his seat.

How late is late?

Mrs. Jones was the third and last speaker for the broadcast. Her remarks ran something like this:

"One of the knotty problems in many families is the question of how often young people should go out at night and at what time they should be home. Some parents do not consider it advisable for them to go out at all on school nights. They point to the need for adequate sleep and for time to do homework, to carry on hobbies, or to be with the family.

"However, young people are often involved in club work, school sports, community-center activities, or church affairs which function on week nights. Since sleep and homework cannot be ignored, and since it is generally recognized that young people have certain social obligations, a family understanding needs to be reached. In most cases it is not difficult for parents and young people to reach an agreement that the hour for getting in on school nights needs to be earlier than on week-end evenings.

"The trouble generally comes on Friday and Saturday evenings when schoolwork and sleep are not so pressing. All too often parents have one idea as to what constitutes a reasonable hour to be home, while young people have another. However, sometimes young people would really like to come home earlier than they do. But because other couples are keeping later hours, they feel that it's important to do the same. If parents are concerned about late hours, they might try holding a discussion among themselves. If a group of parents can agree on what seems a fair hour to be home, they may be able to work out dating hours with their sons and daughters that will satisfy both sides. Or it might be helpful to have a discussion between a group of parents and their teen-agers in which both sides can be presented. The solution to this problem also depends on what there is for young people in a community to do when they are out. Parents worry less about hours when they know and approve of the recreational activities of their boys and girls."

Dating Etiquette

As the students entered the homemaking room on the day scheduled for the second broadcast, they saw a large banner hung across the room with block letters saying, "In Case You Ask." Seated in front of the banner were the four seniors participating in the broadcast.

IN CASE YOU ASK

In case you ask

Paul opened the program with the customary introductions. He explained that the group would answer etiquette questions which had been asked in the recent survey on dating. The answers to these questions would be based on socially accepted procedures for young people. The broadcast proceeded something like this:

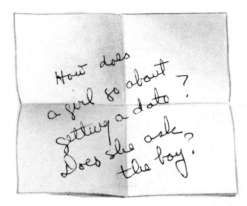

BARBARA SAYS: As a rule, it's customary for a boy to ask a girl for a date, but there are exceptions. A girl or a group of girls may invite boys to a party or to some affair they are holding. Or a girl may invite a boy to a class dance if the boy is not a member of the class and would otherwise not attend. A girl can often pave the way for a date by being friendly toward a boy and showing an interest in something he likes.

How does a boy who is bashful start dating?

GORDON SAYS: You can begin by joining clubs and other groups in which there are both boys and girls. Then start going to mixed parties where you can watch how other boys handle social situations. When you find a girl who interests you, make arrangements for a double or triple date. If possible, plan to include some boy who has already had dating experience. Then you can see how he manages money

matters, escorting, and saying good night. After these experiences, you'll probably have enough self-confidence to date a girl alone. But here's a final bit of advice.

Ask for a date at least several days in advance. If you ask her for the same evening, she may refuse, thinking someone else turned you down at the last moment. No girl likes to feel that she's second choice.

Don't say to the girl, "Are you doing anything Saturday night?" No girl likes to admit that were it not for your call, she'd be at home.

3. Don't ask the girl what she would like to do for the evening. She may suggest something way beyond the range of your pocketbook. Give her a choice of activities you feel you can afford.

4. State the time you will call for her. She may be ready if she knows when to expect you.

5. Check your finances before you set out. Plan to have a little more than the exact amount you think you'll need.

It's up to the girl to tell you when she is expected home. It's up to you to see that she gets there on time.

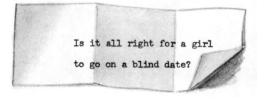

Is it all right for a girl to go on a blind date?

JEANETTE SAYS: A blind date is all right if you can trust the person who is making the arrangements. However, when you accept, it is understood that at least one other couple is going on the date. Don't be disappointed if your dating partner turns out to be just another human being and not the prize package you may have hoped for. You can at least practice your social skills by making the occasion as pleasant as possible.

How do you break a date?

JOHN SAYS: If it is necessary for a girl to break a date, call the boy as soon as possible. Tell him frankly just what the situation is. Failure to offer an explanation may hurt his feelings and give the impression that you do not want to go out with him. Tell him that you are sorry, but hope that you can get together soon.

BARBARA SAYS: When it is necessary for a boy to break a date, he can ease the situation by trying to postpone the date to another definite time. This is important. Otherwise the girl may hesitate before accepting another date with him for fear of being let down again. And there's nothing more embarrassing to a girl than being left in the lurch.

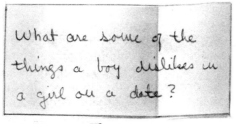

What are some of the things a boy dislikes in a girl on a date?

GORDON SAYS: They are —

Applying make-up in public

Talking loudly or making herself conspicuous in a public place

Being too possessive or too aggressive

Looking bored or not showing enthusiasm for the things they are doing

Trying to make him jealous

Making catty, gossipy, or sarcastic remarks

Trying to trap him into another date by saying, "When shall I see you again?"

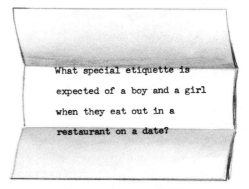

What special etiquette is expected of a boy and a girl when they eat out in a restaurant on a date?

BARBARA SAYS: The girl follows the headwaiter or hostess, the boy bringing up in the rear. If a waiter is not available, the boy helps the girl with her coat and holds the chair for her. The coat may be draped over the back of the chair, or it may be hung on a nearby rack, or in some other place provided for wraps.

The girl's order is given first. She may give it to the waiter herself, or tell the boy what she wants and let him order for both of them. In selecting food, the *à la carte* meal means that you pay for each dish separately. This is usually more expensive than *table d'hôte*, which is a complete meal for the price of the main dish.

If the girl leaves the table during the meal, the boy rises when she gets up and again when she returns. He rises when a girl stops at the table to say hello. He does not rise for a boy but would for an older man. A girl does not rise for another girl but would for an older woman.

When the boy is given the check, he may look it over and add up the total. Tipping varies from place to place, but fifteen per cent is considered acceptable in most places.

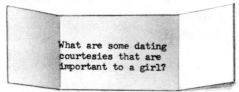

What are some dating courtesies that are important to a girl?

JEANETTE says: They are —

Helping her in and out of a car

Holding open a door for her to enter first

Picking up things she may drop

Helping her with her wraps

Asking her where she would like to sit in a movie, and then telling the usher

Following the usher and her down the aisle. Or if there is no usher, taking the lead in locating seats, and then standing back for her to enter first

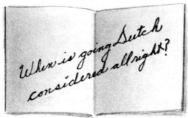

When is going Dutch considered all right?

GORDON SAYS: If a boy asks a girl to go somewhere with him, he is expected to take care of the expenses. But if a girl accidentally meets a boy on her way to the movies, or to some affair at school where admission is charged, she can insist upon paying her own way. Boys and girls who are constantly going places together in a group can either go Dutch or take turns paying.

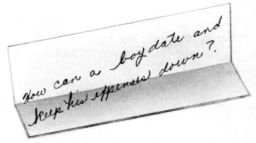

How can a boy date and keep his expenses down?

JEANETTE says: Most girls do not expect expensive entertainment. They are embarrassed when they know that a boy has gone beyond his budget. A boy who wants to keep expenses down can draw up a list of places where he and his date can keep costs low and recreation high. Many girls enjoy an occasional trip to a museum, or merely a walk in the country. But most girls like to go out with boys who are good company even though the boys have little to spend.

Is it all right for a girl to accept gifts from a boy?

BARBARA SAYS: Accepting gifts from a boy is a personal matter, which a girl will need to decide for herself. However, a girl who accepts too many or too expensive gifts from a boy is bound to feel indebted to him. And the question is: does a girl want to become obligated? The boy too may feel that a girl who accepts his gifts belongs to him. If a girl wants to avoid embarrassment, she can tell the boy that she does not believe in gifts during high school years.

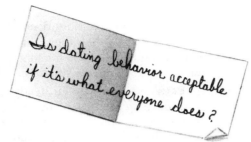

Is dating behavior acceptable if it's what everyone does?

JOHN SAYS: We four seniors believe that something more than "everyone does it" is necessary for personal dating satisfactions and happiness. There are, of course, certain rules of conduct in our society that we must abide by. We can learn about these rules and other forms of social etiquette from our parents and friends, by reading books on the subject, and by observing others. But it is up to each of us individually to develop a standard of dating behavior. We must build up our own sense of values and learn to make decisions which will make us feel at ease within ourselves. Having a high standard of dating behavior will not only lead to personal happiness, but it will create a better understanding with our friends and our families. And so we say, "Happy dating to each and every one of you." (See Book 1 for other forms of etiquette, pages 104–119, 168–170, 321–323, 327–328.)

Going Steady

The broadcast on going steady was held in the form of a debate with two boys and two girls on each side. Paul explained that going steady implied that a boy and girl were having dates with each other exclusively over a period of weeks. He then introduced the speakers. Grace and Mark were to present what might be considered the ad-

vantages of going steady; Tom and Carla, the disadvantages. Their remarks follow:

The advantages

GRACE: "Going steady gives a girl a feeling of security. She doesn't have to sit around the house waiting for a phone call, or stay at home if she doesn't get one. She's usually sure of a date."

MARK: "Having someone to date makes a boy feel secure too. He doesn't have to buck competition for a girl. Going steady gives him prestige in the eyes of the other fellows too."

GRACE: "Dating exclusively gives both the boy and the girl an opportunity to know each other well. This helps to determine whether they want their dating to continue still longer."

MARK: "It costs less money to date only one girl. The boy isn't afraid to tell her what he can afford to spend. And a girl who goes steady is usually considerate about a boy's purse."

GRACE: "Going steady may make the family feel more secure because they know the boy or girl. They are freed from worry that their sons or daughters may be going out with undesirable companions."

The disadvantages

CARLA: "A girl who goes steady may think that she's sure of having a date. But it doesn't always turn out that way. What if something comes up to prevent the boy from taking her out as planned? Maybe the girl has a new dress for the occasion, or it's an affair she has long been anticipating. It's a great disappointment to have to stay at home and miss the fun."

TOM: "It may cost more money to date one girl if she expects the boy to take her out all the time. If a boy is free to date as he pleases and happens to be short of funds, he can go stag or simply not go at all."

CARLA: "Going steady may be disturbing to the girl's family. They may consider the friendship too serious and want to break it up. Or they may not like the boy and want the girl to change. The same may also be true of the boy's family."

TOM: "When a boy and girl date exclusively, they tend to stick pretty much to themselves. They see only each other and lose contact with their friends. Then if they break up, it's hard to get back into circulation again. They both may sit around a long time without a date."

CARLA: "Going steady prevents boys and girls from making new friends. It's important for teen-agers to get acquainted with different types of persons. This gives them experience in evaluating people, which they need before choosing a life partner."

TOM: "All of us respond differently to each person we know. Going steady may limit a boy and girl's experience in responding to a variety of people. Neither person has an opportunity to find out what responses produce the best results or lead to the most happiness. This can only be found by dating a lot of people."

CARLA: "Once a boy and a girl become used to each other, it's difficult to change and adjust to another person. But by dating different people, they learn to make adjustments more easily."

TOM: "The trouble with going steady is that either the boy or the girl may be more serious than the other. One of them may want to carry on too long. This may create a difficult situation."

CARLA: "Boys and girls who go steady are apt to develop feelings of possessiveness toward one another. This may lead to an attempt to dominate and control each other's lives to the extent that they lose their own personal identities."

TOM: "Speaking for all four of us, we feel that the decision of going steady or not going steady is up to you personally. You'll need to weigh all the angles and then decide what seems best. It's a question of values. Boy and girl friendships are valuable experiences. Your success in them is important for your future happiness."

CLASS MEMO:
What can you add to the three broadcasts that will help meet personal dating problems which members of your class may have?

Suggestions for Improving One's Datability

The students believed that the three broadcasts on dating had been quite successful. Several reported that various students in other classes had been asking for information on the subject. In evaluating what they had learned, Miss Corey's group decided to offer some general suggestions for improving

HOW TO IMPROVE ONE'S DATABILITY

- Try to be your ideal self. Cultivate sincerity and straightforwardness. Avoid trying to win dates by putting up a front you cannot afford, or by being a carbon copy of someone else. Be yourself.

- Polish up your social skills and good manners, so that you feel completely at ease.

- Keep on friendly terms with the opposite sex. A person who knows how to make and keep friends gets along well in dating.

- Learn to be sensitive to the welfare of others and to recognize their worth. Respect the feelings of those you are with, and refrain from making unfavorable comments.

- Enter enthusiastically into planning activities with your date or with other couples. Develop your skills and hobbies. Make people feel that you are interesting and fun to be with.

- Work out a high standard of behavior, and make every effort to practice it day by day. Try to establish a reputation for being a person of high principles, and for being trustworthy, courageous, and loyal.

one's datability. These suggestions could be passed on to others who might be interested in having them. At the same time, they would serve as guides for future reference for themselves when they wanted to check up on their own datability. The suggestions were set up in the form of a chart which is given on this page.

HELPING WITH FAMILY ENTERTAINMENT

In opening the class discussion on family entertaining, Paul and Roy told about a movie they had seen at the community club called *Democracy in the Home.* The movie stressed the point that one of the greatest contributions to the democratic spirit in the home is brought about through good times which the family shares together. Both boys felt that this idea tied in with the classwork on entertaining.

During the discussion which followed, the students decided that there are three types of entertaining in which family members can share experiences. First, there is planned entertainment for family friends. Then there are impromptu affairs when friends drop in unexpectedly. Last, but not least are the good times which the family members have among themselves — whether impromptu or planned.

Entertaining So That My Family and Our Friends Have the Best Time Ever

The students recalled that in their previous classwork they had learned a great deal about greeting people and making introductions. Knowing how to be at ease with people, and how to be a good host or hostess were also included. (See Book 1, pages 112–115, 321–323 for these subjects.) All of this, of course, would help them a great deal in entertaining.

However, since their present classwork revolved around the family, it seemed advisable to consider how they could make entertaining fun for the members of their families as well as for family friends. A spirited discussion soon brought out the following points which John wrote on the blackboard:

What it takes for happy family entertaining
- Feeling that all members can offer hospitality to their friends
- Guarding against entertaining special friends so often that other members are prevented from entertaining theirs
- Finding out what kind of entertaining different members like, and trying to meet their preferences in so far as possible
- Spending only what the family can afford, but providing interesting food
- Applying social know-how in such matters as (1) seeing that the spirit of courtesy prevails, (2) getting along with people of different ages, and (3) being pleasant to all guests, and not monopolizing the attention of any special one

Working out individual plans

Keeping these points in mind, the students then began to make individual plans for family entertainment. First of all, they agreed to explain the classwork they were doing to their parents and other members of the family. They realized that it was important to obtain the family's cooperation before making any definite plans. The kind of entertaining different members preferred, the amount of money to be spent, and how to rise to the occasion of impromptu guests needed special consideration. Once these matters were taken care of, each student would then set up a brief plan for family entertaining.

As soon as the plans were completed, they were to be brought to class. But all of them were to be ready by the beginning of the week. In the meantime, questions that might arise with reference to setting up the ideas could be discussed in class.

Presenting some of the ideas for planned entertainment

The students showed considerable thought and ingenuity in setting up their plans. Everyone seemed to be trying to do something that would fit into his or her family situation. For example, a father's business associates, a mother's friends from her old home town, an older sister's boy friend, and a young brother's cub scout group were some of the people included in the plans.

Mary and Bruce's plans are given to show how a family of four and a family of seven might entertain.

MARY'S PLAN

THE FAMILY: Father, Mother, myself, and Bill, ten years old

OVER-ALL PLAN: Some form of entertaining every week or so

Each member to plan the kind of entertaining he or she desires, and to decide who will be guests

Each member to assume certain duties to help make the affairs run smoothly and successfully, the duties to be rotated from time to time if desired

PLANS FOR THE COMING WEEKS:

MOTHER: A dinner party, with our best china, for Mr. and Mrs. Armstrong, our new neighbors

FATHER: A barbecue supper in the back yard for his bowling team

BILL: A Saturday afternoon outing at Lake Cullen, with swimming and boating followed by a wiener roast, for two of his special friends

MYSELF: A Sunday night supper at home for the boys and girls who are serving on the committee for the class dance

BRUCE'S PLAN

THE FAMILY: Father; Mother; myself; George, twelve; Jean, ten; Frances, six; Amy, four

THE PLAN: To celebrate birthdays, holidays, and special events that occur in my family, such as scout awards, or a promotion for my father

Each member to invite a few friends to the home for his or her birthday, and to decide what form of entertainment it will be

On holidays and special events, to serve a dish we all enjoy but do not have too frequently

Carrying out the plans

Once the plans had been set up, everyone was anxious to begin carrying them out. However, in several cases this would not be possible for some time. In Bruce's family, for example, the first birthday and holiday were a month away, and special events did not often occur. On the other hand, Mary said that she hoped to put her ideas into operation within a few days. Several others said they would be ready as soon as some of the details could be arranged.

As the students discussed the situation, they decided to base their reports on family entertainment on the answers to the following questions:

1. Were members of my family satisfied with the entertaining provided? If not, what can be done to produce more satisfaction?

2. Did we keep within the amount of money planned?

3. Did we all do our part in applying social know-how?

4. Did our friends seem to enjoy themselves?

5. Can I make future entertaining more satisfactory? If so, how?

MARY'S REPORT

Mary was the first to tell the class how her plan had progressed. The illustration on page 59 shows how she had jotted down in her notebook the answers to the five questions on her mother's dinner party

SARAH'S REPORT ON IMPROMPTU ENTERTAINING

Sarah reported that two unexpected callers came to see her grandmother one evening. "We were all sitting in the living room at the time," she said. "Dad and Mother were reading the evening paper. My brother David, who is eleven years old, was looking at the funnies. Grandmother was knitting a sweater, and I was looking over some magazines for poster ideas.

"After everyone had greeted the guests, David looked at the clock, said good night, and went up to his room. While the others were talking, I went out to the kitchen to see what we might serve for refreshments. I made a few sandwiches and set out cups for hot chocolate. When I returned to the living room, one of the guests asked me to play the piano. I had a book of songs called *Old-Time Favorites,* and I started with some of them. When Mrs. James began to sing, everyone joined in. Soon they all gathered around the piano, singing first one song and then another. Later, after Mother and I served refreshments, our guests said it was one of the most enjoyable evenings they had had for a long time. Dad said so too after he returned from taking them home in the car."

Before ending her report, Sarah made a few remarks about impromptu entertainment. She said that it could often be more fun than planned entertainment, because of its spontaneity. However, you will need to be ready to apply many of the same techniques used for planned entertainment. For example, cordiality, hospitality, and social know-how are essential for all home entertainment. It is also important to be sure that the guests are having a good time. If conversation lags, it may be advisable to introduce an activity that will interest the group, such as looking at pictures, or showing a hobby. If time permits, some simple refreshments, such as tea, coffee, or hot chocolate, and cookies, will add to the pleasantness of the visit.

Leisure-Time Fun with the Family

When the class began to discuss the third type of entertaining —

MARY'S REPORT

1. Not wholly

Even though I helped, Mother did more than her share of the work and was too tired to enjoy the guests after dinner. Next time I'll try to give her more assistance. My father said he would try to be home earlier the next time we entertained, so that he could help with last-minute preparations.

2. Yes

We actually spent a little less than we planned for, because of a week-end sale at our grocer's.

3. Yes, except Bill

Mother had to remind him to say good night to the guests before he left for his scout meeting.

4. Yes, I think so

Our guests said they enjoyed every minute of their visit. They made favorable comments on the food and on my table service. They also mentioned how handy Bill was in clearing the table.

5. Yes

I'll try to set up a better work schedule for advance preparation.

good times which the family members have among themselves — Paul and Roy again mentioned the film they had seen at the community club.

Fun ideas

"The movie tried to show that the one place where you can really have fun is with the group *you know best* and with the group *who knows you best* — your family," said Paul. "When you're with them, you can be yourself and relax."

"You learn that your mother and father can be friends as well as parents," added Roy, "and that most grownups can be fun."

Several of the other students then told about some of the things their families do together. Birthday celebrations, picnics, and excursions were general occurrences. Before the discussion ended, the class decided to set up some descriptions of various indoor and outdoor activities that might be fun for a family group. When Paul suggested that these descriptions might tie in with some of the classwork they were doing in English composition, he was urged to discuss the matter with Miss Fenton, the English teacher.

Yes, Miss Fenton said that each homemaking student could write a brief, informal description for the English class of an activity that had been enjoyed by his or her family, or a friend's family. Several of the descriptions follow with appropriate tips added by some of the students:

A family excursion in the car can be made more enjoyable for all if play materials and a snack are provided for restless children.

Playing table games together is a popular way of having family fun.

Having summertime supper in the back yard is enjoyed by family members of varying ages.

Broiling one's supper on a skewer over an outdoor grill adds to the pleasure of the family meal.

Here family members share their hobbies. Little Sister collects model horses; Father, liberty head nickels. Brother makes model automobiles. Mother collects cookbooks; Older Sister, interesting souvenirs.

FUN WITH THE FAMILY

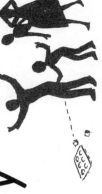

SURPRISE NIGHT AT THE SMITHS'

What fun they have at the Smith home on surprise night! Maybe Mr. Smith puts on a new record, and everybody has to do something in time to the music. Little Janet sings a new song learned at school. Mrs. Smith pretends she's Old Mother Hubbard saying that the cupboard is bare. Then she gives the family ten minutes to hunt in hidden places for peanuts, candy, apples, or popcorn balls. Fifteen-year-old Dennis may have a new game in which he and his parents accept handicaps when Janet participates with them. Yes, there's bound to be lots of fun and laughter on surprise night, which is a weekly affair at the Smiths'.

TIPS

- Try to have some form of family fun at least once a week. The activity may be planned or impromptu.

- Plan some afternoon affairs so that the little ones can join in the family fun.

- Add simple refreshments that everyone likes at some of the get-togethers.

A TREASURE-HUNT PICNIC IN THE BACK YARD

It's difficult to get ahead of the Seward family when it comes to originality. Their most recent idea was a new kind of family picnic in the back yard. Each member was assigned one item on the supper menu. This was hidden somewhere in the yard to be found by other members of the family through clues. A trail of small pieces of paper led to the Thermos jug of lemonade. A limerick posted on a tree gave directions for finding the salad. Numbered slips of paper pointed the way to the potato chips and pickles. Song titles, such as *Where, Oh, Where Has My Little Dog Gone?* gave directions for finding the hot dogs and rolls. *Baby, It's Cold Inside* indicated that the watermelon was in the refrigerator. Small wonder that the Seward family have such good times together all through the year.

SHOESTRING CAMPING WITH THE MAYNARDS

You can see them starting off in the old station wagon every week end during the summer season for a campsite in one of the state parks. There isn't much money in the Maynard family. But during the previous winter, each member earned something extra for the camping equipment. This includes a tent, canvas as the floor, air mattresses, a gasoline stove, an ax, a mosquito net for the front of the tent, a portable ice box, and a first-aid kit. There are no special camp dishes, cooking kits, or camp blankets — old things from home do the trick. That's why they call it shoestring camping. Next summer the Maynards plan to vary the schedule by taking several longer trips instead of going away week ends.

HOMEMADE—BUT IT'S FUN

Sure, if you have the money, you can buy just about anything. But think of the satisfaction you will have if you create something yourself. That's what the Bates family decided to do — have homemade fun. Each week some member of the family prepares a game or some activity that can be shared by the family group, but that is devised from materials that are in the home. The success of each idea is gauged by the ingenuity of the materials used, and the enjoyment the family receives. Here are some of the ideas carried out.

Muffin-Pan Polo

Equipment — One 6-cup muffin pan and five wooden cubes, one inch square, each side numbered, one number to a side, 0, 5, 10, 15 for one cube, 20, 25, 30, 35 for another, and so on

Game — Try to toss the cubes into the cups of the muffin pan from a distance of 6 to 10 feet, depending on the age of the person — the younger, the nearer.

Score — Ten points for each cube in the cup, plus the total of the sides up

JOKE NIGHT AT THE SNYDERS'

Hear the laughter coming from that little home over there? Well, it's the weekly joke night in the Snyder household when every member of the family shares at least one joke with the others during the evening meal. Supper is really the only time when such a busy family can seem to get together. After the meal, they push back their plates and sit around the table for a while, enjoying each other's company. Sometimes they talk about the events of the day – pleasant things that have happened – or discuss ideas for making improvements about their home, which they are all working so hard to pay for. But come what will, Thursday is always joke night. No Snyder would miss it for the world. It's been so much fun that they are considering a riddle night too.

TIPS

- If the family is together infrequently, make the evening meal a special occasion with interesting food and good conversation.

- A family might set aside one evening a week to be at home for a family get-together with entertainment planned for all to enjoy.

TIPS

ON CAMPING

- Limit one day's travel so that you can be in camp four hours before dark. If possible, don't plan to travel two or more consecutive days. Breaking camp in the morning, traveling all day, and then repeating this the next day is work – not fun – for all concerned.

- Look the whole camp area over carefully before choosing your site. Consider the distance from water and other facilities – neither too near nor too far.

- Be prepared for rain, in tents that don't leak, with cooking facilities under shelter, with overshoes, and with things for each member of the family to do when cooped up.

- Know how to cope with bugs, flies, and mosquitoes. Don't let them spoil your enjoyment of being out of doors.

- Plan the meals carefully so that you have a variety of foods.

TV CAPERS

Yes, that's what they are, according to the Chapin family. And it all started one night when there was such poor reception on the television that they could not watch their favorite weekly programs. It was a stormy night, and no one wanted to go out. Sixteen-year-old Jean therefore suggested that they each read different parts in *The Merchant of Venice*, which her class at school was studying. They had two copies at home and borrowed another from one of Jean's friends across the street. The evening was so successful that they tried it again the next time the television reception was poor. Then one day Jean brought home from the library a book of short plays, and the family tried acting out the parts in one of the skits. Now they don't wait for a poor television night. They have a regular time each week for reading a long play or acting out a skit or reading aloud an interesting novel.

Bell-and-Ball Ringer

Equipment – A small bell suspended in a 10-inch or a 12-inch wire hoop, a nail, rope or wire, and an old tennis ball

Game – Suspend the hoop – bell up – from the nail by rope or wire in an open doorway to within 4 or 5 feet from the floor. Then from a distance of 8 to 15 feet, depending upon the age and size of the person, try to toss the ball through the hoop without ringing the bell.

Score – Five trials – 10 points for each time the ball goes through the hoop, and 20 points when it goes through without ringing the bell

Ring Its Leg

Equipment – A kitchen chair, and five rubber rings made from an old bath hose, the rings to measure 4, 5, 6, 7, and 8 inches in diameter

Game – Invert the chair. Try to toss the rings from a distance of 8 to 12 feet, so that they will land around one of the chair legs.

Score – From the smallest to the largest ring, 100, 75, 50, 25, and 10 points

Cartoon Comments on Family Entertaining

One day as the classwork on family entertaining was nearing completion, Michael brought in a large poster. Several students, who knew that Michael was very clever at drawing stick figures, gathered around him as he tacked the poster on the bulletin board.

"I simply couldn't resist the urge to draw some of my impressions of our classwork," he said. The illustration below shows what he drew.

CLASS MEMO: How do your ideas on family entertainment compare with the classwork developed by Miss Corey's group?

FEELING AT HOME WHEN AWAY FROM HOME

THE students believed they were now ready to take up the objective *feeling at home when away from home.* As the discussion opened, Miss Corey brought out the point that most families want to be proud of their boys and girls when they visit other homes. They realize that young people are often embarrassed and ill at ease if they don't know what to do, what to wear, or what is expected of them. She then asked the class whether anyone had a personal experience which might illustrate some of the things they needed to know when away from home.

After a slight pause Mark spoke up. "I recently spent a week end with one of my friends," he said. "It wasn't a very satisfactory visit. In fact, I'm embarrassed every time I think about it. My mother says I certainly made a lot of social blunders."

Urged on by the other students, Mark then told the class about his visit.

MARK'S EXPERIENCE VISITING A FRIEND

"Mom was away visiting her sister when the letter arrived from Gordon asking me to spend the week end with him at his home in Waring. It seemed that his prep school was having an unexpected holiday. Gordon thought it would be a wonderful idea for us to get together and discuss plans for the coming summer. He and I repair boats and canoes at Lake Metake where his family and mine have cottages.

"Since the letter didn't come until the afternoon mail, there was barely enough time for me to throw some things into a suitcase and get down to the bus station. I stopped at Dad's office on the way down town to pick up my weekly allowance and to tell him where I was going.

"When I arrived at Waring, I asked a man how to get to Crescent Avenue. He said he was going that way and would drop me off. Mrs. Renard answered the doorbell and seemed somewhat surprised to see me. In fact, it turned out she didn't even know that Gordon was planning to be home that week end. But when he arrived a half hour later, he explained the whole situation. I didn't hear all the conversation, but I gathered it was inconvenient to have guests at this time. Gordon's father wasn't feeling too well and hoped to have a quiet week end.

"Of course we really didn't mean to cause a lot of commotion. But as soon as Gordon's friends learned he was in town, they began calling him on the telephone. Those who couldn't get in touch with him that way came over to the house. The phone or the doorbell seemed to be ringing most of the time. I never knew that a boy could be so popular. The crowd that night was a jolly group and made themselves right at home. We played records, watched TV, and popped corn. Gordon and I really tried to keep them quiet, but we didn't have much luck. They were having too good a time. After they left, Gordon and I planned to get up early the next morning and clean up the kitchen and living room. But we overslept. Mrs. Renard had it all done by the time we came down.

"Sunday afternoon arrived all too soon, and before we knew it Gordon and I were on our way to the bus depot. One of the neighbors took us in his car, because Mr. and Mrs. Renard were resting. It wasn't until I was nearly home that I realized we hadn't once mentioned the subject of our summer plans. 'Oh, well,' I thought, 'Gordon and I'll get together another week end.' But somehow I had a feeling that it wouldn't be at Gordon's home. That was when I remembered I had forgotten to pack my toilet kit and slippers."

Mark's story brought forth all sorts of comments. However, there was a general agreement that to feel at home when visiting, two things are necessary. First of all, you want your hostess to enjoy having you as a guest. And in the second place, you want to enjoy being a guest. To secure these feelings, Mark or anyone else would need to do certain things before the visit, during the visit, and after the visit.

The students then decided to divide into three groups. Group 1 would find out what needed to be done *before the visit.* Group 2 would assemble material on *during the visit;* and Group 3, *after the visit.* Information would be obtained from people experienced in visiting, from reference materials, and from other sources that might prove helpful.

What to Do Before a Visit

The report given by Group 1 consisted of three parts with appropriate illustrations and demonstrations. Summaries of the report follow:

Making and accepting invitations

An invitation — whether by letter or by telephone — needs to be cordial, and to suggest the time of arrival and the approximate length of the visit. It may also give some idea of the kind of entertainment that will prevail, so that the guest may bring suitable clothing. But the approval of your parents needs to be obtained before you extend the invitation. (See Book 1, page 320, for other suggestions on writing an informal invitation and a reply.)

An acceptance needs to state the time of arrival, and to indicate that you are looking forward to the visit.

Packing knack

This part of the report was accompanied by a demonstration, the students having brought in the articles necessary for it. A summary follows:

1. Take only enough clothes and accessories to go with them to be suitably dressed. (See Book 1, pages 34–37, for suitable clothing for various occasions.)

2. If you need only one bag, place your *shoes* on the bottom at one end of the suitcase. Shoe bags will protect other items against soil.

3. Put your *toilet articles* in a plastic bag or kit at the other end of the suitcase.

4. Put *underclothes, stockings, socks, sweaters, crease-resistant blouses, gloves,* and *other accessories* in the middle section.

5. Then comes a *suit* if you need one. In packing a *skirt*, fold it so that it fits the suitcase on all sides. With gored or full skirts, fold over a small triangle at each side, and then fold crosswise as necessary. Tissue paper inside the folds may help to prevent wrinkling. *Trousers* are folded lengthwise following the leg creases, and then crosswise so that they fit the length of the suitcase. To pack a *jacket* or a *coat*, button the garment, and lay it face down on a flat surface. Put the sleeves into a V across the back, making sure that the shoulders are straight and uncreased. If necessary, then fold the whole thing across the middle, top to bottom. Place in the suitcase with each shoulder at each end of the suitcase.

6. Next come *dresses, blouses that wrinkle easily,* or *shirts.* Before packing a dress, fasten all closings. Then pick up the dress by the shoulders, and lay it front down an a flat surface. Place lengthwise folds in the skirt to make its width fit the suitcase. Fold the sleeves in a V across the back. Then make crosswise folds in the dress so that it will fit into the suitcase. If desired, tissue paper may be placed in the sleeves and between the folds. *Blouses* that are frilly or that wrinkle easily may be packed with the dresses, folding the sleeves in a V and using

as few lengthwise folds as possible. *Shirts* may be packed as they are folded when laundered. *Socks* may be placed in the ring of a starched collar. If unstarched, flatten the collar so that there will only be a crease down each side toward the back.

7. Put *night clothes, slippers,* and *robe* at the top if you expect to use them before completely unpacking the suitcase, such as when sleeping on the train. Otherwise they may be put with the underclothes. It is wise to unpack outer garments as soon as possible to allow time for folds to hang out.

8. *Belts* and *other small items* can go around the edges of the suitcase.

A gift for the hostess

It is not necessary, but it is courteous to take your hostess a gift. If you are visiting someone your own age, the mother of your friend is usually regarded as the hostess. You may want to consult your own mother about something appropriate. But flowers, candy, or fruit are usually enjoyed.

During the Visit

Group 2 presented their report in the form of two imaginary guests, showing what each might do during a visit. The chart on the next page shows the way the group set up the report.

THE PESKY PEST	**THE GRACIOUS GUEST**

Arrives earlier or later than expected

Arrives on time, at the hour suggested in the invitation

Brings too much luggage or too little

Has the right amount of luggage to dress suitably

Is late for meals or stays away without phoning the hostess. Refuses to eat certain foods that are disliked. Monopolizes the table conversation or refrains from talking

Appears promptly at mealtime. Eats what is served without comment and appears to enjoy it. Carries on a share of the conversation during the meals

Makes the visit a hardship for the hostess. Does not offer to help with the extra work. Leaves the bedroom untidy and personal belongings scattered around

Tries to make the visit as easy as possible for the hostess. Offers to help with the extra work. Keeps the bedroom and personal belongings neat and tidy

Expects to be entertained all the time. Is discontented and restless if left alone

Does not feel neglected if left alone, but is willing to participate in various types of entertainment

Centers attention on one member of the family and ignores others

Shows an interest in all members of the family

Stays beyond the time suggested in the invitation without being urged to do so. Or leaves in a hurry, forgetting various items

Leaves at the time suggested in the invitation. Never overstays the visit unless especially urged to do so. Packs leisurely, so that nothing is left behind

See the next page for additional points.

After the Visit

Group 3 gave a brief but important finish to the information on visiting. Their report stressed the point that as a guest you need to do two things after a visit:

1. *Always thank your hostess and your friend promptly.* If you were visiting within your community, this may be done by telephone or in person. If not, write thank-you notes within a day or two after you return home. Write the notes in longhand on notepaper, and make them simple and sincere. The two notes on page 70 are examples of what might be written to a hostess and to a friend. The line in the upper right-hand corner indicates the date the note was written, and that in the lower left-hand corner the writer's address, which may be omitted if it is well known by those visited.

2. *Evaluate your visit to see how you may improve it another time.* You may know the courtesies expected of a thoughtful guest, but you may not be able to perform them as easily as you would like. Gaining skill is acquired by evaluating each visit you make, and by trying to profit by the experience you have had.

The students then decided that the two points given at the bottom of this page could well be added to the summary which Group 2 had made.

> CLASS MEMO:
> If feeling at home when away from home is a part of your classwork, what experiences will your group carry out?

Completing the Classwork on Visiting

After the three reports, it seemed advisable for each student to concentrate on the group material in which he or she needed more help. Several students, who expected to be away for the coming holidays, practiced packing a suitcase with the articles used in the demonstration given by Group 1. Other students recalled visits they had made, and evaluated themselves on how nearly they came to being gracious guests. Still others practiced writing thank-you notes, with the assistance of the members of Group 3. By the time the work ended, all of the students believed that they were now well prepared to feel at home when away from home. They hoped that their parents would be proud of them wherever they went.

THE PESKY PEST	THE GRACIOUS GUEST
Fails to write a thank-you note to the hostess and to the friend. Or writes it poorly or late	Writes a cordial well-written note to the hostess and to the friend promptly
Makes no attempt to improve guest know-how	Evaluates each visit to determine what went well and what might be improved; then tries to profit by this experience

September 22, 19___

Dear Susan,

After such an enjoyable week end with you and your family, I'm having trouble getting back into school routine. My thoughts keep returning to the happy hours we had together. It's difficult to say which ones I enjoyed the most, but the beach party you gave Saturday was something I shall long remember. Thank you so much for including me in your weekend plans.

Affectionately yours,
Vera

September 22, 19___

Dear Mrs. Conant,

Please accept my sincere thanks for the delightful week end spent in your home. It was fun being with Susan and meeting some of her friends. I can't recall when I've had such a good time. Thank you again for your kind hospitality. Mother and Dad join me in sending regards to you and Mr. Conant.

Cordially yours,
Vera

PLANNING YOUR OWN CLASSWORK

THE students in Miss Corey's class made a sincere attempt to meet and resolve some of their personal problems honestly and fearlessly. Setting up a picture of the ideal self, they made consistent efforts to develop a realistic understanding of the kind of person they wanted to become. They learned that people meet their problems in various ways — some desirable, others undesirable. Studying how other people behave helped them to guide and control their own emotions.

As you begin to plan your own classwork on problems relating to the family, you may be wondering what approach to take. You are probably aware that you cannot resolve all the problems that may arise. But perhaps you are planning to select some of the most troublesome ones which members of your class have. No doubt you will try to see these problems from the viewpoint of others — your parents, members of your family, and your friends — as the students in Miss Corey's class did. Your class too may want to use role playing and to make use of movies, filmstrips, and other techniques which make situations seem real. But whatever procedures you use will need to be the ones you consider best for your own group.

SUGGESTED EXPERIENCES

As your classwork progresses, you will need various experiences to help you understand more fully some of the problems you are working on. Since no two family situations are alike, a variety of experiences are suggested. From this list, you may find something that will fit into your own particular problem, and help you meet it more satisfactorily.

1. Hold a "What-Do-You-Think Session" on various situations relating to understanding oneself and others. These are some suggested situations.

SITUATION A: Louis and George were running for class treasurer, and George won the election. Louis claims that his defeat was due to the fact that George's father works in a bank. There might, of course, be other reasons. *What do you think?*

SITUATION B: One day Margaret overheard Moira complain about her low mark in homemaking. Moira attributed this to the fact that she was unable to buy expensive material for the garment she made. *What do you think?*

SITUATION C: Marie is fond of her girl friend, Susan, but she often speaks slightingly about Susan's dates and never approves of Susan's boy friends. Marie rarely has a date herself, but she says that's because she does not care about boys. Susan does not believe that this is true. *What do you think?*

2. Have class members turn in unsigned papers listing their pet peeves about the behavior they have observed in others. A committee can summarize these statements and use the results as material for a class discussion on how desirable or undesirable the behavior is.

3. Hold a class discussion on the following question: How can one's personality be improved by good family relationships? By school experiences? By social activities?

4. Have several members of your class tell about people they know who are happy most of the time regardless of the problems that may confront them. Discuss how they may have developed such an attitude.

5. Study magazine advertisements displaying glamor or good looks. Then try to figure out how other personality traits or desirable behavior could be advertised.

6. Your class may want to work out a list of acceptable ways of releasing feelings of anger. Such a list can be very useful to you or any of your friends who fly off the handle too often.

7. Have a group of volunteers bring to class some questions or proverbs relating to pleasant and unpleasant emotions, such as "The angry person opens his mouth and shuts his eyes," or "The only thing we have to fear is fear itself." Then let each student select and study the quotations which appeal to him or to her.

8. Let several members of the class tell how they would handle these situations.

SITUATION A: Early this evening you gave your kid brother a dollar bribe to stay in his room while you were entertaining some of your friends. Just as the party got in full swing, your brother appeared on the scene, with every intention of entering into the fun.

SITUATION B: You are going skating with your special crowd. Later on it will be your turn to have them in for refreshments before they return home. Your mother has asked you not to include a good friend who made a nuisance of himself at your last party.

SITUATION C: Your parents do not approve of your taking part in school activities. They say you are in school to study, not to waste time acting in plays or decorating for parties.

9. Let each member of the class list five things he or she thinks are most important in getting along with one's family. Then compare and discuss the lists.

10. Discuss a currently popular movie or television program which most of your class has seen. Does it picture family relationships as you think they really are? What suggestions, if any, can you offer for making the program more true to life?

11. Each member of the class may want to plan an experience to be carried out within a week with some member of the family. Some suggestions follow:

EXAMPLE A: Try spending a half hour each day with a younger brother or sister you rarely play with. Note your reactions and those of the person you are with.

Getting along well at school with your studies, and with your class-mates and teachers indicates a healthy personality.

Entering into the fun of making music may help to develop and improve your personality.

Pleasant, happy emotions may be stimulated by a vigorous outing on snowshoes or skis, followed by a warming snack.

EXAMPLE B: Try to help a member of your family get something he or she very much desires that will contribute toward happy living. If the desire is not attainable within a few days, help the person to work out plans for its future attainment. Study the person's reactions to your help, as well as your own feelings in the matter.

EXAMPLE C: Keep a record for two days of the unkind or thoughtless things you say or do to members of your family. Then for the next two days, try to say or do the same number of kind and thoughtful things to these same people. Note your reactions and theirs.

12. Using the role-playing technique, portray the following situations or others you may want to consider.

SITUATION A: How a boy or girl wanting more than his or her share of the family income can become satisfied with a fair share

SITUATION B: How boys and girls can keep square in the matter of treats with friends who have far more spending money than they do

13. Your class may want to hold a "Tell-the-Truth Session." Members can tell what they have done or think they might do at home to bring about more cooperation in family money matters.

14. According to Confucius, regardless of how much money your family has, the following is a safe rule to follow: "If a man would be severe toward himself and generous toward others, he would never arouse resentment." If you agree with Confucius, how could you put this rule into practice?

15. Students who so desire may write out a money problem which they have observed. A committee with the assistance of the teacher can select the most interesting ones for various groups to present to the class in a "Behind-the-Scenes-at-Home Television Program." Here are some examples of problems.

EXAMPLE A: Summer vacation is just around the corner. Henry's parents are expecting him to get work part of the time, but Henry has other plans. He wants to learn to play a better game of golf and to improve his swimming.

EXAMPLE B: Frances and Jean Brown, two teen-agers, live in a family where the father holds the purse strings. Mr. Brown does not believe in taking anyone into his confidence about financial matters. He provides for the needs of the family and for some of their wants. This arrangement is very unsatisfactory because no one knows what the family can really afford. Mrs. Brown and the two teen-agers would feel more secure and could make more satisfactory spending plans if they had some knowledge of the family income. They are wondering what clues would provide this knowledge.

16. Appoint groups representing families of four or five, with children of different ages. Let each group demonstrate how a family council might be conducted.

17. Hold a "Dating-Problem Session." Divide the class into small groups of four to six persons with a chairman for each group. Let each group take a dating problem and discuss it among themselves for six minutes. Then let the chairman report the group's recommendations. Here are some suggested problems.

PROBLEM A: A girl whom Harold has admired for some time has agreed to go out with him tonight. But Harold's finances are down to $1.50. He doesn't believe in borrowing, and there is not time to earn extra money. *How can he make the evening interesting?*

PROBLEM B: Kathleen is very much attracted to John. They have been on the staff of the school paper for several weeks, but John hasn't seemed to notice her. Kathleen, knowing that John is not going steady with anyone, would like to date him. *What can she do to encourage his attentions?*

PROBLEM C: Henry recently made a date to go to a movie with Annette, who said she would meet him on the corner by the drugstore. When they returned from the movie, they had a soda at the drugstore. Then Annette insisted that he leave her on the corner, saying that her home was just down the block. The second time he dated Annette, she followed the same procedure. Henry is puzzled and wonders whether there is any reason why Annette does not permit him to call for her at her home. *What could he do?*

PROBLEM D: During the holiday season, Edward's parents asked him to date Cynthia, the daughter of one of their best friends. Cynthia, who attends a girls' school in another state and travels during the summer vacation, spends very little time at home. Edward feels that he would rather date the girls who attend his school, but he hesitates to turn down his parents' request. *How could he handle the situation?*

18. Several members of your class — both boys and girls — who have had dating experience can write an anonymous description of the best date they ever had. Points, such as what the partner was like, what they did, and why the date was so successful, can be stressed.

The descriptions can be screened by a committee with the teacher's assistance, and the most interesting ones discussed in class.

19. Select a group of students to discuss the advantages and disadvantages of a double date.

20. Jane Simmons and her date have gone in his car to a movie in a nearby town. Before they left, Jane had an understanding with her parents that she would return home by eleven o'clock. Use role playing to portray a home scene with Mr. and Mrs. Simmons in the following situations:

Jane isn't home.

Jane still has not arrived.

Jane comes into the house after saying good night to her date.

After the presentation, the class can discuss the situations, keeping the following questions in mind:

a. Was the situation a realistic one? Why or why not?

b. Were the reactions of the individuals understandable?

c. What can be done on future dates to avoid a similar situation?

21. "Dating Etiquette Then and Now" can serve as a topic for class discussion. Students with grandparents living in the home can ask them about dating customs in former years. Other students can look around for old books on etiquette and see what they can find that is different from present-day situations. Seeing how dating customs have changed and explaining the reasons for these changes may prove very interesting.

22. Hold a series of sociodramas, such as:

a. Being courteous and gracious to guests you do not enjoy

b. Entertaining unexpected guests under difficult circumstances

c. Having fun with a family not interested in home entertainment

23. Hold a "Reminiscing Hour," such as one of the following:

a. The time two groups of callers came unexpectedly about the same time

b. The night you entertained for your mother and discovered there was an extra guest at the last minute

c. The evening your father said was one of the best the family ever had together

24. Your class may want to set up a list of activities that family groups may enjoy. These activities may be personal experiences, ideas from interviews with other people, or from reference sources.

25. Ask people you know to tell you about "Favorite Guests I Have Entertained." Then decide what characteristics these persons have in common that make them so popular.

26. Prepare an exhibit of invitation, acceptance, and thank-you notes related to visiting.

27. Hold a mock or live television program on packing a suitcase.

Meals to Fit
the Family's Needs

Learning more about family food needs

Knowing how to plan meals

Buying and storing food wisely

Preparing and serving balanced meals

IT WAS EARLY EVENING in the Jamison household. The supper dishes were still on the dining-room table. Fifteen-year-old Marta was in the kitchen piling up the soiled pots and pans in order to make room for the unwashed dishes. She sighed audibly as she reached under the sink for the dishpan. "I wonder whether I'll ever get finished," she said to herself.

In the living room Mr. Jamison sat at his desk looking over a stack of bills, which had been accumulating for several weeks. He too sighed deeply as he sorted out the bills, placing in one pile those that simply must be paid, and putting the others that could wait into the top drawer. His face was tired and drawn. Two small ridges formed between his kindly blue eyes. He seemed totally unaware that anyone else was in the living room.

Eleven-year-old Teddy and his pudgy nine-year-old sister, Paula, were talking excitedly as they emptied a box of airplane material on the middle of the living-room rug. They seemed happy and interested in their play.

Presently Mr. Jamison looked up from his work and pushed the bills aside. A feeling of unutterable loneliness and inadequacy overwhelmed him. If only Mrs. Jamison were here. She would know what to do. But she had passed away several years ago, leaving him with three small children. Until recently Mrs. Parsons had been their housekeeper. She had not been entirely satisfactory, but was the best they could afford. However, since the family income had not kept pace with the increase in their expenses, he had let her go. Marta was fifteen and should be able to run the house with his help.

But deep down in his heart, Mr. Jamison knew that he and Marta were going to have difficulty managing the household. Even before Mrs. Parsons left, he had been feeling poorly for some time. He suspected that the trouble was due to too little of the right kind of food. Something must be done, and quickly. He could not afford to become ill.

Later that evening Mr. Jamison called his three children together for a family conference. They often talked things over when important decisions were to be made, such as letting Mrs. Parsons go, or deciding what to do for a summer vacation. The children had been wonderfully cooperative about money matters, seldom asking for the little extras that many of their friends had as a matter of course.

Marta came into the living room drying her hands on her apron. She smiled wearily as she sat down with the other members of the family. But as her father began to discuss the difficulties they were having, Marta's face brightened perceptibly.

"I have an idea," she said. "I don't know why I didn't think about it before. Miss Dodds, my homemaking teacher, knows a lot about problems that families face. I can talk over some of our difficulties with her, and perhaps she will offer suggestions."

The others thought this was a fine idea and urged Marta to see Miss Dodds as soon as possible.

Marta found Miss Dodds very receptive and willing to help the Jamison family. She had a warm, pleasing personality which made it easy for Marta to talk about her difficulties.

"Most of our trouble seems to center around food," explained Marta. "It's planning and preparing the meals, and buying the food which bothers me the most."

"How would you like to discuss the situation with the other members of the class?" asked Miss Dodds. "You know we're planning to take up our classwork on foods very soon. Perhaps your problems can serve as a basis for some of the goals we'll be setting up."

"That's a wonderful idea," said Marta. "Maybe it will work two ways. I'll not only be getting the help I need, but the other members of the class will be learning things they can use in their homes too."

MARTA'S PROBLEMS SERVE AS A BASIS FOR THE CLASS GOALS

ONE day a short time later, Miss Dodds told the students about the Jamison family. She mentioned the fact that until recently they had a housekeeper, but now Marta was preparing the family's meals herself. This was already presenting difficulties, and Marta felt greatly in need of advice. Miss Dodds then asked Marta to tell the class more about the situation.

"My father and I seem to lack energy and tire easily," said Marta.

"Both of us are underweight. I suspect it's because we haven't been getting enough of the right kind of food. My brother Teddy worries me because he spends much of the money he earns from his paper route on cokes and candy bars. And Paula, who is fat and pudgy, eats far too many sweets.

"Mrs. Parsons, our former housekeeper, did the best she could, but the meals she served left much to be desired. Without her, we will have a little more money for food. But I wonder whether my father and I will be able to spend it to the best advantage.

"I've made a little improvement, such as having fruit for breakfast, but there is a lot I don't know about getting meals. I realize that I don't manage things very well either. I have difficulty getting dinner ready on time. And I never seem to be able to do all that needs to be done. Perhaps Teddy and Paula could help more." Marta smiled wanly.

The description of the Jamisons' situation served as a challenge to the class. Everyone was most enthusiastic about helping Marta and her family. It did not take long for the students to decide to take Marta's problems as a basis for their classwork on foods. They all seemed to believe that learning how to meet these difficulties would benefit every member of the class as well as Marta and her family.

After a lively discussion, the following goals were selected:

1. Learning more about family food needs.
2. Knowing how to plan meals
3. Buying and storing food wisely
4. Preparing and serving balanced meals

Miss Dodds then asked for volunteers to assist her in selecting books and pamphlets for the reference shelves. Everyone was urged to bring in any material from home that might be helpful. There was also a general agreement that classwork on the first goal would begin at the next meeting.

CLASS MEMO:
In what way would your class have helped the Jamison family? What similar problems do members of your class have?

LEARNING MORE ABOUT FAMILY FOOD NEEDS

AT the next meeting of the class the students were ready to begin learning more about foods the family needs to eat. Peter opened the discussion by saying that from their classwork the previous year, they already knew quite a bit about what foods a person needs daily.

"And we know in a general way why the body needs these foods,"

he added. (See Book 1, pages 136–150.)

Miss Dodds nodded. "What have you learned about food needs that might serve as a good starting point for this year's classwork?" she asked.

Everyone was thoughtful for a few seconds. Then Lucile spoke up. "We learned," she said, "that the body uses various foods for three purposes: (1) for building and repairing the body; (2) for energy to work and play and for heating the body; and (3) for keeping the body working normally."

"Yes," agreed Bob, "and there are sixteen servings of various foods — or substitute servings — that we need every day to supply those three uses of food in the body. I know because I still check myself, now and then, to see that I'm getting them all. For building and repairing the body, one serving of meat, fish, poultry, dried beans or peas, peanut butter, or nuts . . . ," he said pausing for breath. Given the time and necessary breath, it appeared that he could probably complete the summary all by himself. However, there were others eager to join in the discussion.

"We know all about these food needs," said Rita taking advantage of the pause which Bob had made to catch his breath. "But Marta's younger brother and sister don't. There ought to be some interesting way to show them that cokes, candy bars, and sweets won't make them strong and healthy."

Using the Game—"The Health Chain of Good Eating"

"I have an idea," said Dale quickly. "They might enjoy playing the game 'The Health Chain of Good Eating' that Miss Dodds recently put on the reference shelves. I studied one of the copies, and I know several others did too. I'm sure that Teddy and Paula will get a lot of fun out of the game as we all will when we use it. And it certainly will give them a fine start in

The body requires a variety of foods to supply its needs for building and repair, for energy, and for working normally.

learning about foods that are good for them."

Dale's idea made an instant appeal to everyone. With Miss Dodds' approval, Dale then distributed copies of the game to members of the class so that everyone could see how to use it. A reproduction of the material is shown on pages 84 to 85.

The game represents a chain with two clasps — one to begin with and another to fasten the chain together when completed. The chain itself has sixteen links to be fitted together. For seven of these, substitute links may be used. The sixteen links are shown in gray cardboard and the substitute links in white cardboard. Slits in each link through which tape is inserted help to hold the chain together.

To start the game, people would need to recall what they had eaten that day. If they had eaten one serving of the food listed on each of the sixteen links, or on a substitute link, the links would fit into the chain. The links were keyed to fit only where they belonged in the chain or could act as a substitute. This was to avoid making any mistakes about what servings make up a balanced diet. The goal was to keep making a chain each day, and loop it into the previous day's chain.

Learning About Food Needs Through a Question and Answer Session

The students were well pleased with the game as a means to help Teddy and Paula learn about food

needs. However, Bob soon jolted them out of their complacency.

"That's all well and good for the Jamison children," he said. "The health chain is just a game to them. They are too young to be interested in the how's and why's of the game. But it's different with us. I studied the game, and I can see there's a lot I don't understand about how the body uses foods."

"I'm wondering why certain foods are necessary every day," said Janice, who had also been looking over the game.

"Since questions seem to be in order, I'd like to know what vitamins are, and how they are related to foods," said Edward. "You hear so much about them these days."

"And calories too," added Edith quickly. "People are always saying, 'Count your calories.' I know they have something to do with weight, but what are they?"

"In an advertisement on the television the other day I heard something about protein being an essential nutrient," said Mary. "Just what are nutrients, and what is protein anyway? How do our bodies use it? Why haven't we learned about this before?"

Miss Dodds smiled. "The subject of food and its relation to health covers a great deal of ground," she said. "It seems advisable to start out by learning certain things one year, and then following along with more detailed information the second year. In this way you build up a better understanding than when

(Citrus, etc.)

CITRUS
TOMATOES
SALAD GREENS

(Green Veg., etc.)

GREEN VEGE
YELLOW
(Raw,

½ c

OTHER FRUITS,
OTHER VEGETABLES
(Raw, cooked; fresh,
frozen, canned,
dried)

1 serving

(Citrus, etc.)

CITRUS
TO
SALAD G

2

½ cup

(Green Veg., etc.)

GREEN VEGE
YELLOW V
(Raw, co

froze

OTHER FRUITS,
OTHER VEGETABLES
(Raw, cooked; fresh,
frozen, canned,
dried)

1 serving

GREEN VEGETABLES,
YELLOW VEGETABLES
(Raw, cooked; fresh,
frozen, canned)

1 serving

Here's the last link, ever so bright,
That gives you a happy greeting.
These foods serve your body for
   rest, work, and play,
And complete the chain of wise eating.

THE HEALTH CHA

CITRUS FRUITS,
TOMATOES,
SALAD GREENS, CABBAGE

1 orange
2 medium tomatoes
1 cup raw greens
½ cup orange or grapefruit juice

(Potatoes)

(Bread, etc.)

BREAD
(Who

¾
1 cu

(Bread, etc.)

BREAD
(Who

¾
1 cu

BREAD, FLOUR, CEREAL
(Whole grain, enriched)

2 slices bread
¾ cup cooked cereal
1 cup ready-to-eat cereal
1 griddlecake
½ waffle

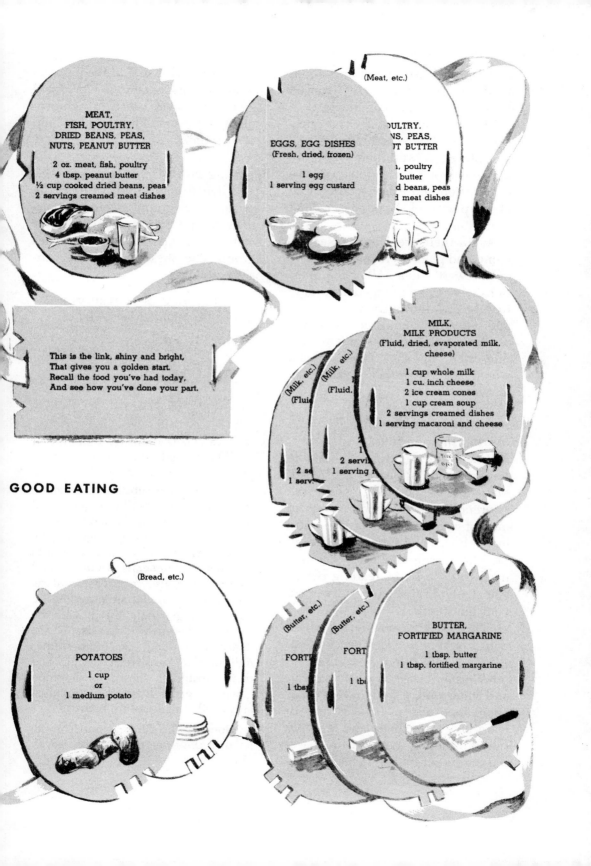

MEAT,
FISH, POULTRY,
DRIED BEANS, PEAS,
NUTS, PEANUT BUTTER

2 oz. meat, fish, poultry
4 tbsp. peanut butter
½ cup cooked dried beans, peas
2 servings creamed meat dishes

(Meat, etc.)

EGGS, EGG DISHES
(Fresh, dried, frozen)

1 egg
1 serving egg custard

OULTRY,
NS, PEAS,
JT BUTTER

n, poultry
butter
d beans, peas
d meat dishes

This is the link, shiny and bright,
That gives you a golden start.
Recall the food you've had today,
And see how you've done your part.

GOOD EATING

MILK,
MILK PRODUCTS
(Fluid, dried, evaporated milk,
cheese)

1 cup whole milk
1 cu. inch cheese
2 ice cream cones
1 cup cream soup
2 servings creamed dishes
1 serving macaroni and cheese

(Bread, etc.)

POTATOES

1 cup
or
1 medium potato

(Butter, etc.)

(Butter, etc.)

BUTTER,
FORTIFIED MARGARINE

1 tbsp. butter
1 tbsp. fortified margarine

you try to learn everything about foods at one time." She paused waiting for further comments.

"There seem to be a lot of questions now that need answering," said Stewart. "And there will probably be more. So why don't we have a 'Question and Answer Session' to clear up some of the points we don't understand?"

Again there were nods of agreement, and plans were made to carry out Stewart's idea. All of the questions were to be grouped according to subject — the nutrients, calories, and the various foods needed daily. Students who had questions or were interested in the same subject would work together getting the answers.

Using source materials for answering the questions

When the matter of suitable source material was mentioned, Miss Dodds nodded toward the reference shelves. "The answers to most of your questions can be found in the books and pamphlets assembled here," she said. "But you may need to do a lot of reading before you can find satisfactory answers to your questions.

"There will be new terms which will probably need to be clarified. It may be difficult at first to see the relationship between what you read and what you are studying at school about food needs. It takes time to learn how to evaluate and to apply the information found in the material on the reference shelves. How-

ever, being able to find the answers to any questions you may have will give a personal sense of achievement. Of course I'll be glad to help at any time."

Reporting on the questions

When it came time to hold the session, each group selected a chairman to report on the questions that were to be answered in his or her group. The questions and their answers follow:

THE ROLE OF NUTRIENTS
[as reported by Edna]

Q. . . . Nutrients is a new word to most of us. I think I understand what it means, but how would you define it?

A. . . . Nutrients are substances or materials which our bodies require and which are found in the foods we eat daily. They are usually listed as proteins, fats, carbohydrates (starches and sugars), minerals, vitamins, and water. Fiber, also known as cellulose, roughage, or bulk, although not a nutrient is generally listed with the nutrients because it assists in the digestion of food. Scientific studies indicate that the sixteen servings and their substitutes shown in the food game will generally provide the nutrients needed daily in the body.

Q. . . . How are the different nutrients related to the three purposes served by food?

To keep food costs down, meat, fish, and poultry — expensive nutrients — may be stretched by using them in casserole dishes. (See page 102.)

Using eggs more frequently when they are low in price is another way of providing a needed nutrient at a reduced food cost. (Again see page 101.)

NUTRIENTS	PURPOSES		
	For building and repairing the body	*For energy to work and play and for heating the body*	*For keeping the body working normally*
Proteins	+	+*	+
Fats		+	
Carbohydrates		+	
Minerals	+		+
Vitamins	+		+
Water			+
Fiber			+

* Expensive source of body heat. See chart, page 96.

A. . . . Each nutrient serves one or more purposes when taken into the body. But all require the presence and assistance of the others if they are to be put to the best use. The summary above shows the purposes which the nutrients serve.

Q. . . . How are the vitamins named?

A. . . . When vitamins were discovered, they were designated by names of the alphabet, starting with A. Now, since more is known about vitamins, some of them have been given names that indicate what they are chemically.

Q. . . . What are some of the vitamins about which information is known?

A. . . . The following vitamins are fairly well known and understood.

Vitamin A

The B vitamins — thiamin or vitamin B_1; riboflavin or vitamin B_2; niacin

Vitamin C or ascorbic acid

Vitamin D

Q. . . . What minerals are considered necessary for body use?

A. . . . Calcium, phosphorus, iron, copper, and iodine are the ones most commonly listed.

A WEIGHTY MATTER
[as reported by Peter]

Q. . . . I don't understand what calories are. Can you explain them?

A. . . . Calories are measurements of energy stored in foods, and used for body activities. We measure weight in pounds, height in inches, and energy in calories. In one sense we do not eat calories. We eat the foods which supply the calories. Our energy needs — the calories we require — depend on various factors, such as age, body build, occupation, and climate. When we eat the number of calories that our energy demands, then our weight does not change. If we eat more than we need, our weight increases, and the leftover calories are stored in the body as fat. When we do not eat enough to meet our energy demands, we lose weight.

Q. . . . Is there any way to know what foods contain a lot of calories?

A. . . . There are certain characteristics of flavor and texture which may serve as a general guide to calorie values. Foods that are relatively high in calories are likely to be compact or concentrated. Some may also be sweet, sticky, gooey, or greasy. Foods that are low in calories are generally watery, often bulky with lots of fiber or coarseness. Such foods as cakes, pies, thick malted milk shakes, fat meats, cheese, and nuts are generally high in calories. Sherbets, fresh fruits, lean meat, skim milk, and crisp vegetables are relatively low in calories. Of course the most accurate way of knowing whether foods are high or low in calories is to consult a calorie chart. Your family doctor, insurance companies, the United States Department of Agriculture, and many other sources have such a chart.

Q. . . . Is it necessary to count calories every day to maintain normal weight?

A. . . . No it isn't. If you eat the sixteen servings from the food groups recommended in the game and already have normal weight, you probably do not need to worry about counting calories. But if you are in doubt about what you should weigh for your age, height, and sex, then you can consult a weight chart. This information may be obtained from the same sources as those given for a calorie chart. If your weight varies considerably from the figures given in the chart, it may be wise to consult your family doctor. He may give you a calorie chart to guide you in the amounts and kinds of food to be eaten to attain normal weight.

THE LOW-DOWN ON MILK
[as reported by Harold]

Q. . . . Why are three servings of milk a day recommended in the game?

A. . . . Few if any other foods supply more nutrients than milk. It is one of the most nearly perfect foods we have. It is superior in calcium and phosphorus but not a good source of iron. It is an inexpensive source of protein of good quality, and a good source of vitamin A and riboflavin. In fact, it is a good source of nearly all vitamins except C and in some cases D, although the latter is often added to milk commercially.

Q. . . . What about substitutes for milk?

A. . . . Since milk is readily available in most sections of our country, it is not desirable to look for substitutes unless you are allergic to milk. Finding substitutes would mean using a lot of other foods for one single food — milk. For example, it would take two cups of baked beans — the kind with molasses — to supply the calcium, and three hamburgers to furnish the riboflavin that one glass of milk supplies.

Q. . . . Suppose a family can't afford the amount of fresh whole milk needed daily; what then?

A. . . . An economical solution may be to use other milk compositions, such as the following:

1. *Fresh skim milk and nonfat-milk solids,* plus extra portions of butter or margarine. These products contain practically all the food value of whole milk except for fat and vitamin A, which butter or margarine would supply.

2. *Buttermilk,* which is similar to skim milk except for the acid content.

3. *Evaporated milk,* a canned milk prepared from whole milk with 50 to 60 per cent of the water removed. When used, it needs to be diluted with an equal amount of water.

A SURVEY OF THE MEAT SITUATION
[as reported by Evelyn]

Q. . . . The game recommends meat once a day. Is that enough? I know people who have it at every meal.

A. . . . Yes, once a day is enough. One serving will give sufficient protein if an egg, whole-grain-cereal products, milk, or milk products are also used. People who eat meat more than once a day may be spending an undue proportion of their food money for meat, and going without other foods that are needed in the diet.

Q. . . . Do different kinds of meat and the edible parts vary in nutritive value?

A. . . . Yes, to some extent. Meat, such as beef, veal, lamb, mutton, and pork, is an excellent source of protein. It also supplies significant amounts of iron, phosphorus, niacin, thiamin, and riboflavin, with pork the richest natural source of thiamin. Organ meats, such as liver, heart, and kidney, are even richer in nutrients. They also provide vitamin A which is not found in other meats, except for traces in the fat. If there is not too much bone or fat, the tougher parts of meat provide the same food value as the tender parts.

BREAD-AND-BUTTER FEATURES
[as reported by David]

Q. . . . In the game, bread, flour, and cereal are labeled "whole grain or enriched." What is meant by enriched?

A. . . . Enrichment was developed as a partial remedy for the losses occurring in the refining of flour and other cereal products. When amounts of thiamin, riboflavin, niacin, and iron approximating those present in the whole grain are added, the product may be labeled "enriched."

Q. . . . Some people won't eat butter or margarine for fear of gaining weight. Don't they need some fat?

A. . . . Everyone needs a certain amount of fat in the diet — even the overweight person who has fat stored in the body. Our richest source of heat and energy is fat, which often carries vitamins A and D with it. Fat also contains essential fatty acids necessary for body growth and healthy skin. In addition, fat acts as insulation to prevent the loss of heat from the body. It also protects the vital organs by serving as cushions for them. Furthermore, there is a prolonged feeling of satisfaction after eating a meal containing some fat. People who do not eat butter or margarine will need to get some fat from other sources, such as fat meat, whole milk, cream, or salad oils.

Q. . . . Why is margarine labeled "fortified," and butter not so labeled?

A. . . . Margarine is high quality fat made from such products as peanut, cottonseed, soybean, and corn oils. The fat is churned in pasteurized skim milk to form a product similar to butter. Since none of the oils mentioned contain vitamin A, manufacturers add generous amounts of this vitamin. The amount of vitamin A in butter will vary according to the food which the cows eat and with the seasons — being less in winter than in the summer.

A CASE FOR EGGS
[as reported by John]

Q. . . . I see that eggs are a good source of protein. Why aren't they grouped with meat in the game?

A. . . . Eggs are so high in other nutrients, as well as protein, that they need to be eaten regularly along with meat.

Q. . . . What nutrients other than protein do eggs have?

A. . . . Eggs are a good source of several minerals — phosphorus, iron, and copper. They also contain the B vitamins (see page 98) and vitamin D. The yolks are especially high in fat and a good source of vitamin A.

REPORTS ON THE FRUIT AND VEGETABLE MARKET
[as reported by Rita]

Q. . . . Why are there no substitutes for fruits and vegetables?

A. . . . Because, in general, as a group fruits and vegetables make the following contributions to the diet that cannot so easily be found elsewhere.

1. They are primarily useful to supply minerals and vitamins.
2. They supply bulk in a desirable form.
3. They add flavor and variety.

Q. . . . Why can green and yellow vegetables be substituted for other fruits and vegetables, but the reverse not be true?

A. . . . Green and yellow vegetables are higher in certain minerals and vitamins than other fruits and vegetables. (See page 98, vitamin A especially.)

Q. . . . Are potatoes and bread needed at the same meal?

A. . . . Since potatoes and bread are both good sources of carbohydrate, some adults may not need both of these foods at the same meal. But growing

Fruits and vegetables—particularly citrus fruits and green and yellow vegetables—are excellent sources of minerals and vitamins.

boys and girls, whose energy requirements are higher than those of adults, may need both.

Q. . . . Why are citrus fruits, tomatoes, salad greens, and cabbage grouped together?

A. . . . Citrus fruits, such as oranges and grapefruit, and the vegetables named are all excellent sources of vitamin C.

Q. . . . What are the differences in the vitamin C content of fresh, frozen, or canned orange juice?

A. . . . The vitamin C content is essentially the same for all three, with a slight difference in favor of fresh orange juice.

Q. . . . Why do some people say that an apple a day is good for one?

A. . . . Many fresh fruits although not especially high in nutrients are valuable in other ways.

1. Their delicious flavors stimulate chewing and start the flow of digestive juices, which are important in good digestion.

2. They supply roughage in the desired form.

3. They have a cleaning effect on the teeth.

Summarizing Food Needs

The students thoroughly enjoyed the Question and Answer Session. However, several remarked that it seemed less easy to fit the information together as compactly as the game had done. For example, Evelyn said that she had trouble remembering what food or food groups provided what nutrients. David added that he would like to know what happens to the body when a person does not get enough of the nutrients that are needed. These remarks and others led to a decision to consult references and then to summarize — in more detail — the points that had been brought out in the Question and Answer Session.

The summary worked out by the class with Miss Dodds' assistance is given on pages 96 to 99. It lists the nutrients, gives their uses in the body, and indicates the results of a mild deficiency. It also shows the distribution of the nutrients in food groups and in individual foods. The students believed that this summary would be helpful to other classes in organizing their knowledge of the body's uses of food.

The class enjoyed a final surprise before their classwork on this first goal was completed. The committee currently in charge of the bulletin board prepared a far less serious summary of their own. They posted it on the bulletin board without the others knowing it until they came to class. This summary is reproduced on the next page. Everyone enjoyed the surprise, and felt that the work on body food needs had been especially interesting.

CLASS MEMO:
What plans will your class make for learning about food needs?

KNOWING HOW TO PLAN MEALS

ONE day when the summary of the food nutrients was nearly completed, Peter happened to mention an article he had recently read about a country where fishing is an important industry. "There the people eat large amounts of fish instead of meat," he said.

"And those countries that manufacture lots of cheese use cheese rather than milk," added Rita.

"There's also a difference in the number of meals that are eaten," said Dale. "I understand that in some countries it's customary to have four or even six meals a day."

"The time of day that meals are eaten also differs," added Janice. "Sometimes the evening meal is not until nine thirty or ten o'clock."

"That's true," said Miss Dodds. "No two countries eat all of the same foods in exactly the same ways. People tend to plan their meals around the foods that are available to them and that fit the conditions under which they live. Gradually they build up what is called a 'food or meal pattern,' which is usually carried over from one generation to the next. When we are ready for our next goal —

WHY EAT?

All the foods which we eat and which make us grow
Are often called nutrients, as you may well know.
By eating the foods which contain all this wealth,
We have a balanced diet and maintain good health.

Carbohydrates
Fats
Proteins*

We eat some foods to make us go,
We're much like an engine, as you know,
And fuel is needed to help us along,
And to keep the whole body comfortably warm.

FUEL FOR MOTION AND HEAT

Proteins
Minerals
Vitamins

We need other foods, for we're constantly growing,
We're building bones and tissues without even knowing
That as they wear out they must be restored,
And producing them both cannot be ignored.

MATERIAL FOR BUILDING AND REPAIRING THE BODY

Proteins
Minerals
Vitamins
Water
Roughage**

Since disease and infections don't lead to much wealth,
We eat certain foods to keep in good health.
They make our eyes sparkle, our step very light.
Without them we'd droop and become a sad sight.

SUBSTANCES FOR KEEPING THE BODY WORKING NORMALLY

*Sometimes used, but expensive for heat and motion

**Technically not a nutrient but is included because it assists in the digestion of food.

knowing how to plan meals — it might be a good idea to start off by examining our food patterns in the United States."

Discussing Meal Patterns

Thus it was that the classwork on the new goal opened with a discussion of eating three meals a day in our country. It brought out the point that for the majority of people, breakfast is usually between seven and eight o'clock in the morning, the noon meal between twelve and one o'clock, and the evening meal between six and seven. However, many people like a snack in the middle of the morning, in the afternoon, and again before they retire.

One of the students also mentioned that here in the United States our meals are generally eaten in one or two orders: (1) breakfast, lunch, and dinner, or (2) breakfast, dinner, and supper.

Young children often have their heavier meal — dinner — at noon followed by a lighter meal — supper — in the evening. Some families follow this procedure for all of their members. However, after children enter school, their noon meal may be a lunch, with dinner in the evening. This is especially true where the father cannot be home for the noon meal.

What we eat at our meals

As the discussion turned to the kinds of foods eaten, it soon became apparent that in our country there is little uniformity in what we eat at our meals. In some parts of New England, such foods as baked beans and brown bread are served regularly. In the South, hominy grits are popular, and hot breads are a must.

However, in order to have a basis for future menu planning, the students decided to set up the meal pattern which seemed to come the closest to what most people in our country follow. This is what they agreed on:

Breakfast
Fruit or fruit juice
Egg and/or meat — sometimes omitted
Cereal, toast or hot bread, or both
Beverage

Lunch or Supper
Main dish — soup and/or the following foods in combination or alone — eggs, cheese, fish, meat, vegetable, or fruit. These may be used as casseroles, sandwiches, salads, or plain
Vegetable or salad — if vegetables are not included in the main dish
Bread, and butter or margarine
Dessert — may be fruit
Beverage

Dinner
Soup or appetizer, or both, or neither
Meat or meat substitute
Vegetables — usually one starchy vegetable and a salad or a green or yellow vegetable or two of these
Bread, and butter or margarine
Dessert — may be fruit
Beverage

Ways of planning meals

During the discussion on meal patterns, Howard brought out the point that families not only differ in the foods they eat, but also in the way they plan their meals. Some of the students said that their mothers found it easier to make out in advance, menus for the whole week. At the same time they made up a list of the foods needed, and shopped on Friday or Saturday when special foods were generally on sale. Some families, who had considerable freezing space, kept frozen a supply of meat, poultry, fish, vegetables, and other items. These families usually planned their meals from day to day around what they had in the freezer. Other families, who had limited storage space, shopped several times a week, planning two or three days' meals in advance.

It soon became evident that various factors affected the length of time which was best for meal planning. Each family would need to work out a system which fitted its own situation. Miss Dodds pointed out that how meals are planned is not as important as seeing that they include foods which make up a balanced diet. In most cases it is easier to do this by planning meals in advance rather than one meal at a time.

General Guides for Menu Planning

Marta then suggested that perhaps the class might be interested in discussing some of the meals served in the Jamison home when they had a housekeeper. "I know we didn't have a balanced diet," she said, "but having some real meals to study — instead of patterns — might help."

Everyone including Miss Dodds agreed that this plan would be helpful not only to Marta but to each of them.

"I'll prepare some menus of typical meals which Mrs. Parsons, our former housekeeper, served," added Marta. "They'll be ready in a day or so."

"In the meantime we can be finding out more about menu planning," said Howard. "Then we'll be better able to discuss Mrs. Parsons' meals."

"What did you have in mind?" asked Miss Dodds.

Howard thought for a moment, and then replied. "There's more to menu planning than fitting a balanced diet into meal patterns," he said. "Marta brought out some of the other things when she first told us about her difficulties. For instance, she spoke about not being able to manage very well. You need to plan meals that you can manage. We learned something about that last year."

"That's right," said Evelyn, "and you need to plan balanced meals that you can afford. Why can't we work out some guides that we can use to evaluate Mrs. Parsons' meals?"

There were nods of approval by the others.

Some time later after consulting references, the students set up four general guides.

1. Follow the meal patterns customarily used in our country, using foods that are essential for a daily balanced diet.
2. Use foods that you can afford.
3. Select foods that will make the meals interesting, appetizing, and satisfying.
4. Take time, energy, and equipment into consideration.

ESSENTIAL FOOD NUTRIENTS

Usefulness in Body, and Distribution in Food Groups or in Individual Foods

Name of Nutrients	Usefulness in Body	Result of Mild Deficiency	Distribution in Food Groups	Distribution in Individual Food
1. PROTEIN	Builds and repairs the body just as building materials build and repair a house Helps regulate body functions, such as the circulation of the blood and the digestion of food May be used as heat and energy, but this is not the main function. When used as energy, it can be compared to burning mahogany wood for heat.	Lack of growth Weak muscles Physical tiredness Mental tiredness Anemia More susceptible to disease	°MILK AND MILK PRODUCTS MEAT, POULTRY, FISH, DRIED BEANS, PEAS, NUTS, PEANUT BUTTER EGGS °°Bread, flour, cereal (whole grain or enriched)	
2. FAT	Is our richest source of heat and energy Often carries vitamins A and D with it Contains acids called "essential fatty acids." These are necessary for body growth and healthy skin. Prevents the loss of heat from the body just as certain insulating materials prevent the loss of heat from outside a house	Underweight Hunger Tiredness	BUTTER AND FORTIFIED MARGARINE	FAT MEATS CREAM SHORTENING VEGETABLE OILS MAYONNAISE SOYBEANS EGG YOLKS NUTS
3. CARBOHYDRATES (Starches and Sugars)	Are the cheapest and most plentiful source of heat and energy When fat burns alone in the body, bad effects, such as headaches, nausea, and irritability, result. If both carbohydrate and fat are burned in the body, there are no bad effects.	Underweight Hunger Tiredness	BREAD, FLOUR, CEREAL Potatoes	Root vegetables, such as carrots Sweet fruits HONEY SUGAR CANDY
4. MINERALS Calcium	Is one of the materials used in making and repairing strong bones and teeth Necessary for normal clotting of blood in case of body injury	Bone deformities, such as bowlegs or knock-knees Poorly developed	MILK AND MILK PRODUCTS	Green leafy vegetables Broccoli Molasses

	Function	Deficiency	Food Sources
	do their normal work. Helps maintain a normal heartbeat Essential for milk production to nourish the young	(top cut off) of the blood	Oranges Dried fruit
Phosphorus	Is one of the materials used in making and repairing strong bones and teeth Normal blood is neutral – neither acidic nor basic. Phosphorus helps maintain this neutrality. Is necessary for the normal use of carbohydrates and fats by the body	Bone deformities Poor teeth	MILK AND MILK PRODUCTS Meat, poultry, fish, dried beans, peas, nuts, peanut butter Eggs Bread, flour, cereal (whole grain or enriched)
Iron	Is essential in forming the red coloring matter found in the red cells of the blood. These red cells carry oxygen from the lungs throughout the body. Is necessary in the body to burn foods which supply heat and energy Is necessary for normal healthy skin	Anemia Poor skin color Tiredness	Green and yellow vegetables Potatoes Other vegetables and fruits Muscle and organ meats, poultry, fish, dried beans, peas, nuts, peanut butter Eggs Bread, flour, cereal (whole grain or enriched)
Copper	Is essential for the conversion of iron into the red coloring matter of the red blood cells, and for the growth of the cells	Unknown	Is found in most of the foods which contain iron. See above.
Iodine	Regulates the energy needs of the body	Goiter Slow growth	DRINKING WATER TO WHICH IODINE SALTS HAVE BEEN ADDED IODIZED SALT COD-LIVER OIL SEA FOODS Vegetables, cereals, fruits, and dairy products produced on soil high in iodine content

*Capital letters indicate excellent source.   *Small letters indicate good source.

Continued on page 98

Name of Nutrients	Usefulness in Body	Result of Mild Deficiency	Distribution in Food Groups	Distribution in Individual Food
5. VITAMINS *Vitamin A*	Promotes growth Is essential for normal adjustment of the eye when it is exposed to extreme changes in light Is essential for the maintenance of healthy tissues that cover the body and line its cavity. For example, it guards against infections by maintaining healthy respiratory tissue. Is necessary for healthy teeth, bones, and hair	Slow growth Inability of the eyes to adjust to changes of light – night blindness Increased number of respiratory infections	GREEN AND YELLOW VEGETABLES Citrus fruits, tomatoes, cabbage, salad greens Milk and milk products Butter and fortified margarine	Fish-liver oils Egg yolk Organ meats
Thiamin or *Vitamin B₁*	Promotes growth by helping to maintain normal appetite, and by aiding in the digestive breakdown of carbohydrates and fats into energy for body use Helps in the control of the nervous system, and relieves fatigue, irritability, and depression	Loss of appetite Tiredness Constipation Headaches	BREAD, FLOUR, CEREAL (WHOLE GRAIN OR ENRICHED) Eggs	PORK; ORGAN MEATS LEGUMES NUTS Meat Leafy vegetables
Riboflavin or *Vitamin B₂*	Promotes growth and lengthens the general life span Is essential for maintenance of the nervous system	Slow growth Cracking at the corners of the mouth Eyes that are very sensitive to light	MILK AND MILK PRODUCTS Muscle and organ meats, poultry, fish, dried beans, peas, nuts, peanut butter Eggs Bread, flour, cereal (whole grain or enriched) Green and yellow vegetables	
Niacin	Promotes growth Helps maintain normal skin and normal functioning of the digestive tract	Diarrhea Skin eruptions Mental depression	Muscle and organ meats, poultry, fish, dried beans, peas, nuts, peanut butter Eggs Bread, flour, cereal (whole	

Nutrient	Function	Deficiency symptoms	Sources	Sources
Vitamin C or *Ascorbic Acid*	Is essential for healthy and normal cells throughout the body. Forms the "cement substance" that holds the cells together in the bones, teeth, and connective tissues. Promotes wound healing. Helps protect against certain types of infections. If infection has already occurred, liberal amounts of the vitamin seem to speed up recovery.	Sore joints; Sore and bleeding gums; Slow wound healing	CITRUS FRUITS, TOMATOES, CABBAGE, SALAD GREENS; Green and yellow vegetables; Potatoes; Other vegetables and fruits	
Vitamin D	Helps regulate the use of calcium and phosphorus, and so is necessary for normal development of bones and teeth	Poor teeth and bones		IRRADIATED FOODS, VITAMIN-D MILK, HALIBUT-LIVER OIL, COD-LIVER OIL, HERRING, MACKEREL, TUNA, RED-SALMON OIL, SARDINES, Eggs
6. WATER	Acts as a transportation system for carrying foods and other valuable substances to cells in all parts of the body. Helps to remove waste products from the body in the form of perspiration and urine. Maintains normal body temperature by acting as a cooling system. Acts as a lubricant for all moving parts in the body, just as oil is used in lubricating an automobile. Makes up three fourths of the body weight			WATER, MILK AND MILK DRINKS, SOUPS, FRUIT AND VEGETABLE JUICES, ICE CREAM
7. *FIBER* or *bulk* or *roughage* or *cellulose*	Forms bulk, which aids in removing waste products from the intestines	Intestinal disorders		PEELINGS AND FIBROUS PARTS OF FRUITS AND VEGETABLES, BRAN OR COATING OF GRAINS

* Fiber, although not a nutrient, is generally listed with the nutrients, because it assists in the digestion of food.

Shaping a balanced diet into our country's meal patterns is a matter of knowing the food needs of the human body; using foods that you can afford; selecting interesting, appetizing, and satisfying combinations; and taking time, energy, and equipment into consideration.

However, much discussion had gone on before they had set up the four general guides. A brief résumé of the main points follows:

Shaping a balanced diet into our country's meal patterns

The students believed that the meal patterns they had agreed upon as customarily used in our country would serve as the framework for planning their menus. Then they could use the food and the servings recommended in the game, the question-and-answer material, and the summary chart for setting up and evaluating menus.

Using foods that you can afford

When the subject of cost came up, Marta reported that she and her family were in agreement that it was important to have a balanced diet. Mr. Jamison had recently gone over the household accounts very carefully to get a better idea of where they stood. He was planning to keep a record of the money spent. Then at intervals she and her father would go over it in an effort to keep the expenses for food within reasonable limits. If it proved necessary to increase the amount even more to maintain a balanced diet, they would cut down on something else.

Miss Dodds said that this was a wise procedure. She added that it was difficult to say in advance just what a family's food would cost. The amount of money needed is affected by the number of persons in the family, their ages, occupations, and health. The number

of meals eaten away from home and the amount of entertaining done in the home also affect the budget. Other factors involve price variations among stores, seasonal price changes, and shopping and cooking skill. It is well to keep a record of food expenditures, and to examine it regularly to determine where money might have been spent more wisely. In this way a family can know more definitely just how much money is needed for a balanced diet.

The students realized that the amount of money spent for food was not only important to the Jamison family but to others as well. Most people planning meals are interested in finding ways of keeping food costs within reasonable limits. By consulting the materials on the reference shelves, the students hoped to find some helpful ideas on the subject. Marta could make good use of the information now, and the class would benefit when it came time for them to make purchases for the meals at school. However, the more detailed aspects of marketing would be taken up as the classwork on buying foods wisely got under way.

Before long, after a lively discussion, the following suggestions were offered.

- Check the current market prices — especially week-end specials — in the newspapers or in other advertisements. Watch for substitutes in food values, and choose the less expensive of these.

- Buy economical cuts of meat, such as hamburg, stew, chuck, short ribs, or flank. Organ meats, such as kidney, heart, and liver — except calves' liver — are also economical to use.

- Stretch meat, fish, and poultry by adding rice, noodles, macaroni, spaghetti, or vegetables to casserole dishes.

- Use eggs more frequently when low in price. Include occasionally dishes featuring peanut butter, dried beans, peas, and nuts when plentiful.

- Use nonfat milk solids or evaporated milk for cooking. Instead of drinking fresh whole milk, use nonfat or whole-milk solids. But if you use nonfat milk — either solids or liquid — be sure to get in extra servings of butter or margarine during the day. (See page 89.)

- Buy vegetables and fruits that are in season or that are plentiful throughout the year.

- Use home-prepared products instead of buying partially or wholly prepared ones when time is not a problem.

- Include leftovers in the menus. Meat, poultry, fish, and vegetables can be used in scalloped dishes, in salads, as stuffing in peppers, and in many other ways.

Selecting foods that will make the meal interesting, appetizing, and satisfying

At one point in the discussion on menu planning, Harold remarked that he judged a meal by the way it tasted. Then he added, "But some meals taste better than others. I wonder why."

Everyone seemed to have a different opinion on the subject. However, the reference materials revealed a number of points that affect the way meals taste. The students organized this information under the general guide of meals that are interesting, appetizing, and satisfying. A summary of the points follows:

- Plan for a variety of color, considering each food in relation to the whole meal. A menu in which cream soup, mashed potatoes, cauliflower, and cornstarch pudding are served has too much sameness in color to be interesting.

- Offer a variety in flavor, but avoid having more than one strongly flavored or highly seasoned food at a meal. Plan combinations that are not too sweet, too acid, or too bland. The combination of a bland food with a sharp food, such as macaroni and cheese, or rice and tuna, is generally pleasing to the taste.

- Arrange for a variety in texture, with some foods that are soft and some that are crisp. A meal consisting of all soft foods is likely to be unappetizing to a well person. Such combinations as soup and crackers, bread and butter, ice cream and cake offer contrast in texture.

- Plan for a variety in form, avoiding more than one chopped food, stuffed food, or creamed food in a meal. Use natural rather than artificial shapes.

- Avoid serving the same food in more than one way at a meal, such as cooked cabbage and cole slaw.

- Include at least one hot food in a meal. Serve cold foods cold, and hot foods hot.

- Plan a meal that can be easily digested. Avoid too many fried foods or too rich a combination of fatty foods. A meal that is difficult to digest is not satisfying.

- Do not introduce more than one new food preparation at a meal. Some people do not like a new preparation the first time it is served. They may be willing to taste a little of it, and then eat more of the other foods they prefer. But to be expected to try more than one new preparation at a time would tend to make the meal less enjoyable.

*Taking time, energy, and
equipment into consideration*

The students knew that Marta's schedule was a busy one. On school days there was not time for meals that required extensive preparation. Then too, part of Marta's schedule involved other household duties. On days when these tasks consumed considerable energy, plans would need to be made to lighten meal preparation. The question of having adequate equipment for preparing the different foods she might want to serve was also important.

Keeping these points in mind, the students believed that the following suggestions they had found would be helpful not only to Marta but to other people preparing meals:

- Plan menus in advance which can be prepared in the time available.
- Plan baked foods which require approximately the same oven temperature, so that they can be cooked at the same time.
- Plan some foods that can be used for more than one meal, such as a meat loaf, a roast, cookies, cake, or cooked fruit. Some of these foods can be served a second time — perhaps in a slightly different form — on days when the schedule includes energy-consuming tasks.

- Plan meals for which you have adequate equipment for preparing the different foods. Otherwise too much time may be spent improvising equipment or waiting to use the same equipment twice.
- Plan some meals that younger members of the family can assist in preparing.
- Encourage all members of the family to suggest foods they particularly enjoy. This will save you time in menu planning.
- Plan the marketing so that whatever is needed for the day's menus is available. Last-minute changes are often necessary and are to be expected occasionally. But if they occur too frequently, they are not only disturbing, but the meals may not meet nutritional requirements.

*Evaluating Some of
Mrs. Parsons' Meals*

A short time later, Marta gave each member of the class a copy of a week's menus of typical meals that Mrs. Parsons had served. She explained that Miss Dodds had recommended showing a week's menus. This would give a better picture of the diet than one day or a few days' menus would give.

MRS. PARSONS' INADEQUATE MEALS

What would have improved each day?

Sunday

Breakfast
Doughnuts
Coffee

Dinner
Fried Steak
Fried Potatoes
Hard Rolls   Margarine
Crisp Chocolate Cookies

Supper
Peanut Butter and Lettuce
Sandwiches
Chocolate Cake
Iced Cocoa

Monday

Breakfast
Cooked Cereal
Bread   Margarine
Tea

Lunch at School
Peanut Butter Sandwiches
Coke

Dinner
Fried Hamburgers
Fried Potatoes
Biscuits   Margarine
Banana Cake with Thick Frosting

Tuesday

Breakfast
Ready-to-eat Cereal
Toast   Honey
Tea

Lunch at School
Peanut Butter Sandwiches
Coke

Dinner
Beef Stew without Vegetables
Boiled Potatoes
Apple Pie

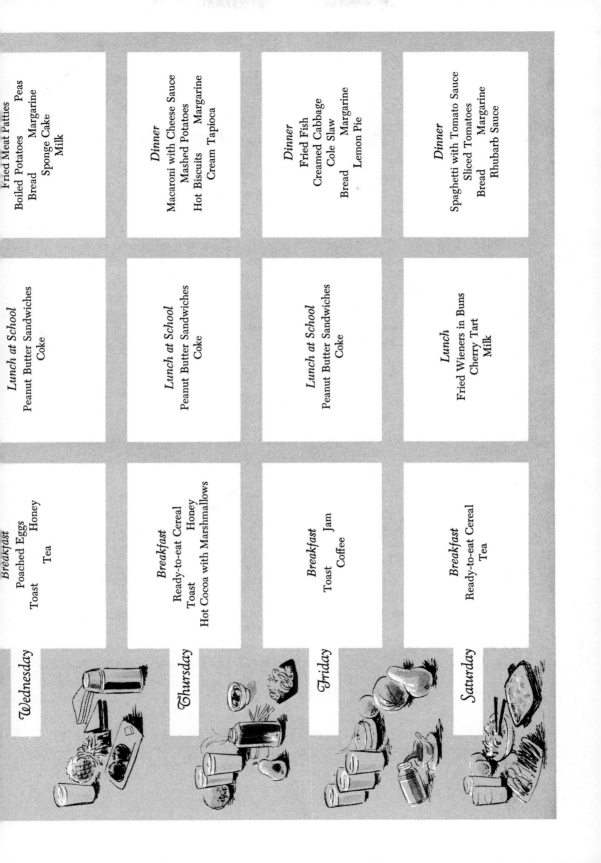

Wednesday

Breakfast
Poached Eggs   Honey
Toast   Tea

Lunch at School
Peanut Butter Sandwiches
Coke

Dinner
Fried Meat Patties
Boiled Potatoes   Peas
Bread   Margarine
Sponge Cake
Milk

Thursday

Breakfast
Ready-to-eat Cereal
Toast   Honey
Hot Cocoa with Marshmallows

Lunch at School
Peanut Butter Sandwiches
Coke

Dinner
Macaroni with Cheese Sauce
Mashed Potatoes
Hot Biscuits   Margarine
Cream Tapioca

Friday

Breakfast
Toast   Jam
Coffee

Lunch at School
Peanut Butter Sandwiches
Coke

Dinner
Fried Fish
Creamed Cabbage
Cole Slaw
Bread   Margarine
Lemon Pie

Saturday

Breakfast
Ready-to-eat Cereal
Tea

Lunch
Fried Wieners in Buns
Cherry Tart
Milk

Dinner
Spaghetti with Tomato Sauce
Sliced Tomatoes
Bread   Margarine
Rhubarb Sauce

What the students found

Mrs. Parsons' meals aroused considerable interest in the class, as each student evaluated the week's menus. The food game, the question-and-answer material, and the summary chart of food needs were used as the basis for the evaluation. There was general agreement that the meals were nutritionally inadequate. However, some of the students were more discerning than others in locating fine points in certain meals, such as their being too sweet or too bland, or lacking variety in color. But both Miss Dodds and the students believed that it had been a helpful experience.

A summary of the main points found lacking in the week's menus as a whole follows:

1. Few, if any, of the day's meals provide adequate nutrients for a balanced diet.

a. Most of the breakfasts are inadequate for growing boys and girls and for an adult.

b. There is need for more fruit and fruit juices.

c. The diet is low in milk and milk products.

d. There is a general lack of salad and green vegetables throughout the whole week's meals.

e. Lunches at school are inadequate and lack variety.

2. Several of the meals are too bland or too sweet.

3. Some of the meals include the same food served in more than one way at a meal.

4. There is not enough variety in texture and color to make the meals interesting and appetizing.

5. Some meals contain too many fried foods which might be difficult to digest.

Improving the Jamisons' Meals

The students were so interested in evaluating Mrs. Parsons' menus that they agreed the next step was to try to improve the Jamisons' meals. While they were considering what references to use, Miss Dodds gave each student a copy of a booklet called *Recipes to Fit the Family Budget*. She said that other homemaking classes who had used it liked the way the material was organized. They had also found the recipes and the general information very helpful in planning meals.

After studying the booklet, the students decided that it would be just what they needed for improving the Jamisons' menus. It would also make a good addition to *Fun in the Kitchen for Teen-Agers*, which they had used in their classwork the previous year. (See Book 1, pages 185–212.) A reproduction of *Recipes to Fit the Family Budget* may be found in this book on pages 167 to 200.

When all of the source materials had been agreed on, the class divided into small groups of three to four students. Each group took the week's menus which Mrs. Parsons had served, and made whatever changes they believed would improve the meals. Current food prices were checked through advertisements and visits to the grocery stores in an effort to plan foods that were within reasonable expense limits. The group Marta was in paid special attention to her problems of time, equipment, and skill in food preparation.

After the meals had been revised by the different groups, a class discussion was held to evaluate the changes and to make any remaining improvements. Both Marta and the students were pleased with the menus which were finally agreed on. They were now much more con-

fident that they could follow the guides for menu planning. However, it was realized that more experience was needed before they could prepare some of the meals in class. This experience would develop as the goal on preparing and serving meals was carried out.

CLASS MEMO:
How would you improve Mrs. Parsons' menus? What approach will your class make in learning how to plan meals?

BUYING AND STORING FOOD WISELY

Now that the students knew how to plan menus, they were all eager to begin preparing some well-balanced meals. However, they realized that the successful preparation of most meals depends to a considerable extent on purchasing the food. And food bought for either school or home use needs to be well stored. Everyone could see that an extensive study of source materials and a lot of personal experience would be needed to carry out these activities efficiently. But the best approach did not appear to be to try to learn all this at once. In fact, the more they discussed the situation, the less advisable it seemed to hold up the classwork on meal preparation until they learned all about buying and storing food.

Certainly some sort of a plan could be worked out so that they could get started as soon as possible on preparing meals.

Planning the Classwork

With a sigh of relief that meal preparation might not be as far away as it had first appeared, the students began to offer suggestions. After considerable discussion, and with Miss Dodds' assistance, they set up the following plan for carrying out the goal — *buying and storing food wisely* — as they worked on their other goal — *preparing and serving balanced meals:*

THE PLAN

• Committees would be appointed for buying and storing food for class use, but these activities were to be rotated among the different students in the class. Everyone would get some experience, although not at every meal being prepared.

- Each group of students preparing a meal would be responsible for making out a list of the supplies — and the amounts — needed for the meal. From this list, the group would check off the items already on hand in the home-making room. Then they would list the other items that needed to be purchased, and give the list to the shoppers assigned to do the marketing for that meal.

- After the shoppers received all of the lists from the various groups, they would make up a master list of all the items to be purchased. The committee on storing the food would be on hand to take care of the supplies when they were brought into the homemaking room.

- The meals to be served were to be kept within the limitations of the school budget. The students and Miss Dodds would decide how much was to be spent on a particular meal. Then it was up to the shoppers to get the best buys within the limit set. How successfully the food was bought and stored would be a part of the evaluation for each meal.

- The students assigned to do the marketing and storing were to consult references if their knowledge seemed incomplete to carry out a particular task. However, as the work on meal preparation progressed, time would be provided for the whole class to learn how to shop advantageously, and how to buy and store specific foods. Marta, and other students purchasing supplies for home use, could contribute helpful information. Field trips to some of the stores, and talks by grocery men or butchers might augment the personal experiences of the students and the written source materials.

- When it came time for a final evaluation, committees would be appointed to make summaries of what had been learned about buying and storing food wisely. The summaries would be presented in any form the committees desired. After they had been approved by the class, they were to be filed in a loose-leaf booklet. This would provide a convenient reference for other classes, even though some of their problems might be different than those of Miss Dodds' group.

Offering General Buying Information

Fairly early in their marketing experience, the student shoppers realized the importance of knowing how to make a good market order. Several family groups had failed to list some of the items needed. Others had listed them in such a haphazard way that it took the shoppers undue time to make up the master list. Students marketing for their families had also reported that a good market list was a prerequisite to good shopping.

As food was purchased for school and for home use, a need arose for ways in which to save time, energy, and money, and yet get good values. This brought up such questions as how, where, and when to shop. Later, other matters about shopping economically came up. These included whether to buy in package or bulk, in large quantities or small, and in fresh, frozen, or canned form.

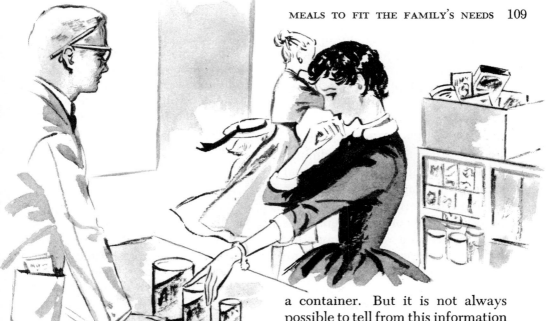

All of the questions on shopping were cleared up in class as they arose. Eventually the information gathered was summarized and filed. See page 120 in the booklet.

Learning About Labels and Can Sizes

The importance of reading labels cropped up time after time and in a variety of ways. One day Stewart brought up the subject by saying, "When I was buying some canned tomatoes the other day, I read the label. But I wasn't at all sure that I had made the best buy."

"I've had trouble with canned goods too," said David. "There are times when I don't know what size to buy."

Miss Dodds spoke up at this point. "Canners are required to give the net weight or liquid measure in a container. But it is not always possible to tell from this information exactly how much will be needed in a particular recipe. However, as you all know, recipes in the booklet "Meals to Fit the Family Budget" give the amounts to be used in terms of a cup. But the recipes also indicate the size of the can in ounces or in common can sizes. In some cases, it may not be possible to buy the exact amount needed for a recipe. Then a larger size will have to be purchased and the excess used in some other way."

Using the opaque projector for learning about labels

Several of the boys were so interested in the subject of labels that they volunteered to consult references and bring back information that would be helpful to the shoppers. Needless to say, this suggestion met with the approval of everyone.

Some time later, the group gave their report, with Stewart acting as spokesman. He announced that arrangements had been made with Miss Dodds to use the opaque projector. However, before this was done, Stewart explained about the Federal Food and Drug Administration. He said that among other things, this organization sets up regulations pertaining to canned products. Some of these regulations concern health guards, information that must appear on labels, and what a shopper may expect to get when the container is opened. In addition to the information required, canners may add other valuable data for the shopper's convenience. All of this makes it possible for the shopper who develops label reading as a habit, to buy canned products more easily and thriftily.

A series of cutout pictures and clippings were then shown, describing important information about labels and can sizes.

Grading standards

One of the points brought out concerned grading standards for canned fruits and vegetables. These standards are not classification of wholesomeness or nutritional value, since this has already been done by regulations. They are standards of quality and identity, and give the shopper an idea of the use that can be made of the product. For example, Grade A or Fancy, or Grade B — Choice or Extra-Standard — on a container of canned peaches would indicate high quality. Peaches of these grades could be used for dessert. Grade C or Standard peaches might be used in a salad, while Grade B or C vegetables would be suitable for a casserole dish. A substandard grade of tomatoes could be used in a stew.

All of the information gave the students a better understanding of labels and was of great value to them in their shopping experiences. However, since most of the material was incorporated in the final summary, it is not given at this time.

Making the final summary on labels

The data which the group supplied through the use of the opaque projector proved to be so helpful

that the committee used it as the basis for the final evaluation. The summary which the committee prepared is in the booklet on pages 122 to 124.

Buying Eggs and Dairy Products

The students were able to get considerable experience in buying eggs and milk, since these were needed over and over again for the various meals served. Margarine or butter, cheese, and cream were bought fairly often.

The committee making the summary presented it to the class in the form of a bulletin-board display. The summary as it was finally approved by the class is reproduced in the booklet on pages 126 to 127.

Eggs

At one point during their preparation for buying eggs, the students learned that eggs come in four forms — fresh, storage, frozen, and dried. However, frozen and dried eggs — from which the shells are removed — are not available in many markets. They are used mainly by commercial concerns in bakery and other quantity cooking. This led the class to concentrate on learning to buy eggs in the shell. And of course, this is what the committee summarized for the final evaluation on buying.

Cheese

On their shopping trips, the students saw many varieties of cheese. They soon learned that cheese is generally classified into three types, according to texture — soft, semihard, and hard.

The older a cheese becomes, the sharper the flavor. The process of aging is called "ripening," which usually involves changes in flavor and texture. Some very ripe cheese will become quite dry and will need grating before it can be used.

As the students talked with people who used a lot of cheese, they learned that most families have individual preferences for certain types and flavors. However, their experience in buying cheese for school menus was limited. They used cottage and cream cheese in salads and harder cheese grated for various casserole recipes. Therefore these were the only types included in the final summary.

Milk

For the information on milk, the group decided to list and describe the types available. They had had experience in buying various types for various purposes, such as milk for drinking, flavored milk to tempt an appetite, and economical or special forms for cooking.

Butter, margarine, cream

The students also learned that butter comes salted or unsalted, and that preference for either is largely a matter of personal taste. Even though margarine is not, strictly speaking, a dairy product, they decided to class it along with butter. Types of cream available were also listed.

Selecting Fresh Fruits and Vegetables

Many times the students purchased frozen fruits and vegetables for their meals at school, mainly because they were ready to use. This saved time for something else. They also used canned fruits and vegetables for the same reason, or because the canned product was better suited for a particular recipe. They were always careful to read the labels on the packaged and canned products. And when they learned to understand the labels, they found the products relatively easy to buy.

However, buying fresh fruits and vegetables proved to be much more difficult. Here was where both information and experience were really necessary. The need for buying fresh products arose fairly early and continued throughout the class-work on meal preparation. Since it was important to be able to make a good selection of these products, the students arranged a field trip where a fresh fruit and vegetable buyer explained some of the points that indicate quality. This information was very helpful to everyone in the class. Later the committee members decided to concentrate their final summary on how to recognize the good qualities in fresh fruits and vegetables. They also included the approximate amounts of vegetables to buy for a family of four. The summary may be found in the booklet on pages 128 to 129.

Buying Meat

When the students began their work on planning and preparing meals, they had had very little experience in buying meat. During the previous year, ground or left-over meat had been used in casserole dishes for luncheon or supper meals. But that had not posed much

of a problem. However, when they began to include meat as a main course for dinner meals, they soon realized there was much to be learned. This became quite evident when they were improving Mrs. Parsons' menus. They soon learned that the size of a family's grocery bill can be controlled to a considerable extent by the amount of money spent for meat, poultry, and fish. In order to plan and to buy wisely, it is important to know about the kinds of meat available, the cuts of meat, and the grade or quality.

Cuts and grades

Through the study of reference materials, the students learned that the top grades and tenderest cuts cost more than the lower grades and tougher cuts, even though they compare favorably in food value. In general, the ribs and loins — including steaks and chops cut from them — are the most tender cuts and require relatively short cooking time. The round or leg and cuts from them, such as round steaks and roasts from round, or rump and chuck roasts, are less tender and require longer cooking. The toughest cuts are the shanks, flank, plate, brisket, and neck.

In order to buy and use meat to the best advantage, it is necessary to understand the most desirable ways of cooking the different cuts. For example, meat from the ribs or loin is generally broiled, pan-broiled, pan-fried, or roasted, while round cuts are braised or roasted. Flank, shank, and chuck cuts are usually better when they are stewed or simmered. Furthermore, it is not always necessary to buy

the highest grade or the most tender cuts to get a satisfying meat dish. When the tougher cuts are cooked by a method that will make them tender, they may be just as appetizing as the more tender cuts. However, in determining the cost of a cut, waste needs to be taken into consideration. Meat with a lot of bone, or with a high proportion of fat that will not be eaten, may not be an economical buy even though the cost per pound is low.

While the students were studying about meat, Miss Dodds gave each of them sheets of pictures like those shown on pages 114 to 117. After the class believed they were well enough prepared to ask intelligent questions, a field trip was arranged to one of the stores. There a butcher showed them various kinds and cuts of meat, and explained about qualities and grades. The final summary on buying meat is reproduced in the booklet on pages 130 to 131.

Learning About Poultry and Fish

Although the class meals at school did not offer a great deal of experience in buying poultry, they did offer some. The students learned that there are quality grades of poultry similar to those for meat. The amount and tenderness of the flesh, the amount of fat — enough but not too much — and freedom from defects, such as bruises or tears, determine the quality. The method of cooking poultry is also an important consideration when buying. Young chickens, for

BEEF

SIRLOIN STEAK
(2 servings per pound)

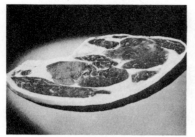

Broil, pan-broil, pan-fry

STANDING RIB
(2 servings per pound)

Roast

T-BONE STEAK
(2 servings per pound)

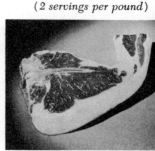

Broil, pan-broil, pan-fry

BLADE POT ROAST (CHUCK)
(2–3 servings per pound)

Braise

FLANK STEAK
(2–3 servings per pound)

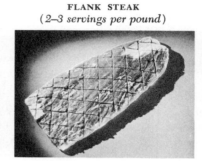

Braise

ROUND STEAK (FULL CUT)
(2–3 servings per pound)

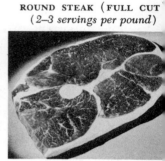

Braise

SHORT RIBS
(1–2 servings per pound)

Braise, simmer

SHANK CROSS CUTS
(1–2 servings per pound)

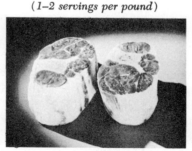

Braise, simmer

TONGUE
(3 servings per pound)

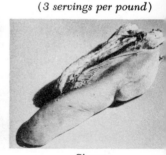

Simmer

HEART
(2–3 servings per pound)

Braise

LIVER
(4 servings per pound)

Pan-fry, braise

KIDNEY
(1 kidney serves 4)

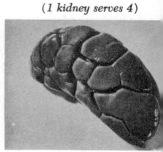

Simmer

LAMB

RIB CHOP
(2 chops per person)

Broil, pan-broil, pan-fry

SHOULDER CHOPS
(1–2 chops per person)

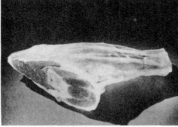

Broil, pan-broil, pan-fry, braise

PATTIES
(1–2 patties per person)

Broil, pan-broil, pan-fry

AMERICAN LEG
(2–3 servings per pound)

Roast

SHANK
(1–2 servings per pound)

Braise, simmer

KIDNEY
(2 kidneys per person)

Broil

HEART
(1 serving per ¾ pound)

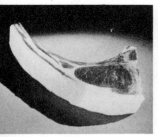

Braise

LIVER
(4 servings per pound)

Broil, pan-broil, pan-fry

PORK

LOIN ROAST—CENTER CUT
(2–3 servings per pound)

Roast

HALF HAM—SHANK END
(3–4 servings per pound)

Bake, simmer

BOSTON BUTT—SHOULDER
(2–3 servings per pound)

Roast

RIB CHOP
(1–2 chops per person)

Braise, pan-fry

CENTER HAM SLICE
(3–4 servings per pound)

Broil, pan-broil, pan-fry

SMOKED PICNIC SHOULDER
(2–3 servings per pound)

Bake, simmer

HOCKS
(1–2 servings per pound)

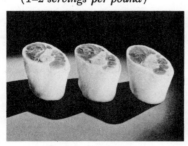

Braise, simmer

SPARERIBS
(1–2 servings per pound)

Bake, braise, simmer

BONELESS RUMP (3–4 servings per pound)	ROUND STEAK—CUTLET (2–3 servings per pound)	HEEL OF ROUND (2–3 servings per pound)
	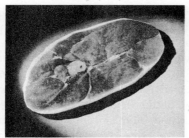	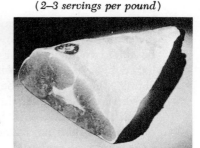
Roast, braise	Braise, pan-fry	Braise, simmer

ARM ROAST—SHOULDER (2–3 servings per pound)	HEART (2–3 servings per pound)	KIDNEY (1 kidney per person)

Roast, braise	Braise	Broil

example, are suitable for broiling and those a little older for frying. Young mature birds can be stuffed and baked, while the older, tougher ones need to be stewed. Again Miss Dodds gave the students some pictures to help identify good quality in poultry for various uses.

Styles of poultry

The students also learned that chicken and turkey, the most common types of poultry, are usually available in the market in two styles — dressed and ready-to-cook. Dressed birds have only the feathers removed. Ready-to-cook poultry has been picked and cleaned. The feet and head have been discarded, and the pinfeathers removed. The giblets — heart, liver, and gizzard — and sometimes the neck are wrapped in paper and placed inside the cavity of the bird. It has been inspected for wholesomeness inside and out. In this form it might come whole or cut up, fresh or frozen, packaged or not. Both chicken and turkey parts are generally available in the markets, as well as turkey halves, quarters, and other parts.

Fish tips

Because of their locality, the class had limited experience with fresh fish. But they realized that it is exceedingly perishable. Unless frozen, it should be used immediately or within a few days at the most when refrigerated. Whenever frozen or canned fish was to be purchased, the labels were carefully read. The students learned that some kinds are expensive, others relatively low in price. Using the lower cost ones — fresh, frozen, or canned — might be a good money saver. But the lower priced products would need to be suited to their use. For example, flaked tuna is less expensive than the chunk style, but may be used in a casserole dish quite satisfactorily. The chunk style tuna would be better in most salads than the flaked tuna. The final summary prepared by the committee on poultry and fish is reproduced on pages 132 to 133.

Storing Food Wisely

Everyone realized that the successful preparation of meals depended to a large extent on storing the food wisely. If foods spoiled before they were to be used, time and money spent in shopping would be wasted. Even before the shoppers began to buy food for the class meals, the students in charge of storing supplies were busy consulting references about suitable storage. They decided that foods requiring refrigeration would need first consideration when they arrived in the homemaking room. Therefore, information was assembled on the placement of these items in the refrigerator.

Placement of food in the refrigerator

Before long, everyone knew that the coldest part of the refrigerator is where the air comes directly from the freezing unit. Items, such as milk, eggs, cheese, meat, poultry, and fish need to be stored near this unit. Other foods can be kept in a less cold place. The students also learned that when the outside of a newly purchased container is not clean, it should be wiped off

before being stored. It is equally important to see that the outside wrappings of meat, poultry, and cheese are removed, and the products covered loosely with wax paper or foil. Fish, of course, would be kept tightly wrapped in the original paper. With so many people working together, various problems in using the refrigerator arose from time to time.

Occasionally the shelves were overcrowded, or food that had been purchased for one family group was accidentally used by another group. Whenever such situations occurred, they were worked out immediately by those concerned.

Foods not requiring refrigeration

During the classwork, the problem of storing foods that did not require refrigeration was also encountered. Keeping these foods in a clean, dry, convenient, cool place was the point brought out in this connection. The final summary prepared by the committee shows in detail suitable storage for the foods needing refrigeration and those that do not. This summary is reproduced on the insert following and page 134.

CLASS MEMO:
What do you find useful in the classwork of Miss Dodds' group on buying and storing food wisely? What other ideas will be helpful to members of your group?

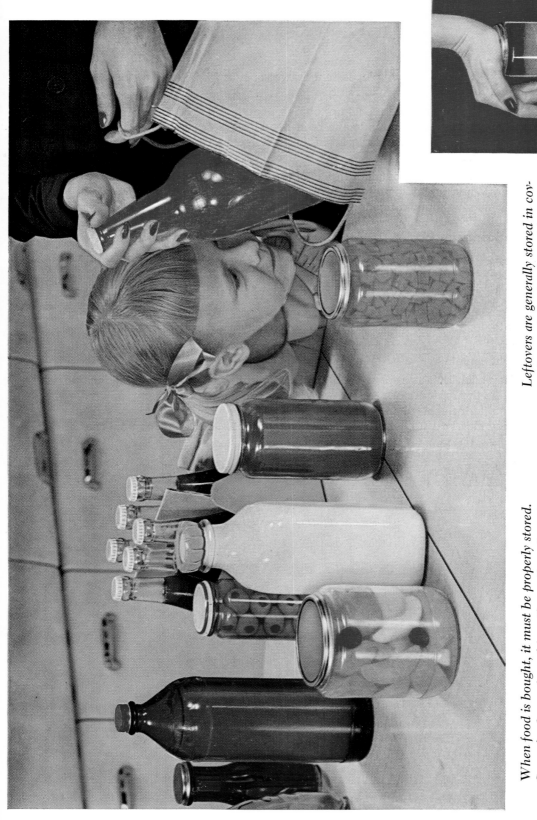

Leftovers are generally stored in covered containers in the refrigerator.

When food is bought, it must be properly stored. Some foods require refrigeration; others do not.

FOODS NOT NEEDING REFRIGERATION

Bread: Store in original wrapping if moistureproof, or in a plastic bag in a cool place. The wrapped bread may be placed in a drawer or bread box, or if the weather is warm in a less cold spot in the refrigerator.

Canned Meats: Keep canned meats up to three pounds in a dry place of moderate temperature. Cans three pounds and over need to be refrigerated. Once opened, a can should be covered and placed in the refrigerator. The contents should be used within a few days.

Cereals: Keep in original container in a cool, dry place, or store in a covered container. When opening prepared cereals, avoid tearing the inner wrapper. Unfold to use the amount needed, and refold to protect crispness of any left. To restore crispness in damp weather, place cereal in shallow pan in a moderate oven leaving door partly open.

Chocolate: Store in a cool place, preferably in an airtight container. During warm weather, keep in refrigerator to prevent color fading.

Cocoa: Store in a cool place, preferably in an airtight container.

Coffee: Store in an airtight container. If bought in paper bags, use immediately or transfer to a container. Refrigeration preserves flavor in very warm weather.

Crackers and Potato Chips: Store in original box or wrapper if moistureproof, or in an airtight container.

Fruits: Keep such fruit as apples, pears, and citrus fruits in a cool place. This may or may not be the refrigerator. Bananas are best when kept at room temperature. They lose their flavor when stored in a cold or even a cool place. Green fruits to be ripened slowly can be wrapped in paper and kept in a dark place until ripe.

Tea: Store in airtight container at room temperature.

Vegetables: Keep such vegetables as potatoes, squash, turnips, onions, and other root vegetables in a cool ventilated place.

Storage of food — and equipment — as near as possible to its point of first use simplifies meal preparation.

BUYING AND STORING FOOD

A Loose-Leaf Booklet of Summaries Prepared
by Miss Dodds' Class

CONTENTS

GENERAL BUYING INFORMATION

HINTS FOR MAKING A MARKET LIST

Keep a pad and pencil in the school or home kitchen to list staples and miscellaneous items, such as soap and other cleaners, that run out during the week. A small bulletin board is convenient for such memos and for messages to others with whom you are working.

Study carefully the meals and recipes planned. Check to see what foods and ingredients you have, and what you need to buy. Plan to have enough supplies on hand to take care of any last-minute changes that may be necessary.

Check the current market prices, especially week-end specials, in the newspapers or in other advertisements.

Organize your list by grouping together the same kinds of foods and supplies, since they are grouped together in the store. If you generally shop in the same store, time may be saved by arranging the groups in the order in which you approach them in the store. But if you expect to do extensive buying, it might be well to list perishables and frozen foods last.

If you are telephoning the order, give specific information, such as the amount or size, the kind, and the quality or grade of the products you want.

HOW TO SHOP

By telephoning your order and having it delivered

Saves time for a person who works and cannot shop while the stores are open.

Stores featuring telephone and delivery service may also extend credit. This may mean a delivery charge or slightly higher prices to absorb the costs of book-keeping and the occasional losses of unpaid accounts.

By the cash-and-carry system in supermarkets or smaller stores

Gives you a chance to make your own selections, and often saves you money.

WHERE TO SHOP

Where you can get the most satisfaction for your money

Where you can get everything in one store if your time is limited

Where the quality of the products suits the needs of the family

Where the products are handled in a sanitary manner, such as butter and bakery goods wrapped, milk in containers, fresh fruit and vegetables separated from those rotting

Where the prices are prominently displayed

Where you can take your time to study the labels

WHEN TO SHOP

For staples

The best time is when the markets are the least crowded—usually the first four days of the week.

For sale items and for fresh fruits and vegetables over the week end

Shop Friday or Saturday. The earlier in the morning, the better, or between one and three o'clock, or on Friday evening if the markets are open.

LARGE OR SMALL QUANTITIES

That depends on:

The size of your family and how soon you can use perishable foods before they spoil

The amount of storage space you have to keep canned goods dry and perishable foods in good condition

A safe rule:

Buy in reasonable quantities to fit the needs of the family. If there is adequate storage, it is frequently possible to save money by buying in large quantities.

PACKAGED OR IN BULK

When packaged

Time is saved in weighing and wrapping products.

Products are more sanitary because less handling is required and the food is protected from flies and other insects.

Cost of waste is cut for fresh fruits and vegetables because they are cleaned before being packaged.

Fresh fruits and vegetables keep better, stay fresh longer, retain more vitamins and often look more attractive.

In bulk

You can be sure of getting the same grade throughout your purchase if the store permits customers to make their own selection.

You can buy in the desired quantity.

Sometimes the products are lower in price than when packaged.

FRESH VERSUS FROZEN VERSUS CANNED PRODUCTS

When fresh:

Generally displayed without identification as to quality, brand, or variety.

Purchaser needs to make selections on the basis of experience or be dependent upon the advice of the clerk.

If purchased when the nearby supply is most abundant, prices may be lower than those of frozen foods.

When frozen:

Easier to use, because all the waste has been removed, and the products are ready for cooking.

May be more economical at times of the year when fresh products have to be shipped in from other sections of the country, and transportation charges are involved.

When canned:

Often the best substitute when fresh or frozen products are not available.

May be preferred by some people and in some recipes.

May be less expensive in price than fresh or frozen products.

BE ALERT WHEN SHOPPING

Select the latest date on dairy products when they are dated. But day-old bread and some bakery goods may be economical buys. However, be sure to read the labels first.

Know when to recognize real bargains. Try to figure out whether the price might be reduced to attract customers, or whether there might be something inferior about the product. Quite possibly there could be an overabundance of the product.

Be sure that you pay the sale price if you decide to buy "specials." The regular price may still be marked on the item.

Watch to see that the cash register or adding machine has been cleared of a previous sale before the clerk starts to check your order. If you think that the total amount is too high for what you have purchased, add the slip yourself immediately. A mistake may be unintentional, but it needs to be brought to the attention of the clerk before you leave the store.

THE LABEL — A GUIDE TO WISE BUYING

WHAT IT MUST SHOW		HOW IT AIDS THE SHOPPER
The name of the product	Quickly identifies the food	The label must be truthful and in no way misleading. The usual name of the product must be on the label. Imitations must be prominently labeled "imitation." Any picture on the label must be a true picture of the contents of the container. If the product is made of two or more ingredients, they must be named in the order of their predominance.
The net weight or liquid measure	Gives accurate amount of contents so that shoppers can purchase the amount needed	If the product is solid or a mixture of solid and liquid, it must be labeled in terms of weight. If the product is liquid, it must be labeled in terms of liquid measure. Food containers must not be made, formed, or filled to be deceiving. The standard of fill for a container is the maximum quantity which can be processed in a container without crushing or breaking the contents. If a packer has not met the standards of fill, the container must be conspicuously labeled.
How the standards of identity and quality or grade have been set	Gives leading information about the characteristics and composition of the products	Packers are required: 1. To designate the style of pack for fruits and vegetables. The style for fruits must include characteristics, such as whole, halves, slices, or chunks; for vegetables, cut, diced, Frenched, or shoestring. 2. To indicate the type of variety of the products, such as red or pink salmon, cling or freestone peaches. 3. To indicate the sweetness of sirups used with fruits—as light, heavy, or extra heavy. 4. To specify when products are processed with little or no sugar. These are sometimes called water packed. 5. To designate when vitamins have been added. Packers must state also the percentage of the minimum daily requirements of the vitamins that a reasonable daily amount of the product will furnish. 6. To indicate when products are substandard.

Government standards of quality for canned fruits and vegetables have been set under the following grades: Grade A or Fancy   Grade B—Choice or Extra-Standard   Grade C or Standard   Substandard

Packers can use these grade designations only when they comply with the standards set by the government. For example, Fancy or Grade A fruits must be uniform in size and degree of ripeness. They must also be good in color, free of blemishes, and of good flavor. Grade A vegetables are those of the highest quality in flavor and tenderness, and the most desired size. Choice or Extra-Standard are of good flavor and tenderness, but are likely to be more mature.

The U. S. Department of Agriculture has a service whereby expert inspectors may be employed by a packer to evaluate the grading of all canned products of that company. The label on the products may then include two shields, stating the U. S. Grade on one, and "Packed under continuous inspection of the U. S. Department of Agriculture" on the other.

Knowing the name and address makes it easy for a shopper to contact a packer or distributor in case such a contact is necessary.

The name and address of the packer or distributor	Lets shoppers know with whom they are dealing

PEAS
PACKED BY
ALLGOOD and CO.
(somewhere, U.S.A.)

OTHER INFORMATION IT MAY OFFER

A brand name	May help as a guide to getting the same product if desired	Some packers process different grades of products, giving a brand name to each. When shoppers are familiar with these brand names and have found the products satisfactory, they can make a selection easily and quickly.
Size of the product	Serves as a guide in selecting a product for particular use	In addition to designating the style of pack, a further description may be given. For example, a label may read "Large pear halves" or "Small pear halves."
Maturity of the product	Helps in selecting the flavor and texture of the product	A label indicating that a fruit was "tree-ripened" might indicate that a more delicious flavor could be expected than that of a fruit that was picked before it had fully matured. The tree-ripened fruit does not hold its shape so well.
Contents—cups or pieces	Gives shoppers an idea of the amount needed	Knowing the contents of a container in terms of cups or pieces makes it easy for a shopper to know how much to purchase for particular recipes or for individual servings.
Recipe suggestions	Helps the shoppers to get the best results from the product	Some people find it convenient to use recipes given on a container. They may also learn new ways of preparing a product.

A GUIDE TO COMMON CAN SIZES

[AMERICAN CAN COMPANY]

6-oz.

Distributed principally in metropolitan areas and used for most fruits and vegetables, as well as for ripe olives.

Approximately ¾ cup
6 fl. oz.

8-oz.

Used principally for frozen concentrated juices, as well as regular single strength fruit and vegetable juices.

Approximately 1 cup
8 oz. (7¾ fl. oz.)

No. 1 (picnic)

Used principally for condensed soups, and some fruits, vegetables, meat and fish products.

Approximately 1¼ cups
10½ oz. (9½ fl. oz.)

No. 300

For specialty items, such as beans with pork, spaghetti, macaroni, chili con carne, date and nut bread, and clams—also a variety of fruits, including cranberry sauce and blueberries.

Approximately 1¾ cups
15½ oz. (13½ fl. oz.)

No. 303

Used more extensively than any other for a complete range of vegetables, plus fruits such as sweet and sour cherries, fruit cocktail, applesauce.

Approximately 2 cups
1 lb. (15 fl. oz.)

No. 2

Used for all vegetable items, plus a wide range of fruits and fruit and tomato juices.

Approximately 2½ cups
1 lb. 4 oz. (1 pt. 2 fl. oz.)

No. 2½

Used principally for fruits, such as peaches, pears, plums, and fruit cocktail, plus vegetables, such as tomatoes, sauerkraut, and pumpkin.

Approximately 3½ cups
1 lb. 13 oz. (1 pt. 10 fl. oz.)

The shopper who develops the habit of reading labels on canned and packaged goods, and of carefully evaluating her purchases once they are made develops skill in purchasing wisely.

INFORMATION ABOUT EGGS

EGGS IN THE SHELL

The "Outside" Story

Eggs in the shell are generally sold in stores as fresh or storage, and graded as to size—Extra Large, Large, Medium, or Small.

Fresh eggs are those that have been delivered soon after they are laid. But a "fresh" egg is no longer fresh after a day of being unrefrigerated. When buying eggs at the store, take them from the refrigerator and not from a bulk display outside.

Storage eggs are those placed in cold storage to be used during seasons of low production.

The size of the egg is not a clue to a good purchase. The largest is not always the most for the money. A good rule to follow is this: Medium eggs are a good buy if priced 1/8 less than Large eggs, Small eggs if priced 1/4 less than Large.

In some sections of the country, white eggs are preferred to brown, or brown to white, but there is no difference in food value or flavor.

The "Inside" Story

There are voluntary gradings for eggs worked out by our Department of Agriculture. These are Grades AA, A, B, and C. Grades AA and C are seldom found in markets.

The higher grade eggs, when removed from the shell, have compact, firm, thick whites and upstanding yolks.

The lower grades have whites that thin out, and flattened yolks.

The nutritive values of Grades AA, A, and B are practically the same. But appearance is important to some people in poaching or frying.

If storage eggs are of good quality when stored, they retain their food value up to nine months. They may have a slightly different flavor from that of fresh eggs, but they can be used satisfactorily in cooking. They are often an economical buy for that purpose.

CHEESE

Types	Examples
Soft-unripened:	Cottage cheese: mildly seasoned milk curd; in fine or large curds; sold in labeled cartons or in bulk
	Cream cheese: milk curd mildly flavored and processed into a soft, smooth product that spreads easily; sold in 3- or 6-ounce packages or by the pound
Semihard-ripened:	American Cheddar: mild to sharp in flavor; varies from cream color to orange inside; outside surface waxed; texture varies from fine to crumbly depending on aging processes.

MILK

Generally two kinds of milk on the market—raw and pasteurized

Raw: milk in its natural form; usually sold in rural areas

Pasteurized: raw milk which has been subjected to heat to destroy harmful bacteria. To be really safe, any milk should be pasteurized.

Certified: has a very high standard of purity; production and distribution subject to strict controls and supervision; may be raw, but is generally pasteurized; higher in price than other milk and not always available; generally used for babies, invalids, and special cases

Homogenized: whole milk so treated that the cream is distributed throughout the milk instead of rising to the top

Skim: whole milk from which most of the fat is removed

Milk solids: whole or skim milk with the water removed; before using, water needs to be added.

Chocolate: milk to which a chocolate sirup is added. When made from whole milk, it is called "chocolate-flavored milk." When made from skim milk, it is called "chocolate-flavored drink."

Buttermilk: churned milk with the butter removed; similar to skim milk except for the acid content

Evaporated, canned: fresh milk with 50 to 60 per cent of the water removed

Condensed, canned: prepared from fresh milk by evaporating half the water content, and adding sugar to about 40 per cent

Malted: a powder prepared from a mixture of fresh milk, barley malt, and wheat flour with salt added; sometimes chocolate also added

BUTTER

Common Types

Sweet: unsalted and may be made from either sweet or sour cream

Salted: salt has been added in the proportion of two pounds of salt to ninety-eight pounds of butter

Quality

Difficult for a shopper to judge quality. A good solution is to buy from a reliable market which carries a consistently good quality

The more protective its wrapping, the better the original quality will be retained

CREAM

Light: generally purchased for table use on cereals or in coffee

Heavy: generally used as whipping cream for desserts

Sour: sometimes purchased for casserole cooking, salad dressing, cakes or cookies; is more perishable than sweet cream

MARGARINE

Prepared from a variety of vegetable oils churned with skim milk

Usually fortified with vitamins A and D

Widely used as a substitute for butter since the cost is considerably lower

BEST BUYS IN FRESH

HINTS ON BUYING FRESH FRUITS AND VEGETABLES

<u>Make your own selection.</u> Personal inspection and selection for the purpose in mind, tends to give greater satisfaction and economy.

<u>Avoid handling unpackaged products unnecessarily.</u> Rough handling when buying causes spoilage for which the shopper ultimately pays. The store must sell at a price high enough to cover such loss.

<u>Remember that the largest is not always the best.</u> They may not be the best quality or the most economical to buy.

FRESH FRUITS

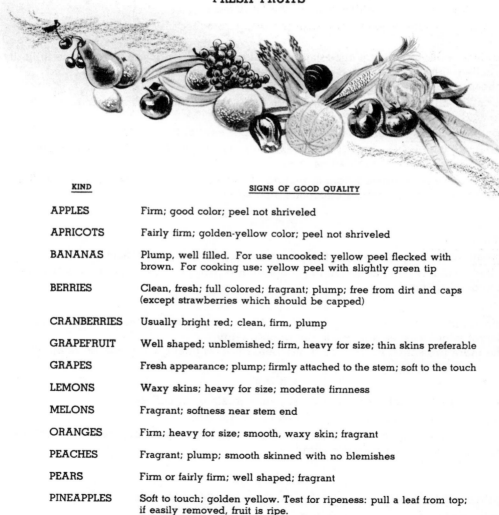

KIND	SIGNS OF GOOD QUALITY
APPLES	Firm; good color; peel not shriveled
APRICOTS	Fairly firm; golden-yellow color; peel not shriveled
BANANAS	Plump, well filled. For use uncooked: yellow peel flecked with brown. For cooking use: yellow peel with slightly green tip
BERRIES	Clean, fresh; full colored; fragrant; plump; free from dirt and caps (except strawberries which should be capped)
CRANBERRIES	Usually bright red; clean, firm, plump
GRAPEFRUIT	Well shaped; unblemished; firm, heavy for size; thin skins preferable
GRAPES	Fresh appearance; plump; firmly attached to the stem; soft to the touch
LEMONS	Waxy skins; heavy for size; moderate firmness
MELONS	Fragrant; softness near stem end
ORANGES	Firm; heavy for size; smooth, waxy skin; fragrant
PEACHES	Fragrant; plump; smooth skinned with no blemishes
PEARS	Firm or fairly firm; well shaped; fragrant
PINEAPPLES	Soft to touch; golden yellow. Test for ripeness: pull a leaf from top; if easily removed, fruit is ripe.
PLUMS	Fresh looking; plump; not shriveled

FRUITS AND VEGETABLES

FRESH VEGETABLES

KIND	SIGNS OF GOOD QUALITY	APPROXIMATE AMOUNTS FOR 4 PERSONS
ASPARAGUS	Straight, fresh green stalks; heavy for size; crisp	1½ to 2 pounds
BEANS—Green	Bright color; firm pods which snap when broken	1 pound
Lima	Fresh; clean; free from decay and dark spots	2 pounds unshelled
BEETS	Uniform in size; dark red color; leaves not too large	1 pound
BROCCOLI	Short, fresh, crisp stems; green color in heads, leaves, and stems	1 pound
BRUSSELS SPROUTS	Firm; good green color; no wilted yellow leaves	1 pound
CABBAGE	Closely packed leaves; only a slight odor	1 pound
CARROTS	Firm; free from decay or cracks; clean	1 pound
CAULIFLOWER	Head firmly packed, white in color; outer leaves green	Large head
CELERY	Thick, crisp stems free from spots; fresh-looking leaves	Medium bunch
CORN, sweet	Fresh, green husks; golden to brown silk; kernels juicy; ears filled to tip; no wormholes	6 to 8 ears
CUCUMBERS	Crisp; solid; deep green; long, straight without tapering ends	1 medium to large
EGGPLANT	Firm; fairly smooth; well shaped; glossy; purple color	1 large
GREENS—Spinach	Fresh, crisp leaves flat or crinkled; deep green color	1 to 1½ pounds
Swiss chard	Crisp, tender, fresh green leaves	1 pound
LETTUCE	Round, firm heads; crisp; tender	1 medium head
OKRA	Firm, fresh, thick meaty pods	1 pound
ONIONS—Dry	Round; crackly skin; no green streaks or sprouts	1 pound
Scallions	Thick neck, small bulb	1 to 2 bunches
PARSLEY	Bright green leaves; fresh and fragrant	1 small bunch
PARSNIPS	Firm; smooth; well trimmed	1 pound
PEAS, green	Young, tender, fresh pods well filled; fresh peas crush easily	2 pounds
PEPPERS, sweet green	Fairly well formed; glossy; bright color	2 pounds
POTATOES	Firm; well shaped; shallow eyes; no sprouts	2 pounds
SQUASH	Fairly heavy for size; free from blemishes; smooth rind	2 pounds
SWEET POTATOES	Firm; well shaped; free from decay, bruises or cuts	2 pounds
TOMATOES, red	Rich red; fragrant; solid; smooth skin	1½ pounds
TURNIPS	Smooth skin; well shaped; firm; heavy for size; free from rot	1 pound

GUIDES TO BUYING MEAT

HOW SOLD

Meat may come prepackaged—fresh or frozen—wrapped in transparent wrappings and displayed in refrigerated cabinets for self-service. The label on the wrapping indicates the name of the animal and the cut. It also gives the price per pound, total price, total weight, and sometimes the use for which it is best suited. Packaged meats may not show grade on the label; so it is important to know indications of quality or grade.

Different kinds of meat may be displayed unwrapped in a refrigerated showcase, in large or small cuts. The shopper makes a selection and tells the clerk the quantity needed. If a desired cut is not on display the clerk may have it in the storage refrigerator.

QUALITY—GRADE

Meat shipped in interstate commerce must be inspected and passed by federal law. The purple stamp placed on each wholesale cut means that the meat is safe for food. See the illustration. Meat not shipped in interstate commerce is usually under state and local laws for inspection and approval. Some meat may also have a government grade stamp. The grades for beef are U. S. Prime, U. S. Choice, U. S. Good, U. S. Commercial, and U. S. Utility. Beef previously graded U. S. Commercial is being divided into two grades—Standard for that from younger animals, and Commercial for that from mature animals.

Top Qualities	Lower Grades
Fine grain with a generous marbling of fat; exception, veal which is too young to be marbled; proper color for type of meat	Coarser grain; little or no marbling; little or no fat; poor color for type of meat
Beef—a cherry red color	Beef—dark red to purplish
Young pork—grayish pink	Old pork—a rosy pink
Lamb—pink	Yearling to mutton—varied from light to dark red
Veal—grayish pink almost white in color	

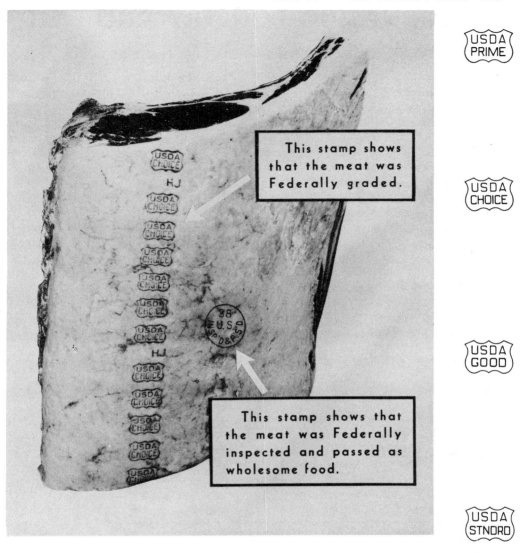

This stamp shows that the meat was Federally graded.

This stamp shows that the meat was Federally inspected and passed as wholesome food.

A stamp appears on each retail cut—in this case "choice," as shown on a whole-sale cut. The stamp shows that the meat was inspected for wholesomeness. The number—38 in this instance—indicates the packing house.

PURCHASING POULTRY AND FISH

POULTRY STYLES—FRESH OR FROZEN

BROILERS
(½ chicken per person)

Broil, pan-broil

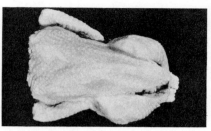

Good quality
chicken

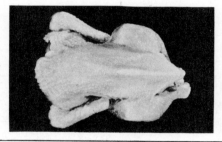

Poor quality
chicken

FRYERS
(2 servings per pound)

Pan-fry

FOWL
(2 to 3 servings per pound)

Stew

ROASTERS
(2 to 3 servings per pound)

Roast

TURKEY
(2 to 3 servings per pound)

Roast

DUCKLING
(2 servings per pound)

Roast

BUYING GUIDES FOR POULTRY—FRESH OR FROZEN

General appearance of ready-to-cook style
Needs to be clean and well dressed, with very few if any pinfeathers, no bruises or discolorations, and no food in the crop

Body
Needs to be wide, plump, full breasted with the breastbone well covered. A bird which has a long, thin body has a greater amount of bone and less meat.

Skin
Needs to be soft and smooth with few if any long hairs or pinfeathers. The color may be white or yellow depending on the breed. Dark-colored flesh and skin usually indicate that the bird is not fresh. The skin of mature birds may be coarse and dry.

Fat
Needs to be under the skin and down the back, over the thighs and along the sides, indicated by light yellow or white streaks. Poultry that is not well fattened may show flesh through the skin. Overly mature birds may have an excess of fat.

Legs and thighs
Need to be well covered with flesh

Breastbone
Needs to be soft and flexible at the tip in young birds. As birds age, it becomes firmer. In old birds it is hard.

BUYING GUIDES FOR FISH

FRESH

The flesh: needs to be elastic, firm, and moist. Impression made by the finger should disappear quickly.

The color: needs to be bright and clear, not faded

The odor: needs to be a fresh, fishy odor, not stale

DRESSED—Small or Split
(2 servings per pound)

Broil, Bake, Pan-fry

FROZEN

Generally comes packaged, ready to cook

Allow same amounts as for fresh fish

STEAKS OR FILLETS
(3 servings per pound)

CANNED

The higher grades: better for salads or for serving plain

The lower grades: satisfactory for creamed dishes or fish cakes

Broil, Bake, Pan-fry, Boil

STORING FOOD

FOODS NEEDING REFRIGERATION

IN THE COLDEST LOCATIONS

Frozen foods: Keep in original packages in the freezing compartment until ready to use.

Meat, fish, poultry, and cheese: Remove outside wrapping and cover loosely with wax paper or aluminum foil, with the exception of fish, which needs to be kept tightly wrapped in original paper; store near or under freezing compartment.

Milk, cream, and beverages: Wipe containers with a damp cloth to remove any soil; place near the freezing unit.

Butter, margarine, salad oils, or fats: Keep in original containers near freezing unit; in addition, place partly used butter and margarine in a tightly covered dish.

Eggs: Store not far from freezing unit. Eggs keep best when retained in original carton. If removed, be sure that the large end of the egg is up. Never wash eggs until ready for use.

Leftovers and food prepared ahead of time: Put in covered containers or cover with wax paper or foil. Keep cooked meat and poultry in as large pieces as possible. Store dressing and gravy separately.

IN OTHER LOCATIONS

Soft fruits, such as berries or grapes, and watermelon: Keep berries in the same boxes in which purchased. Cover top of cut watermelon with waxed paper or aluminum foil.

Most fruits desired cold: Keep in humidrawer or in a ventilated container.

Vegetables: Clean and trim salad greens, young carrots, cauliflower or broccoli, and place in humidrawer, a covered container, or in a moistureproof bag. Leave peas and Lima beans in pods until ready to use.

HINTS FOR THE CARE OF THE REFRIGERATOR

Keep the temperature between 32 degrees and 45 degrees. Anything lower may cause food spoilage. Watch that no more than one-quarter inch of ice forms on the freezing unit.

Open the refrigerator door as little as possible.

Avoid overcrowding the shelves. A free circulation of cold air is necessary.

Keep the refrigerator clean inside and out. Wipe up spilled food immediately.

PREPARING AND SERVING BALANCED MEALS

Now that the students knew how to plan menus and had set up plans for the classwork on buying and storing food, they were ready to take up the goal — *preparing and serving balanced meals.* Needless to say, everyone was delighted. It brought back memories of the previous year when they had prepared simple lunches and suppers. Marta commented on how helpful the experiences had been to her in her present situation. Others mentioned the classwork on setting a table and using good table manners, and how they were applying what they had learned. Evelyn said that a copy of the check list they had made for desirable work habits was still posted in her kitchen at home. She and members of her family often referred to it. Yes, everyone agreed that they had learned a lot last year. (See Book 1, pages 126–212.) Now they were ready and eager to tackle new problems on meals.

Presenting a Sequence of Meal Patterns

The students had realized when they improved Mrs. Parsons' meals that they would be learning about many new foods this year. Some of the meals they had planned for the Jamison family sounded very appetizing. Everyone was anxious to plan equally attractive menus for the meals to be prepared in class. But as they began to think about the various new foods they might use, David raised a serious question.

"Do you remember how careful we had to be last year not to include more than one new preparation in a meal?" he asked. "And those meals were simple in comparison to some of the menus we will probably be planning this year."

"That's true," said Dorothy, "but we managed to work things out quite well. I'm sure we can plan something this year that will be equally helpful when we begin to learn new preparations."

There were nods of agreement throughout the room, but no one offered any suggestions. Finally Edward gave them a lead. "We could begin the classwork with the simpler meals of the day and work up gradually to the more difficult ones," he said.

Explaining the sequence

This was all the students needed to start a lively discussion. Sometime later, they decided that the best way to handle the situation was to set up a sequence of meal patterns. Miss Dodds helped them work out the details. When they completed the sequence, everyone believed that the problem of learning new processes could be met quite satisfactorily. This is what the sequence of meal patterns offered:

1. *A series of patterns progressing from simple ones to those more difficult.* The sequence began with some processes previously learned, and one simple new process. As the series progressed, more difficult new processes were introduced, gradually leading — in some cases — to more than one in a meal pattern. The final pattern was quite inclusive, offering an opportunity to use much of what had been learned both this year and last.

2. *An opportunity to have experience with a process already learned, and to try out different recipes for the same process.* For example, they already understood the process used for quick breads, and had made biscuits and muffins. This year they could start off with these or other recipes for quick breads. They had learned how to prepare certain casserole dishes, but now other recipes for casserole dishes could be used. This would make it easy to gain experience with a familiar process, using the same type of food but not necessarily the same recipes.

3. *An arrangement whereby the students could work together on the same new process at the same time.* This would facilitate the use of demonstrations and the assembling of important reference materials. For example, if the new process was fruit pie, the whole class could learn about making pastry and about other related information at the same time.

4. *Opportunities for the students to make good use of their new learning.* A new process would be considered "learned" after it had been used in a meal. Then it could be repeated — as desired — in other meals. But it would not be thought of as a new process, since no new principles would need to be learned.

5. *Page references to Book 1 and Book 2 to make it easy to plan menus.* References to Book 1 referred to information and recipes for preparations already used. References to Book 2 indicated where additional recipes would be found for the processes previously learned, and for new preparations and related information.

The sequence of meal patterns which the students and Miss Dodds set up follows on page 137:

MEAL PATTERNS		REFERENCES	MEAL PATTERNS		REFERENCES

1

	Book	Pages
Fruit	1	208–209
Eggs if desired	1	194–195
Quick bread	1	189–190
	2	186; 188–189
Beverage	1	188
	2	199–200

2

	Book	Pages
Vegetable plate	2	182–185
Eggs	1	194–195
Quick bread if desired . .	1	189–190
	2	186; 188–189
Dessert	1	198–209
	2	190–198
Beverage if desired . . .	1	187–188
	2	199–200

3

	Book	Pages
Casserole dish	1	192–194
	2	177–179
Vegetable or salad	1	195–197
	2	182–185
Quick bread if desired . .	1	189–190
	2	186; 188–189
Dessert	2	190–198
Beverage if desired . . .	1	187–188
	2	199–200

4

	Book	Pages
Meat, broiled, pan-broiled, or pan-fried	2	169–171
Vegetable and/or salad . . .	1	195–197
	2	182–185
Yeast bread	2	186–187
Fruit dessert	1	208–209
Beverage if desired	1	187–188
	2	199–200

5

	Book	Pages
Meat, roasted, braised, simmered	2	169–174
Vegetable and/or salad . . .	1	195–197
Bread if desired	1	189–190
	2	186–189
Dessert—pastry, fruit pie . . .	2	190–193
Beverage if desired	1	187–188
	2	199–200

6

	Book	Pages
Poultry	2	174–175
Relish or sauce	2	180–181
Vegetables, starchy and green	1	192
	2	182–185
Bread if desired	1	189–190
	2	186–189
Dessert—pastry, cream pie . .	2	190–194
Beverage if desired	1	187–188
	2	199–200

7

	Book	Pages
Fish	2	176
Relish or sauce	2	180–181
Vegetable and/or salad . . .	1	195–197
	2	182–185
Bread if desired	1	189–190
	2	186–189
Sponge cake	2	195–197
Beverage if desired	1	187–188
	2	199–200

8

	Book	Pages
Fruit cup	1	208
Meat, poultry, or fish	2	169–176
Vegetable and salad	1	195–197
	2	182–185
Second vegetable if desired . .	2	182–185
Bread if desired	1	189–190
	2	186–189
Dessert	1	198–209
	2	190–198
Beverage	2	199–200

The students believed that the sequence of meal patterns would greatly facilitate their classwork on preparing and serving the meals at school. Of course, other classes may want to plan a different sequence more suited to their needs. For example, some groups might prefer to learn no more than one new process at any meal. But whatever the situation may be, a sequence of patterns that progresses from simple meals to those more difficult to prepare, is certain to be helpful to any class.

Working Out an Over-all Plan for Preparing and Serving Meals at School

Miss Dodds' group now began to consider the procedure necessary for setting into motion the sequence of meal patterns. As they discussed the situation, one point stood out very clearly. This was that everything they had previously learned — last year and this — as well as the new things to be learned would come into play as they prepared and served meals in class. This meant planning balanced menus, keeping in mind daily food needs. It also meant buying and storing food wisely. Meals would be prepared and served not only repeating what they already knew, but adding something new. Keeping the kitchen clean and neat would contribute much toward successful meal preparation.

The plan

Keeping these things in mind, the students with the assistance of Miss

Dodds worked out an over-all plan for preparing and serving the meals at school. It was agreed that as the sequence progressed and as new problems arose, procedures could be changed to meet the situation encountered. However, the plan is given as it was first set up and used by the students.

- The class will divide into small family groups. The number in a group can vary from time to time, depending upon the difficulty of the meal and the skill to be gained.
- Each family group will plan a menu starting with Meal Pattern 1, and prepare, serve, and evaluate the meal. The same procedure will be followed for the other meal patterns, with everyone in the class working on the same meal pattern at the same time.
- Whenever a new process occurs in a meal pattern, demonstrations — as needed — will be given for the whole class. Also as much time as is necessary for learning the process will need to be provided.
- In planning their menu, each family group will proceed as follows:

1. Except for foods in a new process, decide whether to use (1) the same foods previously prepared, or (2) the same type of food but with a different recipe.

2. Use the four menu-planning guides given on pages 101 to 103. In Guide 1, in order to see the meal in relation to the daily diet, the other two meals of the day will also need to be planned. In Guide 2, plan so that the total cost of the meal does not exceed the amount of money agreed on by the class and Miss Dodds for the meal

pattern being used. The cost can be estimated approximately by checking current prices, and by consulting the buying summaries for the amounts to purchase for certain foods. (See pages 114–117, 124, 129, 132–133.) If the cost appears to exceed the amount previously agreed on for the meal pattern, the menu is to be revised. It will need to include less expensive foods without lessening the nutritive value of the meal.

- Each family group will list the supplies and the amounts needed for the meal to be served. After the supplies are listed, the group will check to see what items are already on hand in the homemaking room. They will then make out a market order of the supplies to be purchased. The order will be given to the shopping committee designated by the class for the meal pattern being used.

- Based on what was previously learned, each family group may choose its own type of meal service. Table setting and table manners will be included as a part of meal service. When new types of service are to be learned, the class as a whole may need to study and observe a demonstration of the new method.

- Each family group will set up a schedule showing activities to be performed in preparing and serving the meal, and indicating when and by whom they will be done. The schedule will need to include all of the work preceding the actual serving of the meal, as well as that to be done on the serving day. But as the meals require more time to prepare and become increasingly difficult, more pre-preparation time will need to be allowed.

- Each family group will take care of the cleanup work in accordance with what was learned last year. (See Book 1, pages 174 to 176.)

- After a meal has been prepared and served according to the procedures described, each family group will make an evaluation. This will include answering the following questions:

1. How well were the four guides in menu planning carried out?

   Were the meals planned adequate for a balanced daily diet?

   Was the cost kept within the limit previously agreed on?

   Did the foods that were served make the meal interesting, appetizing, and satisfying?

   Did the use of time, energy, and equipment receive suitable consideration?

2. How could the food prepared have been improved?

3. How did the table setting, the service, and table manners rate?

4. Was the cleanup work efficiently carried out? This includes the day of serving, as well as the days of partial preparation.

5. How efficiently did the committees on marketing and storing do their jobs in relation to the meal?

6. General comments

Showing How the Over-all Plan Was Carried Out

The over-all plan proved to be very satisfactory. The sequence from simple meals to the more difficult ones was so gradual that learning new processes presented few problems. When the end of the sequence was reached, the students believed that their ability to prepare and serve meals was greatly improved.

Space does not permit a full account of the many interesting experiences which the students had. But one meal pattern — toward the middle of the sequence — has been selected to show how the over-all plan was carried out by one of the family groups. Several pages from Rita's notebook are reproduced on pages 141 to 144.

CLASS MEMO:

If your class plans to use a sequence of meal patterns, what kind of sequence will your group develop? How will this part of the classwork be evaluated?

OUR GROUP: Edna, Dale, and I—Rita; our guest, Miss Dean, who has a free period

MENU TO BE BASED ON MEAL PATTERN 5: meat—roasted, braised, simmered; vegetables and/or salad; bread if desired; pastry, fruit pie; beverage if desired

NEW PROCESSES: roasting, braising, or simmering meat and making fruit pie

DEMONSTRATION HINTS: We'll be using less-tender cuts of meat, so be sure to allow enough cooking time. Watch temperature. Be very careful with piecrust. Cut in fat just right. Don't forget to chill dough. Handle it carefully.

THE MENU, REFERENCES,
AND OTHER MEALS OF THE DAY

The Menu

Braised Pot Roast
Carrots
Vegetable Salad   French Dressing
Fresh Apple Pie
Milk

References

Book 2, page 173
Book 2, page 183
Book 1, pages 195–197
Book 2, page 193

Other Meals of the Day

Breakfast

Fruit Juice
Ready-to-eat Cereal
Poached Egg on Toast
Cocoa

School Lunch

Peanut Butter Sandwiches
Celery Pieces
Apple
Milk

AMOUNTS AND COST OF SUPPLIES NEEDED—OTHER IMPORTANT ITEMS

Supplies and Amounts*	Cost
1 2-pound pot roast at $.69 per pound	$1.38
1 bunch carrots at $.09	.09
1 small head lettuce $.15	.15
½ bunch celery at $.20 per bunch	.10
1 small cucumber $.05	.05
1 bunch radishes $.10	.10
√ 1 onion at $.12 per pound	.04
√ 1 teaspoon dry mustard at $.10 per box	—
√ ⅓ cup vinegar at $.15 per pint	.03
√ 1 cup salad oil at $.24 per pint	.12
√ 1 teaspoon paprika at $.17 per box	—
6 large tart apples at $.10 per pound	.20
√ 2 cups all-purpose flour at $.10 per pound	.05
√ 1 cup sugar at $.10 per pound	.05
√ ⅔ cup shortening at $.32 per pound	.11
√ 2 tablespoons margarine at $.32 per pound	.02
√ 1 teaspoon cinnamon at $.15 per box	—
1 quart milk at $.22	.22
Total	$2.71

Check ✓ indicates food on hand
in the homemaking room

Market Order

1 2-pound pot roast
1 bunch carrots
1 small head lettuce
1 small bunch celery
1 small cucumber
1 bunch radishes
6 large tart apples
1 quart milk

Important Items

Cost of meal: not to exceed $2.75
Table service: serving food on
plates from the kitchen

OUR WORK SCHEDULE

Time	Activity	Student Responsible
Class period on day before meal is served	Prepare apple pie; wrap, and store in freezing compartment of refrigerator	Rita, Edna
	Prepare salad vegetables, carrots, and French dressing, and store in refrigerator	Dale
Day meal is served Free time before class meets	Bake apple pie	Rita
	Prepare and start pot roast cooking	Edna
First half of class period	Cook carrots	Dale
	Combine salad vegetables and French dressing, and put in individual bowls	Edna
	Slice meat	Dale
	Set table	Rita
	Cut pie, and put on individual plates	Edna
	Pour milk in glasses, and set on table	Rita
Third quarter of class period	Act as hostess; greet Miss Dean	Rita
	Put food on plates, and place on table	Dale, Edna
	Clear table, and serve pie	Edna
Fourth quarter of class period	Clear table, and put away leftover food	Edna
	Wash dishes and cooking utensils	Dale
	Dry, and put away dishes and utensils	Rita
	Clean sink and range areas	Edna
	Rinse out and hang up dish towels	Rita

THE EVALUATION

1. MENU PLANNING QUITE SATISFACTORY

Guide 1: The meal we served, and the other two meals we planned made a well-balanced daily diet.

Guide 2: At first we exceeded the amount of money allowed. We planned to have frozen Lima beans, and more kinds of vegetables in the salad. However, a check on prices caused us to change the menu slightly. But we came out all right with no nutritional loss, spending $2.71 on a $2.75 limit.

Guide 3: The combination of foods was not too sweet, too acid, nor too bland. There was a variety in texture, form, and color. Two hot foods were included, and we believe the meal was easy to digest.

Guide 4: The menu was prepared and served according to the schedule, but we had to rush a little on the day we served. Recipes were selected for which there was adequate equipment to prepare and serve the foods.

2. JUST FAIR ON FOOD PREPARATION

The pot roast was tender and moist, because of the low temperature and long cooking time. But it could have been seasoned a little more.

We didn't think the piecrust was as flaky and tender as that made during the demonstration.

The meat and vegetables were not served as hot as they might have been, even though the dinner plates had been warmed. But the salad was crisp with just enough dressing to moisten it, and the milk was cold.

3. IMPROVEMENT NEEDED FOR MEAL SERVICE

Miss Dean commented on how well the table was set. However, the knife was not needed because the meat was so tender.

On the whole, our table manners were good. But the conversation during the meal was mostly shop talk about the food. I should have tried to introduce another subject equally interesting. When the meal was over, Dale realized he hadn't offered to help Miss Dean with her chair.

The table service worked out well. It certainly takes less work to serve a meal on plates from the kitchen than when you use serving dishes.

4. CLEANUP WORK COULD HAVE BEEN BETTER

There was some rushing to get the cleanup work done, probably because we talked too long at the table. But since the meal required fewer dishes and utensils than some other meals, it was possible to get them washed clean, dried, and put away in their regular places.

The kitchen was in good order when we finished, although we forgot to put away the leftover pie.

5. HIGH SCORE FOR THE COMMITTEES ON MARKETING AND STORING SUPPLIES

The students responsible for buying the supplies did a fine job. It was not their fault that the apples for the pie were not as juicy as some we have had at other times. The shoppers had to take what was available.

The meat, milk, and vegetables were suitably stored in the refrigerator, and the other supplies were well taken care of.

6. PLENTY OF ROOM FOR IMPROVEMENT

I hope to learn to make better piecrust.

We all need to be more careful about watching the time. It creeps up before you know it, and then it's a mad rush to get things done on schedule.

Miss Dean said that she enjoyed the meal and hoped that we would invite her again.

All three of us thought the menu was so successful that we plan to try it out at home in the near future.

Learning More About Serving Meals

At various times while the meal patterns were being carried out, the subject of serving meals came up for discussion. During the previous year, the students had learned about three types of table service. One involved serving the plates in the kitchen, and then placing the served plates on the table at the individual covers. Another featured passing the food at the table for people to serve themselves. Still another stressed serving the food at the table, and passing around the served plates. (See Book 1, pages 164–167.) With this experience, the students had a background for serving meals when they began to carry out the sequence of meal patterns.

As progress was made from the lighter meals to the heavier ones, the family groups varied the type of service used according to the kind of foods being served. In this way, the students were able to try out variations in serving which they had learned about last year, but in which they had not gained much skill. Also as the sequence of meal patterns progressed, they studied and tried out new procedures in table service.

Serving more than one course

One of the newer procedures involved serving a first course, such as fruit juice or fruit cup. The students learned that fruit or vegetable juice, or some simple appetizer, is often served in the living room before the family or guests go to the dining room. The juice glasses or cups can be placed on a tray in the kitchen, and then passed — with small napkins — to the various people in the living room. If crackers or some other accompaniment are served with the juice, small plates may be needed.

Reference sources also indicated that fruit cup is generally served at the table in a sherbet glass, or occasionally in a cup on a small plate. When a cup is used, the handle is placed as when serving a beverage. (See the illustration on page 146.) After the course is removed, the table may need to be relaid for the next course. But since this is time-consuming, the silverware to be used for the rest of the meal may be placed on the table when the table is set. However, if silverware is to be laid for the other courses, it is laid from a tray.

The students also studied illustrations for serving cake and pie, and for ice cream or a soft dessert. Cake and pie are usually served on a dessert plate, with the point of the pie facing the person to be served. If silverware

is not already on the table, it can be brought in on the side of the plate as shown in the illustration. As in the case of fruit cup, a small plate is generally provided for ice cream or a soft dessert in a sherbet glass. This is so that the spoon may be left on the plate rather than in the sherbet glass or dessert bowl, in which this kind of

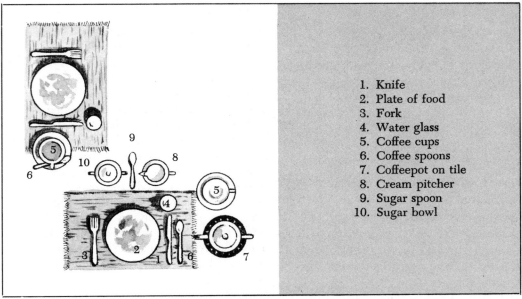

1. Knife
2. Plate of food
3. Fork
4. Water glass
5. Coffee cups
6. Coffee spoons
7. Coffeepot on tile
8. Cream pitcher
9. Sugar spoon
10. Sugar bowl

A simple way of serving coffee at breakfast

dessert is usually served. However, brick ice cream is often served on a dessert plate along with a piece of cake. But in whatever way that ice cream is served, the plate or glass needs to be very cold.

In varying the table service, the first course and the dessert were sometimes served at the table by the hostess. This was done in much the same way that one of the groups the previous year served the casserole dish and the salad. The students thought that this added considerable charm to the meal, provided the necessary serving equipment and sufficient time were available. The same procedures that were learned the previous year were used for clearing the table for the first course and for the dessert. (See Book 1, page 166, items 3 and 4 for clearing the table; page 167 for serving the casserole and salad.)

Serving hot beverages

Learning to make coffee and tea also brought up new serving proce-dures. There seemed to be several ways in which these hot beverages may be served. They can be poured in the kitchen, and the cups and saucers placed on the table at the right of the individual cover. If the person to be served is left handed, the placement would be at the left of the cover. Or the hot beverages might be served at the table. In either case, cream and sugar can be passed at the table.

Coffee may also be served after the dinner at the table. Or it may be served in the living room, although this is not generally done if the first course has been served there. In either case, this type of serving usually re-quires a coffee service. A tray is placed in front of the hostess with a serving pot, cups and saucers, spoons, and perhaps cream and sugar containers conveniently arranged. If a coffee service is not available — when serving in the living room — the cups can be filled in the kitchen, and passed on a tray the same as for fruit juice.

The illustration on this page shows

a simple method used by the students for serving coffee or tea at the table for breakfasts, lunches, and dinners. The pot is placed on a tile at the right of the hostess with the necessary cups and saucers nearby. If lack of space makes it necessary to stack the cups, only two cups are stacked. When serving the beverage, the hostess reassembles the cups and saucers — if they have been stacked — and lifts the pot to each cup to fill it. A spoon may be placed on the saucer before the filled cup is passed, or the spoons may already be laid at each cover. The hostess may also serve the cream and sugar, asking each person his or her preference. Or the cream and sugar may be passed.

Learning to carve

One of the experiences in carving was mentioned in Rita's notebook. This was when pot roast was a new preparation. The illustration on page 148 shows how the carving was done. Later on, another family group planned to serve roast chicken. It so happened that Peter's father had taught him how to carve, so he volunteered to give the demonstration. He said that the same procedures for carving a pot roast can be used for other large cuts of meat. However, carving a roast chicken is more difficult because one must learn where the joints are located.

Peter began his demonstration by telling the class that it was important to have good carving equipment. Holding up the carving set he was to use, the students saw a knife with a thin, nine-inch blade, and a fork with a guard for protecting the hand when cutting toward the fork. Peter said that this type of set could be used for carving roasts of meat and poultry. A smaller set would probably be used for steaks. (See the illustration on page 148.)

Explaining that he was using right-handed procedures, Peter then demonstrated the following steps for carving roast poultry. (See the illustration on page 149.)

1. Place the platter so that the neck of the bird is to the left and the feet to the right of the carver.

2. With the left hand, stick the fork into the bird at the tip of the breastbone. With the right hand, separate the leg and thigh from the nearest side by cutting at the thigh joint and pressing the leg away from the body, as in Step 1 of the illustration.

3. Separate the nearest wing in the same manner, cutting around the joint to locate the dividing point of the joint, as in Step 2 of the illustration.

4. Slice breast meat thin, starting at an angle from the tip of the breastbone and cutting toward the wing joint, as in Step 3 of the illustration.

5. Separate the thigh and the leg at the joint. For small birds, leave the pieces whole. For larger ones, such as a turkey, slice the thigh and leg lengthwise. See steps 4 and 5 of the illustration.

6. Turn the platter and repeat the same procedures for the other side of the bird. Cut enough pieces to serve everyone at the table before transferring the servings to individual plates.

*Offering tips to the carver and
the hostess*

Before the students watched
Peter's demonstration, they had assembled some information of their
own on carving. The tips they set
up for the carver and the hostess,
and used for their own meals
proved so helpful that everyone
wanted a copy to take home. The
material — typed and distributed to
each member of the class — follows:

TIPS TO THE CARVER
- Stand up to carve if it seems easier.
- Be sure that your knife is sharp.
- Remember to "cut across the grain."
  If you cut with the grain, long meat
  fibers give a stringy texture to the
  slices. Steaks are the exception.
- Avoid changing the angle of the knife
  blade while making a slice. Uniform
  slices look better and go farther. Most
  meats are considered more tempting if
  the slices are cut fairly thin.
- Plan the servings before you start putting the portions on the plates, so that
  the choicest parts will be divided

Carving a pot roast

equally among those at the table.
Second helpings cool quickly if sliced
before they are needed.

- It is up to the carver to decide how
  much to serve, when to offer second
  helpings, and to deal with any other
  matters of carving that may arise.

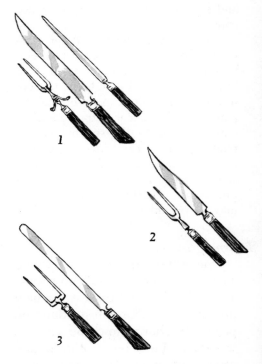

*Carving equipment. 1. Standard set.
2. Steak set. 3. Slicer and helper*

TIPS TO THE HOSTESS
- Give the carver plenty of elbowroom.
  Place glasses and dishes where they
  will not interfere with the carving.
- Give the carver plenty of platter space
  to accommodate the slices. If the platter is not large enough, place another
  dish nearby.
- Be sure that the platter and plates are
  warmed if the food is to be served hot.
- If the carver is inexperienced, try to
  divert the attention of those at the
  table from the carving.

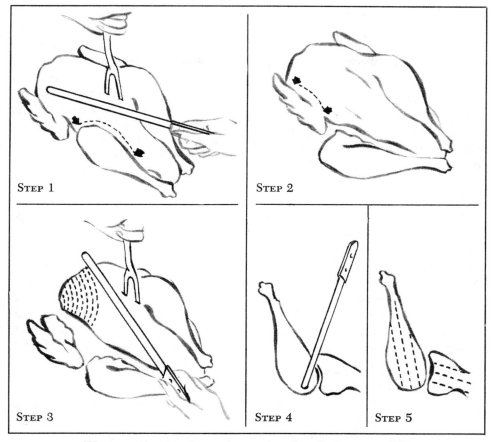

STEP 1

STEP 2

STEP 3

STEP 4

STEP 5

These are the steps in carving poultry described on page 147.

Serving a buffet meal

One day toward the end of the classwork on the sequence of meal patterns, several students who were working together came up with an interesting idea. "Now that we have had so much experience in preparing meals," said Edward, acting as spokesman, "why can't we have a party?"

"A party?" echoed the others. "What kind of a party?"

"We didn't have anything special in mind," replied Edward. "But it ought to be something a little different than serving a family group."

"We had a tea last year," said Edna, "and we wouldn't want to do that again." She paused and then added quickly, "I know what it could be — a buffet meal."

"What's that?" asked several of the boys.

"Well, it's similar to a tea," replied Edna, "except that you serve yourself."

The boys looked a little doubtful, but were quickly reassured when

Janice clarified the situation. "A buffet is really lots of fun," she said. "Everything is put on the table and you walk around helping yourself to what you want."

Miss Dodds smiled. "That's the general idea," she said. "And if you are all interested in learning about buffet service, there's no reason why you can't go ahead and have a buffet party."

There was an enthusiastic response to this suggestion, and tentative plans were soon under way. However, before anything definite was arranged, the students agreed that it was important to find out more about buffet service. The reference shelves supplied plenty of material, and before long the following summary was made:

- A buffet meal is so flexible and practicable that it can be served in a variety of ways. Sometimes the food is placed on the buffet. People serve themselves and then sit down to the dining table. But more often than not, the food is put right on the dining table. Smaller tables are frequently set up nearby or in the living room where people can take their plates. Silverware and napkins may be placed on the dining table, or on the smaller tables. Sometimes trays are used for taking the food to the smaller tables, or for eating with the tray in the lap.

- When it seems desirable to serve as simply and easily as possible, the menu can be composed of foods that do not require a knife. In addition, the foods can be those which may be kept hot without overcooking, or that do not need to be served very hot or very cold. Of course, if a family has appliances that can be used at the table for keeping foods hot or cold, a wider selection of foods is possible.

- The main dish is usually placed at one end of the dining-room table with the serving silver and the stack of plates nearby. Other dishes are attractively spaced on the table, but convenient for people to serve themselves. Water and glasses may be on a side table. Sometimes the host carves or serves the main dish, while the hostess serves the salad. If the group is fairly large, the hostess may ask someone to help her with the serving, so that she can be free to see that foods are replenished when needed. Or the guests may serve themselves to everything.

- The dessert may be placed in advance on the buffet, on a tray cart, or on a side table. If not in individual servings, dessert plates can be nearby for the guests to serve themselves. The beverage may be near the dessert. If coffee or tea, and if suitable equipment is available, it can be made where it is to be served. Or the dessert and the beverage may be served from the kitchen by the hostess. Another method of serving the dessert and the beverage is to do so at the dining table after it has been cleared of the main course. One person may serve the dessert at one end of the table, and another the beverage at the other end.

What especially pleased the students about buffet service were the variations which can be made in table appointments. For example, at a simple, informal get-together a colorful tablecloth, bright-colored serving dishes and silverware, wooden bowls, and other attractive

Menu
Rice and Tuna Casserole
Tossed Green Salad
Hot Buttered Rolls
Strawberry Jam
Coffee   Tea

MAIN COURSE

1. Plates
2. Serving spoon
3. Casserole
4. Hot bread in napkin
5. Jelly spoon
6. Strawberry jam
7. Salad spoon
8. Salad
9. Salad fork
10. Napkins
11. Forks
12. Centerpiece

The menu and service for the buffet meal prepared by the class. Notice how self-service of the main course proceeds around the dining table. A small side table is set up for self-service of coffee and individual servings of dessert.

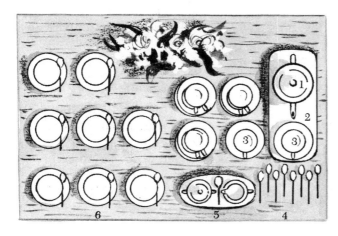

DESSERT

1. Coffeepot
2. Trivet or tray
3. Cup and saucer
4. Coffee spoons
5. Cream, sugar spoon, and sugar bowl on tray
6. Sherbet dish, spoon, and serving plate

utensils can be used. However, the students realized that the appointments selected need to be in keeping with the occasion and the background where they are to be used.

The menus and a diagram of the table setting for the buffet party which Miss Dodds' group held are given on page 151. No further details are included, since other classes may find it more interesting to work out their own plans without being guided by what another group has done.

Arranging Equipment in the School Kitchens

One day while the class was carrying out the sequence of meal patterns, Edna raised an interesting question. "I've noticed that the unit kitchens at school are easier to work in than our kitchen at home. Is there any special reason for this?" Several others added that they too had noticed the same thing.

Miss Dodds smiled and said, "That's a good question. I've been thinking for some time that it might be well to stop long enough to take a careful look at the arrangements in the kitchens. You'll probably find that the answer to Edna's question is tied up with what is called 'management.'"

The students listened attentively as Miss Dodds continued. "These particular unit kitchens were planned not too long ago. A great deal of thought was given to the space and shape for each kitchen

and to the placement of the refrigerator, sink, and range. The amount of counter space needed, and adequate facilities for storage were also carefully considered. Two advanced classes in homemaking participated in planning the setup and in purchasing the small equipment. Both groups prepared summaries which may be helpful to you at this time."

Arrangement of large equipment

The summaries were read and discussed. From them the students learned that the large equipment in the kitchens was placed so as to be conveniently used. Perishable foods would be taken from the refrigerator to a mixing center — where the less perishable items were stored — and then to the nearby range for cooking. Counter space was provided on both sides of the sink and for the mixing center, with storage space both above and below the counters. Counter heights varied, so that the persons preparing the meals could work at heights that promoted good posture. The dinette table and chairs were placed near the range where the foods are cooked, and convenient to the sink where dishes are washed. Storage space for the dishes was near the table, but convenient to the sink. Planning could be done at the dinette table or at a counter not in use. (See the illustration on page 153.)

Arrangement of small equipment

Miss Dodds' group was also interested in the guides for storing small equipment — another part of the summaries. Undoubtedly a convenient arrangement had a direct

Convenient arrangement of both large and small equipment in a kitchen has a direct bearing on how efficiently meals can be prepared.

bearing on how efficiently meals could be prepared. The following guides showed where articles could be placed so that work in the kitchen could go faster and easier:

1. Put small equipment and supplies as near as possible to the area where they will be first used. For example, skillets, lid covers, platters, and serving dishes can be kept near the range since they are generally used there first. Measuring, mixing, and baking utensils along with cooking ingredients can be stored near the mixing area. Knives can be placed in different areas — paring knives at the sink, carving knives at the serving area, and chopping knives at the mixing area.

2. Have all small equipment and supplies that are constantly being used, within bent-elbow distance, and those less frequently used, within full-arm reach. Only those that are rarely used are to go outside these points.

3. Stack articles only one row deep to make them more easily available. This will prevent having to move those in the first row to get to the back row. If space does not permit this arrangement, stack only identical articles of the same size in so far as possible. Otherwise, all have to be lifted to get the largest one.

4. Use dividers to separate articles. This makes each article easy to locate. (See the illustration above.)

After the classwork on the summaries had been completed, Miss Dodds asked Edna whether her question had been answered. Edna nodded and replied, "Yes, it has. I understand much better what is meant by the word 'management.' I'm sure it will be possible to apply some of the things we learned in class to our kitchen at home." The other students who were particularly interested in the same question that Edna had raised, also believed that the classwork had been very helpful.

Working Out Problems of Time

As the sequence of meal patterns began to progress toward heavier meals, the problem of time became even more acute. It seemed necessary to do more and more preparation in advance. This was customary procedure and was to be expected. But what disturbed Miss Dodds was that the students were constantly running in and out of the kitchens at all times of the day. Some solution needed to be worked out to hold these trips to the minimum.

Time solutions

Various possibilities for meeting such problems were then discussed and summarized as follows:

1. Plan more foods that can be frozen or refrigerated until needed. This can be done in the regular class periods any time preceding the meal. Foods to be frozen can be wrapped in treated paper in much the same way as sandwiches are wrapped in wax paper.

(See Book 1, page 211.) It is often easier to use plastic bags — made for quick freezing — for large items, such as a roast of meat or poultry. But in either case, the package to be frozen needs to be tied or sealed, so that air cannot get into it.

2. Make use of a pressure saucepan whenever possible to reduce the time required for cooking some meats and vegetables.

3. Try to make use of the kitchen early in the morning before the regular classes begin, or when a class is not being held.

4. When a preparation is begun but the baking not completed in the class period, set a time clock. Then ask one of your friends who will be in the kitchen during the next class to turn off the range and take the product from the oven when the bell rings.

5. Avoid dawdling while preparing a recipe. By moving right along and perhaps increasing your rate of speed a little, you may be able to complete some preparations sooner than you expected.

6. During the class period when the meal is to be served, make a special effort to keep cooking utensils and soiled dishes cleaned up as you go along.

7. Before the meal is served, get things ready for washing the dishes later on. Set the dishpan in the sink, and make space available for the glasses, silverware, and dishes when the table is cleared.

8. Be time conscious during the meal. Some people become so interested in the table conversation that they slow down their eating. It is not necessary to urge haste. But if the hostess — or host — sets the pace for the meal, the

others will tend to follow and the meal can be finished in the scheduled time.

The Key to Successful Meal Management at School

During the final evaluation of the classwork, Miss Dodds asked the students an important question.

"What do you consider to be the key to successful meal management at school?" she asked.

The summary

After some discussion, the students agreed that the following material might well be the answer to Miss Dodds' question.

- Planning well-balanced, attractive meals that come within the cost prescribed, and that can be prepared and served in the time available
- Setting up and carrying out the work schedule with these points in mind:

1. Plan for as much pre-preparation as is desirable in terms of length of class period and of available free time.
2. See that each person in a family group understands exactly what he or she is to do and when.
3. Arrange small equipment for convenient use.
4. Become time conscious throughout the preparation, serving, and cleanup periods. Move along steadily without confusion and without wasting time.
5. Keep in mind that a meal is not completed until everything in the unit kitchens is in good order.

- Being able to evaluate what you do, and to profit by your own experience as well as the experience of others

Miss Dodds said that the question had been well answered. Then she added, "I'm sure all of you realize the importance of efficient management in preparing and serving the meals at school. And learning how to manage well in your classwork will help to develop your ability to meet management problems successfully in your homes."

Using a Management Problem for a Home Experience

The classwork on management seemed so important that some of the students decided to carry out a home experience involving a management problem. However, space does not permit an account of all of the experiences as they were described in class. But three of the reports are given because of the special interest they may have for other students' families with similar situations.

Working out a schedule for meals

Marta was the first to report to the class. She said that the problem she was going to describe on management was really a part of her home experience on preparing and serving meals for the family. Early in her work, her chief concern had been to have the evening meal on schedule. She usually started out with everything ready, but as she went along too many things piled up. Before she realized it, she was way behind the regular meal hour.

She had tried to use the plan for scheduling work that the family groups set up each time they served a meal. (See the example on page 143.) But she soon realized that the school situation was different from hers. There several people were preparing the meal, whereas at home she was the only one. What she needed was a flexible schedule that could be applied to any meal she might serve.

Since this seemed to be a more difficult problem than she could cope with alone, Marta consulted Miss Dodds. Then two of her friends who were members of the class offered to work with her. Together they set up the following plan:

First of all, the approximate time necessary for preparing the meal would be estimated. This would be based on the foods which require the longest cooking. But it would also include the time it takes a person to assemble the necessary ingredients and equipment, and to prepare the products for cooking. After the total time is determined, it is then broken down into periods.

Marta then showed the class how this plan could be carried out. Selecting one of the dinner menus previously set up by the students for her family, she had worked out a schedule for the meal, as shown on page 157.

Meat Loaf
Baked Potatoes   Canned Tomatoes
Celery
Bread   Margarine
Chocolate Ice Cream
(already prepared)
Tea   Milk

Time required: about 1½ hours

Activities	Periods of Time
Assemble supplies for meat loaf. Heat oven. Prepare meat loaf, and put in oven. Prepare potatoes, and put in oven.	**BEGINNING PERIOD** (*about 20 minutes*)
Prepare celery for table, and put in refrigerator. Wash utensils from previous preparations. Guide Paula in setting table. Put out serving dishes. Relax — read the newspaper or listen to music. Check personal appearance.	**MIDDLE PERIOD** (*about 55 minutes*)
Open, and heat canned tomatoes. Place celery, bread, and margarine on table. Put water on stove for tea. Fill glasses for milk and water. Put hot food in serving dishes, and place on table. Make tea, and put on table.	**FINAL PERIOD** (*about 15 minutes*)
Begin meal preparation about 4:45 **Dinner hour about 6:15**	

Making Harold's kitchen easier to work in

Harold's home experience was, first, making a survey of the kitchen. Then he set up and carried out — with the approval of his family — suggestions for simple changes that could easily be made. He believed that these changes would not only save time and energy, but make the kitchen easier to work in when preparing and serving meals. His re-

HAROLD'S KITCHEN

As it was at time of survey	*Short cuts to easier work*
Small equipment not easily accessible — stored in table drawers or in cupboard	Put up near work area a piece of pegboard with hooks to hold equipment constantly in use.
Cooking utensils not convenient — stored in lower part of cupboard some distance from range	Hang frequently used skillets and pans on hooks near range. Ample space available.
Pot holders too far from range — kept on shelf in cupboard	Hang pot holders nearer range, but not within reach of the heating units.
Sink has only a right-hand shelf. There is no place to put the dried dishes except on a table in the middle of the room.	Use a small table with casters — now in the dining room — as a left-hand shelf for the sink. After the dishes are dried, the table can be rolled over to the cupboard where the dishes are kept.
No rack for dish towels	Put an inexpensive towel rack near the sink area.
Floor area near sink easily soiled by splashing water from dishpan	Use a small washable rug in front of the sink to protect the floor.
No provision made for wiping hands during meal preparation	Buy paper-towel rack with roll of towels. Place on wall near the sink. This is economical because it saves laundry.
Garbage can requires too frequent washing to keep it fresh and clean.	Put paper bag in can, or line with newspapers. These can easily be removed without the necessity of washing the can each time it is emptied. Wrap wet garbage in extra paper.

port to the class included a description of the kitchen as it was when his survey was made. This was followed by suggestions for improvement. The material he presented was lined up on the blackboard as shown on page 158.

*Having more assistance after
the evening meal*

Of course the students were interested in Marta's home experience. They all looked forward to her reports on the progress she was making. One of her recent problems was how to spend less time in the kitchen after the evening meal. Several of Marta's close friends felt that she had managed the situation very well. It occurred to them that it might be fun to present a skit to the class, showing how Marta's work was made easier by securing her family's assistance. Miss Dodds gave her approval and the skit was prepared and given. Stewart acted as the announcer, Bob as Mr. Jamison, Edward as Teddy, and Helen as Paula. Marta was herself. The skit follows:

ANOTHER GLIMPSE AT MARTA'S HOME EXPERIENCE

The scene opens with the Jamison family sitting around the dining table after the evening meal. The action is in pantomime which is coordinated by the remarks of an unobserved speaker. His comments indicate what different members of the family are doing, and run as follows:

"The Jamison family is just finishing a most satisfying meal prepared by Marta. Mr. Jamison and Teddy are profuse with their compliments. Even little Paula sings her praises about the wonderful dessert. Marta is smiling proudly.

"Now you see each member of the family rising and carrying his or her dessert dishes to the kitchen where they are placed to the right of the sink. The serving dishes and dinner plates were removed before the dessert was served by Teddy with some assistance

from Paula. Mr. Jamison and Paula are now returning to the dining room. Paula puts the holders containing the napkins into the sideboard drawer. She is ready to crumb the table after her father has removed whatever was left on it. Look! She sees some crumbs on the floor. She is getting the carpet sweeper to take them up.

"Back in the kitchen Teddy is standing by the sink. It is his turn to scrape, rinse, and stack the dishes. This includes putting the cooking utensils in which there is no food to soak.

"Marta is busy taking care of the leftovers. She puts the drippings from the pan into a special container kept for that purpose. She wipes off the remaining grease with absorbent paper, and puts the pan to soak. Now she is appraising the food left over from the meal and deciding how to

store it. Her thoughts run something like this: '*The rest of the meat loaf can be wrapped in foil and put near the freezing unit in the refrigerator. We can slice the meat and use it for sandwiches tomorrow. The green beans will also go into the refrigerator in this covered bowl. I'll use them in the vegetable salad I've planned for tomorrow evening. These slices of bread seem a little dry. I'll put them in the breadbox, and use them later in a bread pudding.*'

"Now look over toward the sink. Mr. Jamison is taking his turn at washing the dishes. Teddy is drying and putting them away. He is careful to hang the dish towels on the rack when he has finished. Marta has put away the food, and is sweeping the kitchen floor.

"Guess everything is now in order. Those in the kitchen are heading for the living room. Mr. Jamison is sitting down in his favorite chair preparing to read the evening paper. Teddy and Paula are getting out a box of airplane material. Marta stands at the door in the living room half smiling to herself. She is thinking. '*It was a good meal even though the meat loaf was a little dry. Oh, well — I'm learning fast. I've made a lot of improvement since we started the classwork on foods. Who knows, I may become a really good manager one of these days. And now for my homework.*'"

Everyone was pleased with the skit. Some of the comments ran like this:

"It certainly shows that family cooperation can make work in the kitchen easier."

"When each member of the family knows what he or she is supposed to do, there is no confusion. The work is done quickly and effectively."

"Rotating the tasks helps each person to learn to do a variety of things. And by changing the chores, no one task becomes a hardship."

HELPING THE JAMISON FAMILY PROVES TO BE A SATISFYING EXPERIENCE

BEFORE the classwork on "Meals to Fit the Family's Needs" was completed, Marta told the students how much she and the other members of her family appreciated what the class had been doing for them.

"It's wonderful what changes can occur in a few short weeks," she said. "My father is like a new person. He's beginning to gain weight, and he never complains of being tired any more. It was a little difficult at first for Teddy and Paula to cut down on cokes and candy. But after they began playing the food game and eating a more balanced diet, they didn't want so many sweets.

"The menus which the class set up for us when I first started out were a boon. I make use of them quite frequently to save time planning new ones. I still need more experience in preparing certain foods. But I realize this takes practice. My father and I have been going over the food expenses regularly. Now we know that we can afford a balanced diet."

As the students listened to Marta, they felt that helping the Jamison family had been an interesting experience — one that they would long remember with a deep feeling of personal satisfaction.

CLASS MEMO:

What do you find useful in the classwork of Miss Dodds' group on planning, preparing, and serving balanced meals? What other ideas for carrying out your work on foods can your group develop?

PLANNING YOUR CLASSWORK

THE subject of food is always interesting to everyone. But to the students in Miss Dodds' class, it seemed especially important because one of their members needed help with food problems in her home. In fact, the students used these problems as a basis for their class goals. They believed that what would help the Jamison family would also benefit them. An interesting food game and a chart on essential food nutrients were used to learn more about a well-balanced diet. For studying about new foods and new processes, the students followed a sequence of meal patterns. They started with the simpler meals of the day and progressed toward the more difficult ones. This

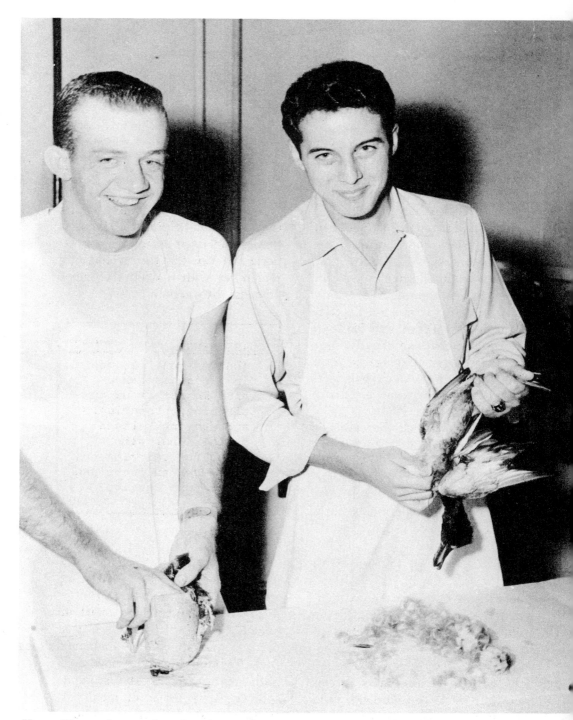

How will your class go about learning to plan, prepare, and serve balanced meals? Here some boys in a homemaking class are preparing a duck dinner.

proved to be an effective method of carrying out the work on planning, preparing, and serving meals. The goal on buying and storing food wisely was also an interesting experience. When all the classwork was completed, the students believed that they had been successful in helping the Jamison family with their food problems. And at the same time, every member of the class had gained a better understanding of meal management in serving a well-balanced diet.

As you plan your classwork on foods, you may have problems similar to those encountered by Miss Dodds' group. However, you need not feel that it is necessary to meet these situations the same way, or to follow the same procedures as those used by Miss Dodds' class. But whatever your plans, you will doubtless strive for the same results. You will want to learn to plan, prepare, and serve meals that build toward the health of yourself and members of your family.

SUGGESTED EXPERIENCES

In making plans for your classwork on foods, you may welcome ideas for various experiences. The suggestions which follow are offered with the hope that they will give you a start toward planning and preparing meals that will meet your family's needs.

1. Members of your class may want to use the food game (shown on pages 84–85) at home, checking the foods served to the family on different days. If certain foods are found to be lacking in the diet, plans can be worked out at school to introduce these foods into the family's meals. The following examples indicate what other students encountered after they used the game at home:

EXAMPLE 1: Joan discovered that green and yellow vegetables were seldom included in the meals, because some members of the family did not particularly like them. Joan learned

new and interesting ways to prepare these vegetables. Then she arranged with her mother to serve them at the evening meal once or twice a week at first. Gradually the family accepted them as part of the meal. Then Joan's mother began to include green and yellow vegetables regularly in the daily menu.

EXAMPLE 2: Lee found that his family was using very little milk. They liked milk in foods, but not as a drink. Lee then collected various pamphlets containing recipes that used milk. He tried out several on the family with success. Then he made a small booklet for his mother containing about eighteen recipes that seemed practical and easy to prepare. Together they planned to use these recipes to meet the daily milk requirements.

EXAMPLE 3: In Alice's family, two of the four members have been unable to eat wheat bread more than once a day because of allergies. Since these two members need food which gives energy, Alice collected recipes of substitutes for wheat bread. Her mother tried out the recipes and found them very satisfactory.

2. Perhaps you have discovered that certain foods are missing in the day's diet. If so, you may find it helpful to study the food chart (shown on pages 96–99) in relation to these foods. For example, if green and yellow vegetables are lacking, note how many nutrients these vegetables supply and how valuable they are to good health.

3. Your class can sponsor the showing of one or more films on better family nutrition. (Consult the *Educational Film Guide,* the H. W. Wilson Company.) Parents and other guests may be invited to the program.

4. Members of your class may find it helpful to bring in problems in meal planning that their families have. Such problems might include:

a. One-dish meals

b. Planning weekly meals

c. Quick and easy guest meals

d. Frozen-food meals

e. Oven meals

f. Low-cost meals

g. Meals adapted to special types of serving, such as a buffet meal

Then the class may plan balanced meals to meet the various family problems. Later each family can help evaluate the meals relating to the problem.

5. Developing some way of evaluating the menus suggested in Experience 4 may prove to be a valuable class experience.

6. It will be interesting to keep a record of what you actually ate during the past week. Then you can ask another member of the class to decide with you how well balanced the meals were and what improvement, if any, is needed.

7. Someone in your class might write a skit showing what balanced meals did for one family. The skit could then be given during one of the regular class periods.

8. Let each member of the class work out a plan with his or her family to use as much as possible of the information on buying and storing food as shown between pages 118 and 135. Examples of what one group did follow:

EXAMPLE 1: Frank arranged to buy the fresh fruits and vegetables for the family. His aim was to become a really expert shopper of these items.

EXAMPLE 2: Mary shopped several Saturday mornings with her mother. After that she did the weekly marketing alone, so that her mother had time to do something else.

EXAMPLE 3: Dean and his mother decided to replan the storage of food in the kitchen and in the refrigerator. Dean also arranged to help with the buying and storing of the food each week.

EXAMPLE 4: Jean planned to learn as much as possible about labels. Once a week she went with her mother to the store. While her mother was shopping, Jean studied labels, taking notes on various products. Before long she was able to make a wise selection of canned goods which not only helped the family budget, but gave more satisfaction.

9. Everyone in the class will enjoy a pantomime session showing what to do and what not to do in buying food for the family meals. Be sure to include

what different members of the family can do to help.

10. Like many other schools, you may have short class periods. If so, you may want to work out plans to provide the most practical experiences in food preparation in the time available. In doing this, it may be helpful to consider how Miss Dodds' class met the problem of time. (See pages 154–157.) You may be able to suggest additional ways of handling a short-period situation. You may also want to consider how the experiences you have planned for school will fit into your home schedule for meal preparation.

11. You may enjoy working out a time schedule for meal preparation at home similar to the schedule shown on page 157. You can use the following menu, or one of your own selection.

Broiled Steak

Mashed Potatoes   Buttered Green Peas

Tomato and Lettuce Salad

Hot Rolls   Butter

Frozen Marlow   Vanilla Sugar Cookies

Coffee

Select from the list which follows a period that would be satisfactory for doing each of the tasks listed below, and indicate the letter corresponding to your choice. All of your answers need not necessarily be the same as those of other classmates serving the same meal.

TIME PERIODS
for 6 o'clock dinner

a. In the morning

b. In the afternoon before 5 o'clock

c. Between 5 and 5:45 o'clock

d. Last 15 minutes before meal is served

TASKS

_____ 1. Prepare lettuce and tomatoes and chill.

_____ 2. Arrange salad on plates.

_____ 3. Put butter on table.

_____ 4. Shape rolls.

_____ 5. Put rolls in oven

_____ 6. Fill water glasses.

_____ 7. Set table.

_____ 8. Make coffee.

_____ 9. Peel potatoes and start water heating.

_____10. Mix dough for rolls.

_____11. Mash potatoes.

_____12. Prepare frozen marlow.

_____13. Start peas to cook.

_____14. Broil steak.

_____15. Make vanilla sugar cookies.

12. Your class may want to arrange with your homemaking teacher to give demonstrations of various procedures. Several members may assist her in such demonstrations as the following.

a. Carving a baked ham

b. Broiling fish

c. Braising short ribs of beef

d. Shaping dough into rolls

e. Making jelly roll

f. Filling cream puffs

g. Lining a piepan with a graham cracker crust

h. Spreading and browning a meringue topping on a pie

13. From educational and commercial listings, volunteers can assemble the names of available films on food preparation. Plans may then be made to show some of the films that are especially interesting to the class.

14. You may want to plan with your mother to try a table service not customarily used in your home. For example, if buffet service has never been used, you could plan a Sunday supper featuring this type of serving. If your family seems to enjoy the change, you can plan to use other types of service occasionally.

15. Holding a mock TV broadcast featuring ways of making work in the kitchen easier might prove very worth while. Members of the class could look over their kitchens at home, and offer suggestions for making simple changes, such as those shown on page 158 for Harold's situation. Parents could be invited to the broadcast as guests.

Recipes

TO FIT THE FAMILY BUDGET

A BOOKLET OF RECIPES USED BY MISS DODDS' CLASS

Chocolate sauce on sponge cake may add pleasure to an already delightful dessert. (See page 195.)

Angel food cake with peaches and whipped cream makes an attractive dessert. (See page 196.)

Here — left to right — is coffee being made by the drip, vacuum, and percolator methods. (See page 199.)

Contents

Main Dishes

Main dishes — MEAT

GENERAL INFORMATION

There are many cuts of beef, veal, pork, and lamb. Each of the cuts, frozen or not, may be cooked by one or more methods: *roasting, broiling, pan-broiling, pan-frying, braising,* and *stewing or simmering.* Sometimes the pressure cooker is used. Temperature and time are important considerations in most meat cookery. Too high heat causes needless shrinking. Meat cooked past the well-done stage becomes dry and unpalatable. Tender cuts — and in some instances those tenderized — are best when cooked by dry heat methods, such as roasting, broiling, pan-broiling, and pan-frying. Less tender or cheaper cuts need longer, slower cooking, and generally require the addition of liquid. This is necessary to soften the connective tissue or the part which may not be tender. Braising and stewing or simmering are the methods generally used.

If meat is started to cook while hard frozen, the cooking time will of course be longer. For defrosted cuts, the same cooking temperatures and time schedules are used as for cuts which have not been frozen. Thick steaks and roasts cook more uniformly if defrosted before cooking.

The cooking time given in charts and in recipes is only an approximate guide. In any case for on-top-of-stove cookery, the person preparing the product needs to evaluate the time and temperature required. In certain electric appliances, such as a frypan, the temperature can be controlled by a regulator. This is true for oven cooking also. For roasting meat, a meat thermometer is an accurate guide for doneness.

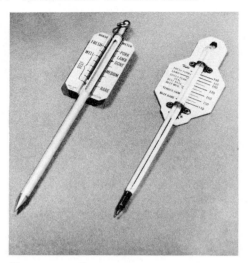

Roast meat thermometers

ROASTING: Roasting is to bake by dry heat, usually in an oven. The steps in roasting meat are as follows:

1. Preheat oven to the temperature required. See the chart below.

2. Wipe meat with a damp cloth.

3. Season with salt and pepper if desired, or season later during the cooking process. Allow ¾ teaspoon salt to each pound of meat.

4. Place meat, fat side up, on a rack in an open pan. If a meat thermometer is used, make a gash in the meat, and insert the thermometer so that the bulb is in the center of the largest muscle. Avoid letting the bulb touch a bone resting in fat. Add no water, and do not cover.

5. Roast to the desired doneness.

Meat loaf is a form of roasting, but is generally referred to as baked. (See page 172 for recipe for Meat Loaf.)

BROILING: The steps which follow describe how to broil.

1. Turn the oven regulator to "broil." Preheat or not as desired.

2. Slash edges of fat on the meat to prevent curling, and place meat on rack of broiler pan, 2 to 3 inches from the heat. The thinner the cut, the nearer it needs to be to the heat.

3. Broil the top side for about half the time given in the chart for broiling (see page 171), leaving the door of the broiling oven open.

4. Season the top side with salt and pepper. Omit seasoning for ham and bacon.

5. Turn, and brown the other side.

6. Season, and serve at once on a hot plate.

CHART FOR ROASTING MEAT				
Meat		Oven temperature in degrees	Approximate minutes per pound	Thermometer reading in degrees
BEEF	rare	325	*22 to 26	140
	medium	325	30	160
	well done	325	35	170
PORK	fresh (always well done)	325	35 to 45	185
	**smoked	325	30 to 35	170
VEAL		325	35 to 40	180
LAMB		325	35 to 40	180

* A rolled roast requires 10 minutes longer per pound.
** Tenderized hams require shorter cooking time. Follow directions available with the ham.

CHART OF
APPROXIMATE BROILING TIME
FOR MEAT

Meat		Total time in minutes
STEAK	1 inch thick,	
	rare	about 10
	medium	about 15
	well done	20 to 25
	2 inches thick,	
	rare	about 25
	medium	about 35
	well done	45 to 50
LAMB CHOPS, 1 inch thick		about 12
HAM SLICE	½ inch thick	15 to 20
	1 inch thick	20 to 30

Only approximate broiling times for various meats can be given because much depends on the broiler, personal preference in doneness of meat, and the meat itself.

PAN-BROILING: Meat suitable for broiling may also be pan-broiled. This method is especially good for meat cut very thin, for small steaks, and when cooking a few chops. Steps in pan-broiling follow:

1. Use a heavy frying pan or griddle. Except for thin meat, such as bacon, the griddle is generally preheated. But this is not essential, since preheating merely starts the meat to cook more quickly. Brush the griddle lightly with fat to prevent sticking. Do not add any more fat or water. Do not cover.

2. Brown meat on both sides, turning occasionally. Pour off or remove any fat that accumulates. Do not overcook. Pan-broiling requires approximately half the time of broiling.

3. Season, and serve at once.

PAN-FRYING: Pan-frying, frying, or sautéing is the same as pan-broiling except that the meat is first browned in a small amount of hot fat, and then slowly fried on both sides. When meat is immersed in fat, the process is known as deep-fat frying. In general, deep-fat frying is probably less frequently used than any other method of meat preparation. Special equipment — a deep kettle and a frying basket — may occupy too much space in the average home to justify the use of this method. The temperature range in frying varies considerably depending upon the size of the pieces to be fried. For these reasons, general directions for deep-fat frying are not given.

Various types of meat may be pan-fried. Tender meat cut comparatively thin, such as "minute" steaks, sliced liver, or chops, is suited to this method. Meat made tender by cubing or grinding, such as "cube" steaks and hamburg patties, may also be pan-fried. Leftover meats ground and combined with other ingredients to make croquettes are generally pan-fried. (See page 173 for recipe for Meat Croquettes.) Some of these types of meat, such as liver, are often dredged with seasoned flour before frying. The seasoning may consist of ¼ to ½ teaspoon of salt and a dash of pepper to ¼ cup of flour. Other seasoning, such as celery salt or onion salt, is sometimes added. Chops, such as veal cutlets, may be dipped in slightly beaten egg — with a little milk added — and then in crumbed dry bread or crackers. When meats are pan-fried, only enough fat to keep the meat from sticking to the bottom of the pan is necessary. But if the meat has a flour or crumbed coating, more fat may be needed than when not coated.

BRAISING: This method is a combination of dry and moist heat. Meat that is braised is first browned in a small amount of hot fat. The meat may or may not be dredged with flour before browning. The pan is then tightly covered, and the meat is cooked slowly — in the oven or on top of the stove — in its own juices, or in a small amount of added liquid. The liquid may be water, milk, soup stock, vegetable juices, or sour cream. Seasoning often consists of salt, pepper, herbs, spices, or one or more vegetables, such as tomatoes, chopped onion, and celery. Any juices remaining in the pan after cooking, may be served as pan gravy or may be thickened for gravy.

Braising is generally used for less tender meat. But some tender cuts, such as chops, steaks, cutlets, and liver, are often braised. This method cooks the meats well without drying them out. Recipes in which braising is used may be found on the following pages: Swiss Steak, page 173; Pot Roast, page 173; Meat Balls — a modified form of braising — page 174.

STEWING OR SIMMERING: Stewing or simmering is a method generally used for cooking less tender cuts of meat. The chief difference between braising and stewing or simmering is the amount of liquid used. Braising requires only a small amount whereas in stewing or simmering, enough liquid is used to cover the meat. Stewing and simmering are similar, except that the term stewing generally refers to small pieces of meat and simmering to large pieces that are to be sliced. Steps for stewing follow:

1. Cut meat into 1- to 2-inch cubes if not purchased already cut.

2. Brown meat cubes in a heavy pan in a small amount of fat on all sides. If a light-colored stew is preferred, omit the browning.

3. Add just enough water to cover the meat. The liquid may be hot or cold. If hot water is used, the meat will start to cook sooner. Season with salt and pepper and other seasonings as desired.

4. Cover the pan, and simmer — cooking just below the boiling point — until meat is tender.

5. If vegetables are to be used with the stew, add them according to the time they need to be cooked. (See Chart of Boiling Guide for Fresh Vegetables, page 183.)

6. When done, remove meat and vegetables — if used — to a pan, platter, or casserole, and keep hot until ready to serve.

See recipe for Beef Stew, page 174.

PRESSURE COOKERY: Meats, vegetables, and other foods cooked in a pressure saucepan usually have a good texture and flavor. The cooking time is greatly reduced, because

the food is cooked at a temperature many times higher than boiling.

A book of instructions comes with each pressure saucepan and should be followed exactly. General guides for pressure-saucepan cooking follow:

1. Place food with the recommended amount of water on trivet in the pressure saucepan.

2. Avoid filling the saucepan more than ⅔ full, or food will clog the steam outlet and prevent safe operation.

3. Adjust cover according to instructions.

4. Place saucepan over high heat, with the steam vent open, until a steady flow of steam comes through.

5. Close steam vent, bringing pressure up to desired degree. Lower heat. Maintain desired pressure by regulating heat under saucepan.

6. When cooking period is over, remove saucepan from heat and reduce the pressure quickly or slowly as indicated in the recipe. *Never try to remove the cover until the pressure gauge registers zero.*

MEAT LOAF
[serves 4]

½ pound beef, ground	¾ cup milk
¼ pound lean pork, ground	1 teaspoon salt
	few grains pepper
1 cup bread crumbs	other seasoning as desired
1 egg, beaten	

Mix the above ingredients thoroughly, and shape into loaf or into individual loaves 1 by 2 by 3 inches. Bake in a moderate oven, 350 degrees, for approximately 1 hour, or somewhat less for individual loaves.

Serve hot or cold as desired.

VARIATIONS:

Ham Loaf: Follow recipe for meat loaf, except use ¾ pound ground fresh pork and ⅜ pound ground cured ham for the meat. Omit salt. Bake in 1 loaf or in individual loaves for approximately 1 hour, or somewhat less for individual loaves.

Beef Loaf: Follow recipe for meat loaf except use ¾ pound beef for the meat. Substitute tomato juice for the milk.

MEAT CROQUETTES
[serves 4]

2 cups cooked meat, ground
1 cup potatoes, mashed
1 tablespoon parsley, chopped
seasoning of salt and pepper

1 tablespoon water
1 egg, beaten
fine dry crumbs or flour for coating
fat for pan frying

Combine meat, potatoes, and parsley. Add seasoning.

Shape into flat cakes, cylinders, or pyramids.

Add water to egg. Dip croquettes into egg and roll in crumbs or flour.

Brown croquettes in a little hot fat, turning to form a good crust all over.

SWISS STEAK
[serves 4]

¼ cup flour
¼–½ teaspoon salt
few grains pepper
1½ pounds round or flank steak (1½ inches thick)

2–4 tablespoons fat
1½ cups canned tomatoes
1 onion, sliced
1 stalk celery, diced

Mix flour, salt, and pepper to make seasoned flour.

Pound seasoned flour into sides of steak.

Brown in hot fat in heavy skillet.

Add tomatoes, onion, and celery.

Cover, and cook over low heat or in slow oven, 300 degrees, until tender (2 to 2½ hours), uncovering the last half hour of cooking time. Serve hot.

POT ROAST
[serves 4]

small amount of fat
2- to 3-pound beef chuck
1 tablespoon flour if meat is to be dredged
1 teaspoon salt
dash pepper
½–1 cup liquid—water, soup stock, tomato juice, or any other liquid desired
vegetables, such as onions, carrots, stalks of celery, or potatoes if desired

Heat small amount of fat in a heavy frying pan or kettle. Do not let the fat smoke.

Add meat, seasoned with salt and pepper. If desired, meat may be dredged in seasoned flour.

Brown well on both sides. Then place on rack to prevent overbrowning.

Add liquid, and cover pan or kettle tightly. More liquid may be added during the cooking if it seems necessary.

Cook slowly on top of stove over low heat, or in a moderate oven, 300 degrees, until tender. Allow 30 to 60 minutes per pound.

Cooking pot roast

If vegetables are to be cooked with the meat, they can be added according to the length of time they need to be cooked. (See Chart of Boiling Guide for Fresh Vegetables, page 183.)

Remove meat — and vegetables if used — to a warm platter, and slice meat. Any liquid left in the pan may be served as pan gravy. Or if a thickened gravy is desired, use 1 tablespoon flour to 1 cup of the liquid. Blend the flour thoroughly with a small amount of cold water before combining it with the liquid from the pan. Then cook over very low heat, stirring constantly until thickened. Cook a few minutes longer, stirring occasionally.

MEAT BALLS
[serves 4]

¾ pound beef, ground	1 teaspoon chili powder
¼ pound pork sausage	¼ cup uncooked rice
1 teaspoon salt	1 cup milk
few grains pepper	2½ cups canned
	tomatoes (No. 2 can)

Mix thoroughly all the above ingredients except the tomatoes.

Heat tomatoes to the boiling point.

Shape meat mixture into loose balls, and drop into hot tomatoes.

Cook slowly with cover for 1½ hours. Uncover, and simmer ½ hour more. Serve hot.

BEEF STEW
[serves 4]

1 pound lean beef, cubed	2 tablespoons fat
¼ teaspoon salt	hot water to cover meat
few grains pepper	2 potatoes, diced
2–3 tablespoons flour	4 small carrots, diced
1 onion, sliced	1 turnip, diced

Sprinkle the meat with salt, pepper, and flour.

Brown it with the onion in the fat.

Add water. Cover pan, and cook just below the boiling point until meat is tender — about 2 hours.

Add potatoes, carrots, and turnips, and cook until tender — about 20 minutes. Serve hot.

Main dishes — <u>POULTRY</u>

GENERAL INFORMATION

Ready-to-cook poultry may or may not need additional cleaning before it is cooked. If cleaning is necessary, wash inside and out in cold, running water. Drain and wipe dry with a clean cloth or absorbent paper. When cleaning the giblets, cut the gizzard — if the inner sac has not been removed — through the thickest part just to the tough, whitish, inner lining. Be careful not to cut this lining. Pull the inner sac loose and discard. If the heart, liver, or gizzard have fat, blood vessels, or blood clots, remove these by cutting carefully. Be sure that the gall bladder sac — greenish in color — is also removed from the liver as well as the oil sac at the base of the tail. Otherwise a bitter flavor may result.

In some cases, poultry may need to be singed if there are fine hairs and down on the outside skin. To singe, hold it at a short distance above a flame until the hairs disappear. Keep changing the position constantly to avoid injuring the flesh.

If poultry is frozen when purchased, defrost completely before cooking, and proceed as above. At room temperature, wrapped in moisture-proof wrapping, the defrosting will require from 2 to 6 hours, depending upon the size of the bird and whether or not it is cut in pieces.

Cooking chicken or other poultry is similar to cooking meat. A young chicken for broiling is usually split — cut in halves. It is broiled first with the skin away from the heat, and is turned frequently. A somewhat larger chicken may be cut in pieces, rolled in seasoned flour, and pan-fried. Young, mature birds can be stuffed and baked. Older ones are often cut in pieces and fricasseed. Fricasseeing is a term generally applied to poultry when it is braised. Older birds may also be stewed, and used in dishes such as chicken pie or creamed chicken. (See recipes for Roast Chicken with Stuffing, below, and Chicken Pie, page 175.)

ROAST CHICKEN WITH STUFFING AND GRAVY
[serves 4]

3–4 pound chicken, whole	stuffing (see following recipe)
⅛ teaspoon salt per pound	3–4 tablespoons fat
	gravy (see following recipe)

Sprinkle the inside of the bird with salt.

Fill neck cavity loosely with stuffing, and fold the skin over the back with a skewer.

Fold wing tip up and over back for a brace when bird is turned over.

Fill the body cavity with stuffing, packing lightly.

Place skewers across opening at regular intervals. Lace a string around skewers, and bring edges of skin together.

Cross ends of drumsticks, tie securely, and fasten to tail.

Brush bird with melted fat. Place bird — breast down — on rack in shallow pan, and roast uncovered without adding water in a slow–moderate oven, 325 degrees. Turn breast up when about ¾ done. Baste several times with melted fat or drippings.

Cook until tender, or about 2½ to 3 hours. Meat is done when the drumstick can be moved up and down easily. The meat thermometer will register 180 degrees.

Simmer giblets and neck until tender while the bird roasts. Cool, remove meat from neck, and chop fine to add to gravy.

Another way to roast a bird is to cover it with aluminum foil, removing the foil the last 20 minutes. The bird will be tender, moist, and brown. When this method is used, a dry stuffing will become somewhat moist.

DRY STUFFING

3–4 cups bread crumbs from at least day-old bread	⅓ cup fat—butter, margarine, or fat rendered from poultry
½ teaspoon sage	¾ cup celery, chopped
½–¾ teaspoon salt	3 tablespoons parsley, chopped
pepper to taste	

Mix crumbs, sage, salt, and pepper together.

Melt fat in frying pan. Add celery and parsley, and cook 2 or 3 minutes.

Add cooked mixture to crumbs, and mix lightly but well.

GRAVY
[makes 2 cups]

4 tablespoons fat from cooked chicken	giblets, chopped fine
3 tablespoons flour	½ teaspoon salt and any other desired seasoning
2 cups liquid—stock from chicken and/or milk or water	

Lift chicken from pan, and place on hot platter.

Allow fat to come to top of drippings, and skim it off. Measure amount needed for gravy. Remove any excess fat.

Blend measured fat and flour in roasting pan, loosening all brown particles.

Stir in measured liquid slowly.

Cook over very low heat, stirring constantly until thickened. Cook a few minutes longer, stirring occasionally.

Add giblets and seasoning. Serve hot.

CHICKEN PIE
[serves 4]

2 cups stewed chicken, boned and cut into pieces	2 tablespoons flour
	2 cups chicken broth
2 tablespoons butter or margarine	seasoning as desired
	unbaked biscuits or pastry

Place pieces of chicken in casserole.

Make gravy as follows: Melt fat in saucepan on top of range. Blend in flour, and mix well. Add chicken broth gradually, and seasoning. Cook slowly until the mixture becomes thick, stirring constantly.

Pour boiling gravy over chicken.

Cover with biscuits or pastry. Make slits in pastry for steam to escape.

Bake immediately in a hot oven, 425 degrees for biscuits, 450 degrees for pastry, for 15 minutes. (See this book, page 190, for pastry, and Book 1, page 189, for biscuits.)

Main dishes — FISH

GENERAL INFORMATION

Most fresh and frozen fish come in convenient fillets and steaks for cooking. In these forms there is no waste, and no preparation is needed for cooking.

Fish is always tender, and therefore requires only a short cooking time. The time is increased slightly for frozen fish thawed in cooking. Careful handling to avoid breaking is necessary. The amount of salt used varies with fresh- and salt-water fish, less being required for the latter.

BROILED FISH
[4 servings]

1 pound fish fillets or steaks or small dressed fish   salt and pepper
3–4 tablespoons melted fat

Preheat broiler about 10 minutes.

Cut fish into serving pieces, or split dressed fish down the back. Sprinkle with salt and pepper.

Place fish skin up in greased broiler pan with rack removed, or in separate greased pan set in broiler pan. Brush with melted fat. Place fish about 2 inches from heat.

Broil 5 to 10 minutes or until brown. Baste with fat. Turn. Baste other side, and broil until brown.

Serve with tartare sauce. (See page 180.)

BAKED STUFFED FISH
[4 servings]

2–3 pound fish, dressed   3 tablespoons melted fat
salt   3 slices bacon, if desired
bread stuffing (page 175)

Wash and dry the fish. Sprinkle inside and out with salt.

Fill cavity of fish ⅔ full with stuffing. Sew the opening with needle and cord, or close with skewers.

Place fish in greased pan, and brush with fat. Lay bacon over top.

Bake in moderate oven, 350 degrees, for 35 to 50 minutes.

PAN-FRIED FISH
[4 servings]

1 pound fish fillets or steaks or small dressed fish
salt and pepper
1 tablespoon water or milk
1 egg, beaten
fine crumbs or corn meal
fat for frying

Cut in serving pieces, or leave small fish whole. Season on both sides with salt and pepper.

Add water or milk to beaten egg. Dip fish in egg mixture, then in crumbs or corn meal.

Heat fat about ⅛ inch deep in a heavy pan.

Fry the fish slowly until brown on one side; turn, and fry on the other side. Cooking time will be 10 minutes or more, depending on the thickness of the fish.

Serve with tartare sauce or cole slaw relish. (See this book, page 180.)

BOILED FISH
[4 servings]

1 pound fish fillet   boiling salted water to cover

Cut fish fillet into serving pieces.

Tie fish in a piece of cheesecloth, and lower into boiling salted water.

Reduce heat, and cook slowly about 10 minutes.

CODFISH CAKES
[4 servings]

1 cup canned codfish   seasoning as desired
2 cups mashed potatoes   fine crumbs or flour for coating cakes
1 egg
fat for pan-frying

Mix fish with potatoes and egg.

Form into cakes of size and shape preferred.

Coat lightly with crumbs or flour.

Pan-fry in hot fat until a golden brown.

Broiled fillets

Main dishes — MISCELLANEOUS

GENERAL INFORMATION

Miscellaneous dishes used as the main part of a meal are generally casserole dishes, often suitable for one-dish meals. Sometimes they are leftovers used in an appetizing way. Or they may be good old family stand-bys which are easily prepared and served, attractive, and well flavored. The dishes given here are based on special information on cheese, egg, milk, and starch cookery. (See Book 1, pages 158–159, especially items 10, 11, 14, and 15.)

CHEESE SOUFFLÉ
[serves 4]

4 tablespoons butter or margarine	1 cup cheese, grated or finely cut
4 tablespoons flour	½ teaspoon salt
1 cup milk	3 egg yolks, well beaten
3 egg whites, stiffly beaten	

Melt butter or margarine; blend in flour; gradually add milk.

Cook very slowly over direct heat *or* over hot water, stirring constantly until thick.

Add cheese and salt, stirring until cheese is melted.

Remove from heat, and cool slightly. Add egg yolks.

Fold egg whites into cheese mixture. Pour into greased casserole.

Place casserole in a pan of warm water about 1 inch deep.

Bake in moderate oven, 350 degrees, until knife inserted in center comes out clean. Baking time requires 50 to 60 minutes.

Serve immediately, since a soufflé tends to fall when left standing.

VARIATIONS:

Cheese Fondue: Reduce butter or margarine to 1 tablespoon, and use 1 cup soft bread crumbs in place of flour. Melt butter or margarine, add crumbs, milk, cheese, salt,

egg yolks. Fold egg whites into cheese mixture and bake as for soufflé. Baking time may be as little as 30 to 40 minutes.

Other Soufflés: Substitute 1 cup of finely chopped meat or vegetables for cheese. Corn, spinach, carrots, tomatoes, mushrooms, ham, or fish may be used. Increase salt for vegetable soufflé, and omit for ham.

Cheese soufflé

CHICKEN SPOON BREAD
[serves 4]

⅔ cup corn meal	2 egg yolks, well beaten
⅔ cup cold water	1 teaspoon salt
3⅓ cups boiling water	¾ teaspoon baking powder
4 teaspoons butter or margarine	2 egg whites, stiffly beaten
⅔ cup cooked chicken, cut up	

Combine corn meal and cold water in a small bowl.

Put boiling water in top section of double boiler. Add corn-meal mixture to rapidly boiling water.

Cook over direct heat until mush thickens, stirring frequently.

Place thickened mush over boiling water and cover. Cook for 15 to 30 minutes, stirring occasionally.

Add to mush the butter or margarine, chicken, egg yolks, salt, and baking powder.

Fold egg whites into mush mixture.

Bake in greased casserole in slow oven, 325 degrees, for about 1 hour.

Serve hot with creamed chicken or mushrooms.

VARIATION:

Spoon Bread: Use milk instead of water if desired. Omit chicken. Use 2 additional eggs.

BAKED BEANS
[serves 4]

2⅓ cups dried navy or pea beans	½ teaspoon dry mustard
1 medium-size onion	⅓ cup molasses
½ pound salt pork or bacon	liquid from cooking beans
1 teaspoon salt	boiling water if needed

Wash beans; discard imperfect ones; cover with cold water; soak over night.

Simmer in same water until tender, about 2 hours. Drain. Save liquid.

Quarter onion, and place in bottom of casserole.

Cut salt pork or bacon into chunks, and place 3 or 4 pieces on top of the onion.

Pour beans into a casserole; place the rest of the salt pork on top.

Sprinkle the salt and mustard over the contents.

Add molasses and enough bean liquid to just cover the beans.

Cover casserole, and bake in slow–moderate oven, 325 degrees, for about 6 hours, or until beans taste tender and are brown. Keep beans covered with hot liquid until last hour of baking. If there is not enough bean liquid, use boiling water. Remove casserole cover the last half hour of baking time.

RICE AND TUNA CASSEROLE
[serves 4]

1 cup uncooked rice	1 cup chicken broth
1 teaspoon salt	1½ teaspoons salt
3 cups boiling water	⅛ teaspoon pepper
3 tablespoons butter or margarine	¾–1 cup tuna (6–8-ounce can)
1 green pepper, minced	dash paprika
¼ cup celery, diced	

Pick over grains of packaged rice carefully. Do not wash rice.

Add salt to boiling water in heavy saucepan. Add rice to boiling water gradually.

Cover saucepan, and cook very slowly for 20 to 30 minutes. When nearly cooked remove cover, and let water evaporate.

Cook the green pepper and celery in melted butter or margarine until they become yellow.

Add the chicken broth, salt, and pepper, and cook slowly for 15 minutes.

Arrange rice in greased casserole.

Stir the vegetable mixture and the tuna gen-

tly into the rice, and bake in a moderate oven, 350 degrees, for 10 to 15 minutes.

Sprinkle with paprika, and serve hot.

VARIATIONS:

Other Casseroles: In place of tuna, use salmon, other fish, chicken, or green peas.

MACARONI, AMERICAN STYLE
[serves 4]

1¼ cups uncooked macaroni	1¼ cups condensed tomato soup (10½-ounce can)
1¼ teaspoons salt	2 teaspoons parsley, minced
5 cups boiling water	
2 tablespoons butter or margarine	bits of bay leaf
1 onion, minced	⅔ cup vegetables, cooked
⅔ cup cooked meat, finely chopped	⅔ cup meat stock
	½ teaspoon salt
¼ cup sharp American cheese, grated	

Cook macaroni in a large saucepan in salted boiling water until tender. Drain.

Melt butter or margarine, and cook onion slowly in it until yellow.

Add meat, and cook slowly for 15 minutes.

Add soup, parsley, and bay leaf, and let simmer 15 minutes.

Add vegetable, meat stock, and salt.

Arrange macaroni in casserole or serving dish. Pour sauce over macaroni. Sprinkle with cheese. Serve hot.

SPAGHETTI ROYAL
[serves 4]

1½ cups spaghetti	½ cup American cheese, grated
1½ quarts boiling water	¼ cup green pepper, minced
1½ teaspoons salt	
¼ cup butter or margarine	¼ cup pimiento, minced
¼ cup flour	4 hard-cooked eggs, chopped
2 cups milk	
½ teaspoon salt	

Cook spaghetti in a large saucepan in salted boiling water until tender. Drain.

Melt butter or margarine; blend in flour; gradually add milk and then salt.

Cook very slowly or over hot water, stirring constantly until thick.

Stir into sauce the cheese, green pepper, pimiento, and hard-cooked eggs.

Mix gently with spaghetti.

Pour into greased casserole, and bake until golden brown in a moderate oven, 350 degrees, for about 30 minutes.

NOODLE GOULASH
[serves 4]

1½ cups noodles	2 tablespoons flour
4 cups boiling water	1¼ cups condensed
¾ teaspoon salt	vegetable soup
1 small onion, finely	(10½-ounce can)
chopped	1 cup canned tomatoes
1 tablespoon butter or	½ teaspoon salt
margarine	dash pepper
½ pound round steak,	
ground	

Cook noodles in a large saucepan in boiling salted water until tender. Drain.

Brown onion in butter or margarine. Add meat, and cook slowly until brown.

Blend in flour, and add soup, tomatoes, salt, pepper, and cooked noodles.

Simmer for 15 to 30 minutes. Or pour into greased baking dish, and bake for the same length of time in a moderate oven, 350 degrees.

Serve steaming hot.

TUNA—POTATO CHIP CASSEROLE
[serves 4]

1 cup potato chips, slightly crumbled

1¼ cups canned condensed cream mushroom soup (10½ ounces)

¾–1 cup tuna, in large pieces (6–8-ounce can)

Sprinkle bottom of baking dish with half the potato chips.

Arrange next a thick layer of mushroom soup and tuna.

Sprinkle the top with remaining chips.

Bake in moderate oven, 350 degrees, for 25 minutes. Serve hot.

CHOW MEIN
[serves 4]

2 tablespoons butter or margarine

½–1 cup onion, cut fine

1 cup celery, cut in bite-size pieces

¾ teaspoon salt

dash pepper

1 cup hot water

2 cups bean sprouts, drained, *or* 2 cups mixed Chinese vegetables (1-pound can)

2 cups cooked pork, beef, veal, or chicken, cut in thin strips

2 tablespoons cold water

2 tablespoons cornstarch

1 teaspoon sugar

½ cup nuts, whole or chopped

garnish, if desired, of shredded green onion, chopped parsley, or a few strips of meat being used

2 cups chow mein noodles (1 can, 3 ounces by weight)

Soy sauce as desired

Melt butter or margarine in skillet. Add onions, and fry for 3 minutes.

Add celery, salt, pepper, and hot water. Cook slowly for 5 minutes.

Add bean sprouts, or mixed Chinese vegetables, and meat. Mix thoroughly, and cook slowly for 5 minutes.

Combine cold water, cornstarch, and sugar. Add to cooked mixture. Stir lightly, and cook 1 minute, or until cornstarch becomes clear.

Serve hot on chow mein noodles. Add soy sauce to suit the individual taste.

VARIATIONS:

Chop Suey: Add 1 teaspoon brown sauce (bead molasses) to the cornstarch mixture. Serve with cooked rice instead of noodles.

Chow Mein or Chop Suey: Add bamboo sprouts and water chestnuts in place of part of the vegetables.

Meatless Chow Mein or Chop Suey: Omit meat, and use both bean sprouts and mixed Chinese vegetables. Add 2 green peppers cut in long strips at the time celery is added.

Tuna Fish Chow Mein or Chop Suey: Use ¾ to 1 cup tuna (10½ ounces) in place of meat.

Easily prepared, attractive, well-flavored casserole dishes are suitable for one-dish meals.

Sauces and Relishes

TOMATO SAUCE
[1 cup]

2 tablespoons butter or margarine

1 slice onion, finely chopped

2 tablespoons flour

1 cup tomato juice

½ teaspoon salt

¼ teaspoon pepper

Melt butter or margarine in saucepan on top of range.

Add onion, and sauté until light brown.

Blend in flour, and mix well.

Add tomato juice gradually, and cook slowly until the mixture becomes thick. Stir constantly.

Add seasoning. Serve with meat loaf, or fish.

TARTARE SAUCE
[4 servings]

⅓ cup mayonnaise

1 teaspoon chopped capers

1 teaspoon chopped green olives

1 teaspoon chopped pickles

1 teaspoon minced parsley

Combine the above ingredients just before serving. Serve with fish.

COLE SLAW
[4 servings]

2½ cups cabbage, finely shredded

1 teaspoon salt

2 tablespoons sugar

2 tablespoons vinegar

⅜ cup sour cream

Sprinkle cabbage with salt and sugar.

Add vinegar and cream.

Toss lightly with fork to blend.

Serve at once. If allowed to stand too long, the cabbage loses its crispness.

CRANBERRY RELISH
[2 cups]

2 cups cranberries, washed and picked over

1 orange, washed, dried, and quartered, with seeds removed

1 cup sugar

Grind cranberries and orange together. Stir in sugar.

Allow mixture to stand in covered jar in refrigerator for a day before serving.

Cranberry relish with chickenburgers

CRANBERRY JELLY
[serves 4]

2 cups cranberries, washed and picked over

1 cup water
1 cup sugar

Cook cranberries in saucepan with boiling water until tender, 3 or 4 minutes.

Put through strainer. Stir in sugar. Place berries on heat, and bring to a boil.

Remove at once, and pour into mold. Unmold when cold and set.

FOAMY SAUCE
[about 1 cup]

1 egg, beaten
1 cup confectioners' sugar, sifted
½ cup butter or margarine
1 teaspoon vanilla extract

Blend egg, sugar, butter or margarine, and vanilla extract in top of double boiler.

Beat with rotary beater until sauce is very foamy, about 3 or 4 minutes.

Keep warm by placing over hot water until time to serve.

Serve over steamed fruit puddings.

VANILLA SAUCE
[about 1 cup]

2 tablespoons sugar
1 tablespoon cornstarch
⅛ teaspoon salt
1 cup milk

1 tablespoon butter or margarine
½ teaspoon vanilla extract

Combine sugar, cornstarch, and salt in saucepan.

Add milk gradually, and cook slowly until the mixture becomes thick. Stir constantly.

Remove from range. Add butter or margarine and then vanilla extract.

Serve warm over steamed fruit pudding or unfrosted butter cake.

Vanilla sauce with cake

$\mathcal{V}egetables$

GENERAL INFORMATION

Many fresh vegetables may be eaten raw as salads or as relishes. Cabbage and salad greens are used frequently, as are carrots, celery, onions, tomatoes, and cucumbers. Peppers cut into strips, turnips sliced thin, and flowerets of cauliflower may be less frequently served raw. Short soaking in cold water adds to the crispness of these vegetables, but may result in the loss of some food value.

Vegetables are cooked either to soften them to make them more digestible, or to give them a more pleasing flavor. They need to be cooked only until tender, and to retain as much of their original form, color, and food value as possible. Boiling is the most common method of cooking vegetables, but baking and steaming are frequently used.

BOILING: In general, it is best to use the smallest possible amount of boiling, salted water that will cook the vegetables without burning. Boiling water can be added if more is needed. Spinach will cook in the water clinging to its leaves. Hard whole vegetables, such as potatoes and beets, will require more water than softer vegetables. A fairly generous amount of water will make the flavor and odor of onions less pronounced, even though some nutrients are lost in the water.

After the vegetables are added, the water needs to be brought back to a boil as quickly as possible. Covering hastens the return to a boil, and speeds up cooking time—both important in preserving food value and flavor. At the same time, cooking green vegetables with a cover tends to destroy their bright color.

Therefore, for some vegetables there may need to be a choice between preserving nutritive value and flavor or attractiveness. Of course a compromise may be satisfactory. The vegetables may be brought to a boil rapidly without covering them. After the first few minutes of cooking, the pan may be covered, the heat reduced, and the vegetables cooked only until tender. (See Book 1, page 159, item 16.)

However, spinach cooks in such a short time and has so much green color that it may be cooked covered throughout. Cooking onions with a cover helps to retain their strong flavor. But when cooked uncovered, the flavor tends to be more delicate. The red or purple coloring in red cabbage and beets requires the addition of a little diluted vinegar or lemon juice and the use of a lid during cooking to preserve the color.

The chart on this page shows the approximate boiling time needed for the most commonly used fresh vegetables. When frozen vegetables are used, directions on the package can be followed.

After vegetables are boiled, they may be seasoned with salt, pepper, butter or margarine, and sometimes herbs, and then served as they are. Or they may be mashed, browned, creamed, scalloped, glazed, or served with a special sauce.

Mashed vegetables may be prepared in the container in which they were cooked after any excess liquid has been removed. A hand masher or an electric mixer may be used. Or the vegetable may be put through a food press. Hot milk or cream, salt, pepper, and butter or margarine are usually added as desired. The vegetables are beaten until fluffy.

Boiled vegetables may be cut in half, sliced, or diced, and then browned in a small amount of fat. Or they may be creamed and scalloped as described in Book 1, page 192.

An example of glazing is given on page 184 in the recipe for Glazed Sweet Potatoes, Carrots, or Onions. Harvard Beets, also on page 184, is an example of a special sauce used with a vegetable.

BAKING: Vegetables are usually baked in their skins. Potatoes baked whole as well as in their skins retain their maximum food value. Certain vegetables, such as eggplant, green peppers, tomatoes, and winter squash, may have their centers scooped out before baking. The centers are replaced with a stuffing, in which all, part, or none of the re-

CHART OF BOILING GUIDE FOR FRESH VEGETABLES

Vegetables	Approximate boiling time in minutes
Asparagus	15 to 20
Beans, green	15 to 30
Beans, fresh Lima	20 to 30
Beets, mature whole	60 to 90
Broccoli	15 to 20
Brussels sprouts	10 to 25
Cabbage, quartered	10 to 15
Carrots, mature whole	20 to 25
Cauliflower, whole	15 to 20
Celery, diced	12 to 15
Corn, on cob	5 to 6
Eggplant	10 to 15
Okra	15 to 20
Onions, mature dry	30 to 35
Parsnips	7 to 15
Peas, shelled green	10 to 20
Potatoes, whole	30 to 35
Spinach	10
Squash, winter	25 to 30
Sweet potatoes	30 to 35
Swiss chard, young	10 to 15
Tomatoes, whole	10 to 20
Turnips, diced	15 to 20

moved vegetable is included. A few vegetables have a better flavor if they are boiled for a few minutes before the stuffing is put in and the baking begins. The recipe on page 185 for Peppers Filled with Leftover Foods is an example. Potatoes may be stuffed after baking, with their own mashed and seasoned contents. Some vegetables with their skins removed, left whole or sliced, can be baked successfully in a covered baking dish. Carrots, onions, parsnips, and tomatoes are examples. Scalloped potatoes, unlike other scalloped vegetables, are generally preferred when prepared from the sliced raw vegetable. Each layer of potatoes in a casserole is sprinkled with seasonings and a small amount of flour. Milk rather than white sauce is used for liquid. Vegetables, such as corn, may be combined with other ingredients and baked, as shown in the recipe for Corn Pudding on page 185.

A chart of approximate baking time and temperature for whole or stuffed vegetables is given below.

CHART OF BAKING TIME OF CERTAIN VEGETABLES		
Vegetables	Approximate baking time in minutes	Oven temperature in degrees
Carrots	35 to 45	350
Onions	50 to 60	350
Parsnips	30 to 45	350
Peppers, sweet green (stuffed and baked after boiling whole 5 minutes)	25 to 30	350
Potatoes, white	60	400
Potatoes, sweet	50 to 60	350
Squash	40 to 60	350
Tomatoes	20	350

STEAMING: There are various ways of steaming vegetables. They may be put over steaming water on a rack or in a steam basket in a tightly covered container. There needs to be at least a depth of 2 inches of water in the bottom of the container. Steaming usually takes place on top of the stove, although it may be done in the oven. In most cases, steaming requires 5 to 15 minutes longer than boiling. Any vegetable that can be boiled in a covered pan is suitable for this type of steaming. Carrots, squash, beets, parsnips, and sweet potatoes are examples.

A pressure saucepan may also be used for steaming. Any vegetable that can be cooked by boiling can be steamed this way. The method requires a very short cooking period in comparison to other methods, but care needs to be taken not to overcook the vegetables. See page 172 for a discussion of pressure-saucepan cooking.

GLAZED SWEET POTATOES, CARROTS, OR ONIONS
[4 servings]

2 tablespoons fat	2 cups cooked vegetables, cut in strips or large pieces
1/4 cup brown sugar	
1 tablespoon water	

Melt fat in skillet.

Add sugar and water, and blend.

Add vegetables, and cook over low heat, turning several times, until the sirup is very thick and the vegetables are well coated— 15 to 20 minutes.

HARVARD BEETS
[4 servings]

1/4–1/2 cup sugar, depending upon desired sweetness	2 1/2 cups cooked beets, cubed
1 tablespoon flour	1 tablespoon butter or margarine
1/4 cup water	1/2 teaspoon salt
1/4 cup vinegar	1/8 teaspoon pepper

Mix sugar and flour; add water and vinegar, and boil 5 minutes.

Add beets to sauce. Cook slowly, stirring occasionally, until beets are heated.

Add butter or margarine; season with salt and pepper.

Grated cheese, white sauce, and partially cooked cabbage to be baked together

Corn pudding garnished with pepper strips; glazed sweet potatoes in individual servings

PEPPERS FILLED WITH LEFTOVER FOODS
[serves 4]

4 green peppers, medium size
1 tablespoon butter or margarine
1 tablespoon flour
½ cup milk
salt and pepper
1 cup leftover food (chopped meat or fish, cooked vegetables, chopped raw celery, grated raw carrots)
buttered bread crumbs for topping

Cut the stem ends from green peppers, and remove seeds and veins.

Cook peppers uncovered in rapidly boiling salted water for 5 minutes. Drain well.

Melt butter or margarine in a saucepan on top of range, or over hot water.

Blend in flour, and mix well.

Add milk gradually, and cook slowly until the mixture becomes thick. Stir constantly.

Add salt and pepper, and combine leftover food with the hot white sauce.

Fill peppers, and cover tops with buttered bread crumbs.

Bake in uncovered casserole dish or in muffin pan in moderate oven, 350 degrees, for 25 to 30 minutes.

CORN PUDDING
[4 servings]

2 eggs
2 cups milk
1 cup soft bread crumbs
2½ cups cream style corn (No. 2 can)
1 teaspoon salt
⅛ teaspoon pepper

Beat eggs.

Add milk, crumbs, corn, and seasoning.

Pour into greased baking dish.

Bake in moderate oven, 350 degrees, for 1½ hours.

Breads

GENERAL INFORMATION

Homemade breads freshly baked are family favorites. They are usually divided into two classes — quick breads and yeast breads, because of the different leavening agents used. Quick breads — biscuits, muffins, griddlecakes, and others — are leavened by baking powder used with milk, or with soda and sour milk. They begin to rise when they are put in the oven. Yeast as a leaven requires time for the bread to rise before it is put in the oven. However, Popovers, on page 187, and Cream Puffs — though not a bread — on page 198, are leavened by steam, which results from a very hot oven and a thin batter. Further information on quick breads is given in Book 1. See page 158 especially.

Yeast bread requires longer preparation time than quick breads. But the trend today toward simple, easy methods can make cooking with yeast a satisfying experience.

Yeast is generally available in two forms. One is compressed yeast which comes in small cakes wrapped in foil. This type of yeast contains active, living yeast cells and needs to be kept in a cold place. In a refrigerator it may keep for one to two weeks. Fresh compressed yeast should be only slightly moist and of a creamy color with a grayish tint. If dark or discolored, it should not be used.

Another popular form is dry granular yeast which comes in moistureproof packages. Each package is equivalent to one yeast cake. This type of yeast may be kept for some time without refrigeration. An expiration date and directions for use are given on the package to insure satisfactory results. When added to the batter, fresh compressed yeast grows and acts more quickly than the dry granular form.

Cooking successfully with yeast is easier when one understands that yeast is a living organism, not a chemical. For this reason, it requires very different handling from baking powder. Being a plant, yeast is sensitive to cold and heat. A low temperature retards its growth. Too high a temperature injures or may even kill the cells. Therefore, the liquid to which yeast is added needs to be lukewarm, or about 80 degrees Fahrenheit when tested with a candy thermometer. Sugar is used to supply quick food for the yeast, to give the bread flavor, and to make it brown quicker. Salt is also added for flavor; and shortening, to improve the tenderness and keeping qualities.

YEAST ROLLS
[1 dozen more or less depending on size]

1 cup milk, scalded and cooled to lukewarm	1 teaspoon salt
*1 cake compressed yeast	4 tablespoons melted shortening
2 tablespoons sugar	3 cups sifted all-purpose flour

Dissolve yeast, sugar, and salt in milk. Use a large mixing bowl.

Add shortening.

Beat in flour until thoroughly mixed, scraping dough from sides of bowl.

Cover bowl with a damp cloth, and let mixture rise in a warm place until double in bulk — about 1½ to 2 hours. If only part of the dough is used, or if all of it is to be used later, put it in the refrigerator. But be sure to grease the top of the dough well, and cover the bowl with wax paper or a cover, or place it in a plastic bag. The dough will keep in the refrigerator about 3 days. Two hours before baking, remove and let rise in a warm place until double in bulk. Then proceed as follows:

Turn dough on a lightly floured board. Flatten with lightly floured hand or rolling pin, pressing out any excess air.

Shape into rolls. (See Variations in Shapes and Kinds of Rolls.) Place on greased baking sheet. Cover with a clean tea towel, and let rise until double in size.

Bake in a hot oven, 425 degrees, 12 to 15 minutes until golden brown.

*NOTE: When dry granular yeast is used, omit ½ cup of milk. Soak yeast in ½ cup lukewarm water for 5 minutes without stirring. Then stir thoroughly, and add to remaining ½ cup milk.

VARIATIONS IN SHAPES AND KINDS OF ROLLS:

Yeast rolls can be made interesting by varying their shape and kind. Equipment for shaping includes a breadboard, a rolling pin, and perhaps a round cutter. These need to be slightly floured and the dough itself lightly handled. Some of the shapes and different kinds of rolls, which have proved popular, follow.

Bowknots: Roll dough about ½ inch thick, and cut into strips about 6 inches by ½ inch. Tie each strip into a knot to resemble a bow. Place on greased baking sheet, and bake as previously directed.

Butter Flake Rolls: Roll dough into a 6- by 9-inch oblong about ⅛ inch thick, and brush with soft butter or margarine. Cut into 6 strips 1 inch wide, and place the strips buttered side up on top of each other in layers.

Then from one end cut into 1½-inch slices. Place a slice in each section of a greased muffin pan with one cut end up. Let rise, and bake as in recipe.

Clover Leaf Rolls: Shape and place 3 small balls of dough into each section of a greased muffin pan. Brush tops with melted butter or margarine. Let rise, and bake as in recipe.

Parker House Rolls: Roll dough about ⅓ inch thick, and cut into circles with a cookie cutter. Brush with melted butter or margarine. Make a crease with the dull edge of a silver knife through the center of each round, and fold over, pressing down lightly. Place on a slightly greased baking sheet. Let rise, and bake as in recipe.

Cinnamon Rolls: Roll dough into an oblong ⅓ inch thick. Spread with 4 tablespoons soft butter or margarine. Sprinkle with sugar and cinnamon mixed together in the proportion of ⅓ cup sugar to 1 teaspoon cinnamon. Roll up tightly lengthwise, and seal edges firmly. Cut into slices about 1 inch wide. Place slices one cut side down on a well-greased baking sheet, and let rise until double in size. Bake in a hot oven, 400 degrees, for 5 to 10 minutes. Reduce heat to quick–moderate, 375 degrees, and bake 15 to 20 minutes longer.

Orange Rolls: Follow recipe for Yeast Rolls, except omit 2 tablespoons milk, and substitute 2 tablespoons orange juice and grated rind of 1 orange. Add to remaining lukewarm milk. Shape as desired.

Graham or Whole-Wheat Rolls: Substitute 1½ tablespoons molasses for sugar, and 1½ cups graham or whole-wheat flour for all-purpose flour in recipe for Yeast Rolls. Shape as desired.

Oatmeal Rolls: Substitute ⅞ cup rolled oats for 1 cup all-purpose flour in recipe for Yeast Rolls. Shape as desired.

POPOVERS
[8 large]

1 cup sifted all-purpose flour	2 eggs
½ teaspoon salt	1 cup milk

Heat oven to 425 degrees.

Beat ingredients together with rotary beater until smooth.

Pour into well-greased deep muffin cups, filling them ¾ full.

Bake 40 to 45 minutes, or until golden brown.

Slip out of cup with aid of a spatula or knife, and serve piping hot.

WAFFLES
[4 to 6]

2 egg yolks	½ teaspoon salt
1 cup milk	⅓ cup melted
1¼ cups sifted all-purpose flour	shortening
	2 egg whites, stiffly
1 tablespoon sugar	beaten
2½ teaspoons baking powder	

Heat waffle iron according to directions, while mixing batter.

Beat egg yolks in a mixing bowl until thick and light yellow in color. Add milk.

Sift together flour, sugar, baking powder, and salt. Add to milk mixture, beating thoroughly.

Stir in shortening. Fold in egg whites last.

Pour batter from a pitcher into center of hot waffle iron. If necessary, spread with a spoon to cover surface.

Cook until steaming stops and waffle is brown. Lift off waffle with a fork.

Serve hot with butter or margarine and sirup, or other spreads. After waffles are served, leave the top of the waffle iron up until the iron cools.

VARIATIONS:

Pancakes: Reduce flour to 1 cup and melted shortening to 2 tablespoons. Beat eggs separately or not as preferred. Mix as for waffles, omitting folded-in egg whites if eggs are not beaten separately. Pour batter from pitcher, in pools a little apart, onto a hot but not smoking griddle. If necessary to prevent sticking, grease griddle very lightly. Cook until under side is browned and the top

A waffle mixture is easier to handle when poured from a pitcher.

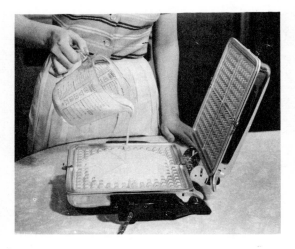

is just set. Turn only once, and brown on other side. Serve hot with butter or margarine and sirup, or other spreads.

Sour-Milk Pancakes or Waffles: Follow pancake or waffle recipe except substitute sour milk for sweet and ½ teaspoon soda and ½ teaspoon baking powder for the 2½ teaspoons baking powder.

Corn-Meal Waffles: Follow Waffle recipe except substitute ¾ cup corn meal and ¼ cup flour for the 1¼ cups flour.

SPOON BREAD

See Variation of Chicken Spoon Bread, page 177.

GOLDEN CORN BREAD
[12 pieces]

1 cup sifted all-purpose flour	2 tablespoons sugar (may be omitted)
¾ cup corn meal	1 egg, well beaten
3 teaspoons baking powder	1 cup milk
¾ teaspoon salt	2 tablespoons melted shortening

Sift flour, corn meal, baking powder, salt, and sugar together.

Combine egg, milk, and shortening.

Add liquid ingredients to dry ingredients. Mix only until the dry ingredients are moistened and blended.

Fill well-greased shallow pan about ¾ full.

Bake in hot oven, 400 degrees, for 25 to 30 minutes. Serve hot.

NUT BREAD
[loaf 4½ by 8½ by 2½ inches]

2 cups sifted all-purpose flour	½ cup sugar
	1 egg, well beaten
3 teaspoons baking powder	1 cup milk
½ teaspoon salt	1 cup black walnut meats, ground

Sift flour, baking powder, salt, and sugar together.

Combine egg and milk.

Add liquid ingredients to dry ingredients. Mix only until all the dry ingredients are moistened and blended.

Stir in nuts.

Fill well-greased loaf pan ⅔ full with mixture.

Bake for 60 minutes in moderate oven, 350 degrees.

Nut-, orange-, or cranberry-bread sandwiches give variety to a school lunch.

ORANGE BREAD
[loaf 4½ by 8½ by 2½ inches]

2 cups sifted all-purpose flour

1½ teaspoons baking powder

½ teaspoon baking soda

½ teaspoon salt

¾ cup sugar

1 large orange—juice and pulp plus water to make 1 cup

rind of 1 orange, grated before juice is extracted

1 cup dates, pitted and cut

½ cup pecans

2 tablespoons melted shortening

1 egg

Sift flour, baking powder, soda, salt, and sugar together in a mixing bowl.

Put orange juice and water mixture into another mixing bowl, and add the rind, dates, and pecans.

Blend shortening and egg, and add to the orange mixture.

Add liquid ingredients to dry ingredients. Mix only until all the dry ingredients are moistened and blended.

Fill well-greased loaf pan ⅔ full with mixture. Bake for 55 to 60 minutes in moderate oven, 350 degrees.

CRANBERRY BREAD
[12 to 16 pieces]

3 tablespoons melted butter or margarine

½ cup sugar

1½ cups whole fresh cranberries, washed and picked over

1½ cups sifted all-purpose flour

½ cup sugar

2 teaspoons baking powder

½ teaspoon salt

1 egg

½ cup milk

3 tablespoons melted shortening

Line the bottom of a greased pan, 8 by 8 by 2 inches, with melted butter, ½ cup sugar, and the cranberries.

Sift flour, ½ cup sugar, baking powder, and salt together.

Blend egg, milk, and shortening.

Stir liquid ingredients into dry ingredients, mixing only until all the dry ingredients are blended.

Pour over cranberries in baking pan.

Bake for 25 minutes in hot oven, 425 degrees.

Desserts

Desserts — PASTRY

GENERAL INFORMATION

Pastry is a stiff dough commonly used for the crusts of pies. Piecrust needs to be tender but not crumbly; crisp, and evenly and delicately browned. Extreme care in mixing, handling, rolling, and baking will help to assure a good product. Four methods of making baked piecrust are given. The first is a cold-water recipe long in use, which produces a flaky crust. The others are newer type recipes. One uses hot water and hydrogenated vegetable shortening; another, cold milk and as shortening a salad oil of the type made from corn. The fourth is commercial piecrust mix. A recipe with variations is also given for unbaked piecrust made with crumbs.

There are two general kinds of baked pies — double crust and single crust. Double-crust pies usually have fruit fillings, with the crust and filling baked at the same time. Single-crust "shells," as they are called, frequently have cream fillings and meringue tops. In such cases, the crust is baked before the filling is put into it. Then comes an egg-white meringue topping, which needs to be gently browned to preserve its moisture and to keep it tender.

FLAKY CRUST
[Two 9-inch crusts]

2 cups sifted all-purpose flour	⅔ cup shortening
1 teaspoon salt	5 to 6 tablespoons cold water

Sift flour and salt together.

Cut in shortening lightly with 2 knives or pastry blender until mixture is coarse but with lumps no larger than a pea.

Add water, sprinkling evenly and mixing lightly with a fork until ingredients cling together.

Chill in refrigerator in covered bowl, or wrapped in wax paper.

Divide dough into two portions.

Roll out one portion on a lightly floured board into a circle ⅛ inch thick and slightly larger than 9 inches. Roll in one direction — from the center to the edge — lifting the roller, not pushing it back and forth. If there is a break in the dough, pinch the edges together.

Fold crust in the center, and transfer it quickly to the pan with the fold along the center of the pan. Be careful not to stretch the crust. Raise folded half, and fit it to the pan so that no air is left between the crust and pan. Trim — with a knife or scissors — ½ inch beyond the edge of the pan.

Add the filling.

Repeat the rolling and folding procedures for top crust, but cut several gashes in center of rolled crust. This allows the steam from the filling to escape during the baking.

The photographs at the right illustrate some of the steps in making flaky pastry for a two-crust pie.

Moisten edge of bottom crust with water, and place top crust carefully over filling. Trim to ½ inch beyond edge of pan.

Fold extra edge of top crust under edge of bottom crust. Press together gently on edge of pan with the floured tines of a fork, or flute the edge with floured fingers. Fluting is done as follows: Push up the crust a little around the edge of a pan. Then place the floured forefinger of one hand on the outside edge, and shape the pastry around it with the floured thumb and forefinger of the other hand. Continue all around the pan.

Bake in hot oven, 450 degrees, according to directions for the filling used.

BEAT-'n-ROLL CRUST
[Two 9-inch crusts]

¾ cup hydrogenated vegetable shortening	2 cups sifted all-purpose flour
¼ cup boiling water	1 teaspoon salt
1 tablespoon milk	

Place shortening in medium-size mixing bowl. Add water and milk, breaking up shortening with a fork.

Beat mixture with fork, tilting bowl and using rapid cross-the-bowl strokes. Continue beating until mixture is smooth and thick, and holds soft peaks.

Sift flour and salt together with shortening mixture. Stir quickly with round-the-bowl strokes until dough clings together and clears the sides of bowl.

Work into a smooth dough, and shape into two flat round pieces.

Roll out as for Flaky Crust. Or place each round of dough between two 12-inch squares of wax paper, and roll lightly into 9½-inch or slightly larger size. Remove top paper.

Fold as for Flaky Crust. If wax paper is used, place bottom crust in pan with exposed side down, and then remove second paper. Trim if necessary.

Continue as for Flaky Crust. If wax paper is used, remove the second paper after placing exposed side of top crust over filling.

Pinching together breaks in the dough

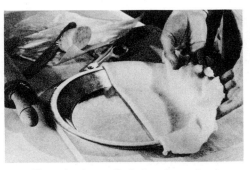

Transferring rolled dough to the pan

Making slits in the top crust

Fluting the two edges together

STIR-'n-ROLL CRUST
[Two 9-inch crusts]

2 cups sifted all-purpose   ½ cup salad oil
  flour   ¼ cup cold milk
1½ teaspoons salt

Sift flour and salt together into a bowl.

Put oil and milk into a measuring cup, but do not stir.

Pour oil mixture into flour mixture, and stir with a fork until blended. Dough will look moist but will not be sticky.

Work into a smooth ball, and cut in halves, flattening slightly.

Roll out with wax paper, and proceed as in Beat-'n-Roll Crust.

VARIATIONS IN TYPES OF CRUSTS:

Pastry Shell for a One-Crust Pie: Divide the ingredients in half in any one of the three piecrust methods previously described. Mix the dough according to directions, but do not divide it in half after it is mixed. Roll and place in pan as for bottom crust. After the crust is trimmed, fold back the ½ inch of dough extending beyond the edge of the pan, making a double edge. Flute all around the edge of the pan. Prick through bottom and sides of crust with tines of a fork. Bake in hot oven, 450 degrees, for about 15 minutes.

Lattice Top Crust: Follow directions for making the crusts in any one of the three methods previously described. But instead of using a single top crust, cut the dough into strips ½ inch wide, and lay them across the filling 1 inch apart. Then cross these strips with others, as shown in the illustration.

COMMERCIAL PIECRUST MIX
Generally comes in a package for two 9-inch crusts. Follow directions on package.

UNCOOKED CRUMB CRUST
[9-inch bottom crust]

½ cup butter or   1½ cups vanilla wafers,
  margarine, melted   rolled fine

Combine butter or margarine and crumbs, mixing thoroughly.

Line sides and bottom of piepan with crumb mixture, pressing evenly to ¼-inch thick with another piepan.

Chill well — at least an hour — before adding filling. Use any cream or chiffon pie filling, ice cream, or a cut-up fresh fruit mixture sweetened to taste. Top with whipped cream if desired.

VARIATIONS:

Other Kinds of Crumbs: Substitute crumbs made from gingersnaps, chocolate wafers, or honey–graham crackers in place of vanilla wafers.

Honey Crumb Crust: Combine 1½ cups graham cracker crumbs, rolled fine, and ¼ cup brown sugar. Blend in 2 tablespoons honey and ¼ cup melted butter or margarine. Proceed as for Uncooked Crumb Crust.

Pricking the bottom and sides of an unbaked shell

Lacing strips together to make a lattice top crust

FRESH APPLE PIE
[9-inch pie]

unbaked pastry for 2-crust pie
6 cups tart, juicy, pared apple slices
3/4–1 cup sugar
1 teaspoon cinnamon or nutmeg
1–2 tablespoons butter or margarine

Line a pan with pastry, and chill while preparing apples.

Mix sugar and cinnamon or nutmeg with apple slices.

Fill the unbaked bottom crust with the apple mixture. Dot with butter or margarine. Proceed as for any two-crust or latticed two-crust pie.

Bake in a moderately hot oven, 400 degrees, for 50 to 60 minutes.

VARIATIONS:

Green-Apple Pie: Increase sugar by 1/2 cup; use only half teaspoon cinnamon or nutmeg; mix 1 to 2 tablespoons flour with sugar if apples are juicy.

Deep-Dish Apple Pie: Use double amount of filling, and a 9-inch baking dish 2 or 3 inches deep. Line sides but not bottom of dish with pastry. Add filling; sprinkle with 1 tablespoon water, and cover with a top crust.

Apple Dumplings: Proceed as for Fresh Apple Pie except roll pastry square in so far as possible, and cut the 1/8 inch-thick pastry into 8 squares. Fill the center of each square with the apple mixture. Dot with butter. Bring opposite points of pastry up over the apples, overlap, moisten, and seal. Place dumplings a little apart in baking dish. Bake until crust is lightly browned and apples are cooked through, about 30 to 40 minutes in a hot oven, 425 degrees. Serve with cream.

Peach Pie: Use 4 cups of sliced peaches. Mix 2 to 3 tablespoons flour with sugar. Omit cinnamon or nutmeg.

Blueberry Pie: Use 4 cups blueberries. Mix 2 or 3 tablespoons flour with sugar. Use 2 tablespoons lemon juice instead of cinnamon or nutmeg.

Blackberry or Raspberry Pie: Use 4 cups berries. Add 4 tablespoons flour to sugar. Use only 1/2 teaspoon cinnamon.

CANNED CHERRY PIE
[9-inch pie]

unbaked pastry for 2-crust pie
3/4–1 cup sugar
3–4 tablespoons flour
1/4 teaspoon cinnamon
*2 1/2 cups pitted red pie cherries and juice
1 tablespoon butter or margarine

Line a piepan with pastry, and chill while preparing fruit.

Mix together in a saucepan the sugar, flour, and cinnamon. Stir in cherries and juice.

Cook over moderate heat, stirring constantly until mixture thickens and boils. Cool slightly.

Pour into pastry-lined pan. Dot with butter or margarine. Cover quickly with top crust.

Bake for 30 to 40 minutes in hot oven, 425 degrees, or until crust is browned and juice commences to bubble through slits in crust.

*NOTE: Water-packed fruit will require more sugar than fruit packed in sirup.

VARIATIONS:

Other Canned Fruit Pies: Use other canned fruit and juice in place of cherries and juice.

COCONUT CREAM PIE
[9-inch pie]

PART 1 — PASTRY
baked pastry shell

PART 2 — FILLING

1/2 cup sugar	2 tablespoons butter or
3/8 cup flour	margarine
1/2 teaspoon salt	1 teaspoon vanilla
2 1/2 cups milk	1/2–3/4 cup moist
3 egg yolks, slightly	shredded coconut
beaten	

Mix sugar, flour, and salt. Stir milk in gradually.

Cook over moderate heat, stirring constantly until mixture becomes thick. Or cook over hot water if preferred.

Stir a little of the hot mixture at a time into egg yolks. Return mixture to the cooking container.

Cook 1 minute, stirring constantly. Remove from heat. Add butter or margarine and vanilla. Add coconut just before filling is poured into shell.

PART 3 – MERINGUE

⅜ teaspoon salt ⅜ cup sugar
3 egg whites

Add salt to egg whites, and beat until frothy. Beat in sugar a little at a time. Continue beating until stiff and glossy.

Pile meringue onto pie filling, being careful to cover all the filling.

Bake until delicately brown, or about 15 minutes in a slow–moderate oven, 325 degrees.

VARIATIONS:

Banana Cream Pie: Omit coconut from filling. Use 2 or 3 large bananas. Arrange a layer of sliced bananas in a pie shell. Cover with cream filling and then meringue.

Chocolate Pie: Omit coconut from filling. Add 2 or 3 squares of grated bitter chocolate with the milk. Or instead of chocolate, add ⅓ to ½ cup cocoa with the dry ingredients. Increase butter or margarine by 2 tablespoons if cocoa is used.

Pouring filling into a baked shell

Piling meringue onto the filling

LEMON PIE
[9-inch pie]

PARTS 1 and 3
Follow directions for Coconut Cream Pie.

PART 2 – FILLING

1¼ cups sugar
⅓ cup cornstarch
½ teaspoon salt
½ cup cold water
1 cup hot water
3 egg yolks, slightly beaten

2 tablespoons butter or margarine
⅓ cup lemon juice
1 tablespoon grated lemon peel

Mix sugar, cornstarch, and salt in a saucepan. Stir in gradually the cold water. Then add hot water.

Cook over moderate heat, stirring constantly until mixture becomes thick.

Stir a little of the hot mixture into the egg yolks. Then blend the egg mixture into the hot mixture.

Cook 1 minute over low heat, stirring constantly. Remove from heat. Add butter or margarine, lemon juice, and lemon peel. Cool.

After the meringue has been delicately browned

PUMPKIN CHIFFON PIE
[9-inch pie]

PART 1 — PASTRY
baked shell, or Uncooked Crumb Crust

PART 2 — FILLING

1 tablespoon unflavored gelatin (1 envelope)	1 ½ cups mashed cooked pumpkin
¼ cup cold water	3 large egg yolks, beaten
¾ cup brown sugar	
½ teaspoon salt	½ cup milk
1 teaspoon cinnamon	3 large egg whites
½ teaspoon allspice	¼ teaspoon cream of tartar
½ teaspoon nutmeg	
½ teaspoon ginger	6 tablespoons sugar

½ cup cream, whipped and sweetened

Soften gelatin in cold water.

Mix together in a saucepan the brown sugar, salt, spices, pumpkin, beaten egg yolks, and milk.

Cook over low heat, stirring constantly until it boils for 1 minute.

Remove from heat, and stir in softened gelatin; cool.

Beat egg whites until frothy; then beat in sugar a little at a time, and continue beating until stiff and glossy.

Beat pumpkin mixture when partially set until it is smooth. Then carefully fold in the egg-white mixture.

Pile into pie shell, and chill until set.

Decorate the top of the pie as desired with whipped cream.

Desserts — SPONGE CAKES

GENERAL INFORMATION

Cakes are divided into two types — those sometimes known as "butter cakes," which call for butter or other shortening (see Book 1, pages 200–204), and sponge cakes, to which no fat is added.

Sponge cakes are also divided into two classes — the white sponge or angel food, and the yellow sponge. The former contains the whites of eggs, not the yolks; the yellow sponge contains both the whites and yolks in varying amounts. The high proportion of egg, the method of combining the ingredients, and the baking are responsible for the light and spongy texture of the cakes — hence their name.

True sponge cakes are made without adding soda or baking powder. As a rule, cake flour produces more volume and a tenderer product than all-purpose flour. Finely granulated sugar is desirable because it dissolves more rapidly and produces a crisp crust. Cream of tartar is added to angel food cake primarily to prevent shrinkage, but it also results in a more tender cake. Lemon juice is commonly used instead of cream of tartar in the yellow sponge as a source of acid and to serve as a flavoring. More often than not, sponge cakes are baked in a tube pan. The pan is not greased, since it is desirable to have the cake stick to the pan until cooled so that it will not have to support its own weight. If removed from the pan when hot, it may collapse. A good product is practically flat or only slightly rounded on top, and is delicately browned. The crust is tender but not sticky. The grain is fine, with a velvety texture. The holes are evenly distributed, and there are no tunnels.

In the mock sponge cake on page 197, liquid and baking powder are substituted for part of the egg. Since there is very little fat in this recipe, the cake is similar in texture to true yellow sponge cake.

TRUE SPONGE CAKE
[10-inch tube pan, 4 inches deep]

6 egg yolks, medium size	grated rind ½ lemon
½ cup sugar, sifted	½ teaspoon salt
3 tablespoons hot water	6 egg whites
1 tablespoon lemon juice	½ cup sugar, sifted

1 cup sifted cake flour

Beat egg yolks until thick and light yellow in color.

Beat gradually ½ cup sugar into the egg yolks until mixture is stiff enough to hold its shape.

Beat hot water and lemon juice gradually into the yolk mixture.

Add salt to egg whites, and beat whites until foamy.

Add remaining half of sugar, and continue to beat until whites hold a stiff peak.

Fold whites and flour, a little of each at one time, gently into stiff yolk mixture.

Pour into ungreased pan, and bake in a slow–moderate oven, 325 degrees, for 1 hour.

Invert pan on a rack for 1 hour or until cake is cold. Remove carefully from the pan with a spatula.

Serve un-iced or with a butter frosting. For Butter Frosting see Book 1, page 204.

ANGEL FOOD CAKE
[10-inch tube pan, 4 inches deep]

1 cup sifted cake flour	1½ cups egg whites
¾ cup sugar	¾ cups sugar, sifted
½ teaspoon salt	1 teaspoon vanilla extract
1½ teaspoons cream of tartar	½ teaspoon almond extract

Sift together 3 times the cake flour and ¾ cup sugar.

Add salt and cream of tartar to egg whites, and beat until the mixture is foamy.

Beat gradually ¾ cup sugar into the whites, and continue to beat until mixture holds a stiff peak.

Fold in vanilla and almond extracts.

Sift flour–sugar mixture gradually over the beaten egg-white mixture, and fold in gently.

Lift batter into ungreased tube pan.

Bake in slow–moderate oven, 325 degrees, until the cake springs back when lightly touched with a finger tip and is a delicate brown, or about 50 to 60 minutes.

Invert pan so that it stands on the tube. Cool thoroughly. Loosen cake with spatula or knife, and remove from pan.

Rolling up the warm cake

Serve plain or topped with fruit, whipped cream, or fruit and whipped cream. Or spread with Seven Minute or Butter Frosting. (See Book 1, page 204.)

VARIATIONS:

Chocolate Angel Food: Substitute ¼ cup cocoa for ¼ cup cake flour. Sift 3 times with cake flour and 1 cup sugar. Omit almond extract. Increase vanilla extract by ½ teaspoon.

Cherry Angel Food: At the last of the mixing process, fold in ½ cup maraschino cherries, drained well and chopped.

Date-and-Coconut Angel Food: At the last of the mixing process, fold in ½ cup coconut and ½ cup dates, chopped finely.

ALTERNATIVE METHOD:

Use Angel Food Cake Mix, and follow the directions on the package.

JELLY ROLL
[Shallow pan approximately 6 by 10 inches]

2 eggs, medium size	½ teaspoon baking powder
½ cup sugar, sifted	⅛ teaspoon salt
2½ tablespoons water	2 tablespoons confectioners' sugar
½ teaspoon vanilla extract	
½ cup sifted cake flour	½ cup soft tart jelly or jam

Beat eggs until thick and light yellow in color.

Beat in sugar gradually; then add water and vanilla extract.

Sift together flour, baking powder, and salt, and beat into egg mixture until smooth.

Pour into pan lined with greased wax paper. (See Book 1, page 201.)

Bake in quick–moderate oven, 375 degrees, until cake tests done, about 12 to 15 minutes.

Loosen sides, and turn out on a dish towel sprinkled generously with confectioners' sugar.

Remove paper immediately, trim off crisp crusts, and roll up, beginning at one narrow end.

Wrap roll in a towel, and set on a cake rack to cool.

Unroll when cold, spread with soft jelly or jam.

Roll up again, and wrap in wax paper until ready to serve. Cut in slices.

VARIATIONS:

Chocolate Cream Roll: Spread with *Chocolate Cornstarch Pudding* (see Book 1, page

198) or *Chocolate Pie* filling (see Book 2, page 194).

Whipped Cream Roll: Spread with whipped cream to which fruit may or may not be added.

MOCK SPONGE CAKE
[1 square pan 9 by 9 inches, or
12 medium-size muffin cups]

2 eggs, medium size	1 teaspoon butter or
1 cup sugar, sifted	margarine
¼ teaspoon salt	1 cup sifted cake flour
1 teaspoon vanilla extract	1½ teaspoons baking
½ cup milk	powder

Grease and flour cake pan or muffin cups. (See Book 1, page 201.)

Beat eggs until very light. Beat in sugar, salt, and vanilla extract.

Heat milk to boiling; add butter or margarine, and beat into egg-and-sugar mixture.

Sift together flour and baking powder, and beat into the above mixture.

Pour at once into prepared pan, or if muffin pans are used fill ⅔ full.

Bake in moderate oven, 350 degrees, until cake tests done. Allow approximately 25 to 30 minutes for square cake, or 20 minutes for cupcakes.

Serve plain or topped with fruit, whipped cream, or fruit and whipped cream, or Butter Frosting. (For frosting see Book 1, page 204.)

Desserts – MISCELLANEOUS

GENERAL INFORMATION

Desserts have long held a place of honor on the menu. Nearly everyone anticipates with pleasure the end of the meal when something sweet will be served. In our country there is a wide variety to choose from. Some of the popular ones have been adopted from other countries, such as steamed puddings from England, and cream puffs from France. But we have developed special ones of our own — refrigerator, oven, and top-of-the-stove varieties. With so many kinds of desserts available it is difficult to make a selection of recipes. But it is believed that the ones in this section will give satisfaction to anyone who enjoys desserts.

FROZEN VANILLA MARLOW
[4 to 6 servings]

¼ pound marshmallows or approximately 12
1 cup milk
1 cup whipping cream or evaporated milk
1 teaspoon vanilla extract
few grains salt

Combine marshmallows and milk; cook over hot water, stirring occasionally until marshmallows are melted.

Cool until slightly thickened.

Whip cream or evaporated milk until stiff; add vanilla and salt.

Fold whipped mixture into marshmallow–milk mixture, and pour into freezing tray.

Set control for fast freezing, and place in bottom of freezing compartment.

Freeze until firm, or 3 to 4 hours.

VARIATIONS:

Chocolate Marlow: Add 1 to 2 squares of unsweetened chocolate to hot milk and marshmallow mixture.

Fruit Marlow: Use ½ pound marshmallows and 1 cup unsweetened pulp and juice in place of ¼ pound marshmallows and milk. Pulp may be from strawberries, raspberries, peaches, or other fruit. Use 2 tablespoons lemon juice instead of vanilla extract.

ICE CREAM SPECIALS

Ice Cream Baskets: Hollow out plain cupcakes. Fill with ice cream, and top with fresh berries, preserves, or appropriate sauce. Use a commercial or a homemade sauce. (See Book 1, page 202 for cupcakes, and page 205 for sauces.)

Ice Cream Sandwiches: Place a slice of ice cream between 2 slices of sponge or angel food cake. Serve with sauce of flavor desired.

Angel's Delight: Fill a pie shell with ice cream. Decorate with fresh fruit or whipped cream.

Orange Surprise: Fill large glass half full of orange juice. Add a dip of ice cream; then fill glass with ginger ale. Garnish with orange slice, and serve with a straw.

LEMON SPONGE
[serves 4]

2 egg yolks	⅔ cup sugar
4 tablespoons lemon	3 tablespoons flour
juice	1 cup milk
rind 1 lemon	2 egg whites, beaten
¼ teaspoon salt	stiffly

Beat egg yolks until thick and light yellow in color. Add lemon juice, rind, and salt.

Mix sugar and flour; add milk.

Add milk mixture to yolk–lemon mixture.

Fold in beaten egg whites, and place in baking dish in a pan of warm water about 1 inch deep.

Bake in slow–moderate oven, 325 degrees, for about 45 minutes. A sponge forms on the top and a custard on the bottom.

POMPADOUR PUDDING
[serves 4]

PART 1 – CUSTARD

6 tablespoons sugar	2 egg yolks, beaten
1 tablespoon cornstarch	½ teaspoon vanilla extract
few grains salt	
2 cups milk	

Mix sugar, cornstarch, and salt.

Combine milk and egg yolks, and blend with cornstarch mixture.

Cook over low heat, stirring until mixture boils. Boil 1 minute. Add vanilla extract. Fill custard cups ⅔ full of mixture.

PART 2 – TOPPING

1 square chocolate (1 ounce)	1½ tablespoons milk
⅜ cup sugar	2 egg whites, beaten stiffly

Cook chocolate, sugar, and milk over hot water until blended.

Fold chocolate mixture into egg whites, and pour over custard.

Bake in a moderate oven, 350 degrees, until topping puffs up and is about to crack open.

CREAM PUFFS
[4 cream puffs]

½ cup boiling water	¼ teaspoon salt
¼ cup butter or margarine	½ cup sifted all-purpose flour
2 eggs, unbeaten	

Pour boiling water over butter or margarine in a saucepan; bring to a boil, and stir until shortening melts.

Stir in salt and flour; cook, stirring constantly until mixture clings to the spoon, leaving the pan clean.

Remove from heat. Cool slightly.

Add eggs one at a time, beating to a smooth paste after each one.

Beat mixture until smooth and velvety.

Drop from spoon onto ungreased baking sheet, forming 4 mounds about 3 inches apart.

Bake in a hot oven, 425 degrees, for 10 minutes. Reduce temperature to a slow–moderate oven, 325 degrees. Continue to bake until well puffed and delicately browned, or 20 to 25 minutes longer.

Cool slowly on a cake rack. Cut off tops with a sharp knife. Scoop out any particles of soft dough.

Fill with sweetened whipped cream, ice cream, or cream filling. Replace tops. Dust with confectioners' sugar.

VARIATIONS:

Chocolate Eclairs: Make just like cream puffs except shape dough with spatula into finger shapes. Bake, cool, and fill as for cream puffs. Frost tops of filled eclairs with *Chocolate Butter Frosting* (see Book 1, page 204).

REFRIGERATOR PUDDING
[serves 4]

1½ cups graham crackers, rolled fine	½ cup nuts
½ cup dates, pitted and cut up	10 marshmallows, cut up
	½ cup milk

Retain ½ cup graham cracker crumbs.

Mix remainder of ingredients together, and form into roll of desired shape.

Coat roll with the retained graham cracker crumbs.

Chill, and then slice when cold. Serve plain or with whipped cream, or ice cream.

STEAMED FRUIT PUDDING
[serves 4]

½ cup boiling water	1 egg, beaten
½ cup figs, prunes, or raisins, ground or cut up finely	½ cup sugar
	¾ cup sifted all-purpose flour
1 tablespoon melted shortening	½ teaspoon salt
	½ teaspoon soda

Pour boiling water over fruit. Add shortening.

Blend in egg and sugar.

Sift together flour, salt, and soda; stir into the egg mixture.

Pour into well-greased pint mold or can with tight lid. Place on a rack over water in a tightly covered container, and steam 1½ hours. Or steam in a pressure saucepan, using the maker's directions and length of time to steam a pudding.

Beverages

Beverages — COFFEE

GENERAL INFORMATION

Coffee has long been a popular beverage in our country, with most families having a favorite method of preparation. The most common methods are the steeped, the percolated, the drip, and the vacuum. But the success of any one of these methods depends upon the following conditions.

1. Having fresh coffee, ground to suit the method used
2. Having the coffee maker absolutely clean
3. Using accurate measurements for the desired strength
4. Starting with fresh cold water
5. Avoiding a product that is boiled or overcooked
6. Serving the coffee immediately after preparation time is completed

Directions are given here for using non-electric coffee makers. For electric makers, either partially or wholly automatic, follow the maker's directions.

COFFEE, PERCOLATOR METHOD
[4 servings]

*½ cup coffee   4 cups water

Add cold water to lower part of percolator.
Put coffee compartment in place, and add percolator-grind coffee.

Cover, and place over heat, allowing water to percolate through the coffee.

Reduce heat, and percolate slowly 7 to 10 minutes depending on strength of coffee desired.

Remove coffee compartment. Replace cover, and serve immediately.

*Note: Use 2 tablespoons coffee to 1 cup water for each serving desired.

VARIATIONS IN METHOD:

Drip: Scald coffee maker with boiling water. Place drip-grind coffee in coffee compartment. Heat cold water to boiling point; pour into upper part of coffee maker; cover. Set over very low heat. When water has dripped through to bottom, remove coffee compartment. Stir coffee; replace cover. Serve immediately.

Glass Vacuum: Heat water to boiling point, and put it into the lower bowl of a glass vacuum coffee maker. Place the filter section in the bottom of the upper bowl of the coffee maker, and add very finely ground or pulverized coffee. Put the upper bowl in place with a slight twist to insure a seal; put cover in place. Apply heat until most of the water has risen through the hollow tube and has reached the upper half containing the ground coffee. Remove the heat, and allow the coffee liquid to be drawn into the lower bowl. Remove the top bowl, and cover the lower one. Serve the coffee at once.

Steeped: Use an old-fashioned coffeepot. Measure water into the pot, and bring it to a boil. Stir all-purpose-grind coffee into the water. Set over heat low enough to keep coffee just below the boiling point. Steep for

7 to 10 minutes. Strain and pour into heated serving pot. Serve immediately. Sometimes when this method is used, a dash of cold water just before serving is added to settle the grounds. Or egg shells, which have been washed before the shell is broken, are used. They are crumpled and mixed with the grounds, and steeped with the coffee to clear it.

Instant: Place instant coffee in a serving cup, using 1 or more teaspoons depending on the strength desired. Fill cup with boiling water, and stir until dissolved. Serve at once.

VARIATIONS:

Iced Coffee: Make coffee in the usual way, except use 3 to 4 tablespoons to 1 cup water. Pour hot coffee over ice in tall glasses. Or use instant coffee that will dissolve in cold water.

After-Dinner Coffee: Make coffee in the usual way, except use 3 to 4 tablespoons coffee to 1 cup water. Serve in small cups, "demitasse," as they are called, after dinner.

Beverages — TEA

GENERAL INFORMATION

Tea is also a popular beverage, with black tea, green tea, and oolong tea the most common kinds used. It is generally purchased in bulk, in packages, or in small tea bags. In-

stant tea is also available. The successful preparation of tea, as with coffee, depends on following certain conditions:

1. Using a teapot made of china, pottery, or heat-resistant glass that is absolutely clean
2. Scalding the teapot by filling it with boiling water just before making the tea, letting it stand for a few minutes, and then pouring off the water
3. Using correct measurements for the strength desired
4. Using boiling water that has just come to a boil

TEA
[4 servings]

*4 teaspoons tea   4 cups water

Put tea leaves in scalded pot, and add fresh boiling water.

Let stand 3 to 5 minutes; strain with tea strainer if desired.

Serve at once, plain or with sugar, and either lemon or milk.

*NOTE: 1 teaspoon tea to 1 cup water for each serving desired.

VARIATION:

Iced Tea: Make tea in the usual way, using 1½ teaspoons tea to 1 cup water. Cool, and pour into a container. Cover tightly and refrigerate. When ready to serve, pour tea over ice in tall glasses. *Or* make tea in the usual way, except use 2 or more teaspoons tea instead of 1. Pour hot tea over ice in tall glasses. *Or* use instant tea that will dissolve in cold water.

Get Well Soon

Caring for a sickroom

Preparing food and serving trays
to a sick person

Learning some simple things to do
for a sick person

Giving prompt attention to any
symptoms of illness

I T WAS a raw, chilly day in early March. As Miss Cameron, the homemaking teacher in the Centerville High School, checked the attendance, she commented on the absence of several students.

"Dorothy and Bob have colds," said John. "And they aren't the only ones either. Nearly everyone in our neighborhood has a cold or is getting over one."

"Martha is in bed with a sore throat and other complications," added Doris. "Mrs. Davenport won't let her have any visitors until they know just what is wrong."

"That's wise," said Miss Cameron, "especially if a person has been exposed to a contagious disease. It's very important to take every precaution to prevent spreading the disease to others."

"This might be a good time for us to take up the class-work on illness which we said we'd include when we set up plans for our year's work," said Bertram. "Right now we might be able to get in some practical experience with sick people." Bertram said this lightly, not thinking that his suggestion would be taken seriously. But much to his surprise there were echoes of, "Not a bad idea," from various sections of the room.

"What better time could we select for learning about illness than when people are really sick?" asked Jane. "Most classes just study and read books about illness. It would be much more interesting — and different too — to be able to have sick people for some of our classwork. In that way we could be helping others at the same time we are helping ourselves."

The students then waited to hear what Miss Cameron would say to these suggestions. They seemed pleased when she said that she heartily approved of them. In fact she agreed that it would be possible to start the classwork on illness soon.

MAKING PLANS FOR CLASSWORK

By the middle of the next week Dorothy and Bob were back in school, and everyone in the homemaking class, with the exception of Martha who was still absent, was ready to make plans for the classwork on illness. The immediate problem, of course, was what to include.

"Let's start with the room that the sick person is in," suggested Cassie. "I think we need to know as much as possible about caring for a sickroom."

There were nods of agreement to Cassie's suggestion.

"Isn't it important for a sick person to have the right kind of food?" asked Phil looking toward Miss Cameron.

"Yes, that's true," replied Miss Cameron. "Preparing food and serving trays to a sick person could certainly be part of the classwork."

"I've been thinking there must be many things that we teen-agers can do when there is illness in our homes," said Carol. "Learning some simple things to do for a sick person would be very helpful."

Again there was agreement.

"We've talked about other people being ill, but what about ourselves?" asked Bob. "I think we need to know what to do when signs of an illness first appear. I heard my mother say just the other day that giving prompt attention to early symptoms of illness often prevents serious trouble later on."

The students and Miss Cameron agreed with Bob. Miss Cameron then suggested that the class summarize what they had already planned. Later on, if time was available, they would consider other problems.

There was a chorus of approval from everyone. Fred, with the assistance of the others, then wrote the following general plans on the blackboard:

1. Caring for a sickroom
2. Preparing food and serving trays to a sick person
3. Learning some simple things to do for a sick person
4. Giving prompt attention to any symptoms of illness

"Now we need a name for our classwork," said Dorothy, who had been busy jotting down words on a scratch pad. "What about 'Get Well Soon'?"

"Fine." "Good." "Right to the point," were heard throughout the room.

Now that general plans for their classwork were made, the students began to consider the details that would need to be carried out to set their plans in motion.

Primarily they were concerned about arranging some of their classwork with people who were really sick. After discussing the matter, they appointed Phil and Jane to consult with Miss Chase, the school nurse, to see what could be worked out. Several other students, with the assistance of Miss Cameron, were to obtain various books, pamphlets, and other helpful materials for the reference shelves.

A short time later, Phil and Jane reported that Miss Chase had suggested three patients whose families were willing to cooperate with the class in some of their experiences in home care of the sick.

One patient was David Crosley, a senior, who had been in an automobile accident and might be in

bed for a couple of weeks. Another patient was ten-year-old Judy Jensen who was recovering from rheumatic fever. The third patient, much to their surprise, was Martha Davenport, their classmate, who had developed a mild case of scarlet fever. All three lived within a short distance from the school.

Miss Chase believed that these three types of illnesses would provide for a variety of experiences.

Even though Martha had a communicable disease, which would prevent personal visits, it would still be possible for the students to do various things to make her comfortable and contented during her illness.

With three real patients and a supply of reference materials, everyone was eager to get started on the first problem. More specific plans must now be made.

CARING FOR A SICKROOM

In setting up their classwork on caring for a sickroom, the students decided to divide into three groups. The boys in the class would work together on David's situation. A group of girls headed by Doris were to plan experiences that would fit into Judy's home. The third group headed by Dorothy could work out something for Martha.

The first two groups would send one, or two students at the most, to talk with the mothers of David and Judy to find out how the groups could be most helpful in caring for the sickroom. Acting on the advice of the mothers, the students would then set up plans and begin to carry them out. The third group could get information about Martha from her mother over the telephone and make plans accordingly. Reports of all the plans were to be given to the class within the next few days re-

gardless of whether the plans had been fully completed.

At David's Home

The boys learned from Mrs. Crosley that David would probably be in bed about ten days longer. He had no broken bones, but since there might be some internal injury the doctor thought it best to keep him quiet for a while. Mrs. Crosley's biggest problems at the moment were cleaning the sickroom and making the bed with David in it. She would appreciate any assistance in these activities and would adapt her daily schedule to that of the students.

The situation was discussed by the boys, who worked out a schedule for making the bed and cleaning the sickroom every day for ten days. Each boy would get experience in both activities. The schedule was posted on the bulletin board in the homemaking room.

Before putting the schedule into operation, the boys consulted references, and then set up guides for making an occupied bed and cleaning a sickroom. Copies of these guides were typewritten on cards and given to each boy.

Making an occupied bed

Although the group already knew how to make a bed (see Book 1, pages 275–276), they learned that somewhat different supplies and procedures may be necessary when the bed is occupied by a sick person. For example, additional bed protection may be desirable. This protection may be a sheet of rubber, oilcloth, or pliofilm placed over the bottom sheet. Over this is placed a folded sheet, called a "drawsheet." It can be drawn out easily and changed or moved from side to side to present a fresh surface. A drawsheet often saves frequent changing of the bottom sheet.

The group also learned that making a bed for a sick person is very important. Not only does the bed need to be comfortable when first made, but it must stay comfortable for a reasonable length of time.

Therefore before going to David's home, the boys not only practiced making an occupied bed, but gave a demonstration to the rest of the class. Copies of the cards containing the guides they had worked out were also distributed. A copy of one of the cards is reproduced as follows:

HOW TO MAKE AN OCCUPIED BED

1. Assemble clean bed linen within easy reach.

2. Remove and fold the spread, placing it on the back of a chair.

3. Remove the upper blanket if there are two, and drape it over a chair to air. Avoid letting it touch the floor. Hold the remaining blanket in place with one hand, and with the other, draw the upper sheet out from underneath the blanket. Be sure that the patient is covered at all times. If the upper sheet is not soiled, it may be folded once and used as a drawsheet.

4. Remove all pillows, except one if needed, and take off soiled pillowcases.

---

5. Have the patient lie on his side at the edge
   of the bed, facing the edge nearest him.

6. On the unoccupied side of the bed, loosen
   the bottom sheet, the rubber sheet, and the
   drawsheet. Fold each close to the patient's
   back. Brush away any crumbs, and smooth
   out any wrinkles in the mattress pad.

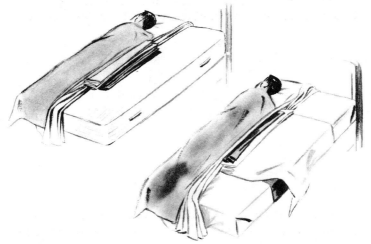

7. Place the clean bottom sheet in position on
   the unoccupied side, mitering the top and
   bottom corners. Pleat the remaining part
   lengthwise, and place it as close as possible to the soiled sheet. Pull the rubber
   sheet back over the clean sheet and arrange
   a fresh drawsheet, folded crosswise. Tuck
   the bottom sheet, the rubber sheet, and the
   drawsheet securely under the mattress.

8. Assist the covered patient to roll back
   over the pleats onto the clean sheet.

9. Go to the other side of the bed, loosen the
   bottom sheet and the drawsheet, and remove
   them from the bed. Smooth out the clean
   sheet, the drawsheet, and the rubber sheet,

and tuck them under the mattress after mitering the corners of the bottom sheet.

10. With the patient in the middle of the bed, place the clean top sheet over the blanket covering the patient. Then pull the blanket from underneath, working from head to foot. Allow enough sheet at the head to come well up to the patient's shoulders, with at least 8 inches to fold over the edge of the

blanket later on. Make a box pleat in the sheet over the patient's toes. Replace the blanket on top of the sheet, and add other blankets if needed. Have the patient draw up his knees. Then miter the corners of the top sheet and the blanket at the foot of the bed. Tuck in only as tightly as will permit the patient to be comfortable.

11. Remove the pillow from under the patient's head, and change the pillowcase. Shake up the pillow and replace it.

12. Put on the spread, tucking it under the mattress at the foot of the bed. At the head of the bed, fold the edge of the spread under the top edge of the blanket. Then bring the top sheet down over both the blanket and the spread.

Cleaning a sickroom

In working out the guides for cleaning a sickroom, the boys learned that cleaning needs to be done once a day, preferably in the morning after the patient has been bathed and the bed changed. A copy of the guides the boys set up and distributed to the other class members is given below, since it may be of interest.

HOW TO CLEAN A SICKROOM

1. <u>Be especially careful about stirring up a lot of dust.</u> Use whatever equipment is available for stirring up the least dust. It may be a vacuum cleaner or a carpet sweeper on the rugs, and a dry mop for the floor. Vacuum cleaner attachments or a cloth can be used for dusting the furniture. But using a vacuum cleaner may depend on whether the noise is disturbing to the patient.

2. <u>Create as little noise and disturbance as possible.</u> Talk quietly, but do not whisper. Whispering suggests anxiety to some people. Since sounds seem to increase during an illness and often cause discomfort, oil anything that squeaks, such as door hinges or bed springs. Prevent windows from rattling by putting a wooden or rubber wedge between the sash and the frame. Do not allow doors to slam.

3. <u>Tidy up the room.</u> Remove soiled drinking glasses, used tissues, waste paper, and the like. Arrange magazines, books, and recreational materials neatly. If there are flowers, change the water, discard withered blooms, and cut the stems. Water plants as needed.

4. <u>Be sure that no unpleasant odors remain in the room.</u> If ventilation has not freshened the air, using a deodorant may help.

At Judy's Home

Jane made the first contact with Judy's home by interviewing Mrs. Jensen to find out what activities would be most acceptable with reference to caring for the sickroom.

Mrs. Jensen said that Judy was able to sit up in bed most of the day. Any ideas that would make the room easier to care for and more comfortable for Judy would be very welcome.

Keeping in mind Mrs. Jensen's suggestions, the group consulted various references. They assembled the information which seemed important, and set up a questionnaire for checking ease of care and comfort of the patient in a sickroom. Cassie and Doris then checked Judy's room. A copy of the questionnaire with what they found out is reproduced on pages 211 to 212.

USING THE QUESTIONNAIRE IN JUDY'S ROOM

IS THE ROOM BRIGHT AND CHEERFUL AND CONVENIENTLY LOCATED?

yes, it is

The room has sunlight part of the day with a pleasant view from the windows. It is convenient to the kitchen and the bathroom.

DO THE FURNISHINGS MAKE IT EASY TO CARE FOR THE SICKROOM?

Not wholly

There is a single-width bed with firm springs and a comfortable mattress. It is located so that it can be approached from both sides, but it is too low for convenient care.

There is a table on one side of the bed. But it does not provide enough room to hold needed articles and still allow space for a tray at mealtime.

The window curtains are simple and easy to launder.

Small nonskid rugs make it easy to clean the floor.

Three chairs seem sufficient — a comfortable lounging chair and two straight ones.

There is a chest of drawers where extra garments and linen can be kept.

DO THE FURNISHINGS CONTRIBUTE TO THE COMFORT OF THE PATIENT?

yes, in some respects

There is a good reading lamp above the head of the bed, and a radio on the table.

Pillows are used as a back rest, but they do not give enough support.

Hobby materials are scattered around and tend to give the room a cluttered appearance.

There are no pictures in the room.

**IS PROVISION MADE FOR
CONTROLLING VENTILA-
TION, LIGHTING, TEMPERA-
TURE, AND HUMIDITY?**

Yes, partly

The room can be ventilated by opening a
window part way at the top and bottom.
But there needs to be some protection to
keep direct drafts from the bed. A screen
would serve this purpose.

At night the light in the room is too
glaring, but it could be shielded behind
a screen.

The temperature of the room is kept comfortably warm — about 70 degrees Fahrenheit.

The humidity is controlled by opening a
window in warm weather and by setting uncovered pans of water on the radiator
during the winter season.

After analyzing the findings on the
questionnaire, the group decided to
make various improvements in the
room.

1. First of all, the bed was too low for
convenient care. Since buying or rent-
ing a hospital bed was not practical,
the students investigated ways of raising the height of the bed in use. They
decided on wooden blocks to raise the
legs, rather than tin cans half filled
with sand or some other means of
elevation. Industrial arts department
equipment was used to bore holes in
the blocks. The illustrations show how
the bed was raised.

2. The next step was to provide more
table space. A large fruit crate, with
the center division providing a shelf,
was painted. The top was covered
with a washable table cover.

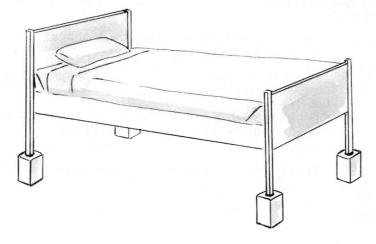

3. Since pillows were used but did not provide enough support when Judy was sitting up, a cardboard-carton back rest was made for her.

4. The group borrowed an unused screen — the type with three panels hinged together — from the school nurse's office. The screen would be used to protect the bed from drafts and to shield it from the glare of the light at night.

5. Since there were no pictures in the room, the group secured several large colorful travel posters. Arrangements were made with Mrs. Jensen to hang one of the posters where Judy could see it. The poster would be changed from time to time.

Since other classes may be interested in making some of the same improvements carried out by Group 2, the materials needed and the directions which the students set up for their own use are given here:

BEDSIDE TABLE
Materials needed:

Large fruit crate with center division
Paint — the desired color
Paintbrush
Washable table cover

Directions:

1. Paint the crate inside and out.
2. Let dry, and then give another coat.
3. Place the crate on end by the side of the bed, and add the table cover.

BED BLOCKS
Materials needed:

4 pieces of hard lumber approximately 8 inches by 8 inches by 12 inches

Directions:

1. Remove the casters from the bed legs.
2. Bore a hole 6 inches deep and wide enough to admit the bed legs in the center of one end of each block.
3. Place the bed legs in the block holes.

BACK REST
Materials needed:

Large cardboard carton approximately 20 inches by 20 inches by 18 inches with cover flaps
Sharp knife
Strong cord or glued tape
Sheet or cloth to cover the carton

Directions:

1. Cut down the two corners to the bottom on one 20-inch side.

2. On the inside of the carton, score — by making a line with the knife — the 18-inch sides of the carton diagonally from the tops of the uncut corners to the bottom of the cut corners. (See the illustration on this page.)

3. Bend the sides inward along the line of scoring, making a sharp diagonal fold.

4. Score excess turned-in sides to fit smoothly on the bottom of the carton.

5. Bend the flap from the uncut corners down, and bring the cut corners and flap up over them.

6. Apply glued tape, or tie the back rest with a strong cord, and cover for the comfort of the patient and for the protection of the bed and bedding.

7. Place on the bed with the slanting side toward the patient. Use with pillows as described on page 233.

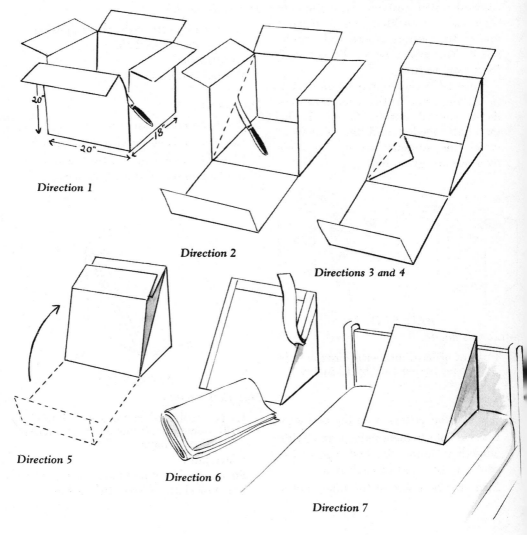

Direction 1

Direction 2

Directions 3 and 4

Direction 5

Direction 6

Direction 7

Martha's Situation

Before contacting Martha's home, Group 3 decided to find out something about communicable diseases. They felt that this would give them a better understanding of Martha's situation. The information would also be helpful in the event that a communicable disease occurred in any of their own families.

To obtain the essential facts, they talked with Miss Chase, the school nurse, and consulted various reference materials. Some of the material they assembled is shown in the chart on this page. It is necessary to study this information to understand why the students decided to do for Martha what they did. Arrangements were then made for Carol to interview Martha's mother by telephone.

Mrs. Davenport said that everything was progressing satisfactorily. Mrs. Adams, the practical nurse

---

PRECAUTIONS GENERALLY PRESCRIBED FOR COMMUNICABLE DISEASES
[For the Nurse or Attendant to Follow]

- *Isolate the patient.* This is to protect the family as well as people in the community. Adults not in contact with the patient are usually allowed to continue their business, unless they are employed in handling food. Exposed children living in the home may or may not be permitted to attend school.

- *Go in and out of the sickroom as little as possible.* Before entering, assemble all the equipment needed for giving the necessary care.

- *Wear a cover-all apron while caring for the patient.* Always leave the apron in the sickroom, preferably on a hook near the door.

- *Turn away from the patient when he coughs or sneezes.* Keep your hands away from your mouth at all times.

- *Wash your hands thoroughly in hot soapy water before and after you care for the patient, and before touching anything outside of the room.* This is to protect the patient from further exposure which you might bring in, and to protect yourself and others from the patient's disease.

- *Keep all articles used by the patient and the nurse inside the sickroom until they can be burned, boiled, soaked in disinfectant solution, or sunned in the air.*

- *Dispose of all refuse from the sickroom either by burning, using a disinfectant solution, or otherwise according to local regulations.*

- *Upon recovery, see that the patient has a warm tub bath, a shampoo, and a complete set of clean clothes before being moved to another room.*

- *Give the sickroom a final cleanup.* This means to wash, air, sun, disinfect, or burn all articles used by the patient as well as to wash all flat surfaces in the room.

who was taking care of Martha, was following the instructions of the health authorities as well as those of the doctor. Anything the group could do to make Martha more comfortable during her illness would be welcome.

After some discussion, the students decided that since the other two groups were working on the care of the sickroom, they too would offer suggestions on the subject. Even though they could not actually visit Martha's room, they believed that it was important to have a better understanding of a

sickroom in which there was a communicable disease. Therefore they agreed to concentrate on three points: (1) the differences between an ordinary sickroom and one used for a communicable disease, (2) the additional care needed for such a room, and (3) what they could do to make it easier to care for Martha. All this called for ingenuity and resourcefulness, but ideas were beginning to come thick and fast. It was not long before Group 3 was ready to give its report.

Differences between an ordinary sickroom and one used for a communicable disease

Acting as spokesman, Doris began her report by referring to a placard posted on the bulletin board. This placard contained the material given in the chart on page 215. It included a list of precautions relating to communicable diseases. The group felt that members of the class might find this information very helpful.

Doris then presented the first of the three points on which her group had decided to concentrate. This was cleverly done by displaying sketches prepared in art class. They were arranged on the bulletin board to show the differences between an ordinary sickroom and one used for a communicable disease. The questionnaire which Group 2 had set up for checking Judy's sickroom (see pages 211–212), and the information obtained from Miss Chase and other sources had been used as a basis for the comparisons. A reproduction of the material is given in the illustrations on pages 217 to 218.

ORDINARY SICKROOM

Bright, cheerful, conveniently located

Easy to care for

Comfortably furnished

Provision for controlling ventilation, lighting, temperature, and humidity

COMMUNICABLE-DISEASE SICKROOM

Isolated from the rest of the household

Sunny, well ventilated, temperature and humidity under control

Sparsely furnished, very easy to care for

Provision for all articles used by the patient and the nurse

Additional care needed for a sickroom used for a communicable disease

The next point, which concerned added care for a sickroom used for communicable disease, was presented by Cassie. It was set up in much the same way as the previous report. The guides that the boys in Group I had assembled (see page 209), plus other reference materials were used as a basis for the report. The information was printed in large type on cards that could easily be seen from the bulletin board. A reproduction of these cards is shown in the illustration that follows:

Use a separate set of cleaning equipment from that used in the rest of the house, and store it in the sickroom. Do not remove it until the final cleanup. Then see that it is thoroughly cleaned and sunned.

Keep a supply of newspapers on hand. Use them for handling anything that is contaminated, or anything you do not wish to be contaminated when your hands have been in contact with the patient.

See that the bedclothing is laundered separately from the family wash. Dishes need to be boiled ten to fifteen minutes before being washed with the family's dishes. Burn partly eaten scraps of food and paper tissues used by the patient. Use a disinfectant with other discharges, and dispose of according to local requirements.

After the patient's recovery, wash floors, window sills, table tops, doorknobs, and shelves with hot soapy water. Air the room thoroughly. Air the mattress, books, and other unwashable articles in the sunlight for several hours. Clean badly soiled articles, or destroy them if they cannot be cleaned. See that all blankets and spreads are laundered before they are used again.

Reporting and carrying out ideas
for Martha's room

When it came time for the third point, Jane gave the report. She said that it had not been easy to find things they could do for Martha's room. However, after consulting various references they found several ideas which they carried out.

The first thing they did was to collect newspapers, since Mrs. Adams would be needing many for Martha's care. Some of the papers were stacked and tied in small bundles for easy handling. Others were cut into fourths and stacked. This was a convenient size for handling contaminated articles. Each small piece could be discarded after one use. The group also made a supply of disposal bags from some of the newspapers. One of these bags was to be pinned to the bed for Martha's tissue discards, and changed whenever necessary.

Other items were a door silencer to quiet the click of the door latch, and a bed cradle to keep the covers from weighing too heavily on Martha's feet.

The bed cradle could be used later on as a bed table. But the item that appealed to the group the most — and to Martha especially — was a phone purchased and installed by Mr. Davenport. It ran from the sun porch to Martha's bedside table. The set was an inexpensive model often used for communication between a house and a detached garage. There were small batteries in the handles of the phone and push buttons to signal either end of the phone. Martha was now able to keep in direct contact with her family and friends.

In presenting the report, samples of the articles sent to Martha were on hand. Jane pointed out that even though the items fitted Martha's situation very nicely, they could be used for illnesses of any type. She explained how they were made and said that the directions worked out by the group were available to anyone who cared to have them. The directions used follow:

DISPOSAL BAG

Materials needed:

Newspapers — double sheet for each bag

Directions:

1. Take a double newspaper sheet folded along the original lengthwise fold.
2. Bring folded edge up and over to form a triangle. Cut off excess paper.

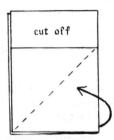

3. Turn triangle fold to bottom. Fold points to center, just overlapping them in a line parallel to bottom.

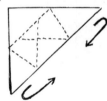

4. Fold half of top over sides to lock in place. Shape into a pouch.

5. Use other half of top to tack on the wall, or to pin to the bed sheet. This half may also be used to cover the bag when time for discarding.

DOOR SILENCER

Materials needed:

Double piece of firm fabric, 3 inches by 5 inches, or 3 inches by 10 inches unfolded

Piece of elastic ½ inch wide and 8 inches long, or two pieces 4 inches long

Thread to match

Directions:

1. Turn in raw edges about ¼ of an inch on three sides of folded material, and pin–baste together.

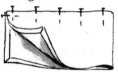

2. Stitch or sew by hand about ⅛ of an inch from the edges. Secure the ends of the stitching.

3. At each end, attach a loop of elastic, using double stitching.

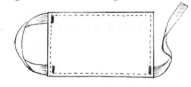

4. Fasten loops over doorknobs with the material covering the latch.

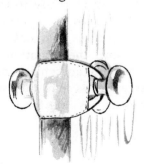

BED TABLE

Materials needed:

Clean, heavy cardboard carton, approximately 24 inches by 10 inches by 12 inches

Sharp knife

Suitable cover — cloth, paint, or wallpaper

Directions:

1. Remove all the top flaps.
2. Cut out the long sides in an arch to make legs and to allow the box to fit comfortably over the patient's thighs. Be sure to hold the knife blade away from your body when cutting.
3. Cut small openings in the upper portion of the short ends to allow easy handling.
4. Cover as desired.

BED CRADLE

This is made the same way as the cardboard table. The size of the carton will depend upon the foot space desired. If a hot-water bag is to be used as extra warmth for the feet, this needs to be taken into consideration in determining the size of the carton.

CLASS MEMO:
What kind of experiences will your class plan in caring for a sickroom?

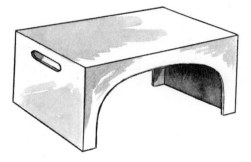

PREPARING FOOD AND SERVING TRAYS TO A SICK PERSON

THE classwork on caring for a sickroom was so well along that the students and Miss Cameron believed they were ready to take up the next problem — *preparing food and serving trays to a sick person.* In discussing the situation, there was a general agreement to plan and carry out as many helpful experiences as possible for the three patients. In this way the students would be preparing themselves for any illness which might occur in their own homes.

Learning About Diets for a Sick Person

"First of all," commented Carol, "I think we need to find out more about what foods a sick person can eat. I know there are limitations when you're sick. And I got the idea when I talked with Mrs. Davenport about Martha's room that Martha was on some kind of diet."

These and other remarks caused the students to begin with a study of diets.

Finding out food needs during illness

From their reading, the students learned that the right kind of food is important for the recovery of a sick person. When a person is ill, the body's power of digestion and utilization of food may be limited, because of lack of exercise, poor circulation, and other factors. The doctor will, therefore, order a diet which he believes the body can digest with ease during a particular stage of an illness.

The students also learned that there are three types of diets generally given during the course of an illness — a *liquid diet*, a *soft diet*, and a *light* or *convalescent* diet. There are special diets that a doctor may order for certain diseases, such as diabetes, heart trouble, or tuberculosis. But since the classwork did not include these illnesses, Miss Cameron suggested that the students concentrate on the three types of diets generally prescribed.

Then too they learned that the reason liquids are usually given at the beginning of an illness is because they are more easily digested than other foods and help to flush the system. Or they might be given if a person is weak following a digestive upset, and also during the course of a fever. A soft diet is usually given for a few days following a liquid diet. Then after a patient begins to recover, a convales-

cent diet can be taken. However, these were general points, since a doctor's orders should be followed in feeding a patient.

Inquiring about their patients' diets

In order to obtain the information they needed about the diets of the three patients, the class decided to have one student interview each of the mothers of the patients. After explaining that they were studying about diets for a sick person, they asked the mothers the following questions: (1) What diet or diets has the patient been given, and what diet is he or she having at the present time? (2) What foods did the doctor recommend for each diet? (3) What foods does the patient especially like in the diet he or she is now having?

After the interviews, the three students pooled their information. The reports they made to the class were in terms of answers to the three questions.

Carol reported that both David and Judy had been on liquid and soft diets, but were now on a convalescent diet. Martha had been on a liquid diet, but was now taking a soft diet. She would be well enough for a convalescent diet in another day or so.

When Harry reported on Question 2, he showed the class a card which Judy's doctor had given Mrs. Jensen. This card contained the kinds of food recommended for the three diets generally given during the course of an illness. Since the card seemed to provide just the information which the students needed, Harry had copies made for each member of the class. A copy of the information is reproduced below.

How to combine family meals with a diet for a convalescent

As the discussion on diets continued, Miss Cameron said that a convalescent patient needs a well-balanced diet —

within the limits of what he or she can eat — just as a well person does. She also pointed out that many foods which form a part of the family's meals are suitable for a sick person. Menus, based on the information recommended by Judy's doctor, could be set up to include foods that would make an adequate diet not only for the patient, but for other family members as well. Such an arrangement would make it easy for a busy homemaker

FOODS FOR LIQUID, SOFT, AND CONVALESCENT DIETS

Liquid Diet	Soft Diet	Convalescent Diet

Strained fruit and vegetable juices
Clear broth
Strained oyster stew
    clam stew
    cream soup
    vegetable soup
Whole-grain-cereal gruels, strained. (Gruel is made by boiling the cereal in water or milk, using more liquid than the directions on the container require.)
Milk, buttermilk, and malted milk
Eggnog
Ices, sherbets, and ice creams
Ginger ale
Cocoa, weak tea
Coffee (for adults)
	Well-cooked whole-grain cereals, strained
	Soft-cooked or poached eggs
	Strained vegetables
	Toast and crackers
	Custards
	Simple cooked puddings
	Gelatin
	Simple cake, plain cookies
	Cooked fruit without seeds
	Liquids as in a liquid diet
		All items mentioned in a liquid and soft diet
		Tender meats, such as
		    chicken
		    lamb chops
		    scraped beef
		Baked fish
		Cooked vegetables, such as
		    asparagus
		    green peas or beans
		    spinach
		    carrots
		    potatoes
		Fresh ripe tomatoes
		Cooked fruits
		Raw citrus fruits
		Avoid
		    coarse or raw vegetables
		    raw fruit other than
		       citrus fruit
		    fried foods
		    rich pastries
		    food rich in fat

Give a glassful of liquid every two or three hours when the patient is awake. At mealtime more than one kind of liquid may be given. Serve hot liquids in the early morning and at bedtime.	Give three meals a day plus between-meal feedings as prescribed by the doctor. Any of the foods in the liquid diet may be served as a between-meal beverage.	

*A tray
for a convalescent*

who might be taking care of a sick person in addition to her regular household tasks.

Miss Cameron's suggestion of adapting the family's menu to that of a sick person appealed to the students, and they decided to see how it could be worked out for their patients. But before they began to plan anything, Bob spoke up.

"I believe this is where I can report on question 3," he said. "I was to find out what each of the patients like in the diets they can have. Since sick people usually have poor appetites, it's important to serve food they like. Anything that stimulates the appetite helps them to get well."

There were nods of agreement to Bob's remarks, and he gave them a summary of the food preferences of the three patients. But since food preferences are an individual matter varying from person to person, the contents of Bob's report are not given.

The students then worked out a day's menus for the families of each patient. These menus were based on (1) many of the foods recommended for a convalescent diet, (2) the preferences of the patients and what they had recently been served, and (3) the guides for menu planning. (See pages 101–103 for guides for menu planning.) The meals for the patients were then adapted from the menus for the families.

These menus — all with roast chicken as the main dish — were then discussed with the mothers of the patients. The students explained how the menus had been set up. They also made arrangements with the mothers for sending in the dinner meal — which would be prepared at school — for the patients. Since the students believed that it was advisable to spend the available time in preparing and serving convalescent meals, the family meals were not prepared.

Since other classes may be interested in learning to combine family meals with a diet for a convalescent, the day's menu worked out for David and his family is given.

Menu for the Family	*Menu for David*

B R E A K F A S T

Tomato Juice	Small glass of tomato juice
Soft-cooked Eggs Buttered Toast	1 soft-cooked egg
Cocoa Coffee	1 slice buttered whole-wheat toast
	1 cup cocoa

D I N N E R

Roast Stuffed Chicken Gravy	1 slice roast chicken
Baked Potatoes Green Beans	1 small baked potato with butter
Cranberry Jelly	½ cup green beans
Clover Leaf Rolls	1 serving cranberry jelly
Baked Custard	1 slice toast
Milk Tea	½ cup baked custard
	1 cup weak tea

S U P P E R

Cream of Asparagus Soup Crackers	1 cup cream of asparagus soup
Toasted Cheese Sandwiches	2 saltine crackers
Lettuce Salad French Dressing	3 halves stewed peaches
Stewed Peaches Cookies	1 cookie
Milk Tea	1 glass milk

Serving a Tray to a Sick Person

The students decided that enough food would be prepared for six trays. Three trays would be taken to the patients and served to them, except in Martha's home where the tray would be sent to her room. Since all of the students could not go to the homes of David and Judy, the other three trays would be served as demonstrations for members of the class who remained at school.

Plans for how they would work were also made. The chicken — without stuffing — would be prepared for roasting the day before it was to be served, and stored in the refrigerator. One of the students would put it in the oven the next day, so that baking time would be completed when the class met. The groups would also time their vegetables to be ready. Other foods, such as cranberry jelly and baked custard for David, would already be prepared. The tea and toast would be made at David's home. (See pages 167–200 for the preparation of these foods.)

*Setting up a check list for serving
a tray*

At one point in the proceedings it became necessary to assemble some information about serving trays.

"Let's find out what to do, and then we'll be able to plan how to do it," suggested Laura. "It will be helpful to have something to check by when we serve the trays. Don't you agree?"

Laura's suggestion appealed to everyone, and it was decided to set up a check list for serving a tray to a patient. The students consulted references, and offered information from their own experiences. Then all of the ideas were coordinated into the check list given below.

POINTS TO CHECK
WHEN SERVING A TRAY TO A SICK PERSON

Is the Patient Comfortable?
1. Has he been given an opportunity to wash his face and hands?
2. Has the bedding been straightened out, and recreational material, such as magazines, books, or other articles, set aside?
3. If he is to sit up, is he well supported by a back rest, with pillows if needed?
4. Does he have something over his shoulders?
5. Is there a bedside table of convenient height ready? Or is there a lap table, so that the person does not have to support the weight of the tray on his knees?

Is the Food Served Attractively and on Time?
6. Is the tray colorful, or is it covered with a clean, attractive tray cloth or a paper mat?
7. Is the arrangement of the tray similar to a place setting at the table?
8. Is the meal itself well planned and well prepared to stimulate the appetite of a sick person?
9. Is there something special on the tray that will please the person, such as a small flower or other attractive decoration?
10. Is the tray ready at the usual time — not too soon after the last meal or too long?

Have Arrangements Been Made for a Quiet, Leisurely Meal?
11. Is the room free from visitors except a member of the family, or a chum who may occasionally have a meal in the room if the patient so desires?
12. Is a bell provided, so that he can call for service; or can ring when he has finished eating?
13. Is someone prepared to remove the tray as soon as notified? And has that person been instructed to avoid comments if he sees that only a small amount of food has been eaten?
14. Have arrangements been made for someone to check the amount of food the sick person has eaten? If the amount is small, will a nutritious beverage be served before the next meal?

Using role playing to demonstrate serving a tray

With a clearer picture in mind of what would be involved in serving the meals to the patients, the students completed their plans. Two students would deliver Martha's tray. Accompanying it would be only that portion of the check list which had to do with the food on the tray. Four other students — two at each home — would take the trays to David and Judy. One person would be in charge of the serving. The other would observe the procedure, checking to see how the points in the check list were being carried out.

In order to make the demonstrations at school as meaningful as possible, the students decided to use the technique of role playing. One section of the homemaking room was arranged as a sickroom. Three students volunteered to act as "Patients for the Day," and three more to serve the trays. After the trays had been served, the patients as well as the rest of the group would evaluate the experience by the check list.

Reporting on the experiences in serving a tray to a sick person

The students who had been at the homes of David and Judy reported that things went fairly well. The chicken and the vegetables, which they had wrapped in foil and transported in a thermabag, had remained hot. Judy was delighted with the crepe-paper doll's hat on her tray, and had cleaned her plate. Both Mrs. Crosley and Mrs. Jensen were pleased with the meals. They indicated that if any of the students needed further experience, they were welcome to come again. At the Davenport home, Cassie and Doris had talked with Martha over the phone on the sun porch. She had not completed her meal, but she told the girls that she would report to them later of her evaluation of the meal.

The comments on the meals at school were favorable for the most part. Fred, who had volunteered to be a patient, said that the potato was piping hot and delicious. His only criticism was that he didn't have enough to eat — a comment which did not come as a surprise, since everyone knew about Fred's fondness for food. One of the groups forgot to put a napkin on the tray and had to keep their patient waiting until one was supplied. However, everyone seemed to agree that tray service could be an agreeable way of eating a meal whether sick or well.

CLASS MEMO:

How will your class handle the problem of preparing and serving food to a sick person? If you plan to take the approach Miss Cameron's group took, what can you add to make the classwork more helpful?

LEARNING SOME SIMPLE THINGS TO DO
FOR A SICK PERSON

Now that the classwork seemed to be going so well, the students were anxious to begin their next goal — *learning some simple things to do for a sick person.* Miss Cameron smiled at their enthusiasm and gave the go-ahead signal.

As the students discussed the subject, they seemed to be primarily concerned with two aspects of the problem: (1) giving a patient the care needed to make him as comfortable and happy as possible, and (2) providing some suitable entertainment when the patient is convalescing, as in the case at present of David, Judy, and Martha. It was finally decided that the girls would work on the first part of the problem, and the boys on the second. Each group would give a report later on.

Giving a Patient the Care Needed to Make Him as Comfortable and Happy as Possible

The girls gave their report first. Dorothy opened the session by explaining that in many illnesses, unless hospitalization is necessary, the mother or an attendant takes care of the sick person. Since teen-agers living in the home are at school most of the day, whatever they do to help will have to be done in out-of-school hours. However, the group believed that young people

need to know what is expected of a home nurse. There may be occasions when they will be called upon to perform some of her duties.

Keeping this point in mind, the girls had used David's illness as the basis for their report. They had learned from Mrs. Crosley, David's mother, who had taken care of David, just what duties she had performed. Then consulting references as needed, they had worked out some simple things which a young person living in a similar home situation could do to help.

The report was presented in parts. Each part described a phase of David's illness, indicating Mrs. Crosley's duties at the time and showing what a teen-ager could do. Several girls took turns reading a description of Mrs. Crosley's situation. Others told what the young person might do and demonstrated some of the procedures.

In order to make the report as meaningful as possible to other classes, it is presented in condensed form on pages 231 to 234. The left-hand column concerns Mrs. Crosley's situation, the right-hand one that of the teen-ager. Other classes may be interested in learning some of the techniques demonstrated. Or different situations may require consulting references and learning other techniques.

WHEN AN ILLNESS OCCURS AT HOME

WHAT A HOME NURSE DOES

WHAT YOU CAN DO

David has had an exciting experience. He was badly shaken up when his car skidded off the road. It was late afternoon, and he was returning from Sackville after doing an errand for his father. The accident occurred on a back country road, and David had to walk nearly a mile to reach a telephone to call for help. By the time he arrived home, he was thoroughly exhausted and chilled. His teeth were chattering — he was so cold. The fact that David could walk seemed to indicate there were no broken bones. However, David had several sore spots and a small swelling where his head had hit the side of the car. While David was preparing for bed, he began to have a severe chill. Mrs. Crosley called Dr. Mead at once, knowing that it was unwise to give any treatment without a doctor's advice. Dr. Mead came over right away and examined David very carefully. He found no broken bones, but said that David should be kept warm and quiet. A hot-water bag should be put at his feet, and an ice cap on the swelling. Mrs. Crosley was to let Dr. Mead know how David was in the morning.

Stand by and be ready to cooperate.
Know how to fill a hot-water bag and an ice cap.

To fill a hot-water bag: Prepare the water to 115–130 degrees Fahrenheit in a container. A pitcher is the easiest to pour from. The water needs to be momentarily bearable to your clenched fist. If the bag is to be placed at the patient's feet, fill it about two-thirds full. For any other part of the body, it will need to be only one third full. If there is air in the top of the bag, rest the lower edge of the bag on a flat surface. Gradually lower the neck of the bag until the water comes almost to the top. This pushes out the air. Screw on the cap; wipe the bag dry, and test it for leakage. Then wrap the bag in a heavy towel, pinning the ends securely with safety pins. In order to be sure that the water is not too hot, see whether you are able to tolerate the covered bag against the inner side of your arm for half a minute. When this test proves satisfactory, carry the bag to the sickroom. Refill the bag when needed. When the patient has finished using the bag, empty it, and hang it upside down with the cap off until dry. Then blow air into the bag; replace the cap, and hang in a cool, dark place.

To fill an ice cap: Fill the cap about half full of ice, breaking cubes into small pieces. Pour water over ice to remove sharp edges. Place the cap on a flat surface in order to prevent air from entering. After wiping the edges of the rim dry, screw on the lid; test the cap for leaks, and wrap it in a towel. The towel prevents moisture from forming on the surface of the cap. Before storing the cap, empty the contents, and fill the cap with absorbent paper, replacing the paper until the inside of the cap is dry. Then fill the cap with air, or leave a little crushed paper inside to keep the sides from sticking together. After replacing the top, store the cap in a cool, dark place.

| WHAT A HOME NURSE DOES | WHAT YOU CAN DO |

During the night David began to have fever, and by morning it was quite high. Mrs. Crosley called the doctor, and he came over. He said that David was on the verge of pneumonia, but that he thought one of the new antibiotic drugs would be effective in preventing it. The swelling on David's head could mean a slight concussion, and even though it wasn't likely, there might be other internal injuries. The best thing to do was to keep David quiet for at least two weeks to see what developed. His temperature, pulse, and respiration rates were to be taken twice daily and reported to the doctor when he called. Necessary arrangements were then made for the medication to be given David as prescribed.

Learn to record a patient's temperature, pulse, and respiration rate.

(See pages 247–250 for how to take temperature, pulse, and respiration.)

Give medication as prescribed.

To give capsules or tablets: Be sure to give them exactly as prescribed — in the amount and at the hour indicated. A glass of water for swallowing the medicine, a spoon, a paper napkin for drying the lips, and the capsules or tablets are all that are needed on the medicine tray. Place the correct number on the spoon, and give them to the patient .from the spoon. If necessary, assist the patient to raise his head to swallow the medicine, holding the glass for him. Boil the glass and spoon if the patient has a contagious disease. Otherwise cleanse them for the next dose.

To give liquid medication: The medicine, a medicine glass, a spoon or a medicine dropper, a glass of water, and a paper napkin are needed on the medicine tray. Something to take away the taste, such as a cracker, a slice of orange, or fruit juice, may be included if the doctor permits it. Shake the medicine well if ordered, and remove the cap or cork, placing it topside down on the tray. Then pour the exact amount into the spoon. If drops are given, count out loud. Assist the patient to take the medicine. Cleanse the equipment used in preparation for the next dose.

Naturally Mrs. Crosley expected to give up some of her household duties while she was caring for David. Bathing a bed patient, seeing that he gets the prescribed medicine and diet, and caring for the sickroom is too much to add to an already full-time job. A nurse needs time to get rested, so that she can be calm and cheerful in the sickroom.

Suggest holding a family council to decide how much help each member of the family can contribute.

You can assist in planning and preparing the meals for the family and for the patient within the limits of your time.

Younger brothers and sisters can run errands and help wash and dry dishes. You can show them how to make their beds too.

Your father can plan to stay in the sickroom evenings, so that your mother can get some rest and recreation.

WHAT A HOME NURSE DOES	WHAT YOU CAN DO

The doctor also said that noise seemed to disturb a sick person and that everything needed to be kept as quiet as possible for a while.

Try to keep the neighborhood children from making too much noise.

Explain in a pleasant way that a sick person needs to rest quietly for a few days.

At first David was not permitted to have visitors, except members of the family. But people began to call on the telephone to find out how he was getting along.

Try to answer the telephone and give information about the illness when you are home.

Tell people pleasantly that the person is getting along as well as can be expected. Naturally you'll keep a list of those who telephone.

Several people sent flowers to David, and there was an avalanche of get-well cards. Mrs. Crosley took in a few at a time — some going on the tray at mealtime or when between-meal beverages were served.

Take care of any flowers that are sent in.

Be sure to write on the cards the kind of flowers sent. Save the cards for the sick person to acknowledge later on. Every day you'll need to change the water in the containers, cut the stems, and discard the faded blooms.

It wasn't long before David's fever was gone. No concussion and no other internal complications developed. Even before he was allowed to sit up, David began to listen to some of the programs on the radio.

Get a daily or weekly schedule of the radio programs with the time and stations they are on.

Put the schedule within easy reach of the patient where he or someone else can check on the programs.

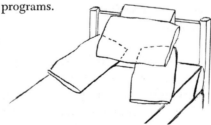

After a while, David was permitted to sit up in bed. He was beginning to take more interest in what was going on. In the evenings, Mr. Crosley discussed sports events with him or told him about incidents that happened at the office. David also showed an interest in his personal appearance. Everyone said that was a sure sign that he was getting better.

Help the patient sit up in bed.

To do this: Use a back rest (see page 213), 2 to 5 large pillows, a small pillow, and a foot support. Slant the surface of the back rest toward the patient. Adjust three pillows as shown in the illustration on this page. Use two large pillows for arm support if needed. Place the small pillow under the knees. Use foot support for upright feet to brace against and to hold the covers off the toes.

WHAT A HOME NURSE DOES	WHAT YOU CAN DO
Mrs. Crosley had brushed David's hair when he was very ill. She had lifted his head slightly and covered the pillow with a towel. She said it was very important to keep a sick person's hair in good condition. Now David was able to brush his own hair.	*Assist the patient in caring for his hair.* Bring him his comb, brush, and a mirror when he is able to brush his own hair. *Keep his comb and brush clean.* Use a soap powder in warm water, and clean the comb teeth and the brush bristles with a discarded toothbrush. Rinse thoroughly. Put both the comb and the brush in the sun to dry. *Assist the patient with the care of his nails.* (See Book 1, pages 18–20 for care of hands and nails.)
As the days went by, David became more like his old self again, gay and cheerful. The doctor said he could now have visitors. It was not long before he was well on the road to recovery.	*Get the names of several friends whom the patient enjoys seeing, and call them on the telephone when visitors are allowed.* Suggest to them that they may want to drop in now that visitors are permitted. Plan other forms of entertainment for him.

What the Boys Suggested for Sickroom Entertainment

The boys had listened carefully to the report given by the girls. Now they were eager to report how their own plans were working out. First of all, they said that they had consulted some references on how to keep a sick person entertained during convalescence or prolonged illness. They had learned that during an illness certain parts of the body may become weakened temporarily. This is often true of the muscles and the eyes. Therefore, it is essential for the patient to avoid fatigue and eyestrain.

There seemed to be so much important information on the subject that the boys decided to summarize their findings. This would give the other members of the class a better understanding of the basis on which they had selected their entertainment for Martha, Judy, and David. They had typed the information on cards, which they distributed to everyone in the class. A copy of the card which the boys prepared is given on the next page.

POINTERS FOR SICKROOM ENTERTAINMENT

- Try to direct the sick person's thoughts from himself and his sickness. Help him to be cheerful and happy by planning entertainment based on his age, interests, and strength.

- In early convalescence, occupations that are entertaining but require little mental and physical effort are advisable.

- As convalescence progresses, a variety of recreations can be planned, but only one at a time carried out. Too much stimulation produces fatigue.

- Occupations which require large and heavy materials need to be avoided, since illness generally weakens the muscles. Discourage too much close work, such as reading, sewing, or crocheting, because of the eyes' weakened condition.

- Plan to have only a few small articles on the bed or bedside table. Too many materials around cause confusion and fatigue. Arrange for storage space within easy reach.

- Plan some listening entertainment, such as radio programs and reading aloud. But limit these activities to no longer than thirty minutes for young people and adults, and less for children.

- If possible, move the bed so that the sick person can look outdoors sometime during the day. Arrange special activities which children may enjoy, such as watching others feed the birds, or make a snowman in winter. Older people will get pleasure from seeing the trees or watching other outdoor life.

- Having live pets, such as a cat or a dog, in the sickroom is not advisable, because they may carry disease germs to the patient. A sick person has low resistance to other diseases. In the case of a communicable disease, there is danger of the pets carrying germs to other people.

- Provide some entertainment that can be carried out by the sick person himself and some that may be shared with one other person. Group activities are likely to be too fatiguing.

What the boys planned for Martha

Martha's situation seemed to call for more ingenuity than the others, since visitors were excluded from the sickroom. But each boy in the class agreed to assume responsibility for carrying out one idea. If the entertainment involved reading, Martha would be guided by the doctor's advice. When it seemed advisable, Mrs. Adams, the practical nurse caring for Martha, would read to her. The line-up of some of the activities looked something like this:

KEEPING UP WITH THE HOMEMAKING CLASS: Bob, who was taking typing, was to give a brief day-to-day account of the happenings in the homemaking class. At first the reports would be very general. But later on when Martha was stronger, he planned to give her a review of the classwork they were doing.

KEEPING UP WITH THE OUTSIDE WORLD: John's activity was to read the newspapers and to clip articles that might interest Martha. News events, styles, household hints, and advice to the lovelorn were some of the items he planned to use.

KEEPING UP WITH THE MOVIES: Phil had learned from one of Martha's chums that she was a movie fan. He therefore planned to attend several movies that Martha had not seen and then to relay the stories to her in the form of brief reviews. The boys knew that Phil had a droll sense of humor, and they anticipated some laughable reviews.

WRITING AND ILLUSTRATING JINGLES: Bertram had a reputation for composing humorous and appropriate jingles for all occasions. He planned to prepare a supply in advance, so that one could be sent up each evening on Martha's tray. He said that he expected to illustrate some of the jingles with stick figures.

PLANNING TRAY DECORATIONS: Harry planned to make an assortment of decorations, one to go on Martha's tray for each luncheon. He was using construction paper and colorful cutouts from an old mail-order catalogue.

MAKING A BIOGRAPHICAL SCRAPBOOK: Fred's activity was a scrapbook to be based on a series of first events, such as the first tooth, the first day at school, and the first date in Martha's life. The supplies he needed included

brown wrapping paper, colored twine, old magazines, scissors, and paste. He planned to make the material going into the book as humorous and colorful as possible.

Get-well Fun for Judy

The boys were a little puzzled to know just what to do for Judy. They consulted reference books in the children's room at the public library and asked several mothers with ten-year-olds what they would recommend. Then they coordinated this information and came up with a novel idea, which made an instant appeal to Mrs. Jensen. Even though the activities involved some eye work, the doctor said that Judy could now undertake them for short periods.

They called the idea "Fun Boxes for Judy." Each boy assembled various articles and put them in a colorful box. The articles were collected from various sources and involved little or no expense. The use for which they were intended was put on the cover of the box. When the boxes were lined up, some of them looked like the following.

FUN BOXES FOR JUDY

For making jigsaw puzzles: Colorful postcards, old Christmas cards, and cutouts from magazines, made firm by being pasted on cardboard—to be cut into simple pieces

For making or trimming doll clothes: Scraps of cloth and felt, pieces of lace and ribbon, bits of trimming

For making animals and birds: Shells, corks of different sizes, small cones, pipe cleaners, colored toothpicks, walnut-shell halves, bird feathers, empty spools, colored yarn

For making stuffed dolls: Old socks and stockings, cotton batting, heavy embroidery thread, bits of colored yarn

For making novelty jewelry: Acorns and grains of dried Indian corn, macaroni in different shapes and sizes, scraps of bright colored material, odd buttons

For staple supplies: Blunt scissors, heavy needles, pins, string, paste, crayons, paper clips, small stapler

For making decorative plates: Plain paper plates of different sizes, construction paper, flower catalogue

How the boys contributed toward David's entertainment

It was a little difficult at first to know what to do for David, because he seemed to have everything he needed to make his convalescence pleasant. He had a radio, various books and magazines, and apparently all the hobby equipment he wanted. His special friends dropped in from time to time and kept him posted on current happenings.

However, as the boys studied the situation they realized that sometimes the less obvious ways of contributing toward a convalescent's entertainment are neglected. They planned, therefore, to do three things for David, and set up a schedule for carrying them out.

1. To deliver a copy of the school paper to him as soon as it comes out

2. To arrange with several of the girls in David's class to write him cheer notes

3. To do errands for him, such as mailing letters, getting books from the library, or buying magazines

CLASS MEMO:

What ways, other than those suggested by Miss Cameron's class, can you offer for making a sick person comfortable and happy?

GIVING PROMPT ATTENTION TO ANY SYMPTOMS OF ILLNESS

ONE day when the classwork on learning some simple things to do for a sick person was drawing to a close, the students noticed a new bulletin-board display. Stick figures were so arranged as to give prominence to a cutout from a popular teen-age magazine. The clipping featured information on giving prompt attention to early symptoms of illness.

"What a clever way to introduce a new problem," said Bob. "I wonder whose idea it was."

"There's only one person around here who can draw stick figures like that," replied Dorothy, looking toward Bertram.

Bertram hesitated and then admitted that he and Miss Cameron had worked out the details together. "While I was illustrating the jingles for Martha's tray, the idea came to me," he said.

*Using a Bulletin-Board Display
as the Basis for Classwork*

"I don't see why we can't use the information on the clipping for the basis of our classwork," said Carol who had been examining the display very carefully. "It seems to include some of the things we need to know about early symptoms of illness."

As the other members of the class studied the clipping, they too agreed with Carol. After a lively discussion, they decided to see how they could apply each item in the clipping to their goal — *giving prompt attention to any symptoms of illness.*

Since other classes may find the information on the clipping helpful, a copy as it appeared on the bulletin board is reproduced below.

BE WISE

GIVE PROMPT ATTENTION TO EARLY

SYMPTOMS OF ILLNESS

BE FAMILIAR WITH SYMPTOMS OF ILLNESS: They give important information on how the body is functioning.

KNOW WHAT TO DO WHEN SYMPTOMS OCCUR: Eat food that is easily digested; get plenty of rest; keep away from other people, especially children.

KNOW WHEN TO CALL A DOCTOR: Let only the doctor diagnose your illness and prescribe medication and treatment.

LEARN HOW TO MEASURE THE CARDINAL SYMPTOMS OF ILLNESS: Temperature, pulse, and respiration rates give important information about how the body is functioning.

Becoming Familiar with Some of the Symptoms of Illness

It so happened that a week end intervened before the students could start their classwork on symptoms of illness. During that period everyone agreed to find out as much as possible about the subject, either through reference materials or other sources.

At the next meeting of the class there was no difficulty in offering various symptoms that might indicate illness. Nearly everyone was able to recall personal experiences of their own or those in their families. The students who had been in contact with the homes of the three patients mentioned the symptoms which had occurred when Judy and Martha became ill and when David almost had pneumonia.

During the discussion, Miss Cameron pointed out that some signs of illness can be detected only by scientific apparatus used by a doctor or a laboratory technician. Furthermore, a doctor sometimes depends as much on the absence of certain signs as on the presence of others. However, for all practical purposes, the students would find it very helpful to be able to recognize a few of the most common symptoms.

The class then decided to make a list of these symptoms. Such a list would include some that were evident to the sufferer, and others evident to an observer.

After the list had been assembled, Phil surprised the group by showing them a poster. In scouting

around for information, he had seen the poster in the office of the school nurse. She had used it with groups of parents and teachers in helping them recognize signs of illness.

"I just thought I'd wait and see how the symptoms we mentioned compared with those on the poster," he explained, holding it up for the class to see.

As the students studied the poster, they found that practically the same symptoms were mentioned as those in their list. Since the poster presents a more graphic picture than the students' list, it is reproduced on page 241.

Knowing What to Do When Symptoms Occur

One of the suggestions offered in the bulletin-board display under knowing what to do when symptoms occur (page 239) was to "eat food that is easily digested." But since diets for a sick person had already been a part of their recent classwork (see pages 222–229), the students believed they were well enough informed to carry out this advice without further study. They therefore decided to concentrate on the other points — getting plenty of rest and sleep, and keeping away from other people.

Getting plenty of rest and sleep

Few, if any of the students, questioned the value of rest and sleep when early symptoms of illness appear. They realized that sleep especially is nature's great restorative. It

COMMON SYMPTOMS OF ILLNESS

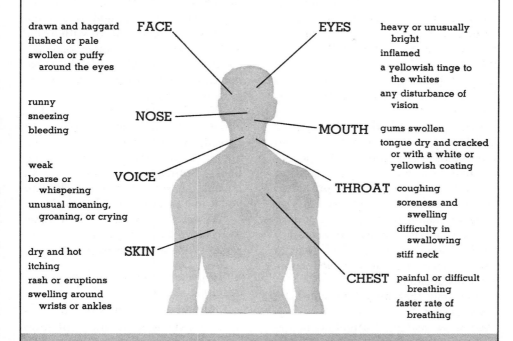

FACE
drawn and haggard
flushed or pale
swollen or puffy
   around the eyes

EYES
heavy or unusually
   bright
inflamed
a yellowish tinge to
   the whites
any disturbance of
   vision

NOSE
runny
sneezing
bleeding

MOUTH
gums swollen
tongue dry and cracked
   or with a white or
   yellowish coating

VOICE
weak
hoarse or
   whispering
unusual moaning,
   groaning, or crying

THROAT
coughing
soreness and
   swelling
difficulty in
   swallowing
stiff neck

SKIN
dry and hot
itching
rash or eruptions
swelling around
   wrists or ankles

CHEST
painful or difficult
   breathing
faster rate of
   breathing

OTHER DISTURBANCES

continued loss of appetite and weight

unusual thirst

headache or severe pain in some other part of the body

soreness in a joint in children following
a throat or chest infection

a general feeling of weakness and discomfort

nausea and vomiting

feeling chilly alternating with feeling hot

diarrhea

is necessary in health for body repair after a day's wear and tear. In illness, recovery may depend as much upon sleep as upon medicine.

In recalling personal experiences, Doris mentioned Martha's situation when she first became ill. Martha remained in bed and was not permitted to have visitors. Later on the doctor said that having plenty of rest and sleep at the beginning of her illness had helped to lessen the attack of scarlet fever.

Laura reported that Mrs. Jensen had kept Judy in bed and had called the doctor when Judy complained of soreness in a joint a week or so after she had a sore throat. This proved to be wise, since an early diagnosis in cases of rheumatic fever is important in order to spare the heart unnecessary work. David, of course, had gone to bed at once after he returned home from his accident.

Bob said that he might not have been absent from school (see page 202) if he had paid attention to the early symptoms of his cold. But instead of remaining quietly at home, he had attended a party. "I hated to miss the affair," he commented. "But I know now that I'd have been better off resting in bed."

Other students reported similar experiences. All in all there was a general agreement that getting adequate rest and sleep when early symptoms of illness appear will pay dividends in the long run.

Why keeping away from other people is important

In discussing the advice — to keep away from other people when symptoms of illness appear — one reason stood out above all others. *It is a precaution against the spread of contagious diseases.*

"Miss Chase told us that contagious diseases are generally most catching during the early stages," said Cassie. "Mrs. Davenport thought at first that Martha was coming down with a cold, and she did not want other people to get it. Even though scarlet fever had not developed, this precaution would have been wise."

"We also talked to Miss Chase about how contagious diseases are spread," added Jane. "I read more about it in some of our reference books, and made notes in case we discussed the subject in class. Perhaps you'd like to hear what I took down."

"We certainly would." "Of course," were heard throughout the room. Her remarks are given on page 243.

How to prevent the spread of contagious diseases

Spurred on by Jane's remarks, the students decided to find out more about the spread of contagious diseases. They already had learned about the precautions generally prescribed for taking care of a person with a communicable disease. (See page 219.) Now they believed it might be worth while to see what they themselves could do to prevent contagious diseases from spreading.

After checking various references, they set up the following guides:

1. In case of epidemics stay away from crowds. Avoid people who cough or sneeze carelessly.

2. Protect others by covering your mouth

and nose when you cough. If you have a cold, use paper tissues or soft clean rags that may be used once and then tucked into a paper bag and destroyed.

3. Wash your hands thoroughly with soap and water before eating, before preparing food, after handling contaminated articles, after going to the toilet, and after handling pets.

4. Keep your fingers away from your mouth, hands, and eyes. Keep articles, such as pencils, pens, pins, and money out of your mouth.

5. Use only your own toilet articles and personal belongings, such as towels, washcloths, toothbrush, hairbrush, and comb.

6. Use only eating and drinking utensils which have been washed in soap and hot water and rinsed with boiling water.

7. Use drinking water, milk, and other food supplies that are believed to be safe. Frequent only those restaurants and food stores which have a reputation for the sanitary handling of food.

8. Obtain from your doctor those immunizations that are available to protect you from diseases to which you may be exposed.

HOW CONTAGIOUS DISEASES ARE SPREAD
[as related by Jane]

"Most contagious diseases are spread by living germs or viruses that enter the body by way of the mouth or nose. In talking, laughing, sneezing, or coughing, tiny drops of moisture are sprayed in the air. If a person has a cold, or an infection of the nose, throat, or lungs, this spray contains germs. A well person nearby may breathe in the germs or take them in by mouth, and thus catch the disease.

"Germs are also spread by dirt and dust brought into the home from the outside. The dust and dirt containing germs settle on the rugs, cushions, and upholstered furniture. Unless the germs are removed by cleaning, they become a health hazard.

"Disease germs are also spread by handling objects used by people infected with contagious germs. Germs picked up by handling infected objects may be carried on the fingers to the mouth, or on food which the fingers have touched. Some people may be infected with disease germs but not be ill themselves. They are called 'carriers.' Their infectious droplets cause others to become sick even though they themselves remain well.

"Some diseases are spread by contaminated water, milk, or other foods. When a communicable disease appears in a community, the health authorities will generally investigate these sources as well as others."

Knowing When to Call a Doctor

It so happened that while the students were discussing symptoms of illness, Dr. Barton was making his monthly inspection of the school. Miss Cameron had met him in the cafeteria and had told him about the classwork the students were doing. He was so interested that he said he would stop in and talk with the students.

Needless to say, everyone was pleased to see him. Bertram showed him the bulletin-board display and the poster concerning symptoms of illness. He said that he and the other students would appreciate a doctor's point of view on the subjects they were about to discuss. These were when to call a doctor,

and why only a doctor should prescribe medication and treatment.

Dr. Barton nodded and said that he would be glad to make a few comments. His remarks on the two subjects as recorded by John, in shorthand and then transcribed, follow:

Calling a doctor

"When to call a doctor is a difficult question to answer, because no two people react to illness in the same way. Some people think they need a doctor for any slight pain or upset. Others wait a few hours to see what develops. Some wait too long.

"When a combination of severe and unusual symptoms appear suddenly, there is generally no question about calling a doctor immediately. Some of these include severe sore throat; vomiting; diarrhea; stiffness or swelling and soreness in the arms, legs, back, or neck; and a high temperature. A fever in itself need not be considered an emergency. It is not necessary to call the doctor in the middle of the night unless the fever is accompanied by other symptoms, such as a severe chill, or severe pain. Nausea after a late party, or a strenuous week end may be the result of overeating or overexertion. It may disappear after a few hours and not necessitate a visit by the doctor.

"When young children show symptoms of illness, it is important for a doctor to know the nature of the illness as soon as possible. Early medical treatment is usually the most effective. And in the case of a communicable disease, a doctor's advice is needed for protecting the patient as well as others in the family.

"Probably the best general advice as to when to call a doctor is this. Whatever procedure gives the most peace of mind and satisfaction to the person responsible for calling a doctor needs to be the primary consideration. However, good judgment based on the prompt attention to early signs or sudden symptoms of illness needs to be acquired. This is built up by experience and by developing confidence and knowledge in dealing with illness."

Why only a doctor should diagnose an illness and prescribe medication and treatment

"In reference to diagnosing an illness, and prescribing medication and treatment, there is one good reason why only a doctor should do these things. He is trained to evaluate symptoms, to make a diagnosis, and to decide what needs to be done. Let me explain this more fully, so that you can see why the judgment of an experienced physician is needed.

"You all know that a symptom is a warning that something is physically wrong. Many of you have doubtless experienced a toothache, which tells you that something is probably wrong with a tooth.

"But not all symptoms are as simple as this. For example, take a headache. The pain does not mean there is necessarily anything wrong with your head. The ache may be due to fatigue, to an upset stomach, to the beginning of a severe illness, or to other causes. Some pain symptoms give little indication of the source of the trouble. Pain from certain heart conditions may sometimes be felt in the arms and fingers. And indigestion is frequently felt as pain in the region of the heart.

"When a doctor is called in, he wants to get as accurate and complete a picture as possible. The patient, or someone acting for him, can help the doctor by giving him certain information:

1. The complaints of the patient
2. The degree of severity of the pain if any
   a. Whether it is a dull ache, an acute or a stabbing pain
   b. Its duration — does it come and go, or is it constant?
   c. When it started
   d. Its location
   e. Whether it is influenced by something, such as eating, or the position of the body
3. The temperature and sometimes the pulse and respiration rates
4. If there is bleeding, its location, color, and amount
5. What if any treatment has been given before the doctor's arrival

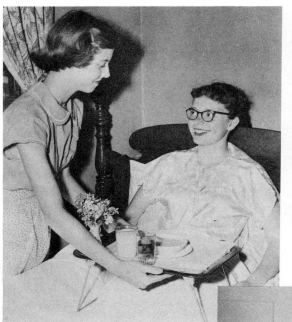

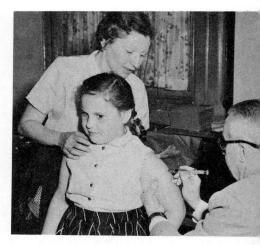

Here a little girl gets polio vaccine for protection against this disease.

Rest in bed and easily digested food will hasten this patient's recovery.

Using your own toilet articles, such as towels, washcloths, and toothbrush, helps to reduce the chance of contagion.

Using your own comb and brush are also good preventive measures.

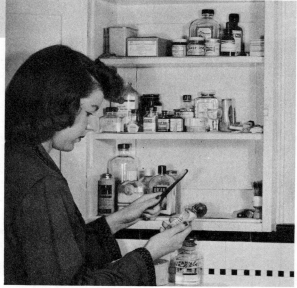

Scalding dishes after they are washed in soapy water helps to assure health.

"The doctor then notes other symptoms, which the sick person may not be aware of," continued Dr. Barton. "As I said before, he knows that people differ in their reactions to illness. Some are likely to exaggerate every little pain or ache, while others minimize any discomfort. He checks the temperature, pulse, and respiration rates. He takes into consideration whether home remedies or patent medicines have been given before his arrival, knowing they may disguise some of the symptoms and perhaps delay a diagnosis. He reviews and weighs all this information as he considers the total picture.

"From what I have said you can see, I am sure, why it is difficult — and even unwise — for an untrained person to evaluate so many complicated factors. Everyone needs to learn to recognize symptoms of illness. But it is best to let your doctor diagnose these symptoms, and prescribe medication and treatment."

The students thanked Dr. Barton for his helpful remarks and indicated they would make every effort to follow his advice.

Learning About the Cardinal Symptoms of Illness

Dr. Barton's remarks about the importance of the cardinal symptoms of illness coincided with the last suggestion on the bulletin-board display. Now the students were ready to learn about temperature, pulse, and respiration rates. By consulting reference materials, they learned the following facts about these cardinal symptoms:

- A normal mouth temperature is 98.6°F., but may vary from 97.6°F. to 99.0°F. and still be normal for certain people. When a temperature is above normal, it is usually caused by disease germs in the body. Fever is nature's way of providing an environment unfavorable to the germs.

- A temperature below normal may be expected when a person is recovering from an illness. This need not cause alarm unless there are other severe symptoms. It may simply mean that the person has not yet returned to normal health, and requires a period of convalescence.

- The pulse is the throbbing of the arteries caused by the contracting of the heart. It indicates the condition of the heart and the blood vessels, and is an important symptom in conjunction with temperature and respiration. The beat will differ in individuals, depending on their age, their activities, their physical condition, and other factors. The rate is more rapid when sitting than when lying, and is increased by standing, walking, or running. It is slower when one is asleep. The normal pulse — when a person is quiet — is about 65 to 70 beats a minute for men, and for women about 75 to 80 beats a minute.

- An untrained person can count the pulse. But it requires the experience of someone like a doctor to recognize the quality, the force, and the rhythm, and to know what kind of a pulse it is.

- Respiration is the inhaling of oxygen and the exhaling of carbon dioxide — one breath taken in, and one breathed out. It goes on continually and unconsciously with about one respiration for every four heartbeats.

- The respiration rate varies in men and women, in children, and in infants. For men the rate in one minute is 14 to 18 respirations, for women 18 to 20, for children 20 to 26, and for infants 30 to 38. The number of respirations per minute increases with strenuous exercise, nervousness, strong emotions, high body temperature, high altitude, and obstruction of the air passage.

A *small jar of warm soapy water*

A *glass of clean cold water*

Learning to Take Temperature, Pulse, and Respiration Rates

During the class discussion on cardinal symptoms, it was suggested that Miss Chase, the school nurse, might be willing to demonstrate to the class how to check temperature, pulse, and respiration rates. Bertram said that he would be glad to ask her. Miss Chase accepted, and the necessary arrangements were made. When the day arrived, the students waited eagerly for her to begin.

A *covered jar containing cotton*

A *container for waste*

Equipment needed for taking the temperature by mouth

On a small table in front of the class, the equipment generally used for taking a person's temperature was displayed. Miss Chase called the students' attention to the following articles:

A *watch with a second hand*

A clinical thermometer

Removing the thermometer from its case, Miss Chase explained that it must be handled very carefully, since it is delicate and breaks easily. It should always be held by the top tip, should never be put in hot water, and should always be kept in the case when not in use. She then passed the thermometer around for inspection.

The students saw a small glass tube containing a column of mercury ending in a bulb. The tube was divided into degrees and tenths of degrees from 94 degrees Fahrenheit to 107 degrees Fahrenheit. When the thermometer is put into the mouth, the mercury expands through the hollow shaft and will remain at the point reached until shaken down.

Cleaning the thermometer

Before and after taking the temperature, the thermometer should be cleaned. Miss Chase demonstrated this procedure as she gave the following directions:

1. Moisten a piece of cotton in the warm soapy water. Working from the tip down, twist the cotton back and forth around the thermometer, so that the entire surface is cleaned. Discard the cotton in the waste container.
2. Rinse the thermometer in the clean cold water, and wipe dry with another piece of cotton. Discard the cotton.

Taking the temperature

Asking Cassie to act as the patient, Miss Chase then demonstrated the following procedures for taking the temperature.

1. With the thumb and first two fingers, grasp the thermometer firmly at the tip. Then give a quick downward jerk of the arm as though you were snapping a whip. This should bring the mercury down to 95.0°F. or lower.
2. Insert the bulb under the tongue, slightly to one side with the tip coming out at the corner of the lips. Have the patient close the lips, but not the teeth, tightly to prevent air from entering the mouth. Leave the ther-

mometer in this position at least three minutes.
3. Remove the thermometer, holding the tip horizontally between the thumb and first finger. Rotate it slowly until you can see what the bar of mercury registers.
4. Clean the thermometer, and replace it in the case.

What to do if the thermometer breaks in the mouth

Harry then asked what to do if a thermometer breaks while a temperature is being taken.

"That's a good question," replied Miss Chase. "I usually caution people not to bite the thermometer, but sometimes they do, despite this advice. However, if it should break, have the person rinse the mouth with plenty of water to wash out all the mercury and particles of glass. Report the matter to the doctor at once. He may want to order an antidote for the mercury, such as the white of an egg. If tiny particles of glass have been swallowed, a piece of bread eaten at once may help to protect the lining of the food canal."

How to check the pulse and respiration

A demonstration of checking the pulse, with Phil as the patient, was then given. Miss Chase said that the pulse may be felt at points on the body where the arteries are just under the skin and over a bone. The wrist at the thumb side is usually used. The rate is generally taken at the same time as the temperature and in the following way:

1. Have the person sit or lie down in a relaxed position. With the watch in

the left hand, place the first and second fingers of the right hand on the inner surface of the wrist just at the base of the thumb. Press just hard enough to feel the rhythmic beats.

2. Count for 30 seconds; stop for a few seconds, and then count for another half minute. Add the two counts to find the rate per minute. If the variation between the two half-minute counts is great, make a recount.

Miss Chase said that she had observed Phil's respiration immediately following the counting of the pulse and while her fingers were still on the pulse. In this way a patient is less likely to be aware that the count is being made and to change his rate of breathing. Phil's count was normal for a man — about 14 to 18 respirations a minute (see page 248). She then said that the count is taken as follows:

1. Observe the rise and fall of the chest. Count for one full minute each rise.

2. Note any unusual condition in breathing.

Practicing Taking Temperature, Pulse, and Respiration Rates

After thanking Miss Chase for the helpful demonstrations, the students were anxious to practice what they had just learned. Miss Chase said that she would leave some extra thermometers. There were several already in the homemaking room, as well as other supplies that would be needed. Some of the students had watches with second hands. Miss Chase added that Miss Cameron was fully capable of supervising the practice.

The students then took each other's temperatures and pulse rates. Those who so desired measured respiration also. One feature of their practice was walking briskly around the room and then counting the pulse and respiration rates. It was interesting to see how this exercise changed the rates.

Impressing Others with the Necessity for Giving Prompt Attention to Early Symptoms of Illness

Later on when the students were reviewing their recent classwork, Bob raised an interesting question. "We all know how important it is to give prompt attention to early symptoms of illness," he said. "But there are some people — and I'm afraid that I have been one of them — who seem to ignore good advice. They hate to take time off to rest, or they simply can't miss that week-end party. Isn't there some way we can impress people with the necessity for taking prompt action when they feel an illness coming on?"

Everyone agreed with Bob that something needed to be done. Right now seemed an especially good time to stress the matter, since colds and other minor illnesses were still prevalent at school. After a lively discussion, the following plan was developed and carried out with the enthusiastic endorsement of the principal.

The bulletin-board display "Be Wise — Give Prompt Attention to Early Symptoms of Illness" (see page 239) was moved to a school

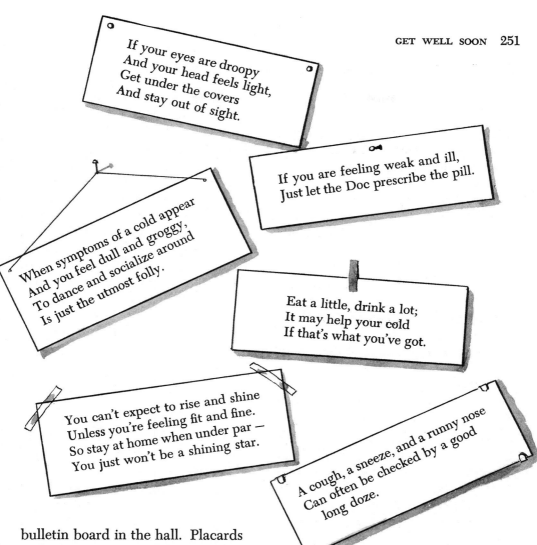

If your eyes are droopy
And your head feels light,
Get under the covers
And stay out of sight.

If you are feeling weak and ill,
Just let the Doc prescribe the pill.

When symptoms of a cold appear
And you feel dull and groggy,
To dance and socialize around
Is just the utmost folly.

Eat a little, drink a lot;
It may help your cold
If that's what you've got.

You can't expect to rise and shine
Unless you're feeling fit and fine.
So stay at home when under par —
You just won't be a shining star.

A cough, a sneeze, and a runny nose
Can often be checked by a good
long doze.

bulletin board in the hall. Placards with appropriate jingles, written by the students, were also posted in various places throughout the school — in the corridors, the library, the homerooms, the clubrooms, and the assembly hall. In fact it seemed that no matter where you looked, your eyes fell upon a jingle, such as shown above.

"Our plan is bound to produce some results," said Bob after the last placard had been posted, "even if it's just among ourselves. You see, each of us will have to live up to the advice we are giving others."

CLASS MEMO:
What plan can you make for doing something effective about early symptoms of illness?

PLANNING YOUR CLASSWORK

You have seen how Miss Cameron's class planned and carried out their classwork on illness. Many of their experiences centered around three young people who were recovering from different illnesses. The students tried to find ways in which they could be helpful. Learning about the care of a sickroom, and how to plan, prepare, and serve tray meals to a sick person were included in the classwork. Making a sick person more comfortable and happy also seemed important to the group. At the same time they believed that it was essential to be able to recognize and to give prompt attention to symptoms of illness. In this way they could protect themselves and others from infectious diseases.

Of course your class may want to stress different aspects of illness. But basically the problems which result from most illnesses are much the same no matter how you approach them. Whatever you learn along these lines will give you a personal feeling of security and satisfaction in being able to help others as well as your family and yourself.

SUGGESTED EXPERIENCES

Since the problems of illness are extensive, you and your class may welcome a few suggestions. Some of the following experiences may be adapted to the classwork which your group is working out.

1. Each student may find it helpful to consider an imaginary situation which might occur in his or her home. Such a situation might be that of a young brother or sister with the measles, or a mother in bed with a virus infection, or a father recovering from an operation, or a grandmother confined to her room. The student can then describe what he or she would do about one or more of the following problems: (a) caring for the sickroom, (b) having a suitable diet for the sick person, and (c) making the sick person comfortable and happy. The class can react to the ideas given and offer additional suggestions.

2. A panel discussion with well-informed people is generally a worth-while experience. Such a panel could include the school doctor, the school nurse or a visiting nurse, a parent, and a student acting as moderator. Each person can outline what he or she does to help keep others well, and to prevent the spread of infectious diseases. Parents and others may be invited to attend the session.

3. Visiting a convalescent and if possible taking something to break the monotony of his day may be a very satisfying experience. Students can report to the class their reactions and those of the convalescent.

4. A worth-while experience might be for each student to list any new words encountered in reference materials on illness. The words could be briefly defined, and the definitions put on the blackboard, so that each person could check his or her understanding of them.

5. The class may set up a schedule of spare-time appointments for members who feel they need more practice in making an occupied bed. Two students can work together, taking turns at making the bed and acting as the patient. Experienced students can volunteer to supervise the practice at school. Additional practice can be carried on at home as long as a student believes it is necessary.

6. Members of your class may find it interesting to arrange a mock or live television program demonstrating ways of making a sick person's tray attractive.

7. With the cooperation of the science department, the class can make cultures showing the presence of bacteria on doorknobs, dishes, and other surfaces. The cultures could then be compared with those made from washed and scalded articles.

8. Members of the class can interview three people who have been ill to find out what might have been done to make their illnesses pass more quickly and pleasantly. The best ideas from these people, along with any others found in magazine articles or other source materials, can be kept in a small scrapbook for future class reference. Additional ideas can be put in the book from time to time.

9. Several students in the class can work out ideas for an article for the school paper on suggestions of what young people can do for their friends when they are ill.

10. An interesting class project would be to assemble "Fun Boxes" (see page 237) for the children's ward in your community hospital.

11. Your class may want to put on a program for the Parent–Teacher Association stressing the importance of giving prompt attention to early symptoms of illness. A playlet or a filmstrip may be used to bring out the main points. Slogans printed on cards and placed around the room may add variety to the program. Examples of such slogans are:

STAY AT HOME — YOU CAN'T BE YOUR BEST WITH A COLD IN YOUR HEAD AND A COUGH IN YOUR CHEST.

A MISGUIDED MISSILE — A PERSON SNEEZING IN A CROWDED ROOM

A SIMPLE RECIPE FOR EARLY SYMPTOMS OF ILLNESS — LIGHT EATING, JUICE DRINKING, MUCH SLEEPING

PATENT MEDICINES MAY BRING RELIEF TO PAIN, BUT WITH A DOCTOR'S DIAGNOSIS, THEY MAY RAISE CAIN.

12. Your class might plan and carry out an "I Can Do It Now Session" for demonstrating ability to take temperature, pulse, and respiration rates. Three first-aid stations, each representing one of these techniques, can be set up in different sections of the homemaking room. Students who already know how to take these rates accurately can be in charge of the stations. The other members of the class can be given check sheets. Then they

can go to each station and demonstrate how well they are able to do the three procedures. Each student can evaluate his or her own performance, and decide with the person in charge of the station whether further practice is needed. When it is believed that the rates can be taken accurately, the sentence "I can do it now" on the sheet is checked.

13. Your class may want to plan a "Do and Don't Pantomime Program," showing ways infectious germs may be spread in a home. Small groups could portray such situations as the following:

EXAMPLE 1:

The Don'ts — using a common towel in the kitchen or bathroom

The Do's — having a handy roll of paper towels

EXAMPLE 2:

The Don'ts — using a common drinking glass in the kitchen or bathroom

The Do's — having a supply of small glasses or paper cups available. Glasses can be set aside after being used, and scalded later with the meal dishes. The paper cups can be discarded in a container.

EXAMPLE 3:

The Don'ts — tasting the baby's food, and then feeding him with the same spoon

The Do's — putting aside the spoon used to taste the baby's food, and getting a clean spoon

14. Each member of the class can report desirable and undesirable practices they have observed in the handling of food by clerks and waitresses.

15. Several members of your group might volunteer to investigate health regulations in your community. They could report on the facilities and services rendered for handling milk and food, for disposal of garbage, and for controlling communicable disease. A discussion might bring out ideas for further improvement in protecting the health of the community.

16. The class may discuss the following statement and explain what it might mean with reference to an illness: "Leisure is priceless, perhaps because we have it so seldom. When it comes our way, we are generally unprepared to use it to its fullest advantage."

Rooms for Happier Living

Making the living area at home meet the
family's needs and desires

Learning ways to improve the living area

Planning storage solutions

Cleaning easily and effectively

I T WAS MISS RAND's opening remarks to her homemaking students that started the class discussion on living rooms.

"I've been wondering whether you and any members of your family have heard about the model-room exhibits that are to be held at Hathaway's furniture store," she said.

"My mother and I read the advance announcement," replied Dorothy. "We thought it sounded very interesting. Mother said that perhaps we could get some ideas for our new recreation room."

"That's what I had in mind," continued Miss Rand. "I believe that we too could get some assistance in the classwork we have planned on improving our homes."

Miss Rand then went on to explain that Hathaway's store was sponsoring a series of room exhibits. Miss Vandermeer, an interior decorator well known throughout the country, had been engaged to supervise them. The exhibits would be open to anyone who cared to attend. Miss Vandermeer, herself, would be available for consultation on problems connected with home improvement.

"What a wonderful opportunity to get some expert advice," said Virginia. "I, for one, believe we need to take advantage of it."

There were nods of agreement throughout the room.

SETTING UP CLASS GOALS

In their preliminary planning the students had decided to focus their classwork on the living area of their homes. By "living area" they meant that part of the house not used primarily for sleeping or for general utility, such as the kitchen or laundry. The living area might be one room with a separate dining room, or a combination living and dining room. A porch, a recreation room, and an entrance hall might also be considered a living area. Miss Rand had said that what they learned about any one of these rooms would generally apply to the others. There had been much interest in improving the appearance of the living area at home. Apparently that interest was still important.

"For a long time I've been wanting to consult someone about our living room," said Russell.

"So have I," chorused several others.

"Our living room is quite small," said Joyce. "There's no place to put anything, and it always seems cluttered."

"I wish ours looked smaller and cozier," added Lewis.

These remarks started a flow of comments from the other students. Several said they wished their rooms didn't look so drab and unattractive. Others said they wished they had better looking furniture. Amy pointed out that her family moved a great deal, and they often had difficulty fitting their furnishings into the new homes.

"What a lot of intriguing problems," said Jerry. "I think they all need to be a part of our classwork."

There were nods of agreement from everyone including Miss Rand. Then other suggestions were also offered. Some of these included repairing and refinishing furniture, and making draperies and slip covers. The possibility of buying new furniture was also mentioned. Learning more about storage and cleaning also seemed desirable.

Interviewing Their Families About Living-Area Problems

Keith then raised an important matter which had occurred to several other students as well. "Before we can make a final decision on what to include in our classwork," he said, "we'll need to find out how our families feel about the problems we have agreed on."

"How right," added Cynthia quickly. "After all, they are the ones who will have the most to say about any changes or improvements to be made. We'll need their cooperation for any classwork we plan to do."

"That's so," chorused the others.

The class discussion then turned to a plan for interviewing their families. At this point Miss Rand showed the group a questionnaire taken from her files. She said that it covered many of the problems mentioned by the class. It was based on living-area improvements most frequently needed by families in general.

The students studied the questionnaire and decided that it could be adapted to one for interviewing their families. Before long they had worked out the interview form shown on this page.

Agreeing on the Goals

The reports from the students indicated that their families had checked various items on the interview form. The parents were also willing to cooperate in the classwork in so far as it was possible for them to do so.

The students decided to group the problems under the first ques-

---

WHAT MY FAMILY AND I MAY DO TO IMPROVE OUR LIVING AREA

DIRECTIONS: Check (√) to indicate *yes* to
any of the questions below.

Do we want to make the living area

☐ more attractive?

☐ appear larger than it is?

☐ appear smaller than it is?

☐ appear brighter and sunnier than it is?

☐ so that it can be used for more family activities?

☐ easier to care for?

☐ so that makeshift furniture can be used to better advantage?

☐ so that we can enjoy it even though we move frequently?

Are we interested in

☐ making draperies?

☐ making curtains?

☐ making slip covers?

☐ repairing furniture?

☐ refinishing furniture?

☐ buying new furniture?

Can we use information on

☐ having better storage?

☐ cleaning more easily and effectively?

tion into one goal which they called *making the living area at home meet the family's needs and desires*. Those under the second question they grouped into a goal — *learning ways to improve the living area*. It seemed best to consider storage and cleaning separately; so the two other goals were *planning storage solutions* and *cleaning easily and effectively*.

"And now," asked Allen, "what about a name for our classwork?"

Several ideas were suggested. "Rooms for Happier Living" was the one finally selected, since it seemed to be in accord with what was desired.

MAKING THE LIVING AREA AT HOME MEET THE FAMILY'S NEEDS AND DESIRES

Miss Rand's earlier suggestion of getting some ideas from the proposed exhibits at Hathaway's store seemed to be the keynote to getting the first goal off to a good start. An appointment was made for Miss Rand, Keith, and Cynthia to interview Miss Vandermeer after school.

They told Miss Vandermeer about the goals that had been set up for their classwork, saying that their families were willing to cooperate in any work they planned. The question was: would it be possible for Miss Vandermeer to give the class some ideas about *making the living area at home meet the family's needs and desires?*

Miss Vandermeer said that she was at Hathaway's store to be of as much service to the community as possible. Not only was she willing, but even eager to help the students with their problems. She was especially pleased to know that so many families were interested in improving what she termed a most important area in the home.

She asked whether the students had had any previous classwork in home improvement. When Keith and Cynthia told her about their experiences in improving a bedroom, she was very much pleased. She said that having this background would save her time and theirs. Knowing the basic facts about color and the selection and arrangement of furniture would give them all a head start with the problems. (See Book 1, pages 41–43; 279–301.)

Planning the Classwork

Keith and Cynthia gave the class a most enthusiastic report of the interview. They said it would be fun to work with Miss Vandermeer. Her ability to make others feel that their problems were hers too seemed unlimited. The students were delighted to have her assistance.

After further consultation with Miss Vandermeer, it was decided to begin with some general ideas about living areas, such as what makes them attractive and suitable to a family's needs. This could be done by studying the model rooms at Hathaway's store and by consulting various references. Later Miss Vandermeer would give assistance on special problems. This would include making a room seem larger or smaller or sunnier, and others which had been checked on the interview form by various families.

The students were enthusiastic as they set about assembling materials on living areas for the reference shelves. All indications pointed to some interesting experiences for them and their families.

Acquiring a Greater Knowledge of Living Areas

The reference sources, the model rooms, and Miss Vandermeer's comments all proved to be very helpful in gaining a better understanding of living areas. Before long the students arrived at four points by which they could determine whether a living area seemed to meet a family's needs and desires.

1. The personality of the members of the family is reflected in the living area.
2. The rooms are attractive.
3. The organization of the rooms shows the various activities carried on by the family.
4. The rooms are easy to care for.

However, much time and effort went into learning the details of how each of these qualities might be achieved. At the conclusion of this part of their work with Miss Vandermeer, the students prepared final summaries which are given here. Appropriate illustrations chosen by the class are also shown.

How a living area reflects the personality of family members

A living area reflects the personality of a family, because it is generally planned around the things which bring satisfaction to its members. But personalities are widely different. Therefore there will naturally be some variation in the things which family members like to have in the living area and want to do there. However, it is through the selection and arrangement of these things that a family's personality may be revealed to other people.

For example, you can tell at a glance that a family is unpretentious when a feeling of informality and simplicity prevails in their living area. When the outward impression is that of formality, you feel that the family members tend to be somewhat dignified and formal. You can tell when a family is creative by the unusual things they do to make the room attractive. On the other hand, a living room that is drab and uninteresting would probably indicate that the family members are unimaginative. They may have little or no creative spirit — at least as far as the living area is concerned. If a room impresses you as being ostentatious and showy, you feel that the members lack sincerity and are trying to impress other people with the family's importance.

You can also tell by looking at the room something about a family's pattern of living. When a feeling of intimacy and companionship is reflected, you are likely to conclude that members of the family enjoy spending much of their leisure time there together. You can easily distinguish between a family who enjoys informal get-togethers and one who prefers the more formal kind of entertaining. The first room is characterized by the availability of the record player and records, and the game table. The floor and furniture are the kind that can

Contrast this room with the one above, and what do you find—a more sophisticated, though cozy room?

What family personality traits do you see reflected in this room—a feeling of intimacy and companionship?

easily be arranged for dancing or other activities. The second room has the appearance of not being used very much except for the formal entertaining of friends or business associates. Still another family may particularly enjoy activities, such as sports, gardening, or travel. This enjoyment is reflected in pictures, hangings, and objects of art that are characteristic of the activity.

Of course all of the families just mentioned have other characteristics too. But it is interesting to be able to see how the living area may reflect some of the traits which contribute toward a family's total personality (Study the illustrations on page 261, and see what family traits seem to be reflected.)

```
CLASS MEMO:
    How will you learn
    about living areas?
    What personality traits
    in addition to those
    mentioned by Miss
    Rand's group do you
    find reflected in the
    living areas you study?
```

What makes a living area attractive

Although families may differ in their personalities, most of them have at least one thing in common. They want the living area to be attractive. But all too often this is not easy to accomplish. For example, a family who prefers simple, unpretentious things may not know where simplicity ceases to be attractive and instead becomes monotonous and unimaginative.

Or if a family likes elaborate, rich furnishings, it is often difficult for them to distinguish between what is rich-looking and what is gaudy.

However, the ability to make a room attractive can be acquired by studying what is considered beautiful, and then trying to apply this knowledge. In a living area this means learning about the shapes and placement of objects, and knowing what colors, designs, and textures go well together in the room. The following material on attractiveness attempts to suggest ways in which this can be done.

• *The form or shape of the objects in the room needs to be (1) suited to their purpose, (2) simple, (3) well proportioned, and (4) suited to the materials of which they are made and not pretending to be anything other than they are.*

For example, a chair that is used in a conversation grouping needs to be comfortable, so that the person sitting in it can relax. Such a chair is more attractive when it is not ornate. Furthermore, if it is also well proportioned it is usually comfortable. This means that the seat is not too deep or close to the floor, and the arms and legs not too large for the frame. Wood or metal that can be rounded to fit the contour of the body would constitute suitable material. In most cases, a chair with these characteristics would not appear to be anything except a chair.

When the form or shape of an object is beautiful and when it is attractive in color and texture, nothing more may be needed. But if decoration is desired, it needs to be used in moderation to strengthen the shape of the

Here students learn how to plan a color scheme for a room,
repeating colors from a fabric to be used in the room.

The living area shown on the next two pages applies the rule of something
dark, something light, something dull, something bright. Notice that light
and dull colors are used in large amounts; dark and bright, in small amounts.

In this large, high-ceilinged dining area a contrast in backgrounds is used to decrease the apparent size. The nice architectural feature — the white dado — is emphasized.

object. It also needs to be so simple that it does not detract from the form of the object itself. Decoration may thus be used in various ways.

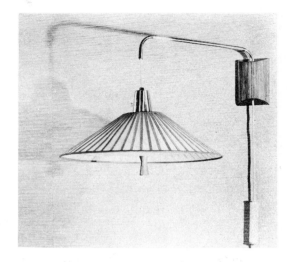

Here surface design on the lamp shade and structural design in the china have been employed.

1. The design may be put on the surface of an object. The illustration of the lamp on this page shows how a simple design has been applied to the surface of the lamp shade.

2. The design may seem to become a part of the form or shape of the object itself. This method as used on a cup, saucer, and plate is shown in the illustration on this page. Note that the decoration is so closely related to the structure of the objects that it appears to be a natural part of their form or shape.

3. The design may be applied so as to stand out on the surface of an object. When it is used sparingly, this decoration enhances the beauty of the objects and does not detract interest from their attractive shapes.

• *Objects in a room need to be related in form and shape to create a feeling of unity or harmony within the room.*

In general, this means that large objects, especially, need to have a strong "family resemblance" to one another, as shown in the illustration on page 267. On the other hand, a large, massive carved piece of furniture would not go well in a room with large, straight-line, light-looking furniture, since there is little or no resemblance in form or shape between the two types.

When small objects are arranged in a group, there also needs to be some family resemblance to one another, as shown in the illustration on page 276.

But when small objects are used for variety or for accent, they may contrast with the larger objects.

• *Colors that are used in the right place and amount, and that are pleasing to the family make a living room attractive.*

Colors may be selected from an object of art or nature, or from generally

Here are two attractive abstract designs both by David Stapler. The one at the right was inspired by a design on a pottery dish.

accepted color combinations. (See Book 1, pages 42–43.) Any of the colors — two or more — appear more attractive when used in different shades and in different degrees of brightness or dullness. A suitable combination would probably include something light, something dark, something dull, and something bright. In

general, light shades and dull colors would be used in the background, and dark shades and bright colors for objects which are to stand out against the background.

The illustrations between pages 262 and 263 show how color may be used in a pleasing way.

The use of color to produce certain specific effects in a room — making it appear larger, smaller, or sunnier — may be found on pages 277 to 281.

- *When patterned material is used, the design needs to be carefully selected.*

  Some designs, known as realistic or naturalistic, imitate real objects. But since it is not possible to copy anything exactly as it is, an attempt to do so generally results in a pattern lacking in beauty. Attractive conventionalized designs originate from realistic or naturalistic forms, but are changed in such a way that they do not wholly resemble the real objects. Abstract designs may be geometric forms, such as plaids, stripes, or checks, or they may be combinations of irregular lines and shapes. But all beautiful patterns, regardless of the designs used, are likely to be simple in form and to present an orderly rather than a rambling, haphazard arrangement.

The conventional design at the left above is "Apples" by Lindberg; the other is by Tiber of Stratford-on-Avon.

But any patterned material needs to be in scale with the size of the room and the area where the pattern is to be used. In general, the smaller the room or area, the smaller the pattern needs to be.

- *A room is more attractive when pattern is used sparingly, when it is in contrast with other patterns, and when it is separated from other patterns by plain areas.*

One can see this point illustrated in the outdoor world. The vast expanse of blue sky has only occasional patterned clouds, while the ocean or other large bodies of water has a plain surface except for occasional whitecaps. These large plain areas with little pattern produce a feeling of relaxation and restfulness, whereas too much pattern would be disquieting and even bewildering.

A living area can reflect the same feeling of restfulness that is felt in nature if pattern is used sparingly. But whatever is used, will show off to better advantage when one pattern is separated from the other patterns by plain surfaces. For example, patterned draperies look best against a plain wall. A chair or sofa with patterned upholstery is more attractive when standing on a plain floor covering. Or if there is pattern on the floor, the objects standing on it need to be plain.

Beautiful pictures and decorative objects show up to better advantage against a plain background. But if it is necessary to use beautiful pictures on a patterned surface, the pictures can be matted with large, plain mats to set them apart from the pattern on the wall. Decorative objects can be separated from a patterned wall by arrang-

ing them against a plain surface, such as a hanging, a tray, or a screen.

When more than one pattern is used in a room, each needs to be different in type and not to vie with one another in importance. For example, one pattern may be conventional, the other abstract. One of the two could have a more striking pattern than the other. But the outstanding design would need to be used in much smaller amounts than the simpler pattern. Each would need to be separated from the other by plain surfaces.

Of course, it is not necessary to have pattern in a room at all. Plain fabrics differing in color and texture can be used in fairly large areas to create the impression of pattern. In such a room, there would need to be a blending and contrast of colors and textures, so that the pattern formed would be effective.

- *A variety of textures — rough or smooth, coarse or fine, shiny or dull, soft or stiff, heavy or light, or something in between each of these — helps to make a room attractive. But the textures need to be harmonious with each other and/or with the colors, the materials, the shapes, the lines, and the patterns in the room.*

Very coarse textures have nothing in common with very fine textures and do not go well with them. For example, a piece of coarse reed furniture would not look well upholstered in fine velvet. Nor would the coarse texture of a piece of oak furniture go well with soft silks, lustrous rayons, or satin fabrics. But coarser fabrics, such as denim, crash, monk's cloth, or similar textures, would harmonize with the coarse pieces of furniture. And woods, such as mahogany or walnut, which have a fine, satinlike grain would harmonize with the fine fabrics. However, there are other fabrics, such as printed linens, cretonnes, and some chintzes, which are in between the coarse and the fine textures, and they may go well with either.

The illustration on this page shows how a variety of textures may be used.

- *Keeping the size of the objects in pleasing relationship or scale with one another, and with the room as a whole contributes toward attractiveness.*

In general, this means evaluating each piece in relation to the pieces used with it, such as not placing a large chair in a large room near a table and a lamp that are proportionately too small. (See Book 1, page 281, *Avoid* illustration, upper left.) It also means using large pieces of furniture in a large room, and smaller pieces in smaller rooms. But if large pieces must be used in a small room, it is desirable to select as few inconspicuous pieces as possible. Large furniture not only creates a crowded appearance in a small room, but the pieces themselves seem larger than they really are. And if the furniture is upholstered, it is important to avoid fabrics with striking colors or patterns. Bright

Notice the variety of textures used in this room. With the drapery drawn back, the arrangement is appropriate for either daytime or nighttime reading.

colors and striking patterns make objects appear larger than when dull colors or inconspicuous patterns are used. On the other hand, if small pieces of furniture appear too small for a room, they can be grouped together, the size of the group to depend upon the size of the room. The illustration on this page shows a furniture grouping that has a pleasing relationship in scale.

- *The wise use of lines to produce rhythmic movement and to create certain effects helps to make a room attractive.*

The lines in a room need to carry the eye smoothly and easily from one place to another, thus tying the objects in a room together. But if too many pieces of furniture or too many patterns have predominately straight lines, the rhythmic movement is not produced. On the other hand, too many curved lines cause the eye to travel too quickly, and create a feeling

of restlessness. There need to be enough straight lines so that the eye can travel smoothly, and enough curved lines to relieve the severity of the straight lines.

If it seems desirable to make objects look taller and more slender than they are, vertical lines may be used. For example, a room with a low ceiling can be made to look higher by the suggestion of vertical stripes in the wallpaper. Or a vertical striped fabric on a chair that is too low carries the eye up and down.

If it is desirable to make a wall seem wider, a horizontal furniture grouping, such as a sofa with low tables at either end and a horizontal wall hanging above, can produce this effect. An unusually long room will seem shorter if long pieces of furniture are placed on the narrow walls. Placing a sofa on the long walls would emphasize their length. The illustrations on page 268 show the use of line to produce certain effects.

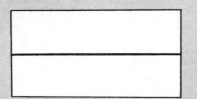

This line
directs the eye horizontally.

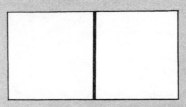

This line
directs the eye vertically.

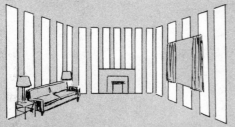

Because the eye is directed vertically, this room appears taller and narrower than it is.

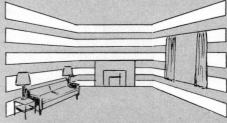

Horizontal stripes make this room appear wider and seem to lower the ceiling.

Transition lines are poor here, because the chair-backs direct the eye away from the window.

Here the tables, lamps, and so on allow the eye to move rhythmically through the grouping.

THE EFFECT OF LINES

- *Attractiveness can be obtained by grouping objects around a center in such a way that the power of attraction is equal on each side of the center.*

  Objects that are identical can be placed an equal distance from the center, producing what is called "formal balance," as shown on page 267. But groupings in which the articles are not all alike call for different treatment. When not identical, objects or groups of objects need to be placed at different distances from the center, but in such a way that they create the same power of attraction. This is called "informal balance."

Some objects in a grouping have more power of attraction than others and generally need to be closer to the center. Unusual shapes, striking colors or patterns, heavy-looking pieces, and the contrast of light or dark colors have more power of attraction than objects that are less conspicuous. But in making any arrangement, the largest pieces need to be considered first.

- *A room is not wholly attractive unless there is some spot on which attention is immediately focused.*

For example, a point of interest may be a part of the room itself, such as a fireplace or a picture window. It may also be an outstanding piece of furniture well placed, or a special arrangement of some of the furnishings. Although other spots in a room may be attractive, they need to be subordinate to the main center of interest. See the illustrations on pages 267 and 271.

CLASS MEMO:

How can your class apply what Miss Rand's group learned about attractiveness to your own work on living areas?

How the organization of the living area can serve various family activities

The organization of the living area is important in order that the room may serve the various interests of family members to the best advantage. For example, some places in a room are generally more advantageous than others for certain activity groupings. It is also important to have furniture suited to the various activities, with pieces that may be used interchangeably if desired. But any furniture for a grouping will need to be arranged for the convenience of the activity going on. Traffic lanes will need to be provided, so that people may go easily from one activity to another without cutting through a grouping. It is also desirable to have adequate general illumination in the room, and local lighting for the various activities. All of this can be done without difficulty by following some general guides for certain activities.

- A good place for a conversation grouping may be around a fireplace, as shown in the illustration on page 261. Or a window or group of windows with a pleasing view may be a desirable location. A sofa, some comfortable chairs, and a place on which to put things make a good conversation grouping. The seating needs to be arranged so that each person can look at the others easily and talk without raising the voice. The illustrations on page 271 show what a difference good furniture arrangement can make.

- Naturally an area for reading needs to be located as far as possible from the conversation area if both activities are to be carried on at the same time. If reading is to be done by daylight, a place near a window is important, as shown on page 266. A comfortable chair for each person reading, a lamp, and an accessible piece of furniture to hold books and magazines are desirable.

- The location for a television grouping needs to be where people watching

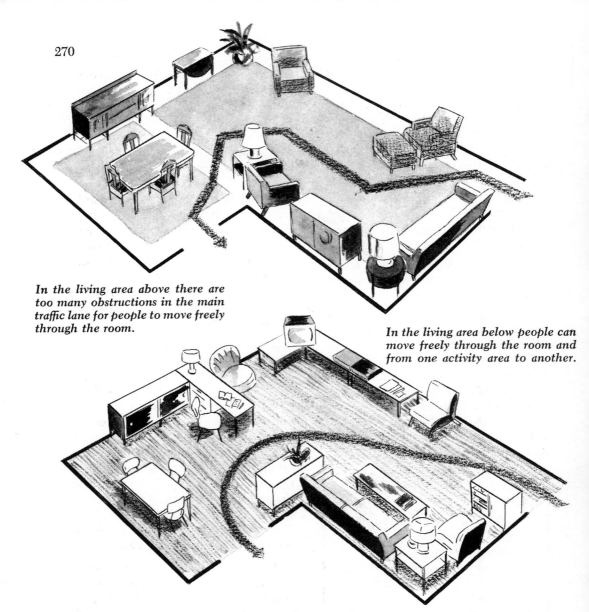

In the living area above there are too many obstructions in the main traffic lane for people to move freely through the room.

In the living area below people can move freely through the room and from one activity area to another.

the programs can get an unobstructed view of the screen. One corner of the room away from people coming and going may be an excellent place. The seating requirements may be left to individual preferences. Children often like low stools or prefer to sit on the floor. In some homes, a conversation grouping may be used for watching television, since it is difficult to carry on the two activities at the same time. But some of the seating equipment will need to be light enough to move easily. Of course everyone watching television needs to face the screen, and to avoid obscuring the view of others. The screen, itself, should be at eye level when the viewers are seated. If the set is a table model, placing it on a swivel stand will give flexibility for viewing a program from different parts of the room. This point is illustrated on this page.

- A separate grouping for listening to music may not be necessary if an area for conversation or for watching television has already been planned. For listening to music, the radio or record player — the most common sources of music — needs to be located at approximately ear level when the participants are seated.

- In arranging traffic lanes, the larger the spaces between the activity areas, the easier it will be to move around the room. Traffic needs to be able to pass through the room without cutting through an activity area. Pieces of furniture can be so placed as to create traffic lanes from one entrance of a room to another. See the illustrations on the opposite page for handling traffic lanes.

- A dining area as near to the kitchen as possible is very desirable. The furniture may consist of a table and the number of chairs necessary for the family and guests. Storage pieces for dining equipment may also be needed. In some dining areas, the table and chairs may be permanently placed. Or

Poorly arranged furniture in this room, which ignores activity areas and a center of interest, gives the room a cold, impersonal, unbalanced appearance.

Using the same furniture, various activity areas and a center of interest around the fireplace are provided. The swivel stand for the television makes it possible to use the conversation area for viewing television.

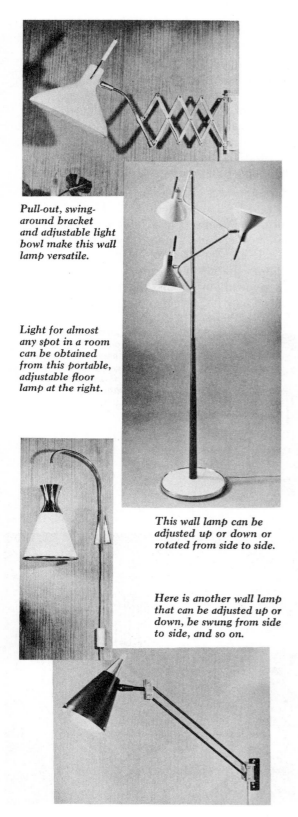

Pull-out, swing-around bracket and adjustable light bowl make this wall lamp versatile.

Light for almost any spot in a room can be obtained from this portable, adjustable floor lamp at the right.

This wall lamp can be adjusted up or down or rotated from side to side.

Here is another wall lamp that can be adjusted up or down, be swung from side to side, and so on.

a table, such as the drop-leaf or gate-leg type, can be put in a permanent position that does not require major moving. The chairs can be used as auxiliary pieces for other activities.

• A table-game grouping needs to be away from conversation, music, and other distractions, since many games call for the concentrated attention of the players. A permanent table with chairs, or chairs nearby, may be desirable for a game area if the room will not look cluttered. When it is not advisable to have permanent placement, a table and chairs that fold up may be used. But storage needs to be convenient, so that the activity can be started with a minimum of preparation.

• Good general illumination is provided by having soft — not intense — lighting throughout the room. Adequate local illumination requires more intense lighting for specific activities that need a good deal of light. (See Book 1, pages 297–300.) Good lighting during the day may be obtained by controlling the daylight with draperies, curtains, shades, or blinds not only for general illumination but for local lighting as well. In the evening, good general or local lighting can often be secured through the use of the same equipment. Flexible lamps that raise or lower, that turn from side to side, that can extend horizontally, and that have different levels of illumination, such as 50, 100, and 150 watts, can perform double duty. They can produce a soft light that will give a feeling of relaxation to a conversation area. Or they may produce more intense illumination for specific activities, such as reading, writing, or playing table games. Other types of double-duty illumination are the inserted ceiling and wall lights. But these are more frequently used for general illumination than for local lighting. (See the illustrations on page 272.)

CLASS MEMO:

What would your class recommend to show how various family activities may be carried on in the living area?

*How to make a living area
easy to care for*

Every living area requires a certain amount of care, depending on various factors. The number and age of family members, and the extent to which they use the room influence the amount of care needed. The proximity to industrial areas or to a dusty thoroughfare, the climate, and the seasons also determine how often cleaning is necessary. Another important consideration is the furnishings used in the room. Some require much more upkeep than others.

In keeping care at a minimum, it is important to provide background finishes and furnishings that (1) resist or do not show soil readily, (2) do not mar or wear out easily, and (3) are easy to clean.

WALLS: Walls that are smoothly plastered generally resist soil more readily and are easier to clean than roughly textured surfaces. Using oil-base paints — with a flat dull finish — on plastered walls may be more expensive than milk-base or water-base paints. But the initial cost will be reduced in terms of longer wear and ease of cleaning. However, less expensive paints may be satisfactory for a room that will not be subject to heavy soil, but they mar more easily than the oil-base paints. No wallpaper that is highly resistant to soil and also suitable for the living room is available. But there are some kinds that can be washed, or cleaned in other ways. One is a washable, plastic-coated type, in which the plastic penetrates the paper but is not visible. It wears longer and mars less easily than some less expensive papers. Another variety is made with a fast-color ink which makes the paper washable. This is not as expensive as the plastic-coated type, but it is also less easy to wash. Then there is ordinary wallpaper, which generally requires special cleaning procedures.

All wall finishes — whether paint or paper — show soil less readily when the colors used are not too light. Patterned wallpaper may help to conceal soil, but its use would need to depend on the extent and kind of pattern used elsewhere in the room.

FLOOR: Although brick, ceramic tile, and cork are sometimes used for floors, the most common type of flooring is wood. Hardwoods, such as oak or hard maple, mar less easily and withstand wear much better than softwoods, such as pine or fir. But the hardwoods are more expensive. However, a good wax finish on any wood floor will protect the surface. And when small rugs are used in places that get the greatest wear, a polished floor — if there is not too much traffic on it — may be very satisfactory.

Wood floors that are to be nearly or entirely covered do not need to be of such good quality as those that are partially or entirely exposed. Composition materials, such as linoleum, asphalt, or vinyl plastic, make an easy-to-care-for covering. But asphalt, vinyl plastic, and inlaid linoleum — which need to be cemented to the floor — are fairly expensive. However, they have good wearing qualities, especially when the surfaces are protected by wax or special preservative preparations. Their colors will last as long as the material itself, since they are impregnated into the mixture. Printed linoleum — in contrast to inlaid — is less expensive and does not need to be cemented to the floor. But it is easily marred and does not have the long-wearing qualities of the inlaid linoleum. However, several coats of colorless varnish or shellac, plus frequent waxing will prolong its use.

A good-quality fabric floor covering either in wall-to-wall carpeting or in a room-sized rug is an expensive investment, but with care it will last for many years. Those that are made of wool or synthetic fibers give longer wear than those made of cotton or grass-matting fibers, but they are also more expensive. Cut pile or nubby textures are more serviceable than the flat smooth weaves. Padding under carpeting or under a room-sized rug also increases wearing qualities. For small rugs, a nonskid type of padding can be used.

One type of flooring is easier to care for than two, but there may be some disadvantages. For example, wall-to-wall carpeting, which is generally tacked to the floor, may have been cut to fit irregularities, such as around a fireplace or a bay window. This makes it difficult to shift it around for wear or to use it in another room. On the other hand, a room-sized rug will require care for the floor around it as well as for the rug's surface. But the rug can be shifted in position to distribute the wear, and can easily be removed for special cleaning. Of course, small rugs can be used on any type of flooring where traffic is heavy to reduce wear and frequent cleaning of the whole floor.

Dark or light colors in floor coverings tend to show footprints and soil more quickly than middle values, while pattern tends to reduce the amount shown. But sometimes it is better to look at a little dirt than too much pattern if it has already been used in other parts of the room.

WINDOW TREATMENT: Window treatment in a living area will vary, depending somewhat upon the preferences of family members. If shades are used, those that do not tear readily and that can be cleaned are the best investment. Venetian blinds require more care and are more expensive than shades, but they also last longer. The types that can be washed in the bathtub, or that have removable slats and plastic-coated tape which can be wiped clean are the easiest to care for.

Draperies that draw may be used without shades or blinds if there is not too much daylight in the room. This treatment probably requires the least amount of care and upkeep, since the draperies serve two purposes. Draw curtains may be used with draw draperies for control of light both day and night. In such case no blinds or shades are needed. When blinds or shades are used with stationary draperies, curtains may or may not be used. Drapery fabrics that can be easily laundered or dry-cleaned are advisable. Some fabrics that are lined may wear longer than those unlined, but more expense may be involved. If curtains are a part of the window treatment, Orlon or nylon fabrics tend to resist dirt and dust readily. They also hold their shape better than rayon or cotton fabrics. (See pages 283–299 for more information on draperies and curtains.)

FURNITURE: A few well-chosen sturdy pieces of furniture that are lightweight and simple in line and construction require less care than those that have intricate, detailed carvings. Lightweight furniture is also easier to move around when cleaning than heavy pieces. Furthermore, less time and effort are needed when large pieces, such as a sofa or bookcase, are high enough from the floor to clean under without being moved, or fit flush to the floor.

Pieces of furniture that are upholstered in materials that can be sponged clean are easier to care for than those that require special cleaning procedures. Plastic and leather are long-wearing materials. Their smooth surfaces resist soil readily, whereas fabrics that are rough in texture accumulate dirt more easily. Materials somewhat dark in color or that are patterned in all-over designs are more practical for upholstery — that cannot be sponged clean — than light, plain materials.

LIGHTING: Simple fixtures and lamps used for general and local illumination require less care than those that are decorative. This holds true for accessories.

Pieces of furniture that can be nested or folded save space in a small room.

A few attractive objects that are easy to care for are more practical than a lot of small knickknacks.

CLASS MEMO:
How many of the suggestions—offered by Miss Rand's class—for making a living area easy to care for would you like to consider for your own homes?

Offering Guides for Special Living Area Problems

One day while the classwork was in progress, Miss Vandermeer and the students discussed the special problems that had been checked on the interview form.

There were five of these problems: (1) how to make a living area appear larger than it is, (2) how to make it appear small and cozy, (3) how to make it seem sunnier, (4) how to use makeshift furnishings to the best advantage, and (5) how to make a living area enjoyable when a family moves frequently.

Miss Vandermeer said that these problems were not new in her experience. In fact, so many people in various communities where she had worked needed assistance on the same problems that she had assembled guides to help them. Each problem started out with a short verse expressing the keynote to the situation. This was followed by suggestions for meeting the problem through the treatment of various aspects of a living area. Families could adapt the guides to their own home situations.

The material had been mimeographed, so that copies were available for each student even though his or her family had not checked all the problems. As the students studied the guides, various questions arose. Miss Vandermeer then suggested that the students might like to try out some of the ideas offered in the guides. This would give them a clearer picture of how they could adapt some of the suggestions to their own use.

Needless to say, Miss Vandermeer's offer received unanimous acceptance. Arrangements were soon made for room space in Hathaway's store where various fabrics and furnishings were available. The students whose families had checked the same problem grouped together to give the demonstrations with Miss Vandermeer's guidance.

It was a rewarding experience. Not only did the students see the actual effect of some of the suggestions, but they were also able to apply much of their previous learning.

An adaptation of Miss Vandermeer's guides is given on pages 277 to 281. References are included to illustrate some of the points.

A few simple accessories that are easy to care for and that have a family resemblance among themselves and to the room are the best choice.

MAKING A LIVING AREA APPEAR LARGER THAN IT IS

You can make a room seem larger without adding to the place.
Just keep things very simple; this will tend to increase the space.

WALLS A single, light color, with a smooth rather than a rough texture, gives a feeling of spaciousness. This is especially true if the woodwork is the same color as the walls. Whenever possible, the same color needs to be used in adjoining rooms, so that the whole area appears as one.

WINDOWS Straight-line draperies that reach to the floor seem to increase the height and apparent size of the room. Having the draperies approximately the same color as the walls also adds spaciousness. If figured draperies are used, a small inconspicuous design in colors similar to the walls is desirable. When the windows themselves are large, they seem to extend the walls and bring in outside space.

FLOORS A bare floor or wall-to-wall covering tends to make a room seem larger because it holds attention all the way to the walls. If small rugs are used, they need to fit the shape of the floor—that is, not be round, oval, or irregular in shape. They also need to be similar in color to the floor. Rugs with patterns, bright colors, and rough textures are not desirable, because they tend to break up the space and make the room seem smaller. Small rugs need to be placed in relation to the furniture groupings, not scattered haphazardly around the room.

FURNITURE It is best to avoid too much furniture in a small room. Light-looking sturdy furniture which appears in scale with the room is better than heavy, upholstered pieces. Furniture that will serve more than one purpose, or that can be nested, stacked, or folded is very practical. (See the illustration on page 275.) Some furniture, parts of which are made of foam rubber, metal mesh, or cotton or plastic webbing, gives a feeling of airiness. If large pieces of upholstered furniture are used, plain fabrics which do not contrast with the walls and floor are best. Such fabrics will tend to make the furniture look smaller, and thus increase the apparent size of the room. In general, if furniture groupings are arranged near the walls, a small room tends to seem larger.

LIGHTING Light gives a feeling of space. A lot of light on the ceiling tends to increase its height, while well-lighted walls make a room seem larger. Using blue bulbs for general illumination at night helps to create an air of spaciousness.

ACCESSORIES A few simple accessories that are similar in type are appropriate for a small room. A large mirror on a wall may be used effectively. By reflecting the plain surfaces throughout the room, it will give a feeling of additional space.

MAKING A LIVING AREA APPEAR SMALL AND COZY

You can make a room seem cozy and small in scale
By creating warmth and cheer in all its detail.

WALLS

Warm colors make a room seem small and cozy. In a large room, if there is adequate lighting, warm, fairly dark colors may be used on one or more of the walls. Or a pattern may also be desirable, depending on the kind and amount used elsewhere in the room. If the ceiling seems too high, it can be made to appear lower by the use of a warm, fairly dark color provided there is adequate light in the room.

WINDOWS

Draperies which hang in full folds, pleats, or gathers tend to make a room seem cozy. Any contrast of color, pattern, or texture between the walls and draperies will also make the room appear smaller.

FLOORS

The floor space can be broken up by using a rug that will come to within a foot or so of the walls. Or smaller rugs may be placed in the different areas of activity. A contrast in color between the rug and the floor, or a patterned rug—if the pattern is not too pronounced—will decrease the apparent size of the room.

FURNITURE

More furniture and larger pieces than used in a smaller room are appropriate. Upholstered fabrics may contrast in color with the walls or floors, or they may have a pattern provided too much has not already been used. Dark furniture against light walls, or light furniture against fairly dark walls produces a contrast that decreases the apparent size of the room. Furniture groupings may be set out from the walls, producing broken areas that also make the room appear smaller.

LIGHTING

Lamps or wall brackets that call attention to the far corners of the room need to be avoided. If the ceiling is high, general illumination that reflects the light downward rather than across a large ceiling area, tends to lessen the height of the room. Using pink bulbs for general illumination will add a feeling of warmth.

ACCESSORIES

Pictures will tend to bring the walls closer in, while plants, even large ones, give a room a cozy feeling. Equipment for several kinds of activities, such as a game table or musical instruments, can be left out in a large room without giving it a cluttered appearance.

MAKING A LIVING AREA SEEM SUNNY

If your living room is gloomy,
And you want it to be bright,
The keynote to such a problem
Is to keep things very light.

WALLS   A very light bright yellow on the walls and ceiling will do more to make the room seem sunny than almost anything else.

WINDOWS   Draperies hung at the sides of the windows rather than across the glass will let in a maximum of daylight. But a very sheer yellow curtain across the glass of a window will usually make the daylight coming into the room look sunny.

FLOORS   Floors need to be light and warm in color. Wood floors in their natural finish are sunshiny in color. However, their smooth finish may not add as much warmth to the room as a soft-textured rug or carpet in a warm, fairly light shade.

FURNITURE   Furniture that is light in weight and color helps to brighten a room. Woods, such as birch and oak, in their natural finish are almost sunshiny in color. Some plastic upholstery fabrics are practical even in white. However, a few pieces of dark furniture will make the others seem brighter by contrast. The furniture needs to be so arranged as to admit what natural daylight there is and to receive the best artificial illumination. A light, or a bright warm-colored, sofa rather than a dark chest needs to be near a lamp, since light, bright colors reflect light, and dark colors absorb it.

LIGHTING   There needs to be good illumination throughout the room. Sun-gold bulbs that give a warm, sunny color are better for a dark room than bulbs that give a cold blue light.

ACCESSORIES   Pictures or paintings that are light in color and merry and gay in content will help to brighten a room. A large well-placed mirror to reflect light also helps. Accessories made of copper or brass, as well as arrangements of certain flowers, give the appearance of sunshine.

USING MAKESHIFT FURNITURE TO THE BEST ADVANTAGE

If you have a makeshift living room, and things don't seem quite right,
The keynote to improvement can be something very slight.
Try to make the total picture just as pleasing as can be,
For it's really but a matter of what the eye can see.

WALLS   The color of the walls needs to be much the same as that of the furniture. In this way the makeshift pieces will not stand out against the walls.

WINDOWS   If a window or a group of windows is attractive, it may be possible to make the window the center of interest in the room to direct attention away from the makeshift furniture. An attractive patterned fabric may be used, or the draperies might contrast with the color of the walls. When windows vary in size and are poorly placed in a room, it may be possible to drape them so as to conceal their proportions, thus making them attractive. (For ideas, see pages 284 and 288.)

FLOORS   A large fiber rug or simple wall-to-wall covering—if harmonious with the furnishings—may help to unify makeshift pieces in the room especially if it is similar in color to the large pieces of furniture.

FURNITURE   Some makeshift furniture can be covered with good-looking slip covers. Or it may be possible to paint the pieces. If a piece seems too large for the room, or if its shape is unattractive, a color as near the color of the walls and floor will reduce its apparent size and make its shape less conspicuous. The furniture can be arranged so that the best pieces are the easiest to see, such as when you enter the room or as you sit in a conversation grouping.

ACCESSORIES   Interesting accessories can be used to draw attention away from unattractive furnishings. These need not be expensive so long as they are in keeping with the room. A pleasing effect can be obtained by using an inexpensive print, a block of interesting wallpaper, an attractive travel poster, or even a lovely flower arrangement.

MAKING A LIVING AREA ENJOYABLE WHEN A FAMILY MOVES FREQUENTLY

It can be fun to move around,
To make new friends and see new faces,
And if you have a flexible plan,
Life can be happy in these places.

WALLS   If the walls have too much pattern, a simple background can be attained by using hangings or movable screens. The hangings can be the type that fold or roll up. A large mat for a picture can provide a simple background and at the same time display the picture to advantage. Screens may be used for various purposes. For example, they may hide ugly architectural details. Or they may be used to divide too large a room, or to give the feeling of an entrance hall where there is none.

WINDOWS   Solid-color drapery fabrics that look well with other furnishings are adaptable to most situations. Fairly thick fabrics through which the light does not show may be sewed together to fit a variety of window sizes. A nubby texture may help to conceal the piecing.

FLOORS   Small rugs that may be grouped together or used separately are more likely to fit any situation than a room-sized rug or wall-to-wall covering.

FURNITURE   Sturdy, simple, unornamented pieces of furniture that come in sections, such as a bookcase or a chest of drawers, can be both attractive and easy to pack. Lightweight folding and extension types, as well as pieces that can be nested or stacked are also practical. (See the illustration on page 275.)

LIGHTING   Simple, adjustable lamps, such as the gooseneck or telescopic kind, provide maximum flexibility for frequent moving. Floor lamps that can be raised or lowered will help to give adequate light in any room. But all types of lamps need to be easy to pack and not too fragile.

ACCESSORIES   A few accessories of simple form and of interest to members of the family can give long-lasting satisfaction. But they too need to be easy to pack and not too fragile.

Setting Up Short-Term and Long-Term Plans with Their Families

The students believed that with Miss Vandermeer's guidance they had acquired a fairly good understanding of living area problems. They then decided that the next step was to discuss with their families how the ideas and suggestions they had assembled could be adapted to their own homes. In some cases it would be possible to use only a few of the suggestions, in others many more.

However, there was a general feeling that many of the suggestions could not be carried out until the students had taken up their second goal. Certain improvements probably could not be made until they had learned more about draperies, curtains, slip covers, repairing and refinishing furniture, and buying new furniture.

Therefore, while the second goal was in progress, the students and their families would set up short-term and long-term plans of what might be done. Short-term plans would show suggestions that were being carried out at once. Several students thought that their families might want to regroup the furniture to better advantage for the activities being carried on. Others mentioned providing for more adequate traffic lanes and trying out different arrangements for balance. Long-term plans would include doing whatever they could from time to time as the budget and the assistance of family members permitted. Reports of all plans would be given after the second goal had been carried out.

CLASS MEMO:
What plans will your group make for carrying out improvements at home?

LEARNING WAYS TO IMPROVE THE LIVING AREA

As the students began to discuss the second objective, they realized that it covered a lot of ground. There was a question whether they could do as much as they wanted to in the time available.

Some of the boys then came up with a practical suggestion that seemed to be the answer to the problem. The girls could take the classwork on learning more about draperies, curtains, and slip covers, while the boys took repairing and refinishing furniture. Of course, if any of the girls preferred to join the group repairing and refinishing furniture they could so so. This alternative would also apply to any of the boys who might want to join the group working on draperies, curtains, and slip covers. However, after the two groups had completed their work, then both the girls and the boys could take up together the subject of buying furniture.

There were nods of agreement throughout the room, and Miss Rand gave her approval.

As the discussion progressed, both groups realized that they needed real how-to-do-it experiences for this part of their work. But nobody's plans at home were far enough along to provide the necessary activities immediately. It therefore seemed advisable to look around for things that needed to be done at school. The homemaking budget had an improvement fund, as did the budgets for other departments. The students could check frequently on their home plans to see how the information assembled at school would be most helpful. Special problems developing at home were to be reported to the group handling the situation. Material assembled by both groups would be available to anyone needing the information at home.

Learning About Draperies, Curtains, and Slip Covers

After a lively discussion, it was decided that the draperies in the homemaking living center might well be replaced now. They were beginning to show signs of wear, and they were several years old. The fairly new occasional chair might have its life prolonged by a slip cover for everyday wear. Expenditures for both of these items would fit in with the general overall plan.

A survey of the rest of the school revealed that the nurse's office was ready for new curtains and for slip covers for the day bed and its pillows. Miss Holmes, the school nurse, was pleased that the girls were willing to take over these projects.

In discussing the work to be done, the group realized that they would need to apply what they had learned with Miss Vandermeer's guidance. For example, the personality of a room, its attractiveness, the activities carried on there, and ease of care were important considerations. What they had learned about creating various effects and minimizing undesirable features would also be called into play.

Understanding the terms used in window treatments

While the students were working with Miss Vandermeer, they had learned about various window treatments. They knew that roller shades, Venetian or bamboo blinds, and draw draperies or draw curtains are used to control light. With stationary draperies and blinds or shades, glass curtains might or might not be used. At the model rooms, they had seen several types of fixtures used with various drapery and curtain headings. Now as the group began to discuss this information, several points were raised.

"I still don't understand some of the window terms Miss Vandermeer used," said Cynthia. "I get mixed up on apron and sill."

"I'm confused too," said Lorna. "I can't remember the names of some of the drapery headings we saw."

"It was never quite clear to me how Miss Vandermeer made draperies and curtains draw," said Dorothy.

"Since we're going to hang draperies and curtains," added Joyce, "I think we need to get these matters straightened out."

The rest of the group nodded in agreement. Before long everyone was busy consulting references and looking at illustrations. Later on, the students summarized the terms and treatments they considered most helpful for school and home use, as shown on pages 285 to 287. Of course, the choice of a treatment would depend on the particular room and what seemed best there. The group was also aware that not all home windows were of the sash type used in the summary. However, this double-sash type seemed adequate for illustrating terms and treatments.

Creating different window proportions

One day when the group was considering what window treatments to use at school, the size of windows came up for discussion. The students had learned that some windows are not in proportion to the size of the room or to the wall in which they are placed. The windows may need to appear shorter, longer, narrower, or wider as the case may be. In such instances, it is possible to improve the proportions by the use of lines to produce the effect desired.

Realizing that information on how to create different window proportions might be helpful in many homes, the students consulted references to find out how this could be done. Then they set up the following guides.

WINDOW TERMS AND TREATMENTS

WINDOW PARTS

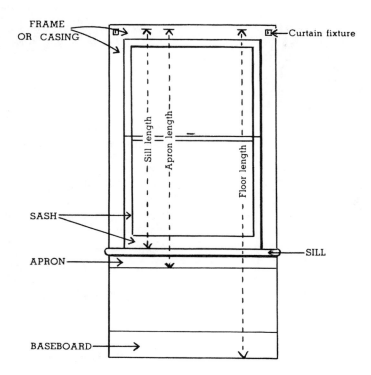

FRAME OR CASING

Curtain fixture

Sill length

Apron length

Floor length

SASH

SILL

APRON

BASEBOARD

DRAPERY AND CURTAIN LENGTHS

Draperies and curtains look best when their length conforms to the structure of the window. They are usually sill length, apron length, or floor length, depending upon the effect desired in the room.

Without a heading

TYPES OF HEADINGS

Gathered on rod — generally used for curtains. May or may not have a heading above gathers. May be used without a heading for stationary draperies under a valance or cornice.

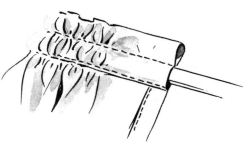

With a heading

Pleated — generally used for draperies — stationary or drawn — without a valance or cornice. Pleats may be pinch, box, or cartridge type.

Pinch

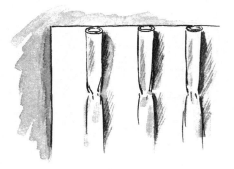

Cartridge

Box

Valance — a horizontal banding of pleated, gathered, or plain material used at the top of a window. Lightweight materials may be gathered. Heavy-weight fabrics are usually pleated or used plain — shaped or not, with buckram as stiffening.

Gathered

Cornice — a wooden or metal covering extending out from the wall across the top of the window. Lower edge may be straight or shaped. Cornice may be painted to blend in with the walls or draperies, or covered with drapery fabric. May be constructed or bought readymade.

Plain, shaped

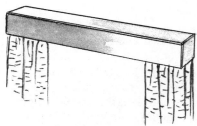

Straight, uncovered

Shaped, covered

FIXTURES

Adjustable Single Rod—for stationary curtain

Adjustable Double Rod—for stationary drapery and valance

Adjustable Triple Rod—for stationary curtain, drapery, and valance

Bay-window Rod—for stationary curtains or draperies

Swinging Extension Rod—for side draperies. May be stationary rather than swinging if desired.

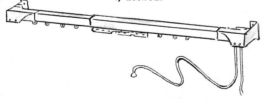

Traverse Rods—for draw draperies and draw curtains. May be single or double.

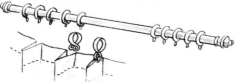

Pole and Rings—allow draperies to be drawn together. Sew-onto or clip-onto fabric rings

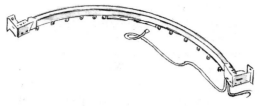

Cut-to-measure Rods—for unusual window shapes—bay, arched, large picture, and so on. Available to accommodate any combination of stationary or draw draperies and curtains, and stationary valances

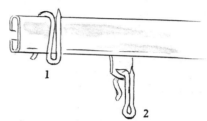

Hooks for Lightweight Fabrics—(1) for stationary use, (2) for traverse use

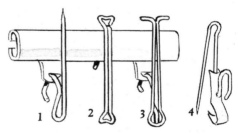

Heading Hooks—for pleat support. Available for either stationary or draw draperies: (1) pin-on type, (2) sew-on type, (3) slip-on type, (4) safety-pin type

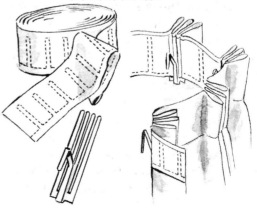

Pleater Tape and Traverse Insertion Hook— for making pleats without sewing them in, as well as for hanging the drapery

- *When a window is short and needs to appear taller.* Straight, floor-length draperies, or a fabric with vertical stripes will increase the apparent height of the window. If feasible, a wooden extension may be set on the wall above the window. The fixtures can be placed on this extension, and a valance or a cornice used to cover the added height.

- *When a window is tall and needs to appear shorter and wider.* Draperies that hang on the wall beyond the window frame, and that extend to the sill or apron will tend to increase the width and decrease the height of the window. To hang the draperies over the wall, the top of the window frame may be extended on both sides with two wooden blocks. The fixtures can be placed on the blocks, and the draperies hung so that they cover the frame and extended portion. A valance or a cornice will also tend to cut the height of the window.

- *When a window is small and needs to appear higher and wider.* A wooden extension of the desired height and width set on the wall above the window will help to create the effect desired. The extension can be covered with a valance or a cornice, and the draperies hung so that they cover the window frame and the added wall space. Using floor-length draperies will also add to the height of the window.

Showing how different types of windows may be treated

Before long, various students whose families were planning new window treatments began to report various problems. Keith said that his family would like some suggestions for treating bay windows. Joyce said that twin windows was the problem in her home.

These and other comments made it seem advisable to assemble information showing how various types of windows could be treated. Although each home situation was different, the students were able to offer general suggestions for each type selected. Magazines, books, and observations of how other people handled the same types of windows were used as reference sources. There was much available information. Several students, with the assistance of Miss Rand, screened the material and presented to the class what seemed most helpful. A reproduction of the information assembled — with illustrations — is given on pages 290 to 291.

Pointing out considerations in the selection of fabrics

When it came time to consider fabrics for the school projects, the students believed they were quite well prepared to make a satisfactory selection. They knew that a fabric needs to be attractive and suitable in color, design, and texture for the room in which it is to be used, and for the purpose it will serve. It also needs to be durable enough to last for several seasons, and easy to care for. The students had examined swatches of material and were now ready to make a final decision.

However, before this was done, several students suggested assembling some information for those at home who were about to purchase fabrics. Of course it would not be possible to recommend specific fabric choices, since home situations would vary. But some general information might prove to be very helpful.

This idea appealed to the group, and before long they had assembled the following material.

- When looking for possibilities, take samples of the colors you are considering with you from store to store. Trying to carry color by eye is very deceptive. With the samples, you can be sure of matching colors or blending shades.

- If a store has a special drapery department, there are advantages in looking there first. Drapery fabrics are planned for home furnishings and are generally more satisfactory in width and texture than those used primarily for clothing. Also, other items needed, such as thread, cording, zippers, and fixtures, are generally in the same department or nearby.

- If possible, try out a swatch of the fabric in the room where it is to be used. This helps in deciding whether it is suitable in color, pattern, and texture and whether it goes with the other furnishings.

- In evaluating the quality of the fabric, you will need to ask yourself or the salesperson several questions.

1. *Is it colorfast to light, laundering, or dry-cleaning?* Fabric furnishings that fade or have colors that run in cleaning are short lived, since they are constantly subjected to soil.

2. *Is it preshrunk?* Draperies, curtains, and slip covers that shrink appreciably after they are made will no longer fit their carefully measured shapes. Shrinking would necessitate tedious alterations or new replacements.

3. *Will it be durable?* A fabric for general use needs to be firmly woven to resist wear and to hold its shape. The fibers should not break easily when bent, as they are in folds of draperies. Fabrics for draw draperies and curtains need to have sufficient strength and flexibility to withstand being pulled back and forth on the rod. Material for a slip cover needs to resist hard wear and the likelihood of threads pulling and catching.

4. *Will it be easy to care for?* Fabrics that wash or dry clean easily are most suitable for draperies, curtains, and slip covers. Special finishes, such as spot, mildew, or crease resistance, will depend upon personal preferences.

- Consider the *pro's* and *con's* of using a lining for draperies. Then decide what seems most suitable for your situation.

THE PRO SIDE

1. Many fabrics need a lining to make them hang better, that is, in soft folds.

2. Lined draperies often look better at a window. The lining prevents the light from passing through the fabric in such a way that it blurs the design.

3. A lining keeps the drapery fabric from fading or showing soil readily.

THE CON SIDE

1. Many drapery fabrics hang in soft folds without a lining.

2. It is less expensive and easier to make unlined draperies.

Types	*Possible Solutions*

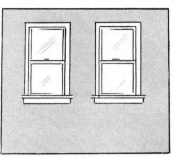

TWIN WINDOWS

Treat as one window with a single cornice or rod placed over the two windows and the wall space, as shown in Figures A, B, and C.

One set of floor-length draperies gives a unified appearance as in Figure A.

The narrow space between the windows may be used for a decorative object, such as a mirror or a hanging as in Figure A. Or another drapery may be used as in Figure B.

If there are radiators or bookcases under the windows, stop the draperies or curtains at the sill or the apron as in Figure C.

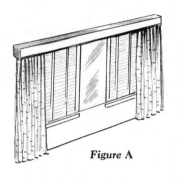

Figure A

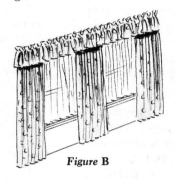

Figure B

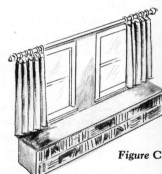

Figure C

BAY WINDOWS

Treat bay windows as a group of windows, with curtains hung in the bay as in Figure A.

Or draw draperies may be hung on the wall that frames the opening of the bay as in Figure B. Curtains may or may not be used.

A curved valance or cornice may be used with side draperies as in Figure C.

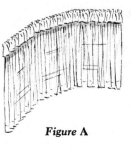

Figure A

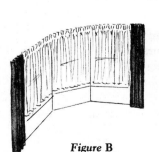

Figure B

Figure C

Types	*Possible Solutions*

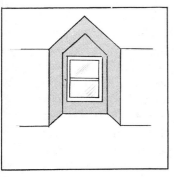

DORMER WINDOW

Simple, sill-length curtains without draperies are generally best, as in Figure A.

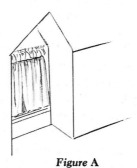

Figure A

PICTURE WINDOW

Draperies need to be hung so they extend over the wall and window frame without shutting out any of the view, as in Figure A. A traverse rod concealed by a cornice can be used to draw the draperies over the windows to close out light and give privacy.

If sunlight is very intense, both draperies and glass curtains, hung on a double traverse rod, may give good control of light, as in Figure B. The glass curtains can soften light without closing it out entirely. They may be concealed behind the draperies when not needed.

A single Venetian blind may be used to control light and privacy as in Figure C. If the view is especially beautiful, draperies or curtains may not be necessary, depending on family preference.

Figure A

Figure B

Figure C

3. Unlined draperies are easier to launder. When lined, they generally need to be dry-cleaned.

Making final decisions for the school projects

As the students appraised the situation in the homemaking living center, they decided to use lined, apron-length draperies with pinch pleats. The draperies would hang from the same rods previously used, with appropriate drapery pins. The size of the windows, the informality of the area, and the activities going on there made apron-length draperies a wise choice. The tailored effect of pinch pleats was also suitable and would cause the draperies to hang gracefully. A colorful print that did not require matching was chosen for the fabric, and a neutral-colored sateen for the lining. The slip cover material for the occasional chair matched one of the colors in the print selected for the draperies. It harmonized with the other furnishings in the living center. Both fabrics were chosen carefully with regard to durability and ease of care.

The fabrics selected for the nurse's office were plain colors. They went well with several colorful patterned accessories which Miss Holmes, the school nurse, planned to continue using. For the curtains, the students chose a sheer Orlon fabric that softened the light yet did not close out too much. They decided to make tailored curtains gathered on the rod. There would be a one-inch heading above the top hem through which the rod would run. For the day bed, they chose a fabric the same color as the plain walls, except that it was a darker shade without offering too much contrast. The students were careful to select a firmly woven, smooth fabric which would resist soil and not spot readily. The slip cover would have inverted pleats (see Book 1, page 439) at the four corners; and the rectangular pillows, a box-type covering. Welting or covered heavy cord would be used around the top edges of the slip cover, and around both front and back edges of the pillows. (See the illustrations on page 294.)

Estimating the amount of fabric needed

Now that the materials had been selected, the next step was to determine how much would be needed. After consulting various references, the students made the following summary for their use at school as well as at home.

DRAPERIES AND CURTAINS

It is desirable to estimate the amount of material needed after the type of drapery and curtain has been decided upon, and after the appropriate fixtures have been installed.

LENGTH ALLOWANCES: An easy way to get the length allowance is to fasten one end of a piece of tape around the rod, and weight the other end. First, measure along the tape with a yardstick from the top of the tape to the length desired — to the sill, to the apron, or to the floor. Then add to these measurements the amount needed for hems. *For draperies with a stiffened pleated heading,* allow 6 inches for 3-inch top and bottom hems plus 2 inches for the heading. *For draperies using pleater tape,* omit the top allowance, adding only ½ inch for attaching the tape. *For curtains,* allow 6 inches for top and bottom hems plus 1 inch for a heading in the top hem. Having the hems alike permits reversing the heading when the lower hem begins to show wear. If double hems in very sheer material are desired, twice the hem allowance needs to be added. For both drapery and curtain fabrics that are likely to shrink, allow 1 inch to the yard.

If the fabric has a pattern that must be matched, allow the equivalent of one extra pattern for each pair of draperies. This extra amount permits moving a design up or down, so that the pattern will be in the same position at the top of each drapery.

WIDTH ALLOWANCES: Both draperies and curtains need to look full to be attractive, but not to the point of appearing bulky. For an average window, 1 width of 50-inch drapery material, or 1½ widths of 36-inch material for each drapery will usually do. Sheer curtains look best when 2 or 3 times the width of the window.

THE LINING: The width may be as much as 5 inches narrower than the drapery material, and the length 8 inches less. Pleater tape (see the illustration on page 287) or drapery stiffening will be needed for the finished — 3 inches less than unfinished — width of each drapery being made.

SLIP COVERS

The width of the material selected needs to be considered in determining the amount needed. Slip cover fabrics usually come in 36- or 50-inch widths. In estimating for large pieces, such as a day bed, the total of all lengths of all sections is generally figured, plus an additional amount for covering cord if used. However, for smaller pieces, such as an occasional chair or the cushions for a day bed, some of the sections may be cut side by side on the same width, especially if a 50-inch width is used. Making a pattern, either from paper, muslin, or an old sheet, is helpful in determining how pieces may be laid out on a minimum amount of material. It is also advisable to use a tape measure rather than a yardstick, since the surfaces to be measured are generally not flat.

THE DAY BED COVER: To estimate the amount of material needed, take the following measurements. (See the illustration on page 294.)

1. The length and width of the top section plus 1 inch on all edges for seams

2. Sides-and-ends section

a. The depth from the top of the mattress to the floor. Allow 3 inches for a hem at the bottom, and 1 inch for a seam at the top.

b. The distance around both sides and both ends of the day bed. Allow 2 inches for a 1-inch seam allowance, and 64 inches for the four inverted pleats — 16 inches per pleat, each pleat 8 inches in total depth. If 50-inch material is used, half this amount plus an additional seam allowance will be sufficient.

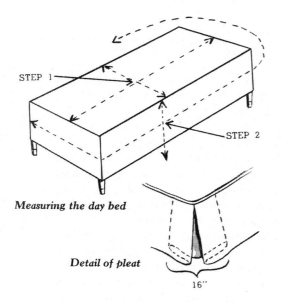

STEP 1

STEP 2

Measuring the day bed

Detail of pleat

16″

THE BOXED CUSHIONS: Directions are given here for measuring one cushion. Three times the amount will be needed for three pillows. Making a paper pattern for the cushions and planning a layout for the width of the material to be used will simplify making the estimate. The following measurements are needed. (See the illustrations on this page and the next one.)

1. Front and back sections

a. The length and width of the cushions — either front or back — plus 1 inch on all edges for seams

b. Allow twice the amount for the two sections.

2. Top-and-upper-sides section

a. The depth of the cushion plus 2 inches for two 1-inch seams

b. The distance around the upper sides and top of the cushion plus 2 inches for two 1-inch seam allowances.

3. Bottom-and-lower-sides section, allowing for a zipper opening to extend across the bottom and 3 inches on each side. Since two strips are needed to insert the zipper, twice the measurements given need to be allowed.

a. Half the depth of the cushion plus a 1-inch seam allowance and a 1½-inch zipper seam

b. The distance around the lower sides and bottom plus 2 inches for two 1-inch seams

c. A second strip equal to a and b in depth and length

CORD FOR THE DAY BED AND CUSHIONS: Measure the distance around the top edges of the day bed, and around either the front or back edges of a cushion, allowing twice the amount for both edges. Three times the total cushion amount will be needed for the three cushions. Allow 1 inch per yard for cutting and joining. Buy the total yardage in one piece if possible. Allow 1¼ to 1½ yards of fabric — over and above the total requirement for the day bed and cushions — for covering the cord.

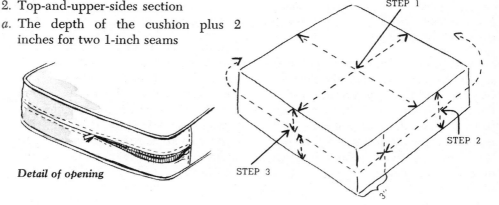

STEP 1

STEP 2

STEP 3

3″

Measuring a pillow

Detail of opening

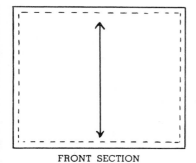

FRONT SECTION

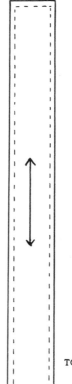

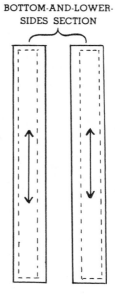

BOTTOM-AND-LOWER-
SIDES SECTION

TOP-AND-UPPER-SIDES SECTION

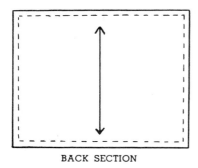

BACK SECTION

Pattern for the boxed cushion

THE OCCASIONAL CHAIR COVER: It is desirable to make a muslin pattern for chairs or a sofa with round or irregular shapes. Not only does this help in estimating the amount of material needed, but it simplifies fitting the cover to the chair. The illustration on page 296 shows how the grain in the muslin pattern is matched to the chair, and the points at which measurements are needed.

1. Back section

a. The length from the top of the chair to the bottom of the seat plus a 1-inch seam allowance at the top and a 3-inch hem allowance at the bottom

b. The width of the chair back plus two 1-inch seam allowances

2. Back-front section

a. The length from the top of the back-front to the top of the seat plus a 1-inch seam allowance at the top and a 3-inch tuck-in at the seat

b. The width of the back-front plus two 1-inch seam allowances

3. Seat section

a. The depth of the seat plus a 1-inch seam allowance at the front and a 3-inch tuck-in at the back

b. The width of the seat plus two 1-inch seam allowances

4. Band section

a. The distance around the front of the seat from side-back to side-back plus two 1-inch seam allowances

b. The depth of the band section plus a 1-inch seam allowance at the top and a 3-inch hem allowance at the bottom

CORD FOR THE CHAIR: Measure the distance over the top of the chair from the bottom of the band on one side to the bottom of the band on the opposite side. Then measure around the top edges of the seat from side-back to side-back. Add the measurements, and allow 1 inch per yard for joining. For covering the cord, an additional ½- to ¾-yard of fabric should be sufficient.

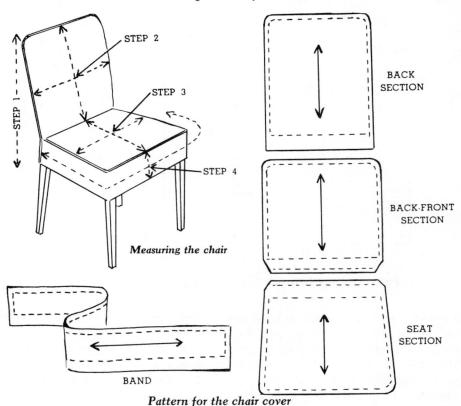

Measuring the chair

BACK SECTION

BACK-FRONT SECTION

SEAT SECTION

BAND

Pattern for the chair cover

Making draperies, curtains, and slip covers

The fabrics which the students selected for their classwork had been preshrunk. However, they realized that if material purchased for home use had not been preshrunk, shrinking would be necessary before the material could be cut. (See Book 1, page 369.) In either case, the grain and the ends of the fabric would need to be straightened before cutting. (See Book 1, pages 394–395.)

With the help of various references, the students worked out the following directions for making draperies, curtains, and slip covers.

LINED DRAPERIES WITH PINCH PLEATS

1. Mark off drapery lengths according to the allowance. Recheck to be sure that the lengths are marked accurately. Cut the lengths by a pulled thread, and trim off the selvages.

2. Mark off lining lengths according to the allowance, and cut by a pulled thread. Make each lining — without selvages — 5 inches narrower than the width of the drapery.

3. Place the right sides of the drapery and lining together, so that the top of the lining is 5 inches below the top of the drapery. The bottom of the lining will be 3 inches above the bottom of the drapery. Baste and stitch the side lengths, starting from the top down. Allow ½ inch for the seams. Clip the seam edges at 4- to 5-inch intervals, and press the seams open. (See Book 1, pages 408–409 and page 410.)

4. Turn the drapery right side out. Flatten the lining to the drapery, so that 1 inch of the drapery extends beyond the seam on both sides. Baste the drapery edge, and press flat with a damp cloth.

5. If pleats are to be sewed in rather than put in with pleater tape and insertion hooks (see the illustration on page 298), cut a strip of drapery stiffening as long as the width of the turned and flattened drapery. Place the upper edge of the stiffening even with the upper edge of the drapery, and baste and stitch along the lower edge of the stiffening. Turn down the top hem of the drapery the full width of the stiffening. Fold the side seams in place, mitering the corners. (See the illustration.) Cut out excess material, and slip-stitch corners in place. Baste or press a ½-inch turn in the top of the lining. Then baste and slip-stitch the lining to the drapery. (See Book 1, page 434 for making a slip stitch.)

6. If pleater tape is used, cut a strip 1 inch longer than the lined drapery for a ½-inch turn-under at both ends. Use

the tape — minus the turn-unders — to locate the position of the pleats on the fixture. See the illustration. Mark the location of the pleats on the tape. Then unpleat the tape. Turn the right side of the drapery up. Turn the pocket-opening side of the tape up and away from the drapery top. Lap the tape to the drapery, covering ½ inch of the drapery and extending ½ inch beyond the drapery at both sides. Stitch. Turn the drapery over, and baste the tape flat against the wrong side of the drapery. Press, and remove basting. Turn under the ½-inch tape overlap at each side, and stitch it to the drapery. Finish the lower edge of

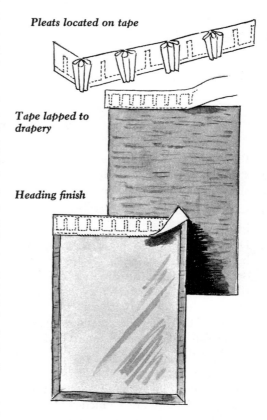

Pleats located on tape

Tape lapped to drapery

Heading finish

Drapery made with pleater tape

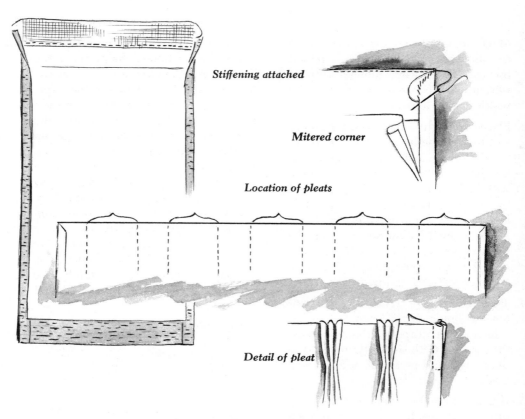

Stiffening attached

Mitered corner

Location of pleats

Detail of pleat

Drapery made with stiffening

the tape to the drapery, machine-stitching across sections for pleats and slip-stitching in between.

7. If the stiffened top is used, make the pleats.

a. Determine the amount of material to be put into pleats in each drapery. To do this, measure the distance on the rod the drapery needs to cover, allowing 3 inches for the curve of the rod to the wall. The width of the drapery minus this measurement is to be taken up in pleats.

b. Plan the number of pleats. Divide the above figure into an odd number. For example, if there are 25 inches of material to put into pleats, divide it into 5 pleats, each pleat to be 5 inches.

c. Using the 25 inches as an example, mark the following pleats with pins.

Pleat 1 — at the curve of the rod,
      3 inches from outside edge
Pleat 2 — 2 inches from center edge
      of drapery
Pleat 3 — center between pleats 1 and 2
Pleat 4 — center between pleats 1 and 3
Pleat 5 — center between pleats 2 and 3

d. Fold each section into a single pleat on the right side of the drapery, and stitch down 1 inch below the stiffened heading.

e. Divide each single large pleat into 3 small pleats. Stitch in place at lower edge of heading by machine, or by hand if material is bulky.

8. Make the bottom hems. If the drapery

material is heavy, it may be advisable to let the draperies hang on the rod a day before putting in the hems. Miter the corners of the drapery hem, and slip-stitch in place. Turn the drapery hem, and put it in by hand. The lining hem may be stitched by machine. When finished, it needs to cover the top edge of the drapery hem by about 1 inch. Press, and hang.

TAILORED CURTAINS

1. Mark off curtain lengths according to the allowance. Recheck to be sure that the lengths are measured accurately. Cut the lengths by a pulled thread, and trim off selvages.
2. Using a gauge, pin, baste, and stitch a 1¼-inch double-turn hem in both sides of the curtain. Remove bastings, and press.
3. Pin, baste, and stitch a 2¾-inch double-turn hem in both ends of the curtain. Remove bastings, and press.
4. Mark a line 1 inch down from the outside edge of the top hem. Stitch on this line to make a casing. Press.

CORDING

1. Cut bias strips of fabric to make cording in the amount needed. (See Book 1, pages 425–426, for cutting and joining bias strips.) The illustration shows a quick way to join several yards at

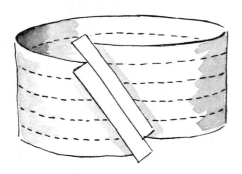

once. The strips need to be 2 inches wider than the circumference of the cord.
2. Place the cord in the center of the strip on the wrong side. Fold the strip over the cord, bringing the edges of the strip together. Stitch close to the cord, using a cording foot on the machine. To be sure that the cording foot hugs the cord closely, hold the strip and the cord well in toward the foot as you guide it under the needle.

DAY BED SLIP COVER

1. Cut top section, and sides-and-ends section according to allowance.
2. Pin and baste cording around the right side of the top section, matching the cut edges. Use a 1-inch seam allowance, and begin on one side or end of the top section. Hold cording slightly full to turn square corners. Join the cording where it meets on the side or end of the top section. Seam the straight ends of the cord covering together, and press open. Clip cord until it barely meets, and whip together.
3. Baste and stitch sides-and-ends section together. Press seams. Turn the joined section right side out. Make an inverted pleat according to the allowance, so that the joining seams fall at one inside edge of the pleat. See the illustration.
4. With right sides together, baste the sides-and-ends section to the top section, placing the center of the inverted pleat at one corner of the top section. Make other inverted pleats at the three remaining corners. Try the cover on the day bed to see how it fits. Stitch if satisfactory.
5. Hem the bottom of the slip cover. Press with a damp cloth.

BOXED CUSHION COVER

1. Place the paper pattern made for the estimate on the fabric. Cut front and back sections, top-and-upper-sides section, and the two strips for the bottom-and-lower-sides section.

2. Baste and stitch cording around the front and the back sections as directed in step 2 for the day bed.

3. Use a running stitch or machine basting (see Book 1, pages 400–401) to join the two bottom-and-lower-sides strips together on the zipper seam allowance. Press the seam open. Turn under 1 inch at both ends of top-and-upper-sides section. Stitch both ends to the ends of the bottom-and-lower-sides section on the seam allowance. Insert zipper in bottom-and-lower-sides section. To do this, turn section to right side. Place the right side of the zipper to the wrong side of the zipper seam, center to center. Pin and baste zipper to zipper seam. Stitch around sides and ends of zipper as close as possible to the zipper chain. Remove bastings, including the one that covers the zipper. Press.

4. Baste the joined top, bottom, and sides section to the front section and to the back section. Try the cover on the cushion to see how it fits. Stitch if satisfactory. Remove bastings and press.

OCCASIONAL CHAIR SLIP COVER

1. Place the pattern made for the estimate on the slip cover fabric. Cut back section, back-front section, seat section, and band.

2. Baste cording around the sides and front of the seat section on the right side of the seat section at the 1-inch seam allowance on both.

3. Join the seat section and the back-front section on the tuck-in edges.

4. Baste the band to the sides and front of the seat section.

5. Baste cording to the back section from side to side over the top.

6. Baste the back section to the back-front section and the band. Try on the chair to test fit. Stitch all seams if satisfactory and if no opening is necessary.

7. An opening is not needed for this type of cover unless the back of the chair is narrower at the seat than at the top. If so, leave one side open, and stitch in snap or hook-and-eye tape, or make a simple placket and sew fasteners on. (See Book 1, pages 437 and 443.)

8. Make a double-turn hem in the bottom of the slip cover according to allowance, and slip-stitch in place. Press.

CLASS MEMO:
    How will your group use the information on making draperies, curtains, and slip covers assembled by Miss Rand's class?

Learning About Repairing and Refinishing Furniture

As the boys surveyed their part of the classwork, Keith suggested that Mr. Glenn, the shop teacher, might give them some ideas. "He's an expert at refinishing furniture," said Keith, "and he probably has lots of reference materials we could use."

There were nods of agreement from the other boys and from Miss Rand. Keith and Alex were then appointed to talk with Mr. Glenn. The two boys soon reported that the interview had been very satisfactory. Mr. Glenn was more than willing to help them. In fact, he had offered some excellent suggestions on the type of work the group could do successfully at this stage of their experience. If special tools were needed, those in the shop could be used. Various references on repairing and refinishing furniture would also be made available when the boys were ready for them.

Setting up a plan for determining the work to be done

Mr. Glenn's remarks led the boys to work out the following plan for determining what kinds of repairing and refinishing could be successfully undertaken.

1. At school Miss Rand and the boys would look around for possible projects. At home each student and a member of his family would do the same.

2. Pieces of furniture were to be examined first from the standpoint of re-

pairs. If a piece was in good condition and considered worth repairing, the necessary repairs would then be determined. When the repairs were minor ones, such as gluing loose joints and removing dents, scratches, or stains, information would be assembled for this work. Major repairs, such as removing a warp, replacing broken or lost parts, or patching damaged areas, would probably require the skill of a woodworker.

3. For pieces in line for something more than repair, the finish or paint covering would be carefully examined. If a piece was made of wood pleasing in grain and color and the lines were good, a finish that showed the grain would be considered. If a piece was made of wood uneven in grain or inappropriate in color, a paint job would probably be recommended. Information on different grain finishes — as the students called them — and on painting would then be assembled.

Making repairs

The problem of furniture with loose joints proved to be fairly common. In addition to what the boys reported from home inspections, some of the girls working in the other group found several pieces in their homes that needed this type of repair. At school one of the dining table chairs in the homemaking unit kitchens had several loose joints.

Scratches and burns on furniture were also numerous. There was a light scratch on one of a nest of tables in the homemaking living center. Some of the cutting tables

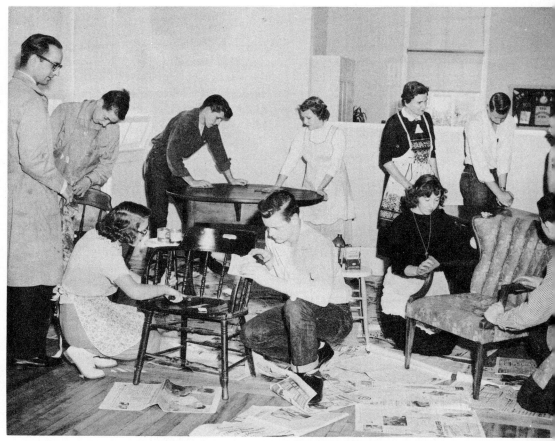

Here a class of boys and girls is carrying out an extensive furniture repairing and refinishing project. Note the shop teacher as well as the homemaking teacher.

in the clothing center had deeper scratches. Several students reported dents, as well as white spots, light rings, and ink and other dark stains on their furniture at home. The desk in the nurse's office revealed a light ring, and a small reading table in one of the English rooms had an ink stain. These and other projects located at school gave the students plenty to do.

The boys then divided into smaller groups — according to their preferences — to repair loose joints, and to remove various scratches,

dents, and stains. The directions and information they assembled for their own use as well as for use at home follow:

GLUING LOOSE JOINTS

EQUIPMENT NEEDED

Small knife or chisel
Narrow strips of firm cloth if necessary
Plastic resin glue
Piece of soft cloth
Clamp, or a heavy piece of cotton clothesline and a stick for twisting the cord tight
Old newspapers

PROCEDURE

1. Test all joints for tightness.
2. Take the loose joints apart. Be careful not to damage or mar the wood.
3. Mark all adjoining parts with a corresponding number. Place numbers on inside of joinings where they will not show. This will help in reassembling the parts.
4. Chip or scrape off all the old glue with the knife or chisel. Avoid cutting into the wood.
5. Assemble parts to see that they fit perfectly. If a joint fits loosely, place one or two strips of firm cloth over the end that goes into the hole. Test to see that it fits tightly. Remove parts again.
6. Warm the parts to be glued in a very low oven or in the sun. This opens the pores of the wood and makes gluing more effective.
7. Apply glue to all parts of the wood to be joined, using strips of cloth over the ends if necessary. Assemble parts, and press together very firmly to squeeze out as much glue as possible. Too much glue may prevent the parts from making contact, and the joints will not hold well. Wipe off excess glue with the soft cloth. Plastic resin glue is especially recommended for beginners. It is waterproof, holds and lasts well, and does not stain the wood.
8. Use a clamp or rope to hold the glued parts together. But first place pads of newspaper under the clamp or rope where it presses on the wood to avoid marring. Hold in position for at least 24 hours until the glue is thoroughly dry. Some people prefer a rope tourniquet to a clamp, because it distributes the pressure more evenly. A single tourniquet is made by placing the rope once around the article, while in the double tourniquet the rope is passed around twice. The ends of the rope are tied together — a bow knot is good — and a stick is twisted in the rope until the desired tension is obtained.

REMOVING SCRATCHES OR BURNS

LIGHT SCRATCHES: These may be removed by rubbing them with a little raw linseed oil, or with a piece of oily nut meat, such as a walnut or pecan. Or commercial scratch removers may be used.

MODERATELY DEEP SCRATCHES: Apply an oil stain that matches the wood to the scratch, using a toothpick or a small brush. Wipe off the surplus oil, and allow the area to dry for 24 hours. Repeat the procedure, this time overfilling the crack. After the stain is dry, rub the spot down with pumice stone and oil.

DEEP SCRATCHES: Be sure that the scratch is thoroughly cleaned out. Then use stick shellac to match the color of the finish. Soften the end of the stick shellac against a heated soldering iron, allowing the melted wax to drop into the depression. Avoid letting the shellac become too hot, so that bubbles form. Before the shellac hardens, flatten it out with the blade of a spatula, leaving the shellac slightly higher than the surface of the crack. Let it stand until thoroughly hard, and then sand it with a fine sandpaper until smooth. When scratches have been removed, go over the area with furniture polish or wax.

RAISING DENTS

Cover the dents with a piece of wet blotting paper. Wet felt or several thicknesses of wet woolen cloth could also be used. Press down on the blotting paper with a hot iron for a few seconds. This produces steam which will make the wood swell, lessening the effect of the dent. To remove the dent completely, lift the iron up and down several times, being careful not to let the blotter become dry lest the wood be burned. This treatment is usually not satisfactory for dents in hard maple, and is not recommended for veneered furniture. In such cases, sanding will probably be needed to remove the dents. This will mean removing the finish, doing the sanding, and then refinishing.

REMOVING STAINS

Speed is necessary in removing liquids from furniture. Sometimes a water spot can be avoided. But the ingredients in beverages, medicine, or perfume may dissolve the finish. When wiped up quickly, the finish is more easily restored. The method used depends to a great extent upon the depth of the stain and the damage it has done. It is best to try to remove the stain by simple methods first. If not successful, then more drastic treatment may be necessary.

WHITE SPOTS, WATER RINGS, OR BEVERAGE STAINS: There are various ways of treating such stains. If one does not work, then try another.

1. Rub with a soft cloth dipped in paste wax, linseed oil, or a mixture of cigarette or cigar ashes and butter.

2. Rub with a piece of flannel dampened with spirits of camphor or essence of peppermint. Or use a few drops of ammonia on a damp cloth. This method is especially good for a varnished surface.

3. Make a thick paste of powdered pumice stone and raw linseed oil, and rub it on the spot with a soft cloth.

If the spot is successfully removed, follow with an application of furniture polish or wax after a brief interval. If the spot cannot be removed, try the procedure for dark stains, or plan to refinish the surface of the entire piece.

DARK STAINS: Dark stains, especially ink spots, are often difficult to remove if the stain has penetrated into the wood. Try an application of pure ammonia, or a saturated solution of oxalic acid. Apply with a brush, and allow it to stand until dry — about an hour. It may be necessary to repeat the application. If the bleached area becomes different in color from the surface around it, remove all of the finish, and use the solution over the entire surface. Then remove all traces of the solution by rinsing the surface with lukewarm water two or three times. Wear gloves to protect the hands if oxalic acid is used. Refinish the surface as desired.

If an ink stain is only on the surface of the finish, it may be removed by using a mixture of ground pumice stone and light oil made into a paste. Rub with the grain of the wood, using a soft cloth. Clean this off with another cloth dampened in turpentine.

Learning about new finishes

Before the boys made any further plans for their classwork, they looked over the interview form that had been used when they were setting goals for "Rooms for Happier Living." They found that quite a few families wanted to know more about refinishing furniture. Although the students themselves had had some previous experience on refinishing furniture (see Book 1, Joseph's Story, pages 302–311), they realized that much remained to be learned.

"Sometimes you can't tell what kind of wood is under the paint," commented Russell, "until you've removed the finish."

"That's right," said Lewis, "and there's a lot I don't know about removers. I've heard that some are better than others."

"I don't understand all the grain finishes Mr. Glenn mentioned," added Keith. "We are thinking about refinishing our dining table, and we don't know which finish to use."

These and other comments led the group to ask Mr. Glenn to talk to the class on applying new finishes. The girls as well as the boys were very much interested in what he had to say.

Mr. Glenn started off by emphasizing the point that three major steps are generally followed in refinishing furniture: (1) removing old finishes, (2) making necessary preparations for the new finish, and (3) applying the new finish. He then went on to comment on these three points. Summaries of what he said follow:

REMOVING OLD FINISHES

Before a new finish is applied, it is usually desirable to remove the old finish first. (See Book 1, page 310.) However, in the case of painted pieces this may not be necessary if the surface is perfectly smooth. Then a new coat may be put on over the cleaned surface. In removing old finishes, the hints given on the following page may be useful:

- It pays to use a reliable paint or varnish remover that does not contain lye or ammonia. Lye tends to burn the wood and to raise the grain, while ammonia bleaches the wood. Follow directions carefully.

- Remember that nearly all removers are flammable. Do not use them around open fires or in rooms that are not well ventilated. An open porch or the back yard is the safest place to work in.

- Wear old leather gloves to protect the hands.

- Burn all rags and papers used in removing the finish.

- Do not allow too long an interval to elapse between the time the old finish is taken off and the new one put on. This is especially important for old wood which is usually dry. When exposed to the air, old dry wood deteriorates rapidly.

PREPARATIONS FOR THE NEW FINISH

This might include making needed repairs, such as gluing loose joints or parts, removing stains or other discolorations, and filling in dents. It would include sanding the surface very smooth, and cleaning away all traces of sawdust. For some of the grain finishes, the addition of a stain might be needed, depending upon the amount lost in removing the finish and the darkness desired.

APPLYING THE NEW FINISH

The best choice of finish is determined by several considerations. Some of these are the kind of wood and the structural lines used in making the piece. Others are the use to be made of the piece, family preferences, and the effect desired in a room. Sometimes it is best to paint; other times, to use a finish that shows the grain. Once a grain finish is determined, another choice is necessary — the type of grain finish. Common types of finishes and some highlights on using them follow:

VARNISH FINISH: This finish has great lasting qualities and resists scratches. It can be made partially or fully resistant to water, heat, and other stains that are acid in nature.

SHELLAC-AND-WAX FINISH: This is one of the most popular finishes, because of its ease of application and the satisfaction it gives from the standpoint of beauty. But shellac stains easily. However, if the surfaces are well protected when in use, many types of furniture may be given this finish, and be satisfactory.

BLOND FINISH: Many of the streamlined modern pieces of furniture have this finish. A strong bleach is used to lighten the color of the wood before it is finished by some method, such as shellac and wax, or varnish. A bleach is most successful on new, light-colored, close-grained hardwoods.

LACQUER FINISH: A good lacquer finish is waterproof, extremely durable, and resistant to mars and scratches. The best results are obtained by spraying the lacquer on. But there are some kinds that can be applied satisfactorily with a brush.

OIL FINISH: This is one of the most satisfactory of all finishes, but it takes time, patience, and willingness to do an endless amount of rubbing to produce a beautiful, rich finish. (See Book 1, page 310.)

HIGHLIGHTS ON APPLYING FINISHES:

* Mahogany, walnut, cherry, oak, maple, and curly birch look best when done in a grain finish, so that the beauty of the wood will not be concealed. The finish acts as a clear, protecting coat that preserves the natural beauty of the wood.

* Thick, glossy coats of finish call attention to themselves instead of bringing out the beauty of the wood.

* When applying new finishes, keep the following considerations in mind.

1. A room temperature of at least 70 degrees is desirable.

2. Use a brush that does not shed its bristles.

3. Keep the can containing the finish tightly closed when not in use. Never leave the brush standing in the finish. When a short period is to elapse between uses, suspend the brush up to the rim of the handle in turpentine or whatever liquid is used for thinning purposes. This can be done by tying the brush to a stick placed across the top of the container.

4. When the final application has been made, clean the brush in turpentine or a commercial cleaner. Rinse well; shake dry, and tie in a paper or plastic bag. Hang or lay the bag so that the ends of the bristles will not turn up.

Carrying out the school projects

The students agreed that Mr. Glenn's talk had been very helpful. Now they were eager to get started on their refinishing projects.

After some discussion, they decided to refinish a small bookcase from Miss Rand's apartment and a drop-leaf table from the teachers' lounge. Chairs from the homemaking unit kitchens would provide painting experiences.

The finish chosen for Miss Rand's bookcase was shellac and wax. It seemed appropriate in the room and to the use made of the bookcase. However, in the process of refinishing, a little darker stain was required. The table in the teachers' lounge was given a varnish finish. Since it was sometimes used for serving coffee and tea, the top was made resistant to moisture and heat. There were no cracks or other rough places in the chairs, and their color was not changed.

Space does not permit a fuller account of how the group worked. However, from the available reference sources, the boys prepared information sheets on staining, on shellacking and waxing, on varnishing, and on painting. These were available to anyone who might use them at home. The sheets are reproduced on pages 308 to 311.

CLASS MEMO:

What kinds of repairing and refinishing projects will your group carry out?

STAINING

Do you know?

There are several kinds of wood stains, but the ones easiest for beginners are oil stains. Since a little goes a long way, they are widely sold in small containers. They come in nonfading colors.

A stain is generally not a finish. A finishing coat must be applied, except in the use of varnish stains, penetrating wood-sealer stains, and lacquer containing stains.

Pieces of furniture in which more than one kind of wood has been used usually look better when all woods are stained to match one of the woods.

Equipment needed

Old newspapers
Stain
Clean soft brush
Turpentine
Lintless, absorbent cloths

Procedures

1. Spread newspapers under or around the piece to be stained.
2. Apply the stain evenly with no overlapping strokes. Keep the brush quite full, but not wet enough to drip. Follow the grain of the wood.
3. Let the stain penetrate 3 to 5 minutes. Then wipe off all excess stain with a cloth. If the wood has more color than desired, wash out some color by going over the wood before it is dry with a cloth soaked in turpentine. If the color is not dark enough after the first application is thoroughly dry, apply a second coat.
4. Allow the stain to dry at least 48 hours before applying the finish.

A SHELLAC–AND–WAX FINISH

Do you know?

Wax should not be applied to bare wood, but always over some kind of finishing material.

White shellac does not change the color of wood, but orange shellac gives a slightly reddish tinge.

Several thin coats of shellac are better than one heavy one.
For best results do not apply shellac on a rainy day.

Paste wax rather than liquid or self-polishing wax is generally used for a shellac and wax finish. It gives a harder, more permanent coating, and has a soft, pleasing luster that results from rubbing the wax.

Equipment needed

Old newspaper
Shellac
Denatured alcohol
Two-inch brush with natural bristles
Fine steel wool
Paste wax
Cheesecloth
Soft polishing cloth or piece of woolen blanket

Procedures

1. Spread newspapers under or around piece to be shellacked.
2. Apply with the brush a mixture of half shellac and half denatured alcohol. Draw the brush once across the surface as smoothly as possible. Do not attempt to go over uneven spots or to remove any air blisters.
3. Let dry thoroughly. The first coat will be dry in 20 to 30 minutes.
4. Rub lightly with steel wool, rubbing with the grain of the wood.
5. Wipe clean with a piece of cheesecloth.
6. Repeat steps 2, 3, 4, and 5 at least three times, allowing several hours between each coat. Let the final coat dry at least 24 hours before proceeding.
7. Place a small amount of wax between layers of cheesecloth, and apply a thin layer to the surface of the furniture, using a circular motion.
8. Let the wax dry 3 to 4 minutes.
9. Polish with soft cloth or woolen blanket until the surface is hard and smooth with a pleasing luster.
10. Repeat steps 7, 8, and 9 if desired.

A VARNISH FINISH

Do you know?

Damp weather is not a good time to apply varnish.

In addition to a room temperature of 70 degrees, there should be good ventilation when varnish is used. An opened window is desirable, but a draft may stir up dust.

It is best to wear clothing that is free from lint or dust.

During a varnishing job, it is best not to sweep or clean the room.

Equipment needed

Old newspapers
Spar varnish if resistance to heat and moisture is desired
Shallow dish
Pan with warm water
Two-inch brush
Fine steel wool
Powdered pumice
Boiled linseed oil
Piece of old woolen blanket or similar material
Soft cloth

Procedures

1. Spread newspaper under or around piece to be varnished.
2. Pour a small amount of varnish into the dish.
3. Set the dish in the pan with the warm water. Keep the water warm while varnishing.
4. Brush varnish onto the surface of the furniture, brushing first with the grain of the wood, then across the grain, and finally with the grain again. Keep the coat thin.
5. Allow at least three days for the varnish to dry.
6. Rub lightly and carefully with steel wool, rubbing with the grain of the wood.
7. Repeat steps 2 to 6 until there are as many coats of varnish as desired, usually two to four.
8. After the final coat is thoroughly dry, rub down as follows:
a. Place a small amount of pumice and a small amount of linseed oil in separate saucers.
b. Make a thick pad of the blanket or similar material.
c. Dip pad in oil, then into the pumice, and rub varnished surface. This develops a sheen instead of a shine.
d. Polish surface with soft cloth. A final coat of wax may be used if desired.

A PAINT FINISH

Do you know?

It is not necessary to remove an old finish of paint or enamel if the surface is smooth and is not scaled or cracked. Painting over cracks, seals, or paint that has dripped will not give a satisfactory effect.

High quality enamel is more economical and will give greater satisfaction in the long run than low grades.

If you are changing the color of a piece of furniture or painting an unfinished piece, white coats under the enamel will be needed.

Equipment needed

Old newspapers
Paint with an oil base — flat white for undercoats; enamel for top coat, color desired
Turpentine
Two-inch brush
Fine sandpaper and pumice

Procedures

1. Spread newspaper under or around the piece being painted.
2. Check to see that the surface to be painted is clean, smooth, dry, and not cracked. Wash and dry if necessary, or remove cracked paint.
3. Apply a coat of thin flat white, thinned with turpentine if necessary.
   a. Be sure that the paint is thoroughly mixed with a stick or paddle.
   b. Dip the brush only ⅓ the length of the bristles. Press off excess paint against the inside rim of the can.
   c. Work with the grain of the wood.
   d. Brush paint out well, avoiding runs and sags.
   e. Let dry, and then sand lightly.
4. Repeat step 3.
5. Apply enamel. If the enamel is high quality, one coat may be used. But two or more thin coats, lightly sanded after each coat — except the last — are recommended. A beautiful finish may be obtained by rubbing down the last coat to a soft polish with powdered pumice or rottenstone and water.

Knowing How to Get the Best Values When Buying Furniture

Learning how to buy furniture turned out to be an interesting experience. The interview form used at the beginning of the classwork on living areas indicated that several families were interested in the subject. And as short- and long-term plans for home improvement developed, buying certain pieces of furniture was included in the setup. As members of the family group, the students whose families purchased new pieces had a share in the selection of what was bought. What had been learned in the class experience with Miss Vandermeer proved helpful in making suitable choices.

However, since buying furniture is a major family investment, there was a general agreement that additional information was needed. This was obtained from various sources. At one point the class heard a talk by a salesman on what constitutes durability and good construction in furniture. References on buying furniture were also consulted. Several students who were interested investigated the possibility of buying used pieces instead of new ones. Eventually the following guides for buying furniture were set up and approved by the class.

1. Select furniture that meets your needs and desires, and that you can afford. It is best to buy furniture as it is needed. If you plan ahead and pay cash, you can avoid carrying charges and the temptation to overbuy. Purchasing something that is not quite suitable simply because it appears to be a bargain is a costly investment. Suites of furniture that are alike in every detail and that are obviously purchased at one time can be dull and uninteresting. Pieces acquired one by one because they fulfill a family's need for comfort or beauty give individuality to a room. Furthermore, knowing values in furniture construction will help you in selecting the best you can afford. Think through clearly what you need and want, and then shop around until you find it.

2. Consider how the room as a whole will look with the furniture. Not only does a new piece of furniture need to be attractive within itself, but it needs to fit into the room where it is used. This means that it needs to have a family resemblance to the other pieces in form and shape, and to be harmonious in texture or pattern. It also needs to fit into the color scheme of the room. Furthermore, it is important for the piece to be in scale with the other pieces and with the room itself. However, judging scale accurately in the store is sometimes difficult. But measuring the piece and comparing the measurements with the space the furniture is to occupy will help to determine a suitable size.

3. Check on observable features. By observable features is meant those parts of a piece of furniture which are exposed. With experience you will be able to judge some of these features by sight. Others will require reading a label or asking the salesman questions. In case there is no informative label, ask the salesman to put his answers in writing on the sales slip if you make a purchase.

a. THE WOOD: Hardwoods are the most satisfactory, because of their strength and durability and because they do not dent easily. Mahogany, walnut, hard maple, birch, oak, and cherry are examples. Gumwood is also hard but dents more easily than some of the others mentioned. It is often stained to resemble mahogany or walnut, and is less expensive than either of these. Furniture may be made of solid wood. Or parts of it may be of veneer — which is a thin sheet cut from sections of the tree where grain is unusually beautiful and glued under pressure over plywood of varying thicknesses. A good, well-applied veneer may be stronger than solid wood of equal thickness, and is less likely to shrink, swell, or warp.

b. THE FINISH: Let the light reflect on the surface to see whether it is smooth and free from rough spots. A good finish has a satiny smoothness rather than a shiny appearance. The finish needs to look as though it had been worked into the wood, not resting on it. Some finishes may be treated so that they are resistant to water, other liquids, and heat.

c. THE CONSTRUCTION: See that the piece stands firmly under pressure. In good furniture, some of the joints are reinforced with triangular corner blocks, which are glued and screwed to the adjoining wood. (See the illustration.) In less expensive pieces, nails are used

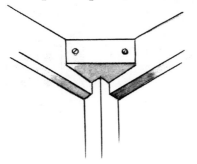

to hold the blocks. Be sure that the wood has not been splintered or cracked by the nailing. Look behind, inside, and outside. In high-quality furniture, the back and underside are smooth and are sealed with varnish or shellac to prevent swelling or shrinking. Pull out drawers, and open doors. Drawers need to be well finished inside, and to slide in and out evenly and smoothly. (The illustration below shows good drawer construction.) Doors should fit well and close easily.

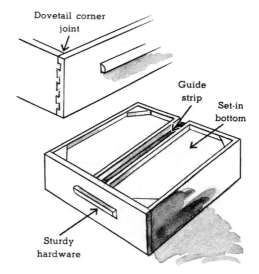

Dovetail corner joint

Guide strip

Set-in bottom

Sturdy hardware

d. THE HARDWARE: Be sure that it is suited to the design of the furniture, that it is smooth and well attached, and that it is strong enough to withstand pull and strain.

e. IF UPHOLSTERED: It is possible to buy a well-constructed piece in one of two ways: (1) covered in muslin and (2) completely upholstered. In the first instance, the piece is priced without the upholstery, which may be selected at the price, in the quality, and in the effect desired. If the piece comes upholstered, the fabric needs to be evalu-

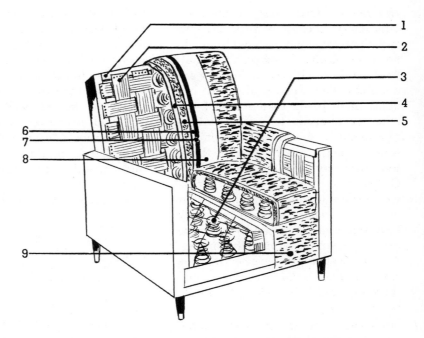

1. Sturdy hardwood frame with dowel joints and corner block reinforcements
2. Firm, closely woven webbing, preferably jute, interlaced closely across back, seat, and arms
3. Closely placed steel springs, tied together at the top in eight directions and securely fastened to the frame
4. Burlap or other heavy fabric over springs
5. New or sterilized hair or moss filling
6. Muslin or burlap filling over stuffing and quilted to it
7. Cotton-felt or foam-rubber padding for smoothness and comfort
8. Muslin cover
9. Upholstery cover

ated for resistance to wear, soil, fading, and suitability in the room. Avoid buying flashy material, which is usually an indication of inferior materials and construction in the concealed parts of the chair. Inferior exposed wooden surfaces also generally indicate poor quality inside the chair.

4. Find out about hidden values. Again read labels, or ask the salesman questions. If you make a purchase, have him write the answers on the sales slip.

a. THE JOINTS: In good construction, joints are either doweled or mortised and tenoned together. A dowel is a wooden pin — preferably grooved — which is glued into holes in the pieces to be joined, thus making them firm and rigid. A double-dowel joint uses two wooden pins instead of one, and

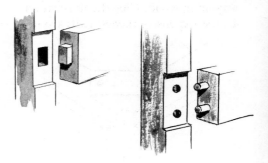

offers greater resistance to strain. A tenon is a rectangular projection which is covered with glue and inserted into the mortise, or hole. All of these provide resistance to strain. (See the illustrations on page 314.)

b. IF UPHOLSTERED: The unexposed portions of the frame need to be made of hardwood thoroughly seasoned to prevent warping and to hold tacks and screws securely. Dowel construction and reinforced corners are also necessary for durability. In good construction, strong jute webbing closely laced across the back, seat, and arms is used to support the springs. In less expensive pieces metal or wooden slats are sometimes used. Springs need to be close enough together to prevent sagging, but not to touch. In good construction, the tops of the coils are tied in eight directions with strong twine. A heavy fabric is stretched over the springs and tacked in place. Stuffing is laid smoothly over the covered springs. Another layer of fabric covers the stuffing, and is quilted to the lower layer to prevent slipping. In the best construction, a second layer of stuffing and another cloth cover are added. Cotton felt is placed over the stuffing to give smoothness and comfort to the rounded arms and back. A muslin cover — a mark of good construction — is applied before the permanent upholstery. (See the illustration on page 314.)

5. Compare values of new and used furniture if cost is important. If the family budget does not permit new furniture, several things may be done to bring satisfaction. Watch for advertisements in the local newspapers. Sometimes good values may be found that way.

Or run an ad of your own. But in either case when you inspect the furniture, be sure to check in so far as possible the four points just mentioned. Occasionally you may be able to attend an auction which offers something you need and desire. But here again, be careful to examine each piece carefully before you consider bidding. At the same time, make up your mind the top price that you are willing to pay. Still another source of supply might be a secondhand shop where manufacturers' seconds are often sold in addition to used furniture. But again be careful to check the points just mentioned.

Evaluating the classwork on buying furniture

Before the work on buying furniture was completed, the students realized that they would need some way of evaluating what they had been learning. After discussing the matter, it was decided that each student would submit one or more comments on buying furniture. These comments would indicate what the student considered either good or poor judgment in buying.

When the comments were handed in, a group of the students and Miss Rand went over them. They chose some of the outstanding examples, and organized them into what they called "The Know-How of Buying Furniture." By making choices — as indicated in the directions — a student could evaluate his or her progress toward understanding the best values when buying furniture. Since other classes may be interested in the device, it is reproduced on the next page.

CLASS MEMO:

Is the subject of buying furniture to be a part of your classwork? If so, how will your group handle different family problems?

Seeing Some of the Improvements Made at Home

Now that the second goal was completed, the students were ready to report on the short- and long-term plans they had made for making the living area at home meet the needs and desires of the family. (See page 282.)

The reports showed much enthusiasm on the part of the students, and indicated that their families had been most cooperative. Of course, everyone realized that it was not possible to carry out all of the desired improvements within the time set aside for this part of the classwork. But even the short-term plans, such as regrouping the furniture, providing better traffic lanes, or creating a center of interest, seemed to give an uplift to members of a family.

Since it is always interesting to see things firsthand, arrangements were made to visit some of the homes. This was done with the approval of the families and to suit their convenience. The students living in the homes showed what had been done and explained any long-term plans the family had made. It was a stimulating experience that everyone enjoyed. But space does not permit a detailed account of all the homes that were visited.

However, one example is given to indicate how some of Miss Vandermeer's suggestions and the information worked out in class were adapted to one situation. A report of what the students saw and had explained to them follows:

AT JERRY'S HOME

MY FAMILY: Father; Mother; Helene, age 10; Marie, age 8; and I

OUR PLAN: To make our living-dining area seem larger and be easier to care for

THE FLOOR: A wall-to-wall covering of inlaid linoleum was put on the floor. This was the first approach to making the total area seem larger and be easier to care for. The linoleum is a plain, medium color that does not show dirt readily. It was given several coats of wax for protection and for ease of upkeep. Mother believes that vacuum cleaning once a week in the living area will be all that is necessary for that section of the room. The dining area

THE KNOW-HOW OF BUYING FURNITURE

The left-hand column describes briefly five factors that need to be considered when buying furniture. The five columns to the right indicate remarks that might be made concerning such purchases. Select the remark on each of the five factors that shows the least know-how. Write the numbers of your answers on a separate piece of paper. Then compare them with the answers given on the next page.

Factors in buying furniture	1	2	3	4	5
A. Decide that it is really needed and that it can be afforded.	"This chair is perfect for Dad and it's to be chiefly his anyway."	"The dusting of this would be too difficult and tedious for anyone in our family."	"This suite of furniture is a great bargain. It's the kind everyone else has."	"I'm sorry. The seat is too high for the comfort of most of our family."	"This piece suits the room to perfection, but it's too heavy to move easily."
B. Consider how the room as a whole will look with this piece.	"This piece is so beautiful that maybe we should take it even though it looks too luxurious for the rest of the room."	"May I measure this chest to see how it will fit into the room? Furniture is likely to look larger in a home than in a store."	"This chair is just what the family has been looking for. It has a high back, but it's still in scale with the other pieces."	"It wasn't what we had in mind. It won't fit in with our color scheme. Thank you, we'll look elsewhere."	"The style and finish will be perfect with the other pieces in the room. In fact it will look as though it belongs."
C. Check on observable features.	"Yes, the finish is smooth and resistant to heat and stains — just what we are looking for."	"This table top shows it is veneer. But if the veneer has been well applied, it should be as satisfactory as a top made of solid wood."	"Yes, the upholstery is colorfast. It won't snag or catch readily. It won't show soil quickly either."	"The piece stands steady on the floor, and the joints are well braced."	"It seems all right even though the legs look fragile. Let's risk it."
D. Find out about hidden values.	"Can you tell us how the inside construction of this upholstered chair differs from that less expensive one? They look very much alike."	"Will you give me a written guarantee that the frame of this chair is made of hard maple with dowel joints?"	"We need to be certain that this piece of furniture is strong at the joints. Can you tell us how it was put together?"	"The label indicates that this chair has mortise-and-tenon joints. It should be sturdy, since the corners are also braced."	"What a beautiful piece of furniture! It's just right even though it doesn't look too sturdy."
E. Compare values of new and old furniture if cost is important.	"Everything seems so expensive. Maybe we can put a want ad in the paper. It might pay dividends."	"If we can't have something that no one else has used, it's better to do without anything."	"It's worth seeing what we can buy that cherry table for at auction. After all, it's exactly what we'd like to have."	"That new secondhand shop has both used furniture and manufacturers' seconds. It won't hurt to take a look before we decide."	"Let's investigate these three for-sale ads before we buy. We might save something for the trip we hope to take next summer."

can easily be swept as often as need be after a meal.

THE WALLS: An oil-base paint, with a flat dull finish that goes well with the floor covering, was put on the smooth plastered walls and on the woodwork. Spots and finger marks can easily be wiped off the walls with a damp cloth. The plain color also makes the room seem larger.

THE WINDOWS: Simple, washable draperies were made for the windows. They are the same color as the walls and woodwork, which tends to give a feeling of spaciousness.

THE LIGHTING: In the dining area there is a covered ceiling fixture set against the ceiling, directly above the table. It gives adequate light for our meals, and is inconspicuous from the living area. However, we plan to replace it later on with one that can be raised and lowered. This type of lamp will draw more attention toward the dining area than what we now have. But it will be more useful for recreational activities that we may want to carry on at the table. In the living area there is also a ceiling fixture, which spreads a soft light over the ceiling, making it seem high. In addition, there are two lamps that can be used for reading or for close work — one that can be moved around, the other on a table. All of the lamps and the ceiling fixtures are simple and require minimum care.

ANSWERS: to *The Know-How of Buying Furniture* on page 317

A	3	D	5
B	1	E	2
C	5		

THE FURNITURE: In the dining area we have a drop-leaf table and six chairs. By closing the table when it is not in use and pushing it near the wall, the dining area seems larger. Two of the chairs sit at either end of the closed table, and the others are used in various living area groupings. This arrangement makes it easier to brush up any crumbs that fall from the table. My two sisters like it too, because it gives them extra space to play in. The only other piece of furniture in this area is a cabinet holding china, linen, and glassware. My father says that someday he will make the top of the drop-leaf table resistant to stains and heat. This will cut down some of the time we spend polishing it.

After we studied Miss Vandermeer's suggestions, we realized that the living area was too crowded, which made the room seem smaller than it really was. I moved a large overstuffed piece up to my room where it will make a good lounging chair when my friends come to call. A sectional bookcase which we really didn't need was divided and put in the girls' room, so that each one could have more storage for hobby equipment. A tall antique chest of drawers, containing odds and ends of no importance, was moved to my parents' room. After these pieces were removed, we rearranged the other furniture. We made the area where the sofa is the center of interest. As you enter the room, your attention is attracted to a colorful picture above the sofa. A coffee table containing current magazines is in front of it, and two comfortable chairs nearby make it a good conversational area. If there are several guests, chairs from other groupings can be added. The television set is placed so that it can be viewed from the sofa, yet one can walk through the room without bumping into furniture.

ACCESSORIES: There was too much bric-a-brac in the living area — too many small articles to dust and keep clean. We moved everything out, except a few selected pieces, which we plan to change from time to time. It is amazing how much more spacious the room seems to be. And we've already noticed that cleaning time and energy have been cut down a whole lot.

COMMENTS: We are all pleased with what has been done and feel that we owe Miss Vandermeer and the students our thanks for their helpful assistance.

PLANNING STORAGE SOLUTIONS

WHEN the students were setting up their goals, it seemed desirable to learn about storage for a living area. The subject became even more important when the students and their families began to make short- and long-term plans for improvements. As changes in living areas were being considered, the problem of storage became a real issue in many homes.

Since the subject of good storage was new to most of the students, they wondered how to approach the problem. After some discussion, they decided to find out first of all what factors influence the kind and amount of storage needed for a living area. At the same time, they would try to get some ideas about what constitutes good storage. This information could serve as a basis on which to check their storage situations at home. Then after they found what specific problems were involved, they would assemble suggestions for meeting these difficulties.

Miss Rand said there was considerable material on the reference shelves and that more could be added if necessary. Before long, everyone was busy looking up references and jotting down notes. All indications pointed to some interesting classwork.

Estimating Storage Needs for Living Areas

When the students believed they were prepared for a class discussion, they took up the subject of storage needs. It soon appeared that two major factors influenced the requirements of most families.

1. The extent to which the living area is used. Is it the social center for the entire family? Are such things as entertaining, reading, listening to the radio, watching television, playing games and musical instruments, and working on hobbies the principal activities carried on in the room? If so, more storage space will be needed than in a room used primarily for relaxation and occasional entertaining.

Here using space under a stairway for storage, as described on pages 324 to 326, is shown.

This is one of the storage solutions for a game table and chairs described on page 324.

As described on pages 324 and 325, a cabinet for musical instruments and other living-area articles may be a good storage solution.

Pegboard on the inside closet door increases storage space, as described on page 326.

2. The number and age of the members of the family group. If the room is used for many activities and the family is large, the need for storage space will be greater than in a small family. This is especially true if there are several children with lots of toys, and game and hobby equipment. Unless there is adequate storage space for these things, the room will tend to have a cluttered look. Space for outdoor wearing apparel will also depend on the size of the family and the sports activities they participate in. Some outdoor activities call for special clothing and equipment, which may be stored in the living area or in the person's own room.

Characteristics of Good Storage

The students then began to discuss what constitutes good storage. Miss Rand felt that the following comments indicated thoughtful consideration.

"I read that good storage needs to be convenient," said Jerry. "If the living area is used for various activities, you want to have the equipment for these activities nearby."

"You also need a place where you can see articles easily, either by daylight or artificial light," said Alice. "Our hall closet hasn't any light, and I waste time on a rainy day looking for my rubbers and umbrella."

"Half the time we are never quite sure what is in our hall closet," said Alex ruefully. "If you know where certain things are supposed to be kept, you can put them away quickly and find them easily."

"Reaching things easily is also important," added Virginia. "For example, if you are storing things on shelves, you can put the articles used most often within convenient reach. The things used less often can go a little higher. And those seldom used can go still higher on shelves that can be reached by a small stepladder."

"Speaking of having things within reach, it's a good idea to put hooks at a height where young children can reach them," said Lewis. "And there also needs to be a low shelf for such things as their caps, gloves, and scarfs."

"Storage space should be easy to clean," said Lorna. "Shelves with smooth surfaces that can be wiped off easily with a damp cloth are recommended."

"What about well-constructed storage space?" asked Russell. "We have a built-in cabinet for our dining area, but the sliding parts stick and don't open easily."

Joyce then added another point. "I think good storage needs to be dry," she said. "We had some things stored in a closed place under a window and the dampness caused mildew."

All of the discussion is not given here. But when Miss Rand suggested that the students summarize their findings on good storage, Keith offered to put the outstanding points on the blackboard. Here is the way the summary appeared.

GOOD STORAGE

- Needs to be convenient to the activity it serves
- Needs to be where you can see and find things easily and store them quickly
- Needs to be within easy reach for all members of the family for things that are frequently used
- Needs to be easy to clean
- Needs to be well constructed so that parts do not stick or bind
- Needs to be dry

Checking Storage at Home

Using the information they had assembled on storage, the students decided to check with their families the living-area storage in their own homes. In so doing they would list the articles that needed better storage, and those for which no storage was provided. These lists would be brought to class and would serve as a basis for further classwork on storage solutions.

The survey revealed a number of improvements that could be made. In some instances simple rearrangement and family cooperation in keeping things in their place would bring about the desired improvement. But in several homes more detailed planning would be needed. How to make available storage more suitable, and how to provide more space were problems faced. Facilities were needed for such items as game equipment, books and magazines, musical instruments, toys, hobby equipment, outdoor wraps, and in some instances sports equipment.

Again, as in the case of other living-area improvements, each student was to work out with the family short- or long-term plans for what could be done to improve storage. In homes where no storage was available or where considerable improvement was needed, each family would decide whether its budget could include improvements, and if so how much. However, concrete suggestions for what could be done to improve existing arrangements would be welcomed by practically all the families.

Keeping these ideas in mind, the students then grouped themselves according to their special interests. For instance, some of those who had younger brothers and sisters and who felt that storage of toys or hobby materials was a special problem would work on solutions for storing these items. Of course, some families needed improved storage for more than one type of article. But it was believed that in many instances suggestions made for one type would be adaptable to others.

Offering Suggestions for Storage Problems

Various sources were used to get helpful ideas and information. Interviewing people who had worked out successful storage solutions, and consulting books and magazines featuring storage in the home revealed numerous possibilities.

In some cases it was necessary for the groups to visit the students' homes to see how the living areas were arranged. They looked around for space that might be used, such as on a wall, under a stairway, or on a closet door. Before these visits were made, the parents were consulted in advance. This was done so that a definite time which was convenient for members of the family could be set for the visit.

Everyone enjoyed assembling material for the various storage problems. Making the solutions as practical as possible for each home situation was challenging. The chart on pages 324 to 326 shows typical situations encountered and the solutions recommended. Illustrations showing some of the solutions are given on page 320.

Making Use of the Suggestions on Storage

A number of the ideas presented by the groups were eventually used in various homes. Some of the families with the ability and willingness for do-it-yourself activities carried out the building suggestions on their own. Others had the work

done by a carpenter, or purchased items already made. Still others bought knock-down units and assembled them at home.

Even though a complete evaluation of the work done is not given here, there were numerous evidences of family cooperation in meeting storage problems. It did not matter whether the problem was providing additional space or making better use of that already available. The keynote was "A place for everything, and everything in its place."

CLASS MEMO:
Do members of your class have storage problems in their homes? If so, what solutions can you offer in addition to those suggested by Miss Rand's group?

CHART ON STORAGE SOLUTIONS

ARTICLES STORED	PRESENT SITUATION	WHY UNSATISFACTORY	SUGGESTED SOLUTIONS
Card table and folding chairs	Stored in a living area closet when not in use	Will not remain in upright position when folded	• Make a small rack on the closet floor to prevent chairs from slipping down. A divider may be placed between the table and chairs if desired. (See page 320.)
		Closet too crowded with out-door wraps	• Leave standing in the living room if desired and if the room is large enough so that it will not look cluttered.
	Stored in a back hall closet	Too far from activity; space needed for other things	• Build a cabinet in the living room, separate or as part of a larger storage unit.
	Folded when not in use, and placed behind door in living room	Soils wall and makes cleaning floor difficult	• Make a cupboard under a stairway — if there is room — by cutting into the face of the stairs.
Games	Stored with table in back hall closet	Too far from activity; space needed for other things	• Provide a shelf or shelves in the living-area closet of convenient height near the entrance. Be sure there is adequate lighting.
	Left lying around in living room	Makes living room look un-tidy	• If space permits, build a drawer in the side wall under the stairway.
			• Make space in a cupboard by putting in another place articles not frequently used.
			• Allow space for games in a storage cabinet that you may be building or buying

Books and magazines	Extra books not in bookcase; stacked on floor	Gives untidy appearance to room; makes floor difficult to clean	• Make space in a bookcase for books on the floor by taking out some books and putting them in bedrooms. Clear a space for magazines. • Make a bookcase of bricks and boards to hold books and magazines. (See Book 1, page 267 for making such a bookcase.)
	Magazines left lying around in living room, on tables and in chairs; back numbers stacked on floor	Makes room look cluttered; takes additional time and effort to clean room	• Build or buy a bookcase. In a long narrow room, one narrow wall might be used for building shelves and cabinet space if needed. Or a smaller bookcase might serve as a room divider. • Build a magazine rack on the wall, or purchase a portable one. • If there is space under the stairs, cut into the face of the wall to make open shelves for books and magazines. (See page 320.) • If a stairway is wide enough, make a bookcase on one side of the stairs.
Toys	Left lying around on floor or stacked in corner when not in use	Safety hazard; makes room difficult to clean	• Build or purchase several low cupboards for young children to keep their playthings in when not in use. • Paint a wooden box or chest the same color as the woodwork for storing toys. • Arrange for a low shelf in the hall closet where toys may be stored when not in use. • Put a chest in the hall area for storing toys. The chest may also be used as a seat.
Record player	Placed on end table when in use; put on floor when not in use	Not convenient – takes time and effort to move player from one place to another	• Build or purchase a cabinet or combination cabinet and bookcase so that all musical equipment can be in one area. Sections can be interchangeable and may be arranged as desired.
Records	Left lying around wherever there is room	Records may get broken; not easy to find the record you want	• Use extra space in a cabinet or bookcase already in the room for radio, record player, and records.
Radio	Sitting on table; electric cord hanging down side and extending along floor to wall outlet	Safety hazard – cord may be caught in cleaning equipment; someone may trip over cord on floor	• Set aside a section of the living-area closet – if there is room – for musical instruments. Be sure that they are well protected. (See page 320.)
Musical instruments	Left standing against wall when not in use	May get knocked down and damaged; also safety hazard	• Make a special cabinet for musical instruments.

ARTICLES STORED	PRESENT SITUATION	WHY UNSATISFACTORY	SUGGESTED SOLUTIONS
Hobby equipment	Left wherever used	Leaves less room for other activities; makes cleaning difficult; parts may get lost or damaged	• Build or purchase a cupboard for equipment when not in use. Needs to be of convenient height for size of persons using it. • Arrange for space in the living-area closet if there is room. • Make a cabinet or drawer under the stairs by cutting into the face of the wall. • Arrange for older members of the family who may prefer privacy to use and store hobbies in their own rooms.
Outdoor garments	Coats, jackets, and sports wear hanging from rod in closet without regard to kind; no provision made for wraps of small children	May be difficult to find garment you want; inconvenient for children to reach their wraps	• Put pegboard on inside closet door. Hooks can be inserted to hold hats, mirror, umbrellas, whisk broom, and children's coats. A shelf hung on hooks can hold gloves and scarfs. A rack can hold rubbers. (See page 320.)
	Hats, caps, gloves, and scarfs put haphazardly on shelf above rod	Articles may be damaged if put one on top of the other; may take time to find what you want	• Rearrange the closet. Hang everyday wraps together on rod, sports wear on another section. Use a metal hat separator on the shelf, so that hats can be placed one over the other without crushing each other, and at the same time save space. Have a container for gloves and scarfs. Make or purchase a rack for rubbers. Provide a container for umbrellas.
	Rubbers, overshoes, and the like on floor in no particular order	Makes cleaning difficult; takes time to find what you want	• If there are small children, put up a rod for their wraps and a shelf for gloves, scarfs, and caps — at a convenient height.
	Umbrellas leaning against back or side wall of closet	Wet umbrellas may damage garments; umbrellas may slide to floor	
Sports equipment	Put in closet wherever there happens to be room	May soil garments; equipment may become damaged if not suitably stored when not in use	• Provide a special cabinet, rack, or cupboard for sports equipment if members of the family participate in sports that require various kinds of equipment. • If there is a special storage cabinet or closet for sports equipment, sometimes room for sports wear may be arranged. • Use a pegboard for sports equipment in combination with wraps. See solution for outdoor garments. • Arrange to have equipment stored in one's room. If a change of clothing is required for an activity, it will be convenient to have the equipment needed in the same room.

CLEANING EASILY AND EFFECTIVELY

THE students believed that their classwork on storage solutions was a good background for their final objective. They could see that by following the theme "A place for everything, and everything in its place," cleaning would be easier than when there was disorder, caused by things being out of place or by there being no place for them.

Everyone realized, of course, that cleaning is considered a necessary activity in every home. Most families enjoy clean, orderly rooms. And they want to have dust and dirt removed not only to protect their health but to conserve the furnishings as well. To accomplish all this is often difficult, as some of the students learned when they talked with their families about living-area cleaning problems. But they all believed that it was important for them to try to help their families meet this particular situation.

Making Cleaning Interesting and Worth While

Although everyone admitted that cleaning was desirable, several members of the class commented on how dull and uninteresting it was.

Miss Rand then pointed out that it need not be monotonous if it is approached with an aim in mind. "You can make it a personal thing — something that will give you individual satisfaction," she said. "Decide what you want to do for your own pleasure and then work out the most effective way of doing it. Of course what you do will need to be based on your habits and experience. It will also need to fit into the circumstances which exist in your family. But you will find that certain tasks which seem to be necessary for keeping the living area clean and orderly can be made interesting and worth while."

Setting up a plan

The students found these remarks very challenging. After a brief but lively discussion, they agreed on the following plan: Before the next meeting of the class each person would decide carefully in what way cleaning could give personal satisfaction.

The answers turned in seemed to please Miss Rand as well as the students themselves. The subject of cleaning began to have a more personal meaning. Perhaps it wasn't going to be as dull as they had first thought. It might even be fun. This attitude was reflected in the answers which the students gave, some of which follow:

A SURPRISE FOR MOTHER: "My mother seems to dislike polishing the brass equipment around the fireplace. She sighs every time it needs to be done. I think I'll learn how to do it and surprise her by offering to relieve her in the future."

EARNING EXTRA MONEY: "Cleaning is one way I can earn extra money. I know a number of places where I can get that type of work. The more efficient I become, the more demand there will be for my available time."

MAKING WORK MORE ENJOYABLE: "I have always helped with the cleaning, but I don't particularly enjoy it. Maybe if I look for short cuts to cleaning efficiently, the work will be more interesting."

NEWER WAYS OF CLEANING: "My mother says she has always used the same methods of cleaning her mother did. But we all think that some of these methods could be greatly improved. Now my mother is willing to change. Together we're going to see whether a new approach to an old task may mean greater efficiency."

USING A MECHANICAL APPLIANCE: "I've never done any cleaning. But the new vacuum cleaner we have with all of its attachments intrigues me. I think I would get personal satisfaction from using it in the living area when cleaning is needed."

WHY CLEANING FATIGUES: "My mother says that cleaning wears her out more than any other kind of housework. There must be some reason for this. I'll not only try to find out the answer, but will do the cleaning that fatigues her the most."

Using Time and Energy Wisely

The students had learned through previous experience that scheduling tasks and practicing time and energy savers paid dividends in the long run. Now they were ready to try to apply this knowledge to cleaning procedures.

One of the first questions to come up for discussion concerned the best time to do various cleaning tasks in the living area. Of course the class realized that home conditions vary. What might seem a desirable time in one home might not be at all suited to the setup of another family. However, in order to use a family's time and energy wisely, it seemed advisable to assemble some general suggestions that might be adapted to fit individual home situations.

Various sources were used to obtain information. Books and pamphlets on the reference shelves were consulted. The students also interviewed at least one family other than their own about scheduling cleaning tasks, and how to save time and energy. The material was then discussed in class, and the following summaries made.

Tips on cleaning schedules

- *Work out a schedule that spreads cleaning tasks over a period of time — daily, weekly, when needed, and seasonal if desired.* Daily care may include tidying the room, surface dusting, and the use of the carpet sweeper, vacuum cleaner, or broom. Weekly care may involve more thorough dusting to include radiators, lamps, and accessories. Mirrors, glass in pictures, and the inside of windows may also be wiped off. A more thorough cleaning of the floors and rugs may also be done. Tasks that involve walls, ceiling, and woodwork can be taken care of on the when needed basis. Seasonal cleaning can depend on the individual situation. In mild climates where heating equipment is not used, it may even be eliminated.

- *Avoid scheduling too many activities in any one period.* Alternate light and heavy tasks. But do not enforce any schedule to the extent that you feel rushed or nervous. Rather let it seem like an orderly arrangement to make cleaning tasks go smoothly.

- *Fit the tasks into the daily and weekly requirements of the family.* For example, if the week end is a time for entertaining, more cleaning may be necessary on Fridays and Mondays than on other days.

- *Consider the energy and the time available for the family members doing the tasks.* For example, dusting every day may be highly desirable. But if energy must be conserved for other more important things, it may be advisable to dust only once or twice a week.

- *Make cleaning tasks flexible to provide for unavoidable delays.* After a time-consuming interruption, avoid trying to crowd an unfinished task into a shorter period than is needed to do the task efficiently. Postpone the task until another time.

Time and energy savers

- *Wear comfortable clothes and shoes.* Tight-fitting garments hinder free motion, and uncomfortable shoes will ruin your disposition.

- *Learn to use both hands for some tasks.* If you are right-handed, it will be fun to educate your left hand to be of more help to you. For example, if you are using a dust mop around the edge of the floor, keep a dustcloth in your pocket. When you come to a window, you can wipe the sill with your left hand without dropping the dust mop or retracing your steps.

- *Use continuous and circular motions rather than abrupt, jerky ones.* As you proceed from place to place, try to make the motions rhythmical. This saves time and energy. People who hum, whistle, or listen to music often find the work easier too.

- *Dovetail tasks by easing one into another.* For example, while a window cleaner is drying, do something else, such as wiping off the sills or wood-work. But avoid feeling that you must hurry. People who move quickly do not always accomplish more than those who move at a slower pace. Keep to your natural speed.

- *Plan task combinations.* Keeping an eye on the baby and doing a pickup job in the living area can easily be combined. Or you can do some head-work while you are polishing the brass accessories.

- *Allow for short rest periods at least every hour if much cleaning is to be done at any one time.* Resting before you get too tired makes the total cleaning job less fatiguing.

Having Suitable Equipment and Supplies

During one of the class discussions several students commented on the subject of equipment and supplies. George mentioned their importance in making cleaning tasks easy and efficient. Alice added that some are better adapted than others to saving time and energy, as well as to cleaning more efficiently. Taking good care of equipment, having it ready to use, and storing it conveniently were also mentioned. Since all of these points seemed important, the students decided to assemble some helpful information on equipment and supplies. This would be summarized in much the same way as had been done with the material on using time and energy wisely. The summaries that were prepared follow:

The equipment

- *If possible, get equipment that can be used for more than one task.* A vacuum cleaner with various attachments, such as a rug nozzle, floor brush, dusting brush, and fabric brush, is this type of item. In homes where it is not possible to have a vacuum cleaner, substitute equipment would need to include a carpet sweeper or a floor broom, a dust mop, dustcloths, and a dustpan.

- *Consider equipment for efficiency, ease of operation, and care.* For example, a long-handled, self-wringing mop is easier to operate than one which must be wrung by hand. There are string-mop and cellulose-sponge types. The string mop covers a wider area than the sponge mop. But it seldom cleans evenly the full length of the strings. This means that to do an efficient job, it is usually necessary to go over the same spot several times. Then too, after the strings have been used, they tend to break off during the mopping. It takes time and effort to pick up the loose pieces. However, if a string mop is used, choose a wringer for it that does not require stooping. In many cellulose-sponge mops the water can be extracted by pulling a lever which presses a simple wringer against the sponge, forcing out the water. Stooping or bending is not necessary, and the wringing can be done very quickly. The sponge-type mop can be cleaned more easily and dries more quickly than the string type, which is apt to become sour unless thoroughly cleaned and dried.

See that handles of equipment are convenient in length for good posture while using them. Too short a handle may cause backache and fatigue. If young children are to help with cleaning tasks, they will need equipment suited to their size, such as a small broom and dustpan. Otherwise they may soon tire of what they are doing.

- *Weigh the cost of equipment in terms of saving time and effort.* A dustpan with a long handle may cost a little more than the flat-type pan, but it eliminates stooping. A vacuum cleaner, of course, is more expensive than the combined number of items needed for the same type of cleaning. But it is well worth the extra expense — if a family can afford it — in terms of the time and effort saved.

The supplies

- *Get supplies that may be used for more than one purpose.* Less storage space will be required than when several items are purchased. For example, a mild detergent may be used for washing dishes and for cleaning linoleum and painted surfaces. It may even be used as a rug or upholstery shampoo. Glass wax also has several uses, such as cleaning windows, mirrors, porcelain, and metal.

- *Experiment with cleaning supplies to find those that are best suited to your needs and preferences.* For example, one kind of brass or copper cleaner may give a higher gloss than another. Therefore, the one that produces the luster preferred will give the most personal satisfaction. Again, some people may be unable to use certain detergents or soaps because of a resulting skin irritation. In such cases, it may be necessary to experiment to see whether one can be found that does not cause irritation. Another example might be a product to clean windows.

What may be effective on the inside may not be equally satisfactory on the outside in certain localities where salt, soot, or grease are deposited on the outside windowpanes.

Tips on using equipment and supplies

- *Assemble all equipment and supplies that are to be used in a convenient place before you begin cleaning.* Use a basket for carrying small equipment, such as dustcloths, brushes, furniture polish, and other cleaning articles. It may mean fewer steps as you go from one part of the living area to another.

- *Handle all equipment carefully.* For example, when disconnecting an electric appliance, grasp the connecting plug firmly and pull gently without wiggling it. Avoid jerking or yanking it. Wind the cord loosely if it is attached to the appliance. If detachable, loop it loosely over two rounded supports placed six to eight inches apart. This will prevent the cord from kinking or bending.

- *Make sure that all equipment is in good operating order before you put it away.* It's discouraging to begin a cleaning task and find something in need of repair.

- *Keep the equipment and supplies for cleaning in one place.* Storage in a hall closet or in a place near the center of the house is convenient for cleaning other areas. Some people have duplicate supplies on the second floor.

Presenting Cleaning Procedures

One day while the students were working on cleaning techniques, Keith made a thought-provoking suggestion. "I've been thinking that it would be a good idea for us to give a series of skits," he said. The students listened attentively, always eager to hear about anything that involved role playing.

"We could give four skits," he continued, "showing daily, weekly, when needed, and seasonal types of cleaning. In fact, the whole thing could be a sort of summary of what we learn about different cleaning procedures."

The other students nodded in agreement, and Miss Rand encouraged the class to go ahead with any plans they might want to make.

After some discussion it was decided that the skits would coordinate all that was being learned about cleaning techniques, managing time and energy, and using suitable equipment and supplies. Four groups were formed to demonstrate what might be done in daily, weekly, when needed, and seasonal types of cleaning.

Of course, everyone realized that there is more than one way of doing a cleaning task. The type of equipment and the kind of supplies used generally set the pattern for the way the task is done. However, it would not be practicable to demonstrate all of the methods that could be used for the kinds of cleaning portrayed in the skits. Therefore, one method of doing a specific job

would be presented. But whenever it seemed advisable, other ways of doing the same task would be pointed out.

The skits were to be set up on the basis of a family of four members, showing how the family as a group might meet their cleaning problems.

The plan seemed to work out so well that the students decided to invite their parents to school to see the skits. It proved to be an interesting experience, and everyone enjoyed it. Needless to say, parents were delighted that their sons and daughters were learning the techniques of cleaning. They expressed the hope that what the young people had learned would be applied at home as easily and effectively as it had been carried out in the skits at school.

Since other classes may be interested in seeing how the skits were presented, a detailed account follows:

Skit 1 — *The Daily Pickup*

THE SCENE: *Four members of a family in the living room just before bedtime. You can hear the voice of the narrator as he says:*

"This is the Morrison family. Over there in the easy chair is Mr. Morrison with a magazine in his lap, but with his eyes half closed. Nearby is Mrs. Morrison darning socks. Sixteen-year-old Bill has just turned off the television, and his older sister, Jane, sitting on the sofa, is knitting a sweater.

"Presently Mr. Morrison yawns as he looks at the clock and says, 'Bedtime, I guess.' He closes the magazine and puts it on a table nearby, arranging other reading material in an orderly way. Picking up the ash tray, he empties the contents into a metal wastebasket. Then he opens a window for a few seconds to air out the room.

"Bill is putting away the television program and some records he has played earlier in the evening. Now he empties the contents of the wastebasket into the evening newspaper, which everyone has read, and takes it to the back porch where he will put it into a large covered metal trash container. He says good night to everyone as he leaves the room.

"You can see that Jean is busy too. She has folded the sweater and put it in a knitting bag. Now she is getting the carpet sweeper from the hall closet. She runs it lightly around the area where the activities have been going on, and then returns it to the closet. Now she smooths out the slip cover on the sofa and plumps up the pillow. Slipping the knitting bag over her arm, she too says good night.

"In the meantime Mrs. Morrison has not been idle by any means. She has tucked the darning into a sewing cabinet. Now she is going around the room putting away odds and ends, and straightening out a little here and there. She soon indicates to Mr. Morrison that she is ready. They turn out the lights and go upstairs.

"This is what is called a quick, over-all pickup job. It takes very little time when each member of the family assumes some responsibility. And what a satisfying feeling it is to come down in the morning and see an orderly living room."

SKIT 2 — *The Weekly Routine*

THE SCENE: *The Morrison living room on a Saturday morning in late winter after the breakfast dishes have been washed. The narrator says:*

"Here comes Mrs. Morrison wearing comfortable clothes and shoes. She is carrying a basket containing polishing cloths, a cellulose sponge, a jar filled with a solution of a rinseless detergent, and an oil-type paper bag — the kind often used in disposal containers. She opens a window and turns down the heat.

"Now she is doing a once-around-the-room pickup job, somewhat different from that done at bedtime. She looks over the magazines and periodicals, putting the ones to be discarded in the wastebasket. She makes a pile of the others that are to be kept but stored elsewhere. When she reaches the fireplace, she wets the ashes with water from a container taken from the radiator where it is kept filled to humidify the room. Now the ashes will not fly around when she puts them in the oil-type paper bag. When she has completed the tour of the room, she sets outside the door the wastebasket and the pile of articles to be stored. Then she prepares to take a plant to the kitchen sink where she will wipe the dust from the leaves and let the plant soak in water for a while. She will also refill the container on the radiator.

"As Mrs. Morrison leaves the room, she calls to Bill saying that he can use the vacuum cleaner. Presently Bill arrives with the necessary equipment. Watch him now in a series of once-around-the-room routes as he cleans various areas:

First trip — with the dust-brush attachment

  Window sills and window-sash moldings, Venetian blinds

  Radiators — where dust shows

  Walls — where cobwebs and any dust show

  Exposed area of bookcases, including backs of books

  Exposed baseboard moldings

  All furniture — except upholstered portions

  Books, magazines, larger decorative accessories, lamp bases and shades, lifting each object to dust underneath

  Mantel and fireplace fixtures

Second trip — with the upholstery-cleaner attachment

  Draperies and curtains, cleaning them, shaking them into position, and lining them up

  Upholstered furniture

  Small rugs

Third trip — with floor-brush attachment

  All exposed floor areas, including those in closets

Fourth trip — with rug-cleaner attachment

  Rugs, cleaning under furniture

"All the time that Bill is working, his mind is busy too. Among other things, he has decided how he will write a composition for English class. He has thought of several suggestions to offer to the committee for the spring festival when he meets with them the following week. And he has just about made up his mind to ask Susan for a date.

"Now he has finished his part of the weekly cleaning. But wait. Before he stores away the vacuum cleaner and its attachments, he checks to see whether it needs emptying. He wants it to be ready for use next week. It proves to be all right this time; so Bill is off for a date with his chum.

"Of course, if the Morrisons did not have a vacuum cleaner, Bill would have used a carpet sweeper or a broom and dustpan for the rugs, a dust mop for the floor, and soft cloths for dusting. A brush would probably have been used on the draperies and upholstered furniture. Had he used a carpet sweeper, he would have checked to see whether it needed emptying before he put it away.

"Now Mrs. Morrison is returning to the living room with the plant and the refilled container for the radiator. After putting them back in place, she takes the basket with the cleaning items and makes a trip around the room. She wipes off a large mirror, cleans the hearth, and polishes the furniture wherever it seems to need it. Now she has finished. Picking up the basket of cleaning supplies, she gives the room a final glance of approval. As she does so she says to herself, *'I must not forget to tell Bill what a wonderful job he does with the vacuum cleaner.'* She then leaves the room."

SKIT 3 — *The When-necessary Tasks*

THE SCENE: *The living room on another Saturday morning as the weekly cleaning is about to begin. It is raining outside. Mrs. Morrison and Bill are talking together. The narrator says:*

"Mrs. Morrison and Bill have decided to add a little more cleaning time today to their regular routine. Bill has canceled a tennis date, because of the weather, and is willing to spend part of the time doing a few extra tasks. Here are the things they plan to do — some today, others at another time when they seem necessary. They include: (1) a more thorough job with the vacuum cleaner, (2) washing the windows, (3) waxing the floor, (4) polishing the brass, and (5) removing the books, dusting them, and cleaning the shelves. Mrs. Morrison thinks that Jean will find time some week end to give the desk and hall closet a thorough overhauling. She is sure there are many unnecessary articles in both places that can be discarded.

"Now Bill is going to start doing a more thorough job with the vacuum cleaner. Using a crevice nozzle, he will clean the narrow spaces in the radiators. Then he will remove the cushions from the chairs and sofa, and clean the crevices there. With a dusting brush, he will go over the pictures,

lamps, and light bulbs. He will probably use the sweeping attachment on the reverse side of the rug.

"In the meantime Mrs. Morrison will wash the inside of the windows as her share of the extra work. She has a container of glass wax and a supply of lintless cloths plus a sturdy stepladder. Watch her now as she goes to work. Standing on the stepladder, she applies a thin coat of glass wax on the upper pane. She descends and does the same to the lower pane. Placing the container of glass wax on the window sill, she stands on the stepladder again and wipes off the upper pane with one of the cloths. (See the illustration below.) She repeats the same procedure for the lower pane. Then she moves on to the other windows, replacing a soiled cloth with a clean one whenever necessary.

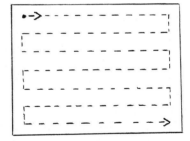

"Of course Mrs. Morrison could have used a liquid spray on the windows instead of glass wax. She would probably wipe this off at once without allowing it to dry, using the same motions as for glass wax. She might even have used clear water with four tablespoons of household ammonia to one gallon of water. But she would need to be very careful to keep the solution from spilling or running onto the finished woodwork.

"Some Saturday afternoon when the weather is good, Mr. Morrison will wash the outside of the windows. He has found from experience that clear, cool water is satisfactory. Using a brush attached to a long handle, he dips the brush into the water and washes off the upper and lower panes. Then with a rubber squeegee — also on a long handle — he makes downward strokes, wiping the edge of the squeegee after each stroke. He says this method is a work saver, but better for the outside of windows than the inside, because of the splashing of water from the brush.

"There are several rules which the Morrisons follow when washing windows. (1) They select a time when the sun is not shining on the windows. Otherwise the windows will look streaky. (2) They never use soap. Soap smears the panes, and the smears are hard to remove. (3) They never sit out a window to clean the outside pane, since there is always danger of losing one's balance. If it is necessary to wash the outside panes from inside the house, they raise and lower the sashes.

"Bill is planning to wax the floor next Saturday morning before his sister Jean's birthday party that evening. He will fold back the edges of the rugs, and mop the floor with clear water, using a long-handled, self-wringing, cellulose-sponge mop and a pail. He will avoid leaving any trace of water on the floor. He will then

apply paste wax to the floor with a soft cloth, and use the attachment on the vacuum cleaner to polish it. Of course without the vacuum cleaner, he could use a self-polishing liquid wax. Or he might use a paste wax, and polish the floor by hand.

"If the brass objects around the fireplace need polishing next week, Bill will try to work that in too. Mrs. Morrison will probably clean the glass on the pictures and a large mirror. These will be cleaned with a minimum amount of moisture to prevent the solution from getting behind the glass. There is an oil painting hanging above the fireplace, but it does not need to be cleaned very often. Mrs. Morrison will use a soft sponge wrung out from mild, lukewarm soapsuds. She will wash a small strip at a time, and wipe it dry with a soft cloth. After the whole picture is washed and dried, she will apply a thin coating of linseed oil with a soft cloth. This will help to prevent the finish from cracking.

"Occasionally the books and shelves need dusting and cleaning. Bill has never done this. His mother explains that after the books are removed from the shelves, they can be dusted with the soft brush–vacuum cleaner attachment. Then they can be placed on a cart with wheels while the shelves are being cleaned. Before the books are replaced, the painted shelves can be wiped off with a cellulose sponge dampened in a mild detergent solution.

"Both Mrs. Morrison and Bill believe that if they can work in extra tasks now and then during the weekly cleaning, the seasonal cleaning will be easier."

Skit 4 — Seasonal Cleaning

THE SCENE: *The living room in late spring after the furnace has been turned off. It is vacation time for Bill, and his sister Jean is taking a few days off from the office. Mrs. Morrison, Bill, and Jean are comfortably dressed. Listen now to the narrator and find out what's going to happen.*

"The members of the Morrison family have set up a plan for the spring cleaning, which they believe is necessary after a long winter. Here are some of the things they hope to do: (1) clean the walls, woodwork, and Venetian blinds; (2) shampoo the rugs; (3) send out the draperies for professional cleaning; and (4) have the room presentable when Mr. Morrison returns in the evening. Can they do all this in one day? Yes, they think so, but let's find out.

"In the first place, they plan to take rest periods of ten minutes every hour, with thirty minutes at lunchtime.

"In the morning after Mr. Morrison left for the office, Mrs. Morrison made sandwiches for lunch. She also arranged to have already-prepared food from the freezer for the evening meal. While she was doing this, Bill and Jean took down the draperies and telephoned a cleaning establishment to call for them. Of course, they could have dry-cleaned them in the back yard.

But Mrs. Morrison had had little experience with flammable fluids, and preferred not to take the risk involved in using them. Bill and Jean also took down the Venetian blinds and the pictures, and moved the rugs to the porch where Bill plans to shampoo them. Now they are moving the furniture into the middle of the room and will cover it with old sheets. But watch how they lift the pieces that are heavy and that would scratch the floor if dragged. They bend the knees, and use the leg muscles as well as the back. (See the illustration on page 338.)

"Bill is now ready to work on the rugs. He has a bottle of good-quality rug shampoo of the type that can be used with a vacuum cleaner. He follows the directions on the bottle, and fills the spray attachment on the vacuum cleaner, turning the motor switch from suction to blow. He sprays the material onto the rug, starting in one corner and working back and forth until the whole surface is damp, with some foam visible. He lets this stand until the rug is about dry. Then he reverses the motor to suction and carefully vacuum cleans the surface with the rug-cleaner attachment. Without a vacuum cleaner, Bill might have used a mild detergent foam on the rug, applying it with a sponge. He would have worked over a small area at a time, rinsing the sponge, and wiping away loosened dirt before moving on.

"While Bill is waiting for the surface of the rugs to dry, he uses the long-handled dusting brush of the vacuum cleaner on the ceiling and walls. A cloth-covered broom could have been used instead of the brush. Bill knew that dust threads and cobwebs are removed most readily by dusting from the bottom of the wall up.

"While Bill is working on the rugs and the walls, Mrs. Morrison and Jean are tackling the Venetian blinds. They put them in the bathtub and are scrubbing them with a mild detergent. Then they tie them on the clothesline to dry. They are able to use this method because the slats are made of metal attached to plastic tape, which does not shrink when wet. Had the slats been made of wood — painted or grain finish — with cotton tape, a different procedure would have been used. For painted slats, they would have cleaned each slat at a time — on both sides — with a sponge wrung out in a mild detergent solution. Had the slats been of a finish showing the grain, they would have cleaned them with liquid wax. An upholstery cleaner or a dry-cleaning fluid would have been used on the tape.

"Now Mrs. Morrison and Jean are back in the living room and about to start washing the walls, which they know are washable and which Bill has just dusted. They have assembled the following supplies: several cellulose sponges, pieces of soft lintless cloth, a container with a detergent especially prepared for painted walls, and a stepladder. They start from the bottom and work up, experimenting first with a small area. Then they clean a larger space — about three feet square — at a time, using a circular motion. They wipe the area dry with one of the soft cloths. Then they proceed to the space above this and repeat the procedure, taking care to overlap the edges of the area just cleaned. They will continue this way until the walls are finished, using the stepladder when necessary.

You will notice that while they are working at a low level, they do not stoop over. They bend their knees or sit on the floor. This helps to prevent backache and fatigue.

"Now it's time for lunch. They wash up, eat slowly, and rest, allowing thirty minutes before resuming work.

"They are back in the living room now where Mrs. Morrison and Jean are ready to wash the woodwork. Again they experiment with a small area first, using the same supplies as when washing the walls. They do the hardest-to-clean spots next and then the entire surface, using long strokes and following the grain of the wood.

"Look, Bill is back in the living room again. He has finished his work on the rugs, and is removing the coverings from the furniture. He hangs the pictures on the walls, and cleans the floor with the vacuum cleaner attachment before he brings in the rugs. Jean and her mother are putting their supplies away.

"Now all three of the Morrisons arrange the pieces of furniture and accessories in their accustomed places and put back the Venetian blinds. It is getting toward the end of the afternoon, but there is ample time to bathe, change clothes, and relax before dinner.

"Mr. Morrison is now entering the living room. He notes the missing draperies but seems pleased with the results of the day's work. When the other members come into the room, he compliments them on a job well done. He even shows his appreciation by offering to do the dinner dishes by himself.

"Yes, the Morrisons are a happy family. They share in the work that needs to be done, realizing that a cooperative spirit among family members contributes toward easy and effective cleaning."

Evaluating the Classwork on Cleaning

When all of the work at school and at home had been completed, the students took stock of what had impressed them most in achieving the goal — cleaning easily and effectively. The following points, which were lined up on the blackboard, indicate a thoughtful and far-reaching appraisal.

The evaluation

• Working out a schedule — daily, weekly, when needed, and seasonal if necessary — eliminates haphazard cleaning and prevents tasks from pil-

ing up to the point of annoyance and discouragement.

• Using efficient equipment within the limits of the family budget can save time and energy, and make cleaning more satisfactory.

• When family members share in the work to be done, a greater understanding of cleaning responsibility is developed.

• Letting young people select the tasks they prefer, and giving them a minimum of supervision encourages a willingness to participate in cleaning activities.

• The attitude a person takes toward the tasks that need to be carried out in everyday living is of great importance. Learning to get personal satisfaction out of any activity is the keynote. When a task is interesting and absorbing, it becomes easy, and more often than not can be done effectively.

CLASS MEMO:
What cleaning problems do members of your class have in their homes? How can the situations be handled to give the most satisfaction to everyone concerned?

PLANNING YOUR CLASSWORK

WHEN some of the students in Miss Rand's class brought up personal living-area problems, it seemed a good opportunity to make

these situations the basis for starting classwork on improving the home. But first, the cooperation of the students' families was obtained through the use of an interview form indicating the subjects that might be studied at school. Then, with the assistance of an interior decorator sponsored by a local store, the class learned many useful things about making a living area meet the needs and desires of the family. They also learned about making draperies, curtains, and slip covers, and how to do some repairing and refinishing of furniture. It also seemed important to get information on buying furniture. Having adequate storage for the living area and knowing how to clean easily and effectively were other procedures worked out by the students. All of this was helpful to members of the class as well as to their families.

In making plans, your class will probably want to help your families with living-area problems. It may be desirable to use some of the same procedures for meeting home situations that Miss Rand's group used. But if you can achieve results that bring satisfaction to you and your family, the approach taken is not important. However, as you make your plans, you may find some of the following experiences helpful in improving the living areas in your homes, or in improving areas of this type at school.

EXPERIENCES YOUR CLASS MIGHT LIKE TO CARRY OUT

1. Your group may want to use an interview form similar to "What My Family and I May Do to Improve Our Living Area," found on page 258, to locate living-area problems among members of your class.

2. It may be very useful to commence a file of clippings from magazines and bulletins on "Helpful Hints for Living Areas." The file can be added to over a long period of time, and be made available to all homemaking classes. You could begin the file with such subjects as the following:

a. Color selections and furnishings to please the family

b. Slip covering for all types of furniture

c. Attractive fabrics to fit the budget

d. Variety in window treatments

e. Accessories for use and beauty

f. Lamps for different purposes

g. General illumination

3. In groups of two or three persons you could wander through the school building at some appropriate time to discover ways in which the school — particularly the homemaking rooms — can be improved. Then you could hold a class discussion to consider suggestions. Those that seem especially interesting to the group, and for which cooperation can be obtained, might be carried out as a class experience.

4. Using the opaque projector might be an interesting way to learn about various subjects, some of which could be:

a. Kinds of finishes used on furniture made of wood

b. Steps in repairing and refinishing furniture

c. Window arrangements including draperies, curtains, Venetian blinds, and shades

5. Your class might want to make a list of questions that a person would ask when buying furniture, such as:

a. Is the finish resistant to liquids and heat?

b. Is the upholstery colorfast?

c. Is this a good grade of veneer?

d. May I see the back and underside of this piece of furniture?

The class might then arrange to visit a furniture store as a group if the class is small, or in several groups to various stores if the class is large. The manager or a salesman could then answer the questions on your list, illustrating if possible his answers with pieces of furniture.

6. An interesting class meeting might be to have several people in the community tell about how they have handled odd-shaped windows. Arrangements might also be made with the speakers to have some of the students who are interested in these special types of windows visit their homes.

7. In small groups, members of your class might find it helpful to look at drapery, curtain, and slip cover materials in the stores. Using the questions for determining quality, found on page 289, you could see how many of these qualities are available within the price range members can afford.

8. An "Experience Session" on buying used furniture may bring out some useful pointers on this subject. The session could end with guides for buying used furniture.

9. Your homemaking teacher may welcome an offer from your group to evaluate the storage situation in the homemaking rooms. If so, the guides on good storage set up by Miss Rand's class, found on page 322, may be used as a basis for the evaluation.

10. Through chatting informally with different members of your family, you may be able to discover certain information about storage: (1) the articles in and near the living area that need improved storage, and (2) the articles for which no storage is provided. Using all the guides you know about good storage, you can offer suggestions for the problems of greatest concern to your family. In so far as possible, help your family carry out the best-liked suggestions.

11. If your group has a file on "Helpful Hints for Living Areas," suggestions and pictures of practical storage solutions would make a good addition to the file.

12. Through talking with your family and reading reference materials, you may be able to add to the list of minor repairs already described by Miss Rand's class on pages 301 to 305. Your group could then discuss these repairs, set up directions for making them, and give demonstrations of how to work.

13. Your parents might enjoy a program in which a series of skits are presented, showing how family cooperation in cleaning might be brought about. A situation, such as the following, could be used as a basis for the skits:

Mr. and Mrs. Smith, whose children are Helene, 8, John, 9, and Marie, 14, would like to have their children learn to share the cleaning tasks in their home. What plans could be made that would teach the children something about daily, weekly, when-necessary, and seasonal cleaning.

Such points as suiting a task to the age and preference of the child, rotating tasks, and supplying suitable equipment could be brought out in the skits.

14. Members of your class may get personal satisfaction from learning and using certain cleaning techniques. Those who are interested in the same tasks can set up directions for these activities. Plans can be made for a two-week interval in which the tasks are carried out. Reports can then be made to the class on how the plans worked out. One group who tried this procedure gave such reports as these:

a. "The fireplace is one of the pleasant features of our living room. My young sister and I like to pop corn over the fire in the evening. But my mother used to sigh a little every time we did it. Now I understand why — we didn't always clean up as well as we could. I worked out a plan to surprise my mother. After each popping session we do a more thorough cleaning job. Then once a week my sister washes the hearth, and I clean and polish the brass equipment. It seems to need polishing more often when we pop corn. My plan worked out fine, and my mother now smiles instead of sighing when she sees us popping corn."

b. "Cleaning seemed a good way for me to earn a little extra money. One day a neighbor who knew that I was interested in this kind of work asked me to dust and tidy up the living room. She was entertaining at dinner that evening and needed to spend her time in the kitchen. I promised to be there at a certain time, and I was. But some-

how I underestimated the time it would take to do the work. By hurrying I just managed to leave by the back door when the guests rang the front doorbell. And even then I didn't do as efficient a job as I could have. Next time I'll plan more carefully."

15. An exhibit of various commercial products used successfully for various cleaning activities may be well worth while. Arrangements can be made with a local store to display such items as cleaning detergents, and cleaning agents for metal and glass, and for wood and paint surfaces. You will want to be sure to include as many brands as are available to a purchaser.

16. Members of your class may want to make a study of cleaning practices in their homes. An outline of what is done daily, weekly, when needed, and seasonally can be made. Activities can be starred as follows: one star for the tasks which a student does occasionally; two stars for regular activities. New tasks that might be done if your mother approves can be underlined. Others members of the class might like to see some of the outlines and to compare them with their own.

17. Making an inventory of cleaning tasks not mentioned by Miss Rand's group could be very helpful to many class members. Techniques and demonstrations for the tasks mentioned could be a part of the experience.

18. As a final, over-all experience for your work on "Rooms for Happier Living," the class is sure to enjoy a series of home visits. Arrangements can be made with several students' families who have recently made improvements in living areas to have the class see what has been done.

5

A Four-Point Plan for My Wardrobe

Planning my clothes

Learning to make my clothes more wearable

Learning to buy some of my clothes

Learning to make some of my clothes

THE CORRIDORS of the Horace Mann High School resounded with mingled voices and hurried footsteps. It was nearly time for the last bell to ring before the classes began. In one of the classrooms, Miss Dennison, the homemaking teacher, was sorting some papers on her desk. Groups of students chattered amicably. Occasionally snatches of conversation could be heard, such as "A wonderful evening," and "An interesting time." Apparently the remarks referred to a debate which had been held the previous evening between the Horace Mann Debating Club and another group from one of the upstate schools. It had been a lively, spirited affair, attended not only by the students but by many parents and other members of the community.

The phrase "How well-groomed the debaters were," caught Miss Dennison's attention. She too had attended the meeting and had been pleasantly impressed with the appearance of the boys and girls in the debate. Clothing and grooming had been on her mind, since some of her students were ready to begin their work in this area. Perhaps the comment she had just overheard would make a good lead for starting off the new classwork.

And so when the last bell had rung, Miss Dennison brought up the subject of the debate. "What did you think of the appearance of the debaters last night?" she asked.

There was an immediate response. Everyone wanted to talk at once. Miss Dennison motioned toward Richard.

"I liked the way the boys wore their clothes," he said. "Their suits seemed to fit just right — not too tight and not too loose. Their shirts must have fitted well too, because they didn't keep fussing or pulling at their neckties the way you often do when things aren't just right. In fact I think having comfortable clothes helps to give a person poise and self- assurance. And the boys certainly had that."

"I sat near the front of the room," said Joel, "and I noticed how well their socks and neckties seemed to go with their suits. It reminded me of our classwork last year when we planned pleasing combinations of shirts, ties, and socks."

"And what about the girl debaters?" asked Miss Dennison.

There was a chorus of "Oh's" and "Ah's."

"They certainly knew how to wear their clothes," said Sharon. "But what struck me most of all was how simple the outfits were and yet how stunning the girls looked."

"And did you notice how few accessories they had?" asked Evelyn. "There seemed to be just enough to give a pleasing effect."

Miss Dennison nodded, saying, "Yes, the boys and girls were well groomed. No doubt they were putting into practice much of what we learned last year about being attractive in appearance. Perhaps we can start planning our classwork by considering how to be suitably and attractively dressed at all times."

SETTING UP PLANS FOR CLASSWORK ON CLOTHING

THERE was a chorus of approval to Miss Dennison's suggestion. In the discussion which followed, everyone agreed that practicing what they had learned last year about clothing was very important. It had certainly been a great help to learn how to keep their clothes clean and neat, and how to select those that are becoming in color, line, and texture. Knowing what clothes are suitable to the occasion and what go well together had proved to be very practicable. (See Book 1, pages 33–59.)

"That's all well and good," commented Joel. "But having the right thing to wear is sometimes a problem. I don't always have it."

"I don't have the money to go out and buy all that I need," added Frances. "I have trouble deciding what to buy first."

"Making your own clothes — if you know how and have time — is a good way to save money," said Evelyn.

"And planning your wardrobe and buying carefully help too," added Sue.

"I have a lot of clothes in my closet that I never wear for one reason or another," said Sharon. "Several are mistakes in buying, I'm sure. Others need repair, and some of them I'm tired of or they seem out of style."

As the discussion continued, there was a general agreement that it is easier for boys and girls to be well dressed at all times if they know how to mend their clothes and how to make simple alterations. Most of the girls — and several of the boys — said that they really wanted to learn how to make some of their clothes. Other students were more interested in buying clothes or making what they had more wearable.

Keeping these points in mind, the students decided to organize their classwork into the following goals.

Planning my clothes

Learning to make my clothes more wearable

Learning to buy some of my clothes

Learning to make some of my clothes

Wardrobe planning, making clothes more wearable, and learning to make new ones appear to be some of these girls' goals.

The students then set up a tentative plan for carrying out the goals. There was a general agreement to try to make it possible for them to spend a large part of their time on the classwork in which their needs and interests were centered. They would all work together on the first goal of planning their clothes, which would point up individual needs. Then as the classwork progressed, all of them would spend a varying amount of time on the other goals, except those boys not making new garments. Details could be worked out as they took up each goal.

"What about a name for our work on clothing?" asked Claude. "I've been thinking that we might call it 'A Four-Point Plan for My Wardrobe.'"

"We couldn't find a better name," said Walter, as the other students nodded in agreement. Miss Dennison smiled and added that she believed the classwork they had planned was going to be very interesting.

```
CLASS MEMO:
   How do the clothing
   interests of your group
   compare with those of
   Miss Dennison's class?
   What goals will you
   set up?
```

PLANNING MY CLOTHES

Now that the goals and a general plan for the classwork had been decided upon, everyone was eager to get started on the more personal aspects of planning a wardrobe. However, the students soon realized that a wardrobe depends on various factors — where you go, what you do, what the seasons are, and what you and your family can afford. Therefore, no two wardrobes will be exactly alike in kind and quality. The problem was to find some way to meet these individual clothing needs.

After some discussion, the students worked out a general plan. In the first place they would list the activities and occasions for which they needed certain clothes. Secondly they would write down the different kinds of clothing needed. Only outer garments plus the accessories to go with them were to be included. The third step would be to find out what they had on hand that was usable or could be made more wearable. Then for the fourth step they would compare what they had with what was needed. The fifth and last step would be to make plans for getting the things they did not have.

It was agreed that each student would consult references on clothing needs, and interview people who made a practice of planning their wardrobes. At the same time they would assemble any ideas they might have on the five steps just outlined. Then through class discussions, summaries would be made of important points that might be

helpful in planning a wardrobe. Activities could be set up and carried out as the classwork progressed.

Determining Clothing Needs

Each student's listing of the activities and occasions for which clothes are needed proved to be pretty much the same as the others. School, church, parties, street or general wear, spectator sports, active sports, and work at home or elsewhere were the items generally mentioned.

The second step in their plan — listing the clothing itself — showed the same general agreement for the kind of garments needed. The main variation was the emphasis which different students placed on the amount of clothing and accessories they considered essential for certain activities or occasions.

The interviews which the students had with people who planned their wardrobes carefully, yielded helpful information. During the class discussion, various ideas were offered for assembling a practical wardrobe.

When it came time to summarize the material on clothing needs, the students decided to set up two columns on the blackboard. One column included general suggestions for planning a wardrobe. The other showed how some of these suggestions might be carried out to fit individual situations. Since the summary may be helpful to other classes, it is shown on pages 349 to 351.

HINTS ON
Planning a Wardrobe

GENERAL SUGGESTIONS	PRACTICAL POINTERS

Build your wardrobe around the places you go and the things you do regularly. But think in terms of the whole ensemble needed for these activities and occasions.

An ensemble for school would include the costume itself plus accessories, such as belts, ties, shoes, purses, head coverings, and wraps.

A swimming outfit might include not only a suit but bathing shoes, a coat, a bag, and a towel as well.

Consider the seasons when you select various articles of clothing. If you live in a climate with definite seasons, you may want to consider each one separately. Or it may be easier to plan for two seasons — winter including fall and early spring, and summer including late spring and early fall. But in all events, you will want your clothing to be comfortable — warm in cold weather, cool in hot weather, and a protection from rain or snow.

One all-purpose coat — neither dressy nor sport — may serve your needs. Or if you live in a climate where both a heavy coat and a light coat are needed, one all-purpose coat of each type may suffice. Or one coat with a zipped-in lining may be used for very cold as well as milder weather.

If the fabric of a coat has been treated to repel water, it may serve for either rain or snow.

GENERAL SUGGESTIONS	PRACTICAL POINTERS

Include in your wardrobe all the garments and accessories you need, but no more than you need. Allow for cleanliness and emergencies. You can never tell when you will have a runner in your stocking or accidentally soil a shirt. Sufficient changes are also desirable to provide for variety. Then too, the frequency of your activities affects the number of garments needed. For example, high school boys and girls usually need more clothes for school than for parties. However, exact numbers will depend on individual circumstances, such as facilities for keeping clothes clean or the ability to make a variety of costumes out of a few clothes.

Some authorities think that at least two pairs of everyday shoes are needed in order to get the most wear out of each pair. By wearing them alternately the life of both pairs is prolonged. You may want shoes for general wear, for sports, and for dress. If you need to cut down on numbers of shoes, a conservative style and color may serve for general wear as well as for simple dress occasions. A black pump for a girl and a black oxford for a boy might meet the needs.

By changing accessories, a suit or dress can often go several places and serve several functions. So-called jacket dresses for girls and women sometimes combine a party dress with what appears to be a suit when the jacket is worn. Changing the kind of shirt and tie can make a boy's suit dressed up or more casual.

A jacket or a cardigan-type sweater may serve as a wrap for school and for sports.

GENERAL SUGGESTIONS	PRACTICAL POINTERS
Build your wardrobe around one or two basic colors. Whatever color or colors you select can be used in a number of ways. That is, a basic color may be used in various degrees of lightness, darkness, brightness, and dullness. Or you may use it with neighboring, contrasting, or neutral combinations. If you select a neutral, such as black, white, or gray, you may use it with another neutral or with an accented color. (See Book 1, pages 42–43 for color combinations.)	For girls, if a basic color was blue, a navy blue suit or two-piece dress might be chosen. Blouses and accessories might include other shades of blue, or possibly aqua, beige, white, or gray. For boys, if brown was a basic color, a dark brown suit might be a good selection. Shoes worn with the suit would preferably be some shade of brown. Shirts, socks, and ties might also be different shades of brown, or they could be other harmonizing colors. An all-purpose coat for either a boy or a girl could be the basic color of the wardrobe. Or it could be a color that harmonizes with the basic color.

Taking a Clothing Inventory

The next step in the clothing plan was to find out what garments the students had that were usable or that could be made wearable. This seemed to indicate that taking an inventory was advisable. However, Miss Dennison pointed out that a satisfactory inventory is something more than merely checking the clothes you have. For example, it involves making decisions about garments that have been outgrown or that are no longer wearable. This saves time and effort later on.

Guides for taking an inventory

The students then decided that it would be helpful to have some guides for finding out what clothes they had on hand. Before long, the information they assembled and discussed was outlined on the blackboard as follows:

1. Assemble all of your clothing in one place, and look over each item carefully. Remember that the length of time you have had a garment is not

necessarily important if it looks well on you, is not definitely dated, and is still in good condition. Try various garment combinations which you have not previously used. In this way you may be able to salvage parts of an outfit, which are still usable, instead of discarding the whole outfit.

2. Separate the clothes into four groups: *a*, those that can be worn just as they are; *b*, those that may need some repairing or altering to make them wearable; *c*, those that you have outgrown but are still wearable by others; and *d*, those that are no longer usable.

3. List the items in group *a* and in group *b*. Use headings, such as coats, jackets, sweaters, suits, dresses, blouses, and other items, and indicate the number of items you have under each heading.

4. Then care for the four groups as follows: Group *a* — hang up or put away in a suitable place. Group *b* — set aside, in a convenient place, for possible classwork on making clothes more wearable. Groups *c* and *d* — consult your parents. They may have definite plans about what should be done with the clothes.

Making a Tentative Clothing Plan

After each student had taken an inventory to determine what clothing was on hand — either ready to be worn or to be made more wearable — the next step was to compare what was on hand with what was needed. This seemed to be a good time to set up a clothing plan. However, everyone was well aware that such a plan would need to be tentative and subject to change.

"I can see how that might be," said Marian. "We might find that some of the clothes we hoped to make wearable wouldn't be worth the time and money spent on them."

"Or someone might give us something as a gift," said Dorothy. "One of my aunts often gives me a birthday present of something to wear. But it's always a surprise; so I can't count on it in advance."

"In any case," Miss Dennison added, "as you work on carrying out your clothing plan, you will probably have many new ideas. Your plan will grow and become more specific as we take up our classwork on buying and making clothes. But a plan, even though frequently improved upon, indicates that you are making a good start in the right direction."

There were nods of approval to these remarks. After a brief discussion, the students agreed that a tentative plan could be made by adding a third column to the listings suggested for the inventory. This would be: 1, *clothes in good condition* — group *a* in the inventory; 2, *clothes I hope to repair or alter at school or at home* — group *b* in the inventory; and 3, *clothes I may buy or make.*

It was then decided that by the beginning of the next week, each student would have completed the inventory and set up a tentative clothing plan.

Deciding How to Get Needed Clothing

When the students first planned their classwork, several had mentioned that, for one reason or another, it was sometimes difficult to get the things they needed. This had led to the inclusion of the fifth step on wardrobes — planning to get the things they did not have.

Planning on the basis of what your family can afford

The students agreed that one big problem in getting new clothing depended upon what their families could afford. However, several members of the class said that they did not know how much their families planned to spend on clothing. Others said that until current bills were paid, it would not be possible to estimate whether any money would be available for new clothing. These and other comments led the class to consult references on how a family might regulate its spending on clothing. A summary of what they learned follows:

- Clothing expenditures are one of a family's flexible expenses. More or less money can be spent, depending upon the size of the family income and the number of members. Everyday expenses, such as those for food and for running the household, are first considerations, as are fixed expenses, such as rent and taxes. These expenditures cannot be cut as much as those for clothing and other flexible items. However, by listing fixed expenses, by keeping account of household expenditures, and by carefully planning flexible expenses, a family can arrive at the approximate amount they can afford for clothing.

- Since clothing needs vary, it is advisable for a family to decide how clothing expenses will be divided. For example, a father who has business demands,

may need a larger share regularly than some of the other members. Because of increased social activities, an older brother or sister may need a larger share than a younger child.

Planning what to do in case your needs exceed what your family can afford

In a further discussion, the students then agreed that no matter what their individual family situation was, there was still another matter to consider. This was what to do if the cost of their clothing exceeded the amount of money they could expect from their families. They had a general knowledge of the cost of some of the articles they wanted. But they knew that much remained to be learned about why, for instance, some coats cost more than others. This would be taken up in the goal — *learning to buy some of my clothes.*

However, in the meantime, they decided to figure out ways in which the problem of meeting their clothing needs could be handled if sufficient family funds were not available. After some discussion, these suggestions were summarized.

- Check back on your clothing plan to see whether by more careful planning you can eliminate some of the items.

- Decide which items are needed most urgently and which ones you can postpone getting until later on.

- Decide to make some of the garments you planned to buy if it will save money.

- Try to find ways of earning extra money. Offer to do some work at home that is ordinarily paid for, do baby-sitting, or find a part-time job after school.

- Make a plan for saving money from an allowance — or from money you earn — to buy the clothing needed.

CLASS MEMO:

What ideas do members of your class have for planning a wardrobe?

LEARNING TO MAKE MY CLOTHES MORE WEARABLE

Now that the inventories and tentative clothing plans had been completed, the students were ready to take up their second goal — *learning to make my clothes more wearable.* As they discussed possible procedures, Evelyn suggested holding a clothing clinic.

"We could bring various garments to the class and get ideas for making them more usable," she said.

"A grand idea," chorused the students. Miss Dennison nodded her approval and suggested that they could start making plans right away.

Setting Up a Clothing Clinic

It was fun getting ready for the clinic. Since some of the clothing would need to be tried on, arrangements were soon made for dressing rooms. Extra clothing racks were also provided for hanging the garments.

As the plans progressed, Dorothy reminded the class that they had learned a considerable amount last year about making clothes more wearable. (See Book 1, pages 48–60; 272–274; 286–287; 382; 415–416; 428.)

"We worked on the problem of keeping clothes clean and neat," said Marian.

"I learned to mend a tear and to make a machine-stitched patch," added Richard.

"Learning to sew on buttons — especially on my overcoat — was a great help to me," said Glen.

"We learned quite a bit about storing clothes in drawers, boxes, and closets," said Sharon.

"Now we can look forward to more advanced problems," said Peter.

"That's right," said Miss Dennison. "I think it would be a good idea for you to look over your clothes that need to be made more wearable. You can leave at home those which you already know how to repair. Bring in only the articles that require new mending techniques or simple alterations."

"How will we go about deciding what to do with the clothing that's brought in?" asked Walter.

A basis for evaluating the clothing

The class pondered this question and after some discussion agreed to proceed in the following manner. Each garment would be examined, tried on if necessary, and then evaluated on the basis of these questions:

1. What kind of repairs or alterations seem desirable?

2. Will the repaired or altered garment give enough wearability to warrant the necessary expenditure of time and/or money?

3. If altered, will the garment serve the purpose for which it is needed?

4. Will the garment give satisfaction after it is repaired or altered?

5. Will the repairs or alterations be minor enough for me to do at school or at home? Or will they need to be done by a more experienced person?

6. Does the garment need to be laundered or dry-cleaned before repairs or alterations can be made at school?

Assembling Information on Repairing Garments

On the opening day of the clinic, the homemaking room resembled a clothing store. Miss Dennison was pleased to see that every student had brought in one or more articles of clothing. Some even came with suitcases filled with a variety of garments. All indications pointed to a busy session for the clinic.

After the clothing had been evaluated and recommendations decided on, the students grouped together the garments requiring repair. They sorted them and listed the following types of work that seemed necessary: (1) repairing broken threads and stitches, small holes, and thin places, and (2) reversing or replacing certain parts of a garment.

The students then decided to divide into two groups, each group to assemble directions for one of the types of work listed. A student could join the group in which he or she needed the most help. Source materials would be available on the reference shelves.

When it was time for the demonstrations, each student was to receive a mimeographed copy of the directions for doing the repair work being demonstrated. The students with considerable skill could use the directions for doing the repairs at home alone. Those with less skill could do the work in class later on.

Repairing broken threads and stitches

When Group 1 was ready to report to the class, Sharon made the opening remarks. She said that broken stitches are likely to occur on a garment wherever there is sewing, especially in seams and hems. She said that no directions had been prepared for repairing a hand-sewn hem, since the stitches had been used last year. (See Book 1, pages 433–434.) Even though repairing a broken seam was similar to previous work, the group had decided that directions and a demonstration might be helpful. How to repair broken threads in sweaters, and runners in hosiery were the other directions assembled for this part of the repair work. These directions follow:

BROKEN SEAMS: Usually it is best to replace a machine-stitched seam — or hem — with machine stitching. Try to duplicate the color and size of the thread as well as the size of the stitch. Sometimes seams, such as those in a glove or some other inaccessible place, are most easily repaired by hand.

If the machine is used, proceed as follows: Begin stitching about 1 inch back of the broken thread, and continue to 1 inch beyond it. Stitch exactly on the line of the seam. Secure the thread ends both at the beginning and at the end of the stitching.

If done by hand, use the backstitch to replace the ripped stitches. From the right side of the garment, a row of backstitches resembles machine stitching. Backstitching is made as follows: Secure the thread. Bring the thread through from the under side one stitch length ahead of where you want the

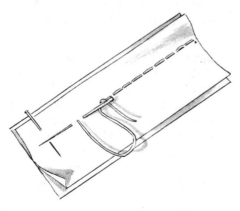

line of stitches to commence. Then insert the needle one stitch back, and bring it out one stitch ahead of where the thread emerges. Continue taking one stitch backward and one stitch forward every time the needle passes under the back of the seam. Make firm stitches uniform in size. Avoid pulling

too tight, or the stitches may break when the seam is stretched. Secure the thread.

BROKEN THREADS IN SWEATERS: Snags in sweaters may be pulled to the inside, and the ends tied or caught together with needle and thread. For a simple break in the knitting, catch the end of each loop with a needle and matching thread. Tie securely on the wrong side. If the stitch is raveled, your teacher may show you how to catch and crochet it in again. If there is a hole, your teacher will advise you as to the kind of repair best suited to the sweater.

RUNNERS IN HOSIERY: If there is a snag, try to keep it from running until the hose can be repaired. A run once begun may be stopped by applying a drop of special run-stop solution. This may be purchased in hosiery departments or hosiery specialty stores. Fingernail lacquer is not recommended since it may make the stocking impossible to repair. The only way to repair a runner so that it does not show is to pick up the stitches which have run. This requires a particular skill and a special needle. Repair shops for mending runners are often available where charges are reasonable. Or you may wish to repair the runner yourself by sewing it together by machine or by hand.

If you use the machine, proceed as follows:

1. Thread the needle and bobbin of the machine with darning thread to match the hose in color and in weight.

2. Working on the wrong side of the hose, make a fold through the center of the runner, and baste or pin-baste it together.

3. Start the machine stitching at least ½ inch beyond one end of the runner, securing the starting stitch.

4. Using a long stitch and a loose tension, make a seam one or two ribs back of the run. While stitching, stretch the stocking as much as it will stretch during wear.

5. Continue the seam at least ½ of an inch beyond the other end of the run. Secure the thread.

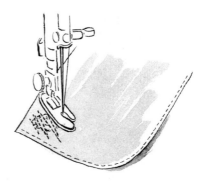

If you do the work by hand, start by fastening the end of the thread on the wrong side a few stitches back of the beginning of the run. Work on the right side, overhanding the run together. Make all of the stitches even in depth and parallel on the right side, slanting the needle underneath. Continue a few stitches beyond the end of the run, and fasten the thread on the wrong side.

Repairing small holes and thin places

Peter acted as spokesman for the remaining types of repair work done by Group 1. He said that various ways had been worked out for taking care of small holes and thin places as inconspicuously as possible. The group had also investigated what might be done with decorative patches. The following directions were made available to the students as the demonstrations progressed.

STITCHING ABOVE A HOLE IN AN INSIDE POCKET: Trim off any frayed threads. But avoid changing the shape of the pocket if so doing will cause it to be unlike a twin pocket. If the hole is in a corner or along the side of the pocket, stitch back and forth several times above the hole. Do not cut off the section of the pocket below the stitching

if it makes the shape unusual or unlike a twin pocket.

APPLYING MENDING TAPE: A quick method of mending is to press a piece of mending tape under a hole or thin place. Find out the brands available at notion counters. Then experiment with the different kinds, following directions for their use. You may discover that some tapes are more satisfactory than others, or that the same tape may be good for one garment and not for another.

DARNING A SMALL HOLE BY HAND: Pull yarns from a scrap of the same material if you have any. Or ravel some from seams or edges where they may be spared. Then proceed as follows:

1. Place your hand, or a darner, or a small piece of heavy cardboard underneath the hole.

2. Outline the area to be darned. Do this by making small running stitches around the hole about ⅛ of an inch from the edge.

3. Using small stitches, work back and forth lengthwise across the hole. See that the needle goes over the first edge of the hole and under the second edge, as shown in the following illustration.

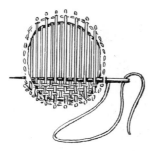

4. Turn the garment around. Weave stitches across the width over and under the foundation stitches already made.

5. Secure the stitches on the wrong side, and press the area.

REINFORCING A THIN PLACE: Baste a piece of sheer material under the thin place. Darn or weave with the grain from the wrong side. Use short stitches on the outside and longer ones on the wrong side. Avoid pulling the work tight. Steam-press the area from the right side.

APPLYING DECORATIVE PATCHES: Small holes or thin places on the elbows of sweaters or jackets, and on the knees of trousers or slacks may be covered with decorative patches. These patches may be purchased at notion counters. They come in various colors, and in several kinds of materials, such as corduroy, felt, and soft leather. They may be cut into whatever shape is desired, and need not necessarily match the color or material in the garment.

Corduroy patches are generally the iron-on variety, but are often stitched around the edge to make them more firm. Directions for applying accompany each patch.

Felt patches are easily applied by stitching them on the machine. Since felt does not ravel, the edges need not be finished.

Soft leather patches may be stitched on by machine or sewed on by hand. In either case a larger size needle than is used for ordinary sewing is needed. This will prevent the leather from becoming weakened by closely spaced stitching or sewing.

Reversing and replacing certain parts of a garment

Group 2's work was concerned with garments which were in good condition except for certain parts. The clothing clinic had revealed shirt collars, collarbands, and inside pockets of trousers that could not be repaired by methods suggested by Group 1. Walter, acting as spokesman for the group, said that sometimes certain worn parts can be reversed if they are still good on the other side. Or the worn sections may be replaced by new parts.

In order to show how this kind of work could be done, the group had assembled several types of shirts. One was the standard dress shirt with a collar attached to a collarband. The others were sport shirts without a collarband. Some of these could be buttoned at the neck and worn with a tie if desired. To save time during the demonstrations, some of the ripping was done in advance. Copies of the directions and comments which follow were carefully noted by the students as they watched the demonstrations.

REVERSING A DRESS SHIRT COLLAR, BUT NOT THE COLLARBAND:

1. Open the seam that joins the collar to the collarband, being careful not to cut the fabric. Do not rip out to the ends of the band, but only from points A to B as shown in the illustration. Remove

These boys appear to be enjoying reversing dress shirt collars or collarbands.

the collar. If the bottom of the collar is attached to the lower edge of the band, cut the collar away carefully.

2. Fold the collar in half, end to end, and mark the center with a pin. Do the same with the collarband.

3. Reverse the collar to its good side, and insert it back into the collarband, centering it as marked. Pin the ends of the collar in place at points A and B.

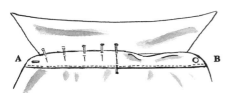

Then pin along the collarband between A and B as shown in the illustration. Baste along the pinned line, being sure that the under side of the collarband is caught by the stitches. Remove pins,

and stitch carefully along the original seam line of the collarband.

4. Secure threads, remove bastings, and press.

REVERSING THE COLLARBAND WITHOUT DETACHING THE COLLAR:

1. Mark the center back of the shirt and the center back of the collarband. Then rip the seam that joins the collarband to the shirt, and remove the band with collar.

2. Reverse the collarband to the good side, and pin it in center back at

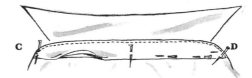

marked points. Then pin the ends of the band to the front edges of the shirt as shown at C and D in the illustration.

Pin the rest of the band in place, slipping the neckline of the shirt inside the collarband. Be sure to place the pins exactly along the old stitching line, but not to overlap more of the shirt than was included in the original seam. Baste, being careful that the under side of the collarband is caught by the stitches. Remove pins.

3. Stitch along the basted line. Secure threads, remove bastings, and press.

4. Draw the opening of the buttonhole together with several small stitches. Remove the button from the other end of the collarband, and sew it over the old buttonhole. Make a new buttonhole on the other end of the collarband. (See pages 422–423, and Book 1, pages 427–428.)

REVERSING THE COLLAR OF A SPORT SHIRT:

1. Mark the center back of the collar, the center back of the shirt, and the collar where it joins the shoulder seams. Study very carefully how the collar is joined to the shirt. Sport shirts vary in this respect, depending upon the way the shirt is made. You will need to put the collar back exactly as it was before. Otherwise the shirt will not fit right.

2. Rip the stitching in the seam that joins the collar to the shirt. Reverse the collar. Pin and baste the under side of the collar to the shirt at the points marked, with the seam on the inside. Remove pins.

3. Stitch on the previous seam line. Secure threads, remove bastings, and press the seam flat, turning the raw edges inside the collar.

4. Baste the top part of the collar to the inside of the shirt on the seam line. Stitch carefully on the original seam line. Secure threads, remove bastings, and press.

USING READYMADE REPLACEMENT PARTS: Replacement parts, such as white dress-shirt collars and cuffs, and inside trouser pockets, may be purchased at notion counters or from mail order houses. Directions generally accompany the parts.

REPLACING THE LOWER PART OF AN INSIDE POCKET:

1. Cut off the worn section of the pocket, and use this as a pattern. Select material similar to the top part of the pocket. Place the folded edge of the old section on the lengthwise fold of the new fabric. Cut a new section, using the original seam allowance on the side and bottom. Add 1⅛ inches at the top for joining the section to the pocket.

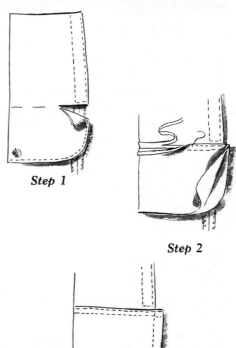

Step 1

Step 2

Step 3

2. Attach the new section to the pocket with a fell seam. (See pages 429–430.)
3. Leave the pocket wrong side out, and place the curved edges of the pocket together. Make a seam, generally plain.
4. Press pocket.

```
CLASS MEMO:
  What problems on
  repairing garments does
  your class have? What
  plans will the group
  make for completing the
  types of repair work
  needed?
```

Assembling Information on Remodeling Clothes

In addition to the garments in need of repair, the clothing clinic contained articles which the students believed could be made more wearable by simple alterations. Some of the boys had grown, so that lengthening their trousers was necessary. Richard had a gabardine suit — a hand-me-down from his older brother — that could be worn if the trousers and sleeves were shortened. The girls also had various skirts and dresses needing to be lengthened or shortened. In addition there were several neckline changes in the girls' clothing that seemed advisable. It was also decided that the service of some dresses could be prolonged by making them into jumpers. All of these alterations were believed to be within the students' ability to do successfully.

It was agreed that the boys would work on information and directions for making the alterations they contemplated, and the girls on theirs. The directions were to be assembled by the time the students were ready to start making some of their clothes. Then each student could decide what activities he or she would like to carry out to complete the classwork in "A Four-Point Plan for My Wardrobe."

This arrangement worked out very satisfactorily. Various source materials were used in setting up the directions. Extension bulletins and other pamphlets were especially helpful. By the time the class was ready for the fourth goal, the following information was available

Altering length

The types of length alterations undertaken by the students were limited to those that could be done at the bottom of a garment, such as those on a trouser cuff, a skirt or dress hem, or a sleeve edge.

LENGTHENING TROUSERS

If 1 inch or less is being added, finish with a plain cuff. If the length requires more than an inch, a French cuff or no cuff may be used. Directions follow for these three finishes:

PLAIN CUFF:

1. Pick out the tacks at the side of the cuff. Then remove the stitches that hold the hem. Open out the cuff and brush away all lint and dust. If the cuffs

have never been repaired or adjusted, there will be three sharp crease lines.

2. Measure down from the top crease the amount you want to lengthen the trousers. Mark the new line. Steam out all old press lines.

Steps 2 and 3

3. From the new line you have marked, measure down 1¾ inches, and mark a second line around the trouser leg. Then mark a third line 1¾ inches below that.

4. Fold along the middle line, and baste.

5. Pin the first and third lines together and baste. Steam-press.

6. Fold to form the new cuff along the line where the third and first lines are basted together. Baste to hold the cuff in place. Press, and then remove the bastings.

7. To finish the cut edge, which is turned up inside the trouser leg, turn the cuff down again. Baste and stitch the cut edge to the trouser leg. If a wear guard is to be used, it needs to be put on before the edge is stitched in place. The guard is usually a ⅝-inch piece of cotton twill tape sewed to the trouser leg just above the fold which forms the bottom of the cuff. A guard of this type helps protect the trouser leg from shoe friction, thus preventing fraying around the bottom of the cuff.

8. Turn the cuff back up, and tack to the sides of the trouser leg.

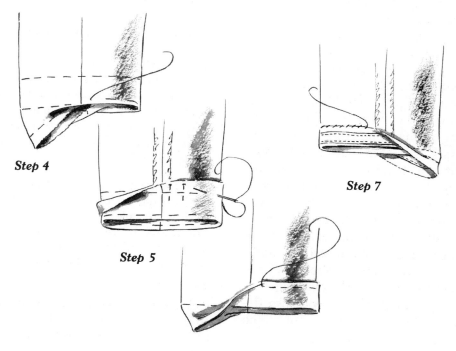

Step 4

Step 5

Step 6

Step 7

FRENCH CUFF:

1–2. Follow steps 1 and 2 for a plain cuff.

3. From the new line, mark two more lines. Make one line 1¾ inches above the new length line, and the other 1¾ inches above the second line.

4. Fold on the center line, and baste. Lay this fold against the top line, and baste. Fold and baste along the lower line, which marks the bottom of the cuff. Steam-press all folds.

5. Turn the cut edge up inside the trouser leg, and fold it under so that the crease just meets the top fold. Trim off any extra material. Join the two folds with slip stitches so that they will not catch on the shoes. If a wear guard is de-sired, follow the last part of step 7 for making a plain cuff.

6. Follow step 8 as for a plain cuff.

NO CUFF:

1. Follow step 1 as for a plain cuff.

2. Steam out the creases. Measure and mark new length. Baste and steam-press a crease on the new line, turning the outside edge toward the inside of the trouser leg.

3. Mark and trim for a 1¾-inch single-turn hem. Baste and stitch cotton twill tape about ⅝ of an inch wide to cover the raw edge of the hem.

4. Hem the top edge of the tape to the trouser leg with a slant hemming stitch. Be careful that the stitches do not show on the right side of the trouser leg. (See Book 1, pages 433–434 for the slant hemming stitch.)

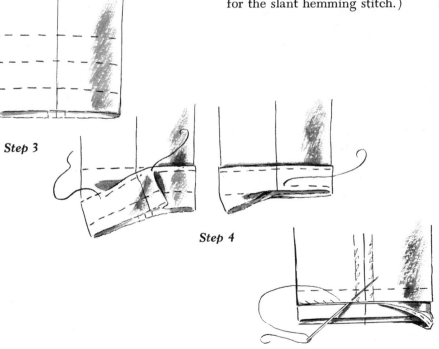

Step 3

Step 4

Step 5

SHORTENING TROUSERS

1. Follow step 1 as for lengthening trousers.

2. Measure up from the top crease of a plain cuff the amount you want to shorten the trousers. Mark the line. Steam out old creases.

3. From the new length line, measure down 1¾ inches and mark. Then measure 1¾ inches below the second line, and mark. Trim trousers off about 1½ inches below what is now the bottom line.

4. Follow steps 4 to 8 inclusive for making a plain cuff.

LENGTHENING A SKIRT
OR DRESS

For slight increases in length, or where a tuck in the hem has been allowed in making the garment, extra length may be gained by letting out the hem. Otherwise a facing for the hem will be needed.

LET-OUT HEM:

1. Take out the old hem. If hem tape is used, it may or may not need to be removed, depending upon whether or not the old hem was straight or even. Clean the crease carefully. Steam-press to remove the crease.

2. Try on the garment and have the new length marked. Proceed in replacing the hem as indicated in Book 1, pages 432 to 433.

FACED HEM:

1. Take out the old hem. Remove hem tape if used. Clean the crease, and remove it by steam-pressing.

2. Have the garment marked for length. Trim below the marking, allowing ⅝ to ¾ of an inch for a seam allowance.

3. Use commercial bias skirt facing, or cut bias strips the desired width. Commercial facing generally comes in different colors in 3-yard lengths with directions for applying. If bias strips are to be cut, see Book 1, pages 425 to 426. Use material that will leave the hem neat and flat. To be inconspicuous, it needs to be as nearly as possible the color of the garment. Join cut strips together to make a continuous strip slightly longer than is needed to go around the bottom of the garment.

4. Baste the right side of the bias strip to the right side of the bottom of the garment, leaving free ½ of an inch at the beginning and end, and using a ½-inch seam allowance. On a straight edge, avoid pulling one side any tighter than the other. On an outward-curved edge, hold the bias strip a little tight to make it fit smoothly. Baste and stitch together the ends of the bias strip. Remove basting, and press seam open.

5. Stitch the bias strip that has been basted to the garment, and trim the edge of the seam to ¼ of an inch. Press, turning the edges together toward the facing.

Steps 6 and 7

6. Turn the facing to the inside of the garment. Ease ⅛ to ¼ inch of the skirt to extend beyond the facing. The thicker the fabric, the larger the ease should be. Otherwise the facing may show, and the garment not hang properly. Baste around this bottom edge of the hem.

7. Finish the top edge of the facing as a hem, and press.

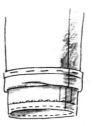

Step 3

SHORTENING A SKIRT
OR DRESS

Follow the same directions as for a let-down hem. If the garment is unusually long, some of the material may need to be cut off from the bottom before the hem can be put in. Or tucks may be used to take up additional length.

LENGTHENING OR SHORTENING
SLEEVES

Dress or blouse sleeves without cuffs are generally hemmed or faced at the bottom. They may be shortened by raising the hem, or lengthened by facing the hem. Sometimes a cuff can be added for additional length. A shirt cuff can be raised to shorten the sleeve, but trimmed seam allowances make lengthening impossible.

SHORTENING LINED SLEEVES: Coat or suit sleeves that are lined can be shortened by turning in new hem lengths as follows:

1. Baste around the sleeve below the elbow to hold the lining in place. Then turn the sleeve to the wrong side, and take out the hem. Free the lining from the sleeve, and remove the interfacing from the sleeve hem. Press out crease marks.

Step 4

2. Try on the garment, and mark the new sleeve length. Trim raw edges of the sleeve 1½ inches below the new length. Pin and baste interfacing to the sleeve, so that the lower edge falls on the new line. Use small loose stitches that do not show on the right side of the garment. Turn the sleeve hem over the interfacing, and baste close to the folded edge. Press. Slip-stitch the raw edge of the hem to the interfacing, and press.

3. Cut the lining the same length as the hemmed sleeve. Turn under the raw edge ¼ of an inch. Baste, and press.

4. Baste the lining to the sleeve ¾ of an inch above the sleeve length. Slip-stitch to the sleeve hem. Remove basting, and press.

5. Turn sleeve to the right side, and remove basting below the elbow.

LENGTHENING LINED SLEEVES: If there is sufficient material, the same directions for shortening a sleeve may be used in reverse. If there is an insufficient amount, then a facing may be applied as for a faced hem. Sometimes a sleeve may show signs of wear along the previously folded edge. If it seems advisable, a row of machine stitches may be placed on the worn part to make it less conspicuous.

CHANGING THE NECKLINE

Sometimes the existing lines of a garment can be changed to make the garment more wearable. Some line changes are difficult to make and require considerable experience. However, neckline alterations on a dress or a blouse, or recutting the neckline and sleeves to make a jumper dress are relatively easy procedures. At the same time, they usually give the renovated garments a new smart appearance.

All neckline changes include removing, refitting, and replacing the finishing already on the neckline. If the neckline is changed to any extent, it will be necessary to apply a new finishing. (See Book 1, pages 434–436 for neckline finishing, and pages 425–427 for applying bias binding and bias facing.)

A NECKLINE TOO SMALL: If there is a sufficient shoulder allowance, decreasing the size of the seam may make the neckline large enough. Or it may be desirable to cut the neckline lower. If this is done, mark the new neckline with pins before cutting.

A NECKLINE TOO LARGE: Increasing the size of the shoulder seams may make the neckline small enough. Or you may want to conceal the large neckline with a detached collar. Sometimes cutting a new yoke for a dress may be advisable. If this is planned, consult your teacher how to proceed. (See page 426 for making a detachable collar.)

RECUTTING THE NECK AND SLEEVES TO MAKE A JUMPER DRESS: Sometimes a dress that is otherwise good wears out at the neck and under the arms. The garment may then be made into a jumper dress to be worn with a blouse. Directions for this procedure follow:

1. Put on the dress, and mark the new neck and arm lines with pins.

2. Remove the dress. Fold the right and left sides together along the center front. Pin to hold in place. Also pin shoulder seams together, and underarm seams. Cut both front sides at once, following the pin lines but allowing a ½-inch seam allowance. Pin in any parts that run into the neckline or armseye. Fold along center back, and repeat the process.

3. Make a paper pattern for a 2-inch — when finished — fitted facing for the neck and armholes. Cut front and back sections separately, so that the material can be cut on the same grain as the front and back of the garment. Make each section the same width throughout. Cut notches to indicate where the pattern pieces fit together.

4. Cut material for the facing according to the pattern, being careful to keep grain lines straight. Use the same or similar material as the dress.

5. Pin front and back sections to the garment to be sure that they fit. Make any necessary adjustments. Remove from garment, and seam together. Press seams open.

6. Baste and stitch the facing to the garment, right sides together. Remove bastings. Clip the edges, being careful not to cut the stitching. Press open.

7. Turn the facing to the inside of the garment, and work the seam out to the

edge. Baste the facing along the edge and back far enough so that it does not show from the right side of the garment. Press lightly, and stitch the seam to the facing close to the edge if desired.

8. Finish the raw edge of the facing as you and your teacher decide.

CLASS MEMO:

What types of altera-
tions are you and the
members of your class
interested in? Are
they within the range
of your experience?

LEARNING TO BUY SOME OF MY CLOTHES

It was a red-letter day when the students and Miss Dennison decided they were ready to take up the goal — *learning to buy some of my clothing.* Everyone was interested in the subject, because it meant one more step in knowing how to be suitably and attractively dressed at all times.

The first thing the students did was to refer back to their clothing plans to see what garments were to be purchased. Both boys and girls wanted to learn about buying suits, coats, and shoes. They all realized that these are expensive items in a clothing budget. They are also the ones which parents are most reluctant for their sons and daughters to purchase without guidance. Hosiery was another item which both groups were eager to learn to buy wisely. It was believed that better buying practices might reduce the total cost of these articles. Some of the girls had already bought dresses and blouses, but even those with experience were anxious to learn more about these garments. A number of boys expected to buy shirts.

The students agreed that their classwork last year and this fitted in very nicely with the objective on buying. For example, they had learned that garments need to be becoming in design and color. They also need to be suited to your age and personality, and to fit the occasion for which they will be worn. (See Book 1, pages 33–47.) Furthermore, having a clothing plan — such as each student had set up — would be very helpful. When you know what you need and want and what you can afford, you have a good start toward understanding buying techniques. The question now was what else needed to be learned to bring about satisfaction in buying.

Planning the Classwork

One of the considerations that seemed important to the students was knowing how to get the best value for their money. Several members of the class told of unfortunate experiences they had had in failing to get their money's worth for certain garments. In some cases the material had not worn well, or the garment did not fit comfortably. Others told how quickly the seams had ripped or how easily the garment got out of shape.

The students finally agreed that to avoid such unsuccessful experiences they would need to learn about fabrics that are used in clothing. They would also need to know how to evaluate the workmanship of garments, and the way they fit. These seemed to be important considerations whether a garment is bought or made.

"I find that I need to learn more about labels," said Evelyn. "I know it's a good practice to look for them and read them. But some garments don't have labels. And even when they do, I don't always understand what the label means. I think that learning about the information on labels would be very helpful."

There were nods of agreement.

Miss Dennison then remarked that there were other points they might want to consider. "There will be some purchases which will not be exactly what you had in mind at the price you hoped to pay," she said. "One garment will meet the picture in everything except price. Another may be ideal except in color. Is price or color more important? Each of you will need to decide what values in buying will bring you the most satisfaction. Then too, as you gain experience, you will find that certain buying practices make it easier to obtain satisfactory purchases."

These and other comments led the students to set up the following over-all plan for what they needed to know about buying clothing.

- Learn all you can about the clothes and accessories you plan to buy before you go shopping. This includes:

  1. How to evaluate clothing fabrics — what they are made of, what services they are expected to give, and what care they require

  2. How to interpret information given on labels

  3. How to evaluate size, fit, cut, and workmanship

- Decide what values in buying will give you the most satisfaction.

- Learn how to improve buying practices.

Deciding How to Carry Out the Classwork

The discussion then centered around the best way to carry out the classwork, so that it would serve everyone's personal needs.

There was much about fabrics and labels that the class as a whole would need to learn, even though various students were planning to buy different types of garments. Personal satisfaction in buying and how to improve buying practices would also need to be considered by everyone in the class. In general, the boys could work separately on setting up guides for purchasing the garments they planned to buy. The girls would follow the same procedure for their garments.

When all of the material on buying clothing was prepared, the mothers of the students would be invited to visit the homemaking rooms to see a store display. The display would feature the different articles the students planned to buy, and the guides they had set up for purchasing these items. During the visit, several members of the class wearing suits, coats, or dresses could exhibit these garments in front of the group. Other students acting as salespersons could point our various characteristics which one needed to consider when buying these garments.

Everyone was quite excited about the store display. It seemed to be a wonderful way to show their parents how much they were learning about buying clothes.

Miss Dennison said that the reference shelves contained books and pamphlets on all of the subjects to be studied. Visiting local stores and having talks by salesmen or buyers were also suggested sources. These and other details could be decided on as the classwork progressed.

Knowing How to Evaluate Fabrics Used in Clothing

The students started their work on fabrics by looking over some swatches of clothing materials that Miss Dennison had on hand. Each fabric was different. Several members of the class were able to point out various ones that were cotton or wool or silk. But there were others they could not identify. And even all of the wool fabrics or the cotton ones did not look alike. It was puzzling, to say the least, and various questions arose.

Miss Dennison pointed out that some of the answers to their questions could be found in the materials on the reference shelves. Others could be learned through experience. Still others could be answered only by information supplied about the fabric. However, knowing what a fabric is made of helps in judging the service it will give and the care it will need. Knowing something about how it is made and finished also helps in evaluating its service and care.

Before long various information was assembled and discussed. With Miss Dennison's assistance, the swatches of material were identified. Final summaries of points that proved helpful follow:

What fabrics are made of

- Some fabrics are made of natural fibers which originate in plant or in animal life. Cotton, linen, silk, and wool are examples.

- Others — made by man — are constructed from chemical fibers. Examples of these are rayon and acetate, Vicara, nylon, and Dacron.

- Some fabrics are made from blends of fibers. Blends are made to give added qualities that would otherwise not be available in a fiber, to produce an unusual texture, or to reduce cost.

How fabrics are made

- Fibers are formed into yarns before fabrics are woven. Short fibers — wool, cotton, and linen, or silk too short to reel and chemical fibers cut into short

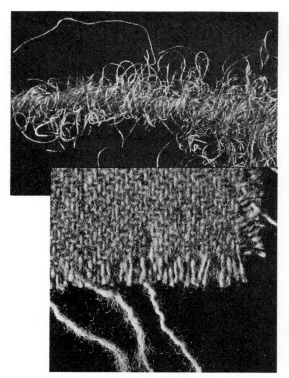

On page 372 fabrics made of wool are classed as woolens and worsteds. Note the short, unstraightened yarns and the character of the woolen fabric at the left. Compare them with the longer, combed fibers and the worsted fabric at the right.

lengths — are spun into yarns. Long silk fibers and chemical fibers are twisted into yarns.

- Yarns made of long fibers are generally smooth, glossy, and strong. Those made of short fibers are irregular in appearance, but are more absorbent than yarns made of long fibers. Yarns that are highly twisted are less lustrous, but have greater strength than low-twisted yarns.

- Weaving is the interlacing of yarns at right angles to make a fabric. Plain, twill, and satin weaves form the basis for all other types. (See the illustrations that follow.) Generally, firm, closely woven fabrics with lengthwise and crosswise yarns equal in number and strength give the best service. In loose weaving, yarns may snag or pull in wear. Also there may be greater danger of shrinkage.

From left to right, greatly magnified, the three basic weaves—plain, twill, and satin—are shown.

• Some fabrics are "fiber dyed," which means the fiber is dyed before it is spun into yarn. This makes possible interesting blends of color, but it is an expensive process. "Dyed in the yarn" means that the yarns are dyed before the fabric is woven. Checks, plaids, stripes, and other designs that show on both sides are examples. "Piece dyeing" means dyeing the cloth after it is woven. This is the least expensive and most commonly used method.

• A pattern or design is put on a fabric in one or more colors by using dyes in paste form. In "block printing," the design is placed on a block, each block containing only one color. The process is slow and expensive. "Roller printing" is a shorter method commonly used. Generally only one side of the material is printed.

Types of finishes

After the fabric is completed, it goes through a number of finishing processes. Some of these improve its appearance or increase its durability or both. Others make the fabric better suited for specific uses. Some finishes are permanent; others are not. One that is not permanent or that cannot be replaced may not be worth the additional cost. It is therefore desirable to consider the purpose for which a fabric is to be used. For example, if you are buying a raincoat, a waterproof or water-repellent finish is important, whereas colorfastness to sunlight may not be. A few of the most common finishes and what they do follow:

COLORFASTNESS: Colors are made fast for special purposes, such as fastness to sunlight, perspiration, washing, or dry-cleaning.

CRUSH OR CREASE RESISTANT: Makes it possible to "shake out" or "hang out" wrinkles

GLAZING: A sheen given to cotton fabrics

MERCERIZING: Makes cotton fabrics stronger, more lustrous, pliable, and absorbent

MILDEW RESISTANT: Fabrics are able to resist parasitic growth due to dampness. The finish may also make the fabrics resistant to odor or perspiration.

MOTH RESISTANT: Repels moths

NAPPING: A process of roughing up or pulling out the ends of fibers to produce a downy or fuzzy surface appearance

SHRINK RESISTANT: Makes fabrics resistant to shrinkage in width and length. (See The Meaning of Preshrunk, Book 1, page 369.)

SIZING: Gives strength, stiffness, and smoothness. Some finishes are not permanent after the fabric is washed or dry-cleaned.

STARCHLESS: Insures crispness or semistiffness without starching

WATERPROOFING: Keeps out air and moisture by closing the pores of the fabric

WATER REPELLENT: Makes fabric resistant to air and moisture, but does not close pores as in waterproofing

Characteristics of fibers and their care

Fibers vary in their characteristics and in the care they require. Making a choice is greatly dependent upon the use intended for the fabric. Warmness or coolness, for instance, depends upon the season or climate. A strong fiber indicates long, hard wear, which may or may not be the prime consideration. Elasticity usually means that a fiber will not wrinkle badly. Low-moisture

CHART OF FIBER CHARACTERISTICS

AND FABRIC CARE

FIBERS	CHARACTERISTICS	CARE

NATURAL

COTTON

Smooth, soft, lightweight, fairly strong. Absorbs moisture easily, but maintains strength when wet. Retains whiteness, but catches dirt readily.

Machine-washable in hot water. If not colorfast to washing, launder and dry separately from white materials. Dampen and iron with a hot iron. Some finishes require little or no ironing. Fibers are weakened by too frequent use of a strong chlorine bleach. Perborate bleaches are recommended.

LINEN

Strong, but lacks elasticity. Absorbs moisture easily. Does not lint, soil, or hold stains readily. Cooler than cotton in equal weight. Wrinkles unless treated.

Washes easily. Pressing requires more moisture than cotton and a cooler iron. Press on wrong side for dull finish. Fibers are weakened by frequent use of chlorine bleach. Some finishes require perborate bleaches.

SILK

Lustrous, strong, elastic. Drapes softly. Dyes and prints well.

Dry-clean unless labeled washable. Launder by hand in warm water with mild soap. Squeeze suds through fabric, rinse, and roll in towel. Do not dry in sun or near heat. Press on wrong side with moderate heat when damp-dry. White silk may be bleached with a perborate bleach.

Pure-dye

Best quality. Has soft, deep luster. Dyes especially well.

Spun

Has no luster, but wears fairly well. Is likely to become fuzzy with use.

Wild, such as shantung or pongee

Coarse. More irregular than other grades, but wears well.

Can be pressed when dry without dampening.

WOOL

Warm; has high moisture absorption. Shrinks easily unless especially treated.

Needs to be aired and brushed often. Preferable to wear wool garments on alternate days. Small articles usually hand-washable; others generally dry-cleaned. In laundering, avoid strong soap and much handling. Use lukewarm water or cold water with a special wool-washing compound. Do not rub, wring, or twist. Dry flat, reshaping the article if necessary. Keep away from heat or direct sunlight. White wool may be bleached with a perborate bleach.

Woolens

Made from short wool fibers, lightly twisted. Have slight natural nap, or may be given additional napping. Thicker, softer, and springier than worsteds; do not wrinkle readily.

Worsteds

Made from long wool fibers, straightened and twisted tightly. Firm, smooth, resilient; have little or no fuzz. Hold their shape, and retain creases well. Some become shiny with wear. A light napping treatment helps prevent this.

FIBERS	CHARACTERISTICS	CARE

CHEMICAL

ACETATE

Soft and silklike. Has pleasing luster; drapes softly; sheds wrinkles easily. Has low moisture absorption. Mothproof; resists mildew, but can be attacked by silverfish and termites.

Wash or dry-clean according to label. Wash in warm water; avoid wringing. Press while still damp with warm iron. Use perborate bleach to prevent graying in white fabrics. Incidental spots, such as nail polish, may be removed with banana oil. Avoid using nail polish remover.

ACRILAN

Strong; warm without weight. Resists shrinkage. Does not wrinkle easily. Does not spot readily. Absorbs very little moisture. Resists moths and mildew.

Generally washable, depending on fabric instructions. Wash in warm water. Drip-dries quickly. Needs little or no pressing. If pressed, do so on wrong side with a warm — not hot — iron.

DACRON

Very strong; fairly soft, and looks like wool. Drapes well. Will not shrink or stretch. Almost no moisture absorption. Creases hold in rain. Moth and mildew resistant.

Generally washable, depending on fabric instructions. Drip-dries quickly. Needs little or no ironing. Spots may be removed with water. Use a perborate bleach to prevent graying in white fabrics.

DYNEL

Soft; looks like wool. Warm, but light and fluffy. Very strong. Will not shrink or stretch. Resists spots. Has little moisture absorption. Holds creases wet or dry. Totally moth and mildew resistant.

Wash or dry-clean according to instructions. Drip-dries quickly. Requires little or no pressing. If ironing is necessary, use low heat. In removing spots, avoid a cleaner with acetone.

NYLON

Light and soft. One of the strongest clothing fibers. Will not shrink if heat-set. Wrinkles hang out easily, but heat-set creases stay in. Mildew and moth resistant.

Washable by hand or machine, but may be dry-cleaned. Drip-dries quickly. Requires little or no pressing. If ironing is necessary, use low heat. Perborate bleach will prevent graying in white fabrics.

RAYON

Has medium strength. Weakens when wet. Stretches somewhat. Higher in moisture absorption than most chemical fibers. Wrinkles easily when wet. Sheer fabrics soft and cool; have tendency to cling.

Washable unless label indicates dry-cleaning. Use warm water with mild soap. Slow drying. Needs to be pressed like cotton.

VICARA

Soft; looks like wool; luxurious. Drapes well. Has higher moisture absorption than most chemical fibers. Less strong when wet. Is moth and mildew resistant.

May be washable. Dries quickly; needs little or no pressing. Dry-clean if label so indicates.

absorption means quick drying. But it may also account for skin discomfort on a hot day, since in closely woven fabrics perspiration is held against the body rather than being absorbed by the fibers. An account of each fiber's characteristics and the care it requires is given in the chart on pages 372 to 373.

Learning About Clothing Labels

One of the features which both the boys and the girls enjoyed was a talk on labels. The talk was given by Miss Hansen, the head buyer of a ready-to-wear department for a local store.

She told the students that labels are still in the developmental stage. There are some government regulations relating to cotton, linen, wool, silk, and rayon fabrics. But there are no general rules covering all fibers. However, some manufacturers — in addition to required rulings — offer other information on the label. For the most part, the information you see is accurate. This applies to bolts of material as well as to readymade garments.

What to look for

Miss Hansen then went on to say that a really good label will contain information on three important points. She explained these points, showing how required regulations applied to different fibers. Here is what a customer wants to know:

1. What the garment is made of, and possibly how the material is made. A label telling what the garment is made of helps you to predict the wear you may expect from the material. If a label gives the name of only one fiber, the fabric is supposed to contain only that fiber. The Federal Trade Commission rulings for silk, wool, linen, and rayon emphasize this point. When more than one fiber is mentioned, it is customary to name them in the order of their amount. Material labeled "cotton and wool" would mean there is more cotton in the fabric than wool. Sometimes the percentage of each fiber is given. This is required in the case of linen and wool.

In some instances you will need to understand the name of the material more fully. For example, "wool" on a label means virgin or new wool that has not been used before. "Reprocessed wool" has been woven, and then

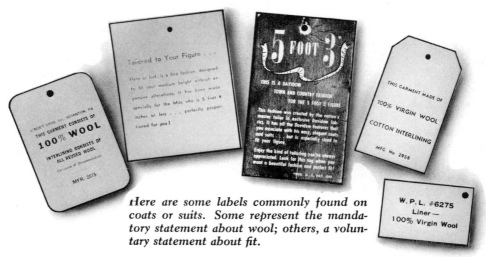

Here are some labels commonly found on coats or suits. Some represent the mandatory statement about wool; others, a voluntary statement about fit.

rewoven without having been used. "Reused wool" has been used and then reworked. Fabrics containing wool must be labeled as to the kind of wool used and the percentage of each. However, this ruling does not apply to carpets, mats, rugs, and upholstery materials. Virgin or new wool fabrics are more expensive than the other two types. A good quality of virgin wool wears well. But a good grade of re-processed wool will be less expensive and probably more durable than a poor grade of new wool.

Or consider silks. A Federal Trade Commission ruling requires that the terms "silk," "pure silk," "all silk," and "pure-dye silk" must contain silk and nothing else except necessary dyes and finishes. "Weighted silk" — silk containing metallic substances — must be so labeled, and must include the percentage of weighting. Over ten per cent may cause silk material to split.

Quite frequently the terms "combed" and "two-ply" or "three-ply" are found on labels. These terms are important when applied to cottons. Fabrics that are combed are fine and smooth. They wear better than those uncombed. Worsted wool yarns are also combed. "Ply" refers to the number of separate strands twisted together to make a single strand. The more strands there are, the stronger the yarn should be. Occasionally the type of weave or the name of the fabric may be given.

2. <u>What service you may expect.</u> The answers to four questions regarding service are desirable on a label. Will the garment shrink? Is it colorfast? What is the finish, and how long will it last? How should the garment be cleaned?

SHRINKAGE: There are some regulations regarding shrinkage. If the term "preshrunk" or "shrunk" is used on a cotton- or linen-fabric label, the manufacturer must indicate the amount of shrinkage remaining in the cloth. Terms, such as "full shrunk," or "shrinkproof," are banned from the label if the products have any further capacity to shrink at all. If the word "preshrunk" or "shrunk" is not used, the label need not indicate the percentage of shrinkage that may occur. This means that if the shrinkage is more than two per cent, or if not known at all, the purchaser needs to take the matter into consideration. More yardage or larger sizes should be bought to take care of the shrinkage that may occur.

Shrinkage in width and in length of rayon fabrics can now be controlled by a process called "Sanforset." To bear this label, a fabric must not shrink or stretch more than two per cent. On good wool fabrics, such terms as "sponged" or "London shrunk" indicate that the fabric has been adequately preshrunk. "Lanaset" is a chemical process used to control shrinkage in wool.

COLORFASTNESS: The term "colorfast" on a label has only a slight degree of guarantee. Unless you have more specific statements, such as "fast to sun and washing" or "fast only when dry-cleaned," you will need to be on guard. Look for the colorfastness with reference to the purpose for which the garment is to be used. For example, if it will need to be laundered, look for that guarantee. Some labels give the dye or dye process used. The terms "vat dyed" or "indanthrene dye" used on a label indicate particular fastness to light and washing. On print materials the term "Aridye" indicates that colorfastness to light, heat, water, and chemicals has been increased.

FINISHES: Look for information on the kind of finish used and what you may expect from it in wear. Some finishes are intended to last the life of the material. Others may improve the initial appearance, but disappear in laundering or dry-cleaning.

CARE: A good label indicates whether the material is washable or is to be dry-cleaned. If washable, you will want to know whether hand-laundering is to be preferred to machine-laundering. The temperature of the water and the way to attain best results in drying and pressing are also important. If the material is to be dry-cleaned, it is highly desirable to have a professional dry cleaner do the work. Home dry cleaning involves great risks. Good establishments use special equipment and supplies. They also reduce the hazards of fumes. Some fabrics prolong their original beauty by being dry-cleaned even though they are labeled washable.

3. The name of the manufacturer and the store at which the garment is bought. This gives you recourse to the maker and the seller if the garment does not live up to claims made for it. This is desirable for all kinds of fibers, but it is required for products containing wool. Either the manufacturer's name or his serial number must appear on the label along with the other required information.

Highlights on Buying Boys' Suits and Coats

One day while the classwork was in progress, Mr. Dean, a buyer from a men's clothing store, gave a talk on boys' suits and coats. The highlights of his talk centered around the different kinds of fabrics and the workmanship that go into the construction of tailored garments. He also emphasized the importance of a good fit in garments of this type. Swatches of materials and several coats and suits were displayed to illustrate the points he brought out.

Needless to say, the boys enjoyed Mr. Dean's visit. Later they summarized what he had said under five topics — outer fabrics, linings and pockets, hidden materials, good workmanship, and fit. This information was to serve as a guide in buying suits and coats. The summaries follow:

Examining the outer fabric

Coats and suits generally have a label giving the name of the fiber that the garment is made of. This will help you to evaluate the quality of the fabric. It will also be to your advantage to find out as much as you can about how the cloth is made and finished. In coat and suit materials, it is important to have a fabric that will resist wear and that will not shrink or fade.

However, there are other factors to consider in examining outer fabrics. You will want to know what kind of wear each is best suited for, which ones wrinkle least, which hold a press, and which are less likely to become shiny. Knowing what to expect from various fabrics will help you select one most suitable for your needs.

SHARKSKIN
A worsted twill

SEMIFINISHED WORSTED
A lightly napped twill

GABARDINE
A worsted twill

TWEED
A rough, bulky woolen

COMMON

SUIT

AND

COAT

FABRICS

FLANNEL
A napped worsted or woolen

TROPICAL WORSTED
ghtweight, plain-woven fabric

TWIST
A plain-woven, rugged woolen

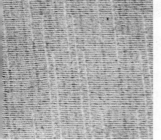

SHANTUNG
ıbby, crosswise-textured fabric

SEERSUCKER
A washable summer suiting

CORD
A washable summer suiting

Notice the difference in closeness of weave and firmness between the good-quality lining fabric at the left and the poor-quality at the right.

It is also desirable to know the names of some of the fabrics used in suits and coats. But the name in itself does not indicate the quality of the material. You still need to know the fiber content, and how the fabric is made and finished. The illustrations on page 377 show some of the most commonly used outer fabrics and their characteristics.

Looking at linings and pockets

Tightly woven rayon twill is one of the most serviceable lining materials. It stands wear better than many other fabrics and is less expensive. You can evaluate the wearing qualities to some extent by examining the closeness of the weave and the firmness of the material.

Find out what you can about shrinkage and colorfastness. A lining that has not been thoroughly shrunk may draw up when wet by rain. This will spoil the shape and fit of the coat. The lining also needs to be colorfast to cleaning and perspiration.

Pull the pockets inside out and look at the material. One of the most durable is closely woven, twilled cotton. Crush some of the material in your

hand. If it feels starchy, it may be heavily sized and will wear poorly. The sizing will come out, leaving the pocket limp and flimsy.

Evaluating hidden materials

Some of the materials in tailored garments are not observable. Yet they play an important part in determining how well the garment will hold its

Closely woven, twilled cotton makes durable trouser pockets.

shape and appearance. If the label does not give information, ask the salesperson about the following hidden features.

FRONT INTERFACING: The material used to interface the coat front determines how well the front will resist wrinkling. High-grade hair canvas is the best material, ranging down through poorer grades to cotton or burlap in cheap garments. With some practice, it is possible to evaluate fairly accurately the quality of the material used. Grasp the front of the coat, and pull your closed hand down over it. If the interfacing is of good quality, it will feel lightweight and soft, not stiff.

Testing good-quality interfacing

When you let go, the front of the coat will spring back into shape without wrinkling. If the material is of poor quality, the front will feel thick, bulky, and crisp. When you let go, you can feel wrinkles in the inside material. After you have learned to evaluate high- and low-grade qualities, it will not be difficult to evaluate those in between.

COLLAR AND LAPEL INTERLININGS: The best material for interlinings is firm linen, but in less expensive garments a sized cotton fabric may be used. This tends to become soft, which affects the set of the collar around the neck. Roll a corner of the collar or lapel up and forward. If the interlining is of good quality, the corner will snap quickly back into place. If poor quality, the corner will turn back slowly.

TAPING: Taping at the lapel edges and armholes prevents stretching or puckering, and preserves a neat look. To find out whether taping has been used, stretch the under part of the armhole and the edges of the lapels. If there is no give, then tape has been used.

SHOULDER PADDING: Good-quality shoulder padding is important in the appearance of a coat. The best quality is soft, lightweight cotton. Poor quality is thick, heavy, and lumpy. You can feel the difference with your hand. You will also notice the difference if you try on the coat. Good shoulder padding fits smoothly and does not exaggerate the shoulders. Poor padding makes the shoulders look abnormally wide.

Looking for signposts of good workmanship

Before making a purchase, it is important to evaluate how a readymade garment is cut and sewed. For good appearance and fit, the garment needs to be accurately cut on the grain of the fabric. The way the garment is cut and the details of the tailoring are as important as the fabric itself.

THE CUTTING: High-grade suits and coats are cut with no piecings or defective places in the cloth, whereas low-grade ones are frequently pieced at the crotch. Flaws in the cloth are ignored or mended or made to fall in the seams. When the fabric has a pattern, the cloth in high-quality garments is cut so that the pattern matches. To check matching, examine the coat at the following points: center back, side seams, armholes, where the edge of the collar rolls over and meets the coat

Notice that the pattern is matched in the collar, lapels, pocket, and sleeve.

in the back, front closing, collar notch, and pocket opening. Matching does not add to the wearing quality of a garment. But it does affect its appearance. In low-grade garments, the pattern is matched in only one direction, and not always with exactness. If you are interested in an inexpensive garment, it is best to select a fabric that has no pattern to match.

THE SEWING: Seams that are stitched by machine give the best wear. Some seams, such as those in the crotch of trousers, are double stitched for strength. Certain other operations skillfully done by hand add to the appearance and comfort of the garment. However, poor handwork may not look as well or last as long as that well done by machine.

Coat linings in high-quality garments are smoothly fitted and finely stitched by hand with matching silk thread. The cut edge of the turned-up portion of the coat is bound, and fastened over the lining. A small pleat along the lower edge of the lining is left for ease or give in fit. In medium-grade garments, the lining is sewed in by invisible machine stitching. In poor-quality coats, the machine stitching is coarse, and no allowance is made for give.

Buttonholes and buttons are important. The best buttonholes are those made with close, even stitches, with a strong bar opposite the eyelet end. In high-grade garments the work is done on both sides by hand with silk twist, which gives a neat appearance. But in other grades good machine buttonholing is better than poor handwork. The best buttons — made of horn — are called "tip horn." They are characterized by dark veining and a natural soft polish. Ivory buttons, which are less expensive, are more commonly used.

Checking on fit

To wear well and look its best, a tailored garment needs to fit perfectly. Try on the garment to get the over-all feel and appearance. Put on and take off the coat yourself to see whether it handles easily. Button it, raise and bend your arms, stoop, and move about. Sit down and see how the garment feels. Then check the following features that make a serviceable, long-wearing outfit.

TOP COAT OR OVERCOAT

- The body of the coat fits smoothly and easily over the suit. No strain when buttoned or in moving about

- The collar sets smooth and close to back and sides of neck. Covers suit and shirt collars

- The shoulder line is firm and unbroken from neck to shoulder point.

- The armholes are cut deep enough to prevent binding.

- The sleeves are comfortably wide. A suitable length is 3½ to 4 inches above the thumb tip when the arm hangs.

- The length extends 1½ to 2 inches below the knee.

SUIT COAT

- Fits easily and comfortably; no strain when buttoned

- The collar sets smooth and close to the back and sides of the neck. Made so that ¼ to ½ inch of the shirt collar shows

- The lapels and neckline hold close to the chest.

- The coat hangs in a straight line with no wrinkles from shoulder to lower edge — front and back.

- Is long enough to cover the seat of the trousers

- The armholes are comfortably large, but not so deep that the coat lifts noticeably as you reach.

- The sleeves taper toward the cuffs; are comfortably wide, but not full enough to cause too many wrinkles. May be long enough to cover the shirt cuffs, or allow ¼ to ½ inch of the cuffs to show, as preferred

- The pockets lie flat and smooth.

Check the fit of a suit by the points given on this page and the next.

THE TROUSERS

- Hang straight front and back, with creases and pleats following the grain of the material. Front waist pleats or unstitched tucks help to prevent baggy knees.

- The waistband feels comfortable and fits snugly when resting on hips.

- The seat is comfortably full, but not baggy. There are no wrinkles that draw through the crotch below the seat or against the front of the legs as you stand or walk.

- The lower edges of the legs are finished so that they either have a slight break at the instep, or so that the cuff edges barely touch the shoes. A deep break makes the trousers look too large. If the trouser legs are too long, they rub against the shoes, and wear out quickly.

Guides for Purchasing Men's Shirts

While the boys were preparing the summaries on suits and coats, they also set up guides for buying shirts. Reference sources indicated that there are two general types — the standard dress shirt and the sport shirt. The boys then set up a chart (below) showing the different features of each type of shirt.

A CHART ON MEN'S SHIRTS		
	DRESS SHIRT	**SPORT SHIRT**
SIZE	Neckband, 14 to 17½ inches, measured around base of neck. Sleeve length, 32 to 36 inches, measured from center back of neck to wrist with arm bent	Measured by neck size: Small . . . . 14 to 14½ Medium . . . . 15 to 15½ Large . . . . 16 to 16½ Extra large . . . . 17 to 17½
COLLAR	Attached to a collarband. Starched, soft, or nonwilt; rounded or pointed; may be buttoned down	Attached to body of shirt. Soft; generally pointed. May be convertible for wear with or without a tie
FRONT CLOSING	**Panel type with** box pleat as left edge finish, or French type with edge turned over and stitched close to fold	French type with edge turned over and stitched close to fold
SLEEVE	Long with single or double cuff, or single cuff with cuff-link openings	Short with no cuff, or long with single cuff
TAIL	Long, rounded	Shorter than dress shirt with squared-off bottom

Quality and fit

   Points to check for good quality fabric, good workmanship, and comfortable fit were also summarized for dress shirts. But the same points would in general apply to sport shirts.

- The fabric will resist shrinkage, be strong, and be colorfast to laundering.

- The neckline fits closely, but not too snug or too loose.

- The width and points of the collar are even in length and appearance.

- The fullness in the back is in pleats or gathers over the shoulder blades, or evenly distributed across a yoke.

- The body of the shirt is smooth fitting, flat on the chest, yet roomy enough for comfort. The tails are rounded and not skimpily cut. They are even in both front and back with a set-in gusset at the side seams.

- The sleeves come to the bend of the wrist, and are about half an inch longer than the sleeves of the coat. Sleeves that are cut in one piece are preferable. But a shirt with a two-piece sleeve will wear as well and may cost less than one with a one-piece sleeve. The sleeve placket is long enough for the cuff to be ironed flat.

- The buttonholes are made with firm, close stitches, with secure backstitching at both ends. The buttons may be made of pearl or hard, durable plastic.

   An appropriate style, a good-quality fabric, a comfortable fit, and good workmanship are important considerations in buying a shirt. Some style and good-workmanship features are shown here.

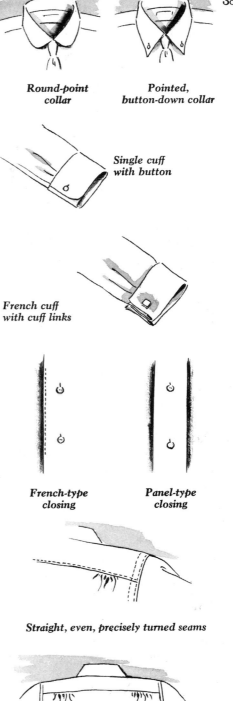

Round-point collar

Pointed, button-down collar

Single cuff with button

French cuff with cuff links

French-type closing

Panel-type closing

Straight, even, precisely turned seams

Generous, evenly divided back fullness

This boy has chosen a well-fitting, well-made, good-quality dress shirt that has a round-point collar with eyelets for the tie pin, and French cuffs with eyelets for the cuff links.

Guides for Buying Girls' Coats and Suits

Arrangements were also made to have a speaker demonstrate some of the important features on buying coats and suits for girls. Miss Valenti, a buyer for one of the specialty shops for women, gave the talk. She stressed the advantage of being able to recognize good quality in materials, cut and workmanship.

"Read dependable fashion books," she also said. "Learn the differences between styles that change little year after year and those that are short-lived. A coat or suit is a good buy if it looks well on you, fits your needs, and promises to stay in fashion as long as you must wear it."

She then went on to say that many tailored garments are designed for general wear. They may be worn equally well for church, social functions, or for street wear, providing the color goes well with other costume parts.

Miss Valenti also showed the girls samples of various materials used for coats and suits. She emphasized the value of reading labels and asking the salesperson for information not available on the tag. Since this information is comparable to that summarized by the boys, it is not repeated here. (See pages 376–378.)

Demonstrations on how a garment should fit and features of good workmanship were also given. Later, this information was summarized as follows to serve as buying guides:

Reading the labels on a coat or suit and asking the salesperson for information not given on the tags is of value in making a wise choice.

Getting the right style and size

Coats are made in fitted, belted, or loose styles. They vary in length from short toppers to full length. Suit jackets come in lengths from above the waist to below the hips. They are made in either fitted or loose styles. Suit skirts are straight, pleated, or gored.

It is best to try on garments in your size range until you find which styles are suited to your figure. Avoid buying a garment that needs major changes. Alterations are expensive and uncertain. A garment cut for one type of figure can rarely be altered to fit another equally well.

Checking on the fit

Take plenty of time to examine the fit. Try the garment on over the same type of clothing you will be wearing under it. This is especially important if you are buying a coat and expect to wear a suit with it. Look at yourself from all angles. The points to check for fit apply in general to coats as well as to suit jackets.

COAT OR SUIT JACKET

- *The collar* fits up close to the base of the neck, but does not rub.

- *The shoulder line* is straight from the neck to the highest point of the sleeve.

- *The shoulder-armhole area* is smooth with no wrinkles. The armhole is deep enough for comfort.

- *The sleeves* hang straight from the shoulders and are roomy enough for the clothing worn underneath. Elbow ease either in darts, small tucks, or gathers is provided in the cut. Long sleeves reach to the wristbone as you touch the lobe of your ear directly above your bent arm.

- *The front and back* fit smoothly with no excessive wrinkles. The front edge of the coat hangs straight with no swing toward either side.

- *The waistline,* if fitted, curves about half an inch below the natural waistline to feel most comfortable and to stay in place.

- *The fasteners* close without strain.

SUIT SKIRT

- *There is easy walking room* to avoid ripped seams and discomfort. The sitting room is ample to prevent strain and crosswise wrinkles. There is also enough room to keep the skirt from pulling up too short when you sit.

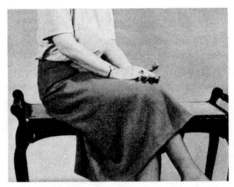

Here room to sit down in a skirt is being checked as one test for determining proper fit.

- *The waistband* fits firmly but not too tightly to the figure and holds the skirt in place.

- *The skirt* fits smoothly and comfortably across the hips with no strain.

- *The side fastening* lies flat and smooth.

- *The back* hangs straight with no cupping under at the seat.

- *The hem* is straight and an even distance from the floor all around.

Evaluating the workmanship

A well-made coat or suit will generally keep its appearance and shape after long wear and many cleanings. But some of the differences between high- and low-grade garments cannot be shown and can only be evaluated on the basis of the purchase price. For example, high-grade coats and suits are carefully cut with regard to the grain of the fabric. Between sewing operations, pressers steam and shape the various sections. This assures the same fit as long as the garments last. Low-grade suits and coats are cut for the greatest economy of fabric with little consideration to grain. There is almost no pressing and shaping as the garments are made, with the result that they often twist or sag. (For other information on hidden values, see pages 378–379.)

However, there are certain observable marks of quality. Check to see whether the following features are present.

Examine the lining and interlining of a coat. In a good-quality coat, the interlining is seamed separately and then tacked to the coat seams. The outer lining is smoothly and neatly fitted to the coat.

- *The outer lining* is smoothly and neatly fitted with a tuck or pleat for expansion allowance in the back. It is tacked securely around the armholes and along the shoulder and side seams. This holds the lining in place and helps to keep the shape and fit of the garment. In a low-priced coat or suit, the lining is stitched up by machine and slipped into place with only a few loose tack stitches. Put in this way, the tack stitches work loose. The lining shifts and soon wears out around the armholes.

- *The inner lining in a coat* — if there is one — can generally be seen from an open lower edge. In a high-grade garment the lining is tacked securely in place to the side seams, the shoulder seams, and around the armholes of the coat. In a low-grade garment, the lining and interlining are seamed together and then put in as one. This results in thick, bulky seams that cannot be pressed flat. Such seams also give the lining an untidy appearance and may cause the wearer discomfort by pressing against the neck and shoulders.

- *The buttonholes* are cut with the grain of the material. If cut off-grain, they will stretch out of shape and soon hang open. Bindings of bound buttonholes and pockets are narrow, squared off securely at the ends, and firmly stitched.

- *The buttons* are smooth edged and slip in and out without straining or wearing the buttonholes.

Pointers in Selecting Dresses and Blouses

Shortly after the talk by Miss Valenti, the girls consulted refer-

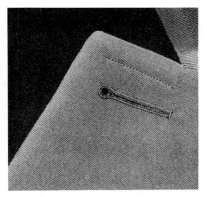

Buttonholes should be cut with the grain and securely worked.

Set-in pockets should be securely squared off at the ends.

Bindings of buttonholes should be narrow but firmly finished.

ence sources on buying dresses and blouses. They learned that much of the information they had assembled for coats and suits would also apply to these other garments. Therefore, instead of repeating the material, they listed additional points that would be helpful in selecting dresses and blouses.

- Select a style that you can wear for some time without being dated.

- When trying on a dress, wear shoes that you plan to use with it. Try on a blouse with the suit that you plan to wear.

- Check carefully on the fit. If a dress is too short or too long waisted, try on a different size. If the garment is too loose at the waist, and the belt is not set in, alterations in some instances may be fairly simple. A dress that is too long may easily be shortened at the hem line unless the bottom is scalloped or specially shaped. It is unwise to get a garment that requires shortening from the waistline.

- Set-in sleeves fit best under a suit jacket. Kimono or raglan sleeves usually have a bulkier armhole and are most comfortable when worn without a jacket.

- A narrow hem is suitable for the lower edge of most blouses. But if the fabric is heavy, the hem may show as a ridge under smoothly fitting skirts. In such cases, the lower edge may be pinked and stitched to keep the fabric from raveling.

- Consider the upkeep necessary for the garment — whether it can be washed or dry-cleaned; how easily it will soil; and how well buttons, belts, and other trimmings will withstand cleaning.

Buying Hosiery

Some of the students who were especially interested in buying assembled information on hosiery. Although the boys and girls worked separately, the material was coordinated so that there would be no overlapping. Summaries which were to serve as guides were made as follows:

Styles and sizes

Hosiery may be full or ankle length or any length between. Women's stockings generally come well above the knee. Men's socks are classified as to wear, such as general or dress socks, sports or athletic socks, and work socks.

Hosiery is sized by length in inches of the stocking or sock foot. In women's stockings, leg length — long, short, or average — is also a part of the size. For comfort and durability, a size at least a half an inch longer than the wearer's foot is advisable. If the foot is unusually wide, a full size larger is recommended.

Methods of construction

In general there are two kinds of hosiery — full-fashioned and circular-knit.

FULL-FASHIONED: This means that the stocking is knitted flat to conform to the shape of the leg and foot, and then seamed. Fashion marks or dots on each side of the seam show that stitches have been decreased to fit the ankle. Thus the original shape and form of the stocking is always retained, giving a superior fit and appearance.

CIRCULAR-KNIT OR SEAMLESS: With this method, hosiery is knit in round tube

Magnified, the 60 loops per 1½ inches in a 60-gauge stocking are shown.

form with the same number of stitches throughout the leg and foot. Shaping is done by means of heat. A mock seam is often made to imitate the full-fashioned style. The circular-knit method is especially suitable and widely used for socks and anklets of all kinds. Stockings made this way — unless nylon yarns are used, which can be permanently shaped by heat — may become baggy and lose their shape after the first washing.

TYPES OF KNIT: The different types of knit are plain, ribbed, and mesh. *Plain knit* is smooth, even textured, and is used in all kinds of hosiery. *Ribbed knit* is distinguished by vertical ridges on both right and wrong sides. It is used extensively in men's hose, because of its durable construction and elasticity. When ribbed knit is imitated, it shows only on one side, and is less elastic and durable. *Mesh knit* is used primarily in women's stockings. The lock-stitched types make the stockings resist runs, but holes may develop at points of strain.

Size of yarns and closeness of knit

There are two terms which are usually given in combination to indicate the size of the yarn and the fineness of the knitting in women's stockings — gauge and denier.

GAUGE: This is the number of crosswise stitches per 1½ inches of stocking fabric. The higher the gauge, the closer

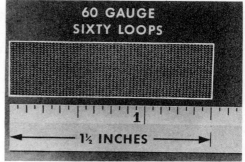

60 GAUGE
SIXTY LOOPS

1

1½ INCHES

the knit. The more stitches, the greater the elasticity and the better the fit. Common gauges are 45, 51, 60, and 66.

DENIER: This term is used to indicate the size of nylon, rayon, and silk yarns. The lower the number, the finer the yarn. Sheer yarns give less service than heavier yarns. However, a sheer

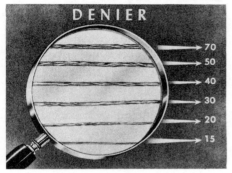

Thicknesses of nylon threads used for 15 to 70 denier hose are shown.

yarn in a high gauge gives better service than one loosely knit. Popular deniers are 30, 20, 15, and 12.

Cotton and wool yarns are also numbered, with the higher numbers producing the finer hosiery.

Pointers on workmanship

Before buying, be sure to examine the hose for careful workmanship.

- Women's full-length stockings of average size should stretch about 12 inches at the top hem. An average size sock will stretch to 7¼ inches through the instep to the heel if it has not been skimped in knitting.

- The ribbed tops of socks and anklets need to be firmly knit. An elastic top should stretch, but still not bind.

- Seams should be flat and firmly sewed with good quality thread the same color as the hose. Fourteen stitches to the inch is considered a good average.

Thread ends on the inside of hosiery need to be securely fastened and clipped to prevent raveling and to increase comfort.

- High-quality hosiery is reinforced at wear or strain points. The top hem may be single or double. The heel — at the back and above it — the sole, and the toe have extra yarn knit into the fabric. The yarn may be of the same fiber as the hose or a combination of fibers. Foot reinforcements come well up along the side of the foot and over the toes for greater service.

Hints for prolonging wear

Good care will add to the wear of hosiery. This will result when you:

- Buy hosiery in the style and weight best suited for the occasion. Be sure that you get the correct size and length.

- Purchase at least two pairs of the same color at the same time. This allows opportunity to match up remaining hose when pairs are broken because of damage.

- Handle hose carefully. Inspect frequently for breaks or weak spots that need mending or reinforcement. Avoid contact with sharp or rough objects.

- Put on stockings correctly. Roll leg of stocking down to the toe, and slip the foot through the roll into the toe. Then straighten the foot seam, and slowly unroll the stocking, smoothing it up over the leg. Straighten the leg seam at the same time. Clasp garters halfway down the top hem, and fasten them so that the seam will remain straight. Never fasten a garter below the top hem.

- Wash hosiery carefully after every wearing to remove perspiration and soil which weaken the fibers. (For how to wash stockings and socks, see Book 1, pages 52–53.)

- Use a utility box with a smooth lining to keep hose in place and to protect them. It is a convenient way to find at a glance the hose you need.

Buying Shoes

When the students were ready to take up the problem of buying shoes, they consulted references, and some of them visited shoe stores. They soon learned that many of the basic considerations, such as fit and construction, were the same for both men and women. Again the information was coordinated into one summary.

Styles and sizes

No one type of shoe can serve all purposes, just as no one outfit can be worn for every occasion. Young people need shoes for walking, for dress wear, for sports, and for leisure-time wear. Appropriateness, comfort, attractiveness, and durability are considerations in choosing any of these types.

Shoes are sized according to length and width. The length is measured numerically from 1 to 13 in adult sizes. There is approximately $\frac{1}{3}$- to $\frac{1}{2}$-inch difference between each whole size. The width varies from very narrow, AAAAA, to very wide, EEEEE, with $\frac{1}{12}$-inch difference between each width letter. However, the size of a shoe is no indication of fit. You need to learn to select a shoe on the basis of how its shape conforms to the shape of your foot. How it feels on the foot is more important than the size markings.

Materials used and construction

Leather, plastic, fabric, rubber, and composition are some of the materials used in shoe construction.

The soles are generally made of leather, rubber, or composition. Rubber and composition are less porous than leather, but more durable. However, porous leather, which admits air, is more healthful for continuous wear.

The uppers are usually made of leather, but fabric and plastic are sometimes used. Even though leather is generally preferable, grades of leather vary. A good quality leather feels firm, but not stiff. One test of quality is to bend the shoe slightly at the part where the ball of the foot comes. A high-quality leather will break into many tiny creases. The creases will be fewer with medium-grade leather, still less with a lower grade.

Fabrics are used in dressy and sport shoes. A firm, close weave is necessary to prevent the shoe from stretching, and to give good service. Plastic, which is nonporous, is best used in shoes with open-toe or open-back construction. This provides for ventilation.

The uppers may be attached to the soles in one or a combination of three processes — sewed, cemented, or nailed. The type of shoe determines the method used. Men's shoes designed for hard wear are often sewed with a leather welt which usually extends about $\frac{1}{4}$ of an inch beyond the uppers. The sewing can be seen on the outside of the shoes. Very heavy soles may be nailed to men's work shoes. Sometimes they are stitched on the outside to resemble welt construction. In dressier types of shoes, the way the soles and uppers are attached generally cannot be seen. Because of the variety of processes used, the feel of the shoe on your foot and the backing of a reliable manufacturer are the best endorsements of quality.

The insoles — lying between the sole and the lining on the bottom of the shoe — help to determine how long a shoe will keep its shape. Insoles made of good-quality leather are the most flexible and durable. Other materials used are fiberboard, cork, and in poorly made shoes sometimes paperboard. Shoes with paper insoles soon become shapeless and shabby. Examine the insole carefully by lifting an edge of the lining on top of the insole.

The linings help to prevent shoes from stretching and need to be smooth to reduce chafing of the foot. Some shoes are leather lined throughout. Others are lined in the back part with leather and with fabric in the forepart. If fabric is used, it needs to be closely woven and not sized.

The counters and toe boxes — lying in between the upper material and the

Toe box and counter

lining of the shoes — reinforce shoes and help to retain their shape. (See the illustration.) High-grade leather is the best material, but good-quality fabric may be more satisfactory than poor leather. Whatever is used needs to be stiff enough so that it does not

bend readily, but springy enough so that it goes back into shape when bent.

The heels may be made of leather lifts or of fiberboard lifts built up to the desired height. In women's dress or general-wear shoes, wooden heels covered with leather or fabric are frequently used. Rubber or composition materials on the part of the heel touching the ground are long wearing and lessen the jar of walking. But they may be slippery on smooth, wet surfaces.

Getting the right fit

A good fit is the most important consideration in buying shoes. One that conforms to your foot in length, width, and shape is essential for comfort and the prevention of serious foot trouble.

It is important to have both feet measured for length and width in a standing as well as in a sitting position. Then both shoes need to be put on to get their feel. Walk around the store, and check on the following points.

- The toe shape of the shoe conforms to the shape of your toes, the great toe lying straight and the toe cap of the shoe not touching the toes.

- The shoes are ½ to ¾ of an inch longer than the ends of the big toes in closed-toe shoes, but may be somewhat less in open toes.

- The widest part of the ball joint corresponds to the widest part of the shoes. The ball is the forward base of the foot on which the weight is borne. It determines the fit more than any other part. When the feet tread evenly, the first signs of wear on the soles should come under the ball of the foot.

- The shoe conforms to the arch of the foot without exerting pressure against the arch.

- The inside line of the shoe — from the heel to the position of the big toe — should be almost straight to conform to the shape of a normal foot. (See the illustration.)

In a well-fitting shoe, the toe shape of the shoe conforms to the shape of the toes, the shoe is longer than the toes, the widest part of the ball joint corresponds to the widest part of the shoe, the inside line of the shoe is almost straight, and so on.

- The fit from the ball of the foot to the heel is smooth and firm without pressure or gaping. The shoe uppers do not cut into the fleshy part of the foot.

- The inside of the heel fits snug, so that the heel of the foot does not slip in walking, or rub up and down inside the shoe. It is wide enough at the base to support the heel.

- The heel height is ½ to ¾ of an inch for general wear. High heels may be worn without danger for short periods on special occasions. But if worn for any length of time, they may produce serious results, since they throw the feet and body out of their normal positions.

- The soles on shoes for general wear are thick enough to cushion the foot and to help absorb the jar of walking. Thin-soled shoes worn constantly tend to cause arches to sag and calluses to form.

Holding the Store Display

After all the buying guides were completed, the students began to make arrangements for the store display. Invitations were sent out to the mothers, and plans were made for assembling various articles of clothing. Some of the items, such as shoes, were borrowed from the stores that had cooperated in assembling the buying information. In other instances well-selected purchases made by older brothers and sisters or by the students themselves were brought in. The supply was adequate for the display.

When the mothers arrived, they found the homemaking rooms divided into various departments. In one section the boys had assembled suits, coats, and shirts. Another department included girls' dresses, blouses, suits, and coats. Shoes and hosiery were together in another section.

The session opened with a suit, coat, and dress display. Several students wearing these garments paraded in front of the group. Others, acting as salespersons, pointed out important characteristics that one would need to check when buying these items. After this event, the mothers circulated among the different departments to see items that had not been modeled. In each section, student salesmen pointed out various features that one would need to consider for satisfactory buying.

One of the surprises of the store display was a larger placard conspicuously placed where everyone could see it. Several students especially interested in buying had worked out the idea together. A reproduction of the placard is given on this page.

Needless to say, the store display was quite successful. The mothers seemed to enjoy the affair as much as the class did. Various comments indicated that they were surprised and pleased that the students were learning so much about buying clothes. Some of the mothers said they had always dreaded shopping trips with their sons and daughters. It had been difficult to agree on what was wanted. Now with a clearer picture in mind, buying

---

SHOPPING KNOW–HOW

- SHOP WHEN THE STORES ARE NOT CROWDED. Then salespeople can give you better service. If your time is relatively free, shop around to get the best values for your money. But don't use up too much energy and get overtired trying to save a few pennies.

- STATE YOUR WISHES CLEARLY. This helps the salesperson to meet your needs, and saves his time and yours.

- HANDLE THE MERCHANDISE CAREFULLY. Careless handling by thoughtless customers costs the store money which is eventually reflected in the price you pay.

- USE STORE SERVICES FAIRLY. Consider delivery costs, and carry small packages. Buy only what you intend to keep. Returning a purchase because you have changed your mind adds to merchandising costs.

- LEARN BARGAIN VALUES. Sales include all types of merchandise, good and poor. Sales may bring you bargains if you buy what you need, and if you know how to recognize quality. It is also important to be able to afford the purchase at this time.

    "Soiled" merchandise may be a good buy if it is not damaged, and if it can be easily washed. But consider the extra cost if it requires dry cleaning.

    "Irregulars" or "seconds" may be satisfactory if the flaws are in places where they do not show and where they will not affect the wearability of the article.

    "Sample merchandise" or "odd sizes" may be bargains if they fit you and your clothing plan.

- IF YOU PLAN TO ATTEND A SALE, GO AT THE BEGINNING. The selection will be greater, the merchandise cleaner, and the service better.

clothes would be easier and more satisfactory for everyone.

Deciding What Values in Buying Will Give the Most Satisfaction

In evaluating the store display in class, the students could not resist various comments about the garments which had been shown. "The dress that Frances modeled," said Catherine, "was just the style I had planned to buy. But the material wasn't what I had in mind. I don't know which is more important to me, the style or the material."

"I liked the coat which Marian had on," said Gwen. "But the color wouldn't fit in with the rest of my wardrobe. If I bought a coat like that I'd need other clothes to go with it. And that would upset my budget."

"That's what is meant by learning to make satisfactory compromises with oneself," said Miss Dennison. "All the way through your work on planning wardrobes and setting up buying guides you have been considering what values will give you satisfaction. But since few purchases are perfect in every respect, there will be many times when you will need to make a compromise. Good judgment in weighing values will help bring satisfaction in buying."

Making decisions

The students then reviewed the values they believed would bring satisfaction in the garments they bought. These were as follows:

- Appropriate to the occasion for which you need it
- Suitable for your age and personality
- Within the cost range you can afford
- Fit of the garment on you and into your wardrobe
- Personally becoming in line, color, and texture
- Suitable in quality of fabric, workmanship, and ease of care for the purpose and amount of wear intended.

Glen then offered a suggestion. "I believe it would be helpful if some of the members of the class with buying experience would give examples of the decisions which have confronted them."

The other students and Miss Dennison agreed. Soon the room was quiet except for the rustling of paper as some of the group jotted down notes. A short time later the following examples were given.

PETER: If I cannot find a suit for the price I want to pay, shall I disregard time and effort and continue looking until I find something? Or shall I pay the price, save time and effort, and do without the new sport shirt I had hoped to buy?

FRANCES: Shall I get an inexpensive outfit of a color I like and which looks well on me, but does not have smart lines? Or shall I get a more expensive one of a color I don't particularly like, but which has smart lines and is within my budget?

MARIAN: Shall I get a bright-colored dress which I can't resist, but which will be socially acceptable only on certain occasions? Or shall I get a color I like less, but which will be socially acceptable on more occasions? If I get the bright-colored dress, am I willing to use an old one I had hoped to discard for occasions when the bright one can't be worn?

GEORGE: Shall I buy one white nylon shirt which I can launder myself, but which will be my only shirt for dress occasions? Or for the same amount of money, shall I get two shirts — one white, one colored — which I'll have to send to the laundry, but which will give me a choice to wear?

EVELYN: The right fit and the durability of a washable dress are important to me. Shall I buy a dress that has these qualities, even though the style and color aren't particularly suitable for me?

CLAUDE: Shall I buy an overcoat of high quality which will last for several years? Or for the same amount of money, shall I get a jacket and an overcoat which may not wear as well as the high-quality overcoat?

Since individual situations differ, the decisions reached by the students are not given here. However, Miss Dennison's closing remarks follow. "Each of you will need to work out your own compromises and decide what qualities will give you the most satisfaction," she said. "The point is to get as many qualities as you can that are considered good and that you yourself value highly. Wise buying is achieved by developing satisfactions and decreasing dissatisfactions."

How to Improve Buying Practices

Various comments throughout the work on buying led the students to consider what they might do to improve buying practices. Of course, they realized that much information and experience were necessary to make wise purchases. And even then one still might make mistakes. But surely something could be done to improve the situation.

At one point in the discussion, the question was raised about garments that do not live up to reasonable expectations. Sue had reported the following incident.

"My cousin was one of a group who bought dungarees from a certain store for a camping trip," she said. "Everyone in the group had trouble with seams breaking. The group went together to the store and showed the dungarees to the manager. They said they knew there wasn't any special guarantee against seams breaking. But the price they had paid should guarantee longer wear than one washing. The manager was very cooperative and said he was glad they had called his attention to the matter. He offered to make an exchange or to give a refund. Later on, the group found out that the manager had sent the dungarees back to the manufacturer. It seemed that a shipment of poor thread was the cause of the seam breakage."

"Sue's illustration shows what can be done when garments do not come up to expectations," said Miss Dennison. "Most stores are reasonable about such returns, especially if there have been other complaints about the same article. The store will usually make an even exchange, or give credit toward the purchase of something else in the store. In some cases the purchase price will be refunded. Returning merchandise for a justifiable reason is a good practice. Not only does it help you get your money's worth, but it may help others. However, a word of advice. When you return a purchase, you'll find that a friendly manner on your part will get more consideration than a demanding, belligerent attitude."

There were other problems brought up in discussion that concerned the students. One was the low-grade quality of some garments with poor designs and decoration. These seemed hardly worth buying even though they were cheap in price. Another problem was the lack of information given on labels. What to do about a garment that does not live up to the claims made in advertising was also mentioned.

After considerable study and discussion, the students agreed that as well-informed purchasers they could improve buying practices in the following ways.

1. Return merchandise that does not live up to reasonable expectations of wear. A reliable merchant will make satisfactory adjustments. He will report the defect to the manufacturer who, in turn — if he is reliable — will stand behind his product. This may lead to higher standards of production.

2. Avoid purchasing obviously shoddy merchandise. Buying it is a vote in favor of it. If people refuse to pur-chase low-grade garments, there will cease to be a market for them.

3. Encourage the use of informative labels. Question the salesperson about garments that are not adequately labeled, and make known your desire for the information. If enough people request these facts, manufacturers are likely to comply with such demands.

4. Keep well informed about new developments in the clothing field. This will help you interpret new information that may appear on labels. It will also help you in making requests for information that is needed.

5. Question advertising that makes false or extravagant claims for a garment. Report complaints to the store's advertising department. Justified complaints may result in more accurate and careful advertising.

6. Be familiar with various agencies or organizations interested in promoting better buying practices. The National Association of Better Business Bureaus — and the various local bureaus — are maintained by business to protect itself and the community against unfair, misleading, or untruthful advertising and selling. The National Bureau of Standards serves as a coordinator between consumer groups and manufacturers in discussing standards for various products. Such organizations as the American Home Economics Association and the General Federation of Women's Clubs are also interested from the purchaser's point of view.

Evaluating What They Had Learned About Buying Clothes

When it came time to evaluate the classwork on buying, the students agreed that what they had learned was very helpful. In fact, problems that had first seemed puzzling were now easier to understand. Students with little or no buying experience appeared willing and eager to assume some responsibility for making purchases in their clothing plans.

However, everyone realized that learning to buy wisely and skillfully is a continuous process. It requires willingness to keep useful information in mind, and practice in applying this knowledge. How successful each student might become could not be determined at this time. But as shopping experience increased, a student could evaluate his or her progress toward becoming a wise and skillful buyer.

With this thought in mind, the students set up a list of questions to be answered as they purchased the articles in their clothing plans. The same list would continue to be useful as long as they were trying to improve their buying skills. The questions set up by the class are given on page 398.

CLASS MEMO:

Is buying clothes one of your class problems? If so, how will your plans for working on this problem differ from those carried out by Miss Dennison's group?

Making Plans for Individual Needs and Interests

Now that the students had carried out the classwork on buying some of their clothes, they were ready to decide how they would complete the work on "A Four-Point Plan for My Wardrobe."

All of the girls and a few of the boys were looking forward to making some new garments. The boys who were not going to participate in this part of the classwork wanted to repair or remodel some of the clothing they had brought to the clinic. Some of the girls also planned to do repairing and remodeling along with making new garments. Several boys and girls hoped to do more work on buying clothes.

As the students discussed their various interests, it seemed advisable to write down in the form of a plan what they wanted to do. Each student then reported briefly on his or her plan, so that Miss Dennison and the other members of the class could help evaluate it. A suitable plan was to be based on a student's needs and interests, past experience and skill, and whether the activities could be carried out in the time available.

Sample plans

Space does not permit an account of all the plans that were made. But several are given as examples of how some of the students were able to meet their special needs and interests. They follow the chart on page 398.

A PROGRESS CHART ON BUYING

AM I A WISE AND SKILLFUL BUYER?	YES	NO
Do I know what I want before I go shopping?	____	____
Do I know the characteristics I want and need in the article I plan to buy?	____	____
Do I decide in advance the maximum amount to spend on the article?	____	____
Do I look for labels and/or ask the salespeople for information not available?	____	____
Do I know what values give me the most satisfaction?	____	____
Do I shop around to get the best value for my money without undue sacrifice of time and energy?	____	____
Do I avoid *bargains* I don't really need?	____	____
Do I avoid crowded rush hours?	____	____
Do I combine friendliness, courtesy, and understanding when dealing with salespeople?	____	____
Do I handle merchandise carefully?	____	____
Do I return goods only when they are defective or unsatisfactory through no fault of my own?	____	____
Do I have a file for buying information and see that it is kept up to date?	____	____

If all of my answers are *yes*, I am on my way toward being a wise and skillful buyer. If some of my answers are *no*, I will find ways of improving these points.

MAURINE: Put a facing on the bottom of a plain wool skirt that is too short; make a dress.

RICHARD: Shorten the sleeves and trousers of a gabardine suit; learn more about buying raincoats and jackets.

EVELYN: Make detachable collar and cuffs for a printed dress; make a blouse.

CLAUDE: Make a sport shirt.

MARIAN: Remodel a dress that is worn at the neck and under the arms into a jumper dress, and make a blouse that can be worn with it.

JOEL: Repair a small hole in an inside coat pocket; apply a decorative leather patch on the sleeve of a jacket; reverse a shirt collar.

DOROTHY: Change a too-large neckline on a blouse; make a dress.

HELEN: Make a plain wool skirt and a blouse; learn more about buying jackets.

CLASS MEMO:
What plans will your class make for meeting the clothing needs and interests of the members of your group?

LEARNING TO MAKE SOME OF MY CLOTHES

Now that the students had a clear picture of how they were going to proceed, those who planned to make new garments began to work on the fourth goal.

The students already had a tentative idea of what they wanted to make. The girls had selected wool skirts, blouses, and simple dresses while the boys had decided on sport shirts. However, they all realized that making these garments would involve new techniques not found in *Simple Construction Processes for Beginners*. This was the bulletin they had previously used when making gathered or fitted skirts, simple blouses, and miscellaneous articles. (See Book 1, pages 423–444.) The problem now was to choose patterns with processes that would not be too difficult to learn at this stage of their experience.

Selecting Pattern Styles

As the students began to discuss the situation, Miss Dennison pointed toward the reference shelves.

"You'll find a number of pattern books there which will be very helpful," she said. "By studying and analyzing the pictures you may find something you like that will be suitable. Some of you may want to bring in examples of garments that you think might be appropriate, to examine the construction processes. There is also illustrative material on the shelves showing steps in making various garments. You can study these steps and evaluate their difficulty."

The girls had limited themselves the previous year to simple patterns for garments requiring a minimum of fitting, and had used the simplest of construction details. A number of them were now ready to take on more difficult construction and fitting processes. As they studied the illustrative materials, and examined several garments, they listed various new techniques that might be undertaken this year. The boys did the same for several types of sport shirts. All of the processes were then discussed with Miss Dennison. The final list included eight new techniques. Of course, those undertaken would depend upon the type of garment being made and the student's own previous experience and skill. The list follows:

1. Joining a skirt and waist
2. Putting an underarm zipper in a dress
3. Setting in sleeves
4. Attaching a collar and cuffs
5. Attaching a yoke
6. Making a flat-fell seam
7. Making bound and handworked buttonholes
8. Making set-in pockets

While the students had been studying the pattern books, they had also made tentative selections of the styles they liked. But before making a final decision, they decided to set up some general guides which might be helpful.

• Select a style with lines that fit your face and figure. (See Book 1, pages 37–39.)

• Consider the number of pattern pieces. A few pieces are easier to handle than many. When new processes, such as joining a skirt and waist and setting in sleeves, are included, more pieces than were used last year are required. But select a pattern with as few pieces as possible for the type of garment you are making.

• Choose a pattern with pieces which can be cut on the straight of the material. Large pieces cut on the bias are difficult to handle and to fit.

• Look for a pattern in which you can use a number of processes previously learned. Then you can concentrate on some of the new techniques agreed on by the class. But keep the new processes as simple as possible. For example, a dress with a normal waistline is easier to fit than one which joins above or below the waistline. Short sleeves are easier to manage than long fitted ones.

Using the material they had assembled, the students began to make a final decision on the pattern to be selected. The girls who planned to make dresses grouped together according to similar figure types for a discussion on which lines and styles were best for them. Those making blouses compared face types to determine the most suitable necklines. The boys making sport shirts discussed whether or not to use a pattern with a yoke. Miss Dennison offered her assist-ance, and before long everyone had decided on the pattern he or she was to use. Since there was some variation in previous experience and skill, the patterns selected showed varying degrees of difficulty. But the selections were believed to be within the scope of each student's ability to achieve.

Determining Pattern Sizes

Using commercial patterns was a new problem for the boys. But the girls already knew from previous experience that it is important to purchase the correct pattern size. They had also learned how to take their own bust, hip, and waist measurements. (See Book 1, pages 391–392.) However, when Maurine suggested that more help might be needed for the classwork this year, there were nods of agreement.

Girls' sizes

Miss Dennison then distributed to the girls copies of a chart of pattern sizes. The chart is reproduced on page 402. She said that it was based on body measurements agreed upon by the pattern industry, and designed to fit various body types. For a dress, the back-waist length and the fullness of the bust are helpful measurements in determining the best pattern type. The back-waist length is taken from the prominent bone at the base of the neck to the waistline.

Then she explained more about the pattern types. She said that the teen type was designed to fit the partially developed, growing figure. It is shorter waisted, narrower in the shoulders, and flatter through the bust than the junior-misses' and misses' sizes. The junior-misses type is for a more mature figure than the teen. But it is shorter in the waist and skirt than a misses' type. The misses' type was designed to fit a fully developed, youthful figure. It is longer in both waist and skirt than the other two types.

Miss Dennison went on to say that with patterns designed for figure types, the problem of locating a pattern that fits you is lessened. Once you determine your figure type, you can take your measurements, and compare them with the chart. Then you may find a size that corresponds to your measurements. Or it may be that your measurements vary slightly from those on the chart. For a dress or blouse, it is best to buy the size in your figure type that most nearly corresponds to your bust measurement. Choose the one slightly larger rather than smaller. The slight additional fullness will not be a serious problem. If necessary, it can be taken out in deeper side seams when the garment is fitted. Alterations in the waistline and in the hip section of a dress are easier to make than those at the

bust. However, Miss Dennison reminded the girls that in the case of a skirt, making the waistline smaller is easier than enlarging the hips. Extra width at the waist can be taken out as shown in the illustration on page 407.

Keeping these points in mind, the girls then began to analyze their figure types, to take their measurements, and to make comparisons with the chart. But before making a final decision on type and size, they checked with one another and with Miss Dennison to be sure they were correct.

Boys' sizes

Miss Dennison also gave the boys copies of a chart they could use for determining the size needed for a sport shirt. (See page 402.) She said that boys' sizes were designed for figures not fully developed. They are narrower through the shoulders and through the chest than men's sizes. In boys' sizes, chest measurement is the deciding factor, whereas for mature figures, the neck measurement is taken. If the best pattern for body type and size is selected, very little pattern altering and fitting is necessary in a sport shirt,

TEEN—SIZE 14	JUNIOR MISS—SIZE 13	MISS—SIZE 14
About 5' 3"	*About 5' 5"*	*About 5' 6"*
34" bust	*33" bust*	*34" bust*
26" waist	*25½" waist*	*26" waist*
36" hip	*35" hip*	*36" hip*
15¼" back-waist length	*15½" back-waist length*	*16¼" back-waist length*

CHART OF PATTERN SIZES

G I R L S

Teen Size

PATTERN SIZE	10	12	14	16		
Bust	30	32	34	36		
Waist	24	25	26	28		
Hip	32	34	36	38		
Back-waist length	14¾	15	15¼	15½		

Junior-Misses' Size

PATTERN SIZE	9	11	13	15	17	
Bust	30½	31½	33	35	37	
Waist	23½	24½	25½	27	28½	
Hip	32½	33½	35	37	39	
Back-waist length	15	15¼	15½	15¾	16	

Misses' Size

PATTERN SIZE	10	12	14	16	18	20
Bust	31	32	34	36	38	40
Waist	24	25	26	28	30	32
Hip	33	34	36	38	40	42
Back-waist length	15¾	16	16¼	16½	16¾	17

SIZES FOR SKIRTS

Teen Size

Waist	23	24	25	26	28	
Hip	31	32	34	36	38	

Junior-Misses' Size

Waist	23½	24½	25½	27	28½	
Hip	32½	33½	35	37	39	

Misses' Size

Waist	24	25	26	28	30	32
Hip	33	34	36	38	40	42

B O Y S

Boys' Size

PATTERN SIZE	10	12	14	16	
Chest	28	30	32	34	
Waist	24	25½	27	29	
Hip	29	31	33	35	
Neck base girth	12½	13	13½	14	

Men's Size

Chest	32	34	36	38	40
Waist	28	30	32	34	36
Neck base girth	13½	14	14½	15	15½
Shirt sleeve length	33	33	33	33	34

since fit does not need to be as exact as in women's garments. Furthermore, she added that the sport shirt industry is fairly well standardized. In general, a boy can buy the same size pattern that he buys in a readymade shirt.

Setting Up a Basis for the Selection of Materials

The students realized that selecting a pattern and material go hand in hand in planning a new garment. The girls making skirts had been considering wool fabrics. The boys had been thinking of easy-to-handle, washable materials for their sport shirts. Several of the girls making blouses and dresses were planning to buy different fabrics from the ones used last year. However, the kind of materials to be used would depend upon the purpose for which the garment was intended, as well as the number of new processes attempted and the student's previous experience and skill. Even though there was more leeway among the girls in choosing fabrics than last year, those presenting difficult problems would need to be avoided.

Points to consider

After referring to source materials and discussing the situation, the students decided to select what they would use on the basis of four points. These were: (1) ease of construction, (2) style of garment, (3) ease of care, and (4) money available. Brief considerations on these four points were summarized as follows:

EASE OF CONSTRUCTION
- Firm, closely woven fabrics with some softness are easier to work with than loosely woven, sleazy materials.
- It is best to avoid fabrics which ravel easily, because they require wide seams and special finishing processes, such as overcasting or binding.
- Thick, bulky fabrics are hard to handle, and make accurate stitching difficult.
- Solid colors, small over-all prints, or pin stripes make cutting and fitting easier than do large prints, plaids, or wide stripes.

STYLE OF GARMENT
- Garments with fullness around the waistline or concentrated in the front call for soft, pliable materials that fall into graceful folds.
- Garments with pleats need smooth, fairly soft, closely woven materials resistant to wrinkling and stretching.
- Fitted garments require materials that will hold their shape, are fairly smooth, and not too stiff.

EASE OF CARE
- Materials which fit your personal preferences in the care of clothes are most satisfactory. If you prefer to launder the garment, be sure that the fabric you select is washable. Remember too that most wool materials look best when dry-cleaned.
- You may find it worth your while to select a fabric that has been treated to resist wrinkling. Such a finish may add to the cost of the garment, but the results may be worth the additional expense.
- In general, medium or dark tones or an over-all pattern tend to show soil

less readily than very light colors. If you want to decrease the cost of dry-cleaning, this may be an important consideration.

MONEY AVAILABLE

* The material you select needs to be within a price range which you and your family can afford. This means being guided by your own financial situation and not being influenced by what others are doing. Some of your friends may be considering materials far more expensive than you can afford. Trying to keep up with these friends may upset your clothing plans. It may also lead to unpleasant financial problems for you, and to unhappy relationships with your family.

* Read labels, ask questions, and get your money's worth in a fabric suited to the type of garment you are making and to your ability to handle it. Select the best quality you can afford. But remember that an expensive fabric may not necessarily be the one best suited for your purpose.

Other supplies

"When we buy our pattern and material," said Maurine, "we might as well plan to purchase our other supplies. We'll need thread, of course, and some of us will be using zippers."

Maurine s suggestion led the students to consider other supplies needed for making their garments. After consulting various references and illustrative materials, the following points were set up.

* Mercerized sewing thread — a slightly darker shade works in best — can be used on wool and other easy-to-handle fabrics. But the size of the thread will depend upon the fabric you are using. (See Book 1, page 367 for sizes, as well as for sewing equipment in general that is needed.)

* If a zipper is used, select one that matches the color of your material as nearly as possible. Get the length which the pattern calls for or which you prefer. Remember that even though an underarm zipper in a dress is set in like a skirt zipper, a different kind is needed. A skirt zipper has one tape end open, and is usually 7 inches long. A dress zipper has both tape ends closed, and is available in 9-, 10-, or 12-inch lengths. (See the illustration.)

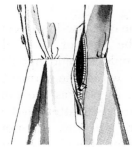

A side-placket dress zipper has both tape ends closed; a skirt-placket zipper, only one.

• For interfacings — often used on collars and cuffs or other garment parts — buy the kind and amount your pattern calls for. Or use suitable material already on hand at home. For medium-weight washable fabrics, interfacings of preshrunk muslin, cambric, or long cloth are frequently recommended.

• Commercial seam tape — sometimes used to make hems in wool skirts lie flat — needs to be as near the color of the material as possible.

• If buttons are used, choose those suitable in size, shape, color, and durability to the type of garment being made.

• If a belt buckle is desired, select one that harmonizes with the buttons, or is suited to the garment.

Preparing Materials That Have Not Been Shrunk

One day while the students were discussing patterns and materials, Frances brought up the subject of fabrics that may shrink.

"Several of us are planning to use wool for our skirts," said Frances. "We learned last year how to shrink cotton fabrics. But since none of us made wool garments, we'll need to know about wool." (See Book 1, page 369, for shrinking cotton material.)

"I'm glad you mentioned the subject," said Miss Dennison. "As you know, most good-quality wool materials have been preshrunk or made shrinkage-resistant. You can look for this information on the labels. However, if you are in doubt about the shrinkage in the piece you buy, it is important to know

how to test it. You don't want your garment to shrink in wear. But you do want to avoid subjecting your fabric to the process unless it is necessary. If further shrinkage is needed, you will want information on how to proceed."

The students who were planning to use wool materials for their garments then volunteered to look up references on the procedures just mentioned. Later, with the guidance of Miss Dennison, the information was summarized as follows and made available to the other members of the class:

How to test wool fabrics to determine whether shrinkage is needed

1. Wet a third of a pressing cloth. Then fold the cloth, and allow it to stand until the moisture is equal throughout.

2. Lay the pressing cloth on a small square of the wool material with the wrong side up.

3. Set the iron control for wool, or use a moderately hot iron. Press the square area until the pressing cloth is dry, lifting the iron from place to place, not sliding it up and down.

4. Lift the pressing cloth, and pat the material with the palm of the hand to let the steam escape. Then inspect the material carefully. If there are no wrinkles running up into the unpressed material, previous shrinkage is sufficient.

How to sponge and shrink wool fabrics

Wool fabrics need to be handled carefully. A commercial establishment which has a pressing machine is much better equipped to sponge and shrink a long length of wool material than an individual person is. The charge for this service is generally small, and is worth the time and effort saved. But for those who may be doing their own sponging and shrinking, the following directions are given.

1. Clip the selvage on each side every 6 to 8 inches.

2. Wring a sheet out of warm water, and lay it out smoothly on a flat surface. Place the wool material — folded lengthwise — on the sheet, keeping the selvages parallel to the edge of the sheet, but 2 or 3 inches in from the edge. Turn the free sections of the sheet over the wool, and then fold the two together smoothly.

3. Let the material remain in the cloth overnight or for several hours until the surface of the wool is evenly dampened.

4. Unfold, and lay the sheet and the wool out smoothly on a flat surface. Let the wool dry thoroughly.

5. Then lay the wool — still folded lengthwise and with the wrong side up — over the ironing board. Spread a damp pressing cloth over the material.

6. Set the iron control for wool, or use a moderately hot iron. Move the iron right and left along the grain of the material with a quick patting motion. Lift the pressing cloth, and pat the material with the palm of the hand to let the steam escape. When the upper layer of the fabric is almost dry, move the material along until another section is on the board. Continue pressing and patting until the entire upper layer has been pressed. Then turn the material over, so that the other layer is on top. Repeat the same pressing and patting procedure.

7. Hang the material evenly over a line to finish drying.

Altering Patterns

Not all of the students were fortunate enough to find pattern sizes that corresponded exactly to their body measurements. After Miss Dennison and the girls had helped the boys understand how to use their patterns (see Book 1, pages 392–393), attention was directed toward those students with pattern alteration problems.

The students whose patterns needed lengthening or shortening through the body of the garment, followed the directions that had been used the previous year. (See Book 1, pages 393–394.) However, lengthening or shortening a sleeve was a new problem, and some of the girls needed to alter their patterns through the hips. Busily they set about to find the help needed.

Directions

Information on how to make the various new types of alterations follows:

SHORTENING A SLEEVE: Fold and pin two tucks across the pattern horizontally, one above and one below the elbow. The width of the tucks needs to measure ½ the amount to be taken out — each tuck ¼ the amount. This is because in making the tuck you fold out twice its width.

LENGTHENING A SLEEVE: Cut across the pattern horizontally above and below the elbow. Spread the pattern to the desired length, putting in ½ the amount to be added at each slash. Pin

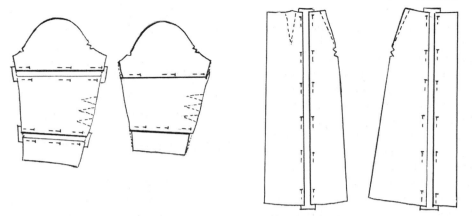

After lengthening or shortening a sleeve or widening the hip line of a skirt, mark new cutting lines as indicated by the dotted lines in the above illustrations.

pattern to paper to hold the slashes apart. See the illustration.

WIDENING THE HIPS: Slash vertically both the skirt front and the skirt back between the side seams and the darts. Make a paper insert from waist to hem, putting in ½ the desired width in the front, and ½ in the back. Adjust the seam line above the hip to fit the waist. See the illustration.

Cutting Out the Garments

The students were now ready to start laying out their patterns. But first, the girls reviewed for the boys what had been learned last year about cutting out a garment, using a commercial pattern. (See Book 1, pages 394–398.) Miss Dennison stressed the importance of being sure that the grain of the material was straight before any cutting was done. The students were careful to pull threads to straighten the ends of the material, and to stretch the fabric diagonally when necessary. Everyone worked diligently to make the folded material lie straight with the edges of the cutting tables.

The layout guides on the patterns were then carefully studied, and the pattern pieces laid on the grain of the material exactly as indicated. A ruler was used to measure from both ends of the grain-line markings to the selvage of the material. Cutting was not done until a trial placement showed the best location for all pieces. Techniques in pinning the pattern to the material, in cutting out by the pattern, and in transferring markings were demonstrated by various girls in the group.

Special points

Miss Dennison also made some comments. She said that it would be helpful to mark the center front and center back of a shirt, a waist or a blouse, and a skirt. These markings help in putting garment pieces together, and are especially important where there is a lapped opening. Furthermore, in fairly straight-cut garments, these center-front and center-back markings indicate the straight of the grain. If the grain falls correctly here, it will be straight in the rest of the piece.

She also recommended marking from the highest point of the sleeve cap straight with the grain to the bottom of the sleeve. This helps to check the lengthwise grain of the sleeve. A similar marking straight with the crosswise grain of the sleeve about 6½ inches below the highest point of the cap makes it easy to check the crosswise grain of a sleeve. These markings are especially helpful for set-in sleeves in blouses or dresses, since the sleeves need to fit much more accurately than those in a sport shirt.

Making General Preparations for Construction Work

After the material had been cut, the students reviewed what they had previously learned about using the sewing machine. They also studied the summaries they had made last year on general and special pressing techniques. Many of these would be used in constructing their garments this year. (See Book 1, pages 401–411.)

Miss Dennison then showed the students a bulletin. She said that it contained the new techniques they would need for their classwork this year. Copies of this bulletin, as well as *Simple Construction Processes for Beginners* (See Book 1, pages 423–444), would be placed on the reference shelves. She also added that new processes could be demonstrated as needed. Time would be scheduled, so that the students using the same new techniques could watch the demonstrations.

The bulletin *Construction Processes for Intermediates* is reproduced on pages 419 to 432. Students in other classes may find it helpful in constructing their garments.

Setting Up Construction Plans for Assembling the Garments

The students already had a general idea how their garments might be put together. Identifying pattern pieces for the style they were to make had helped in this respect. Then too, some of the pattern guides gave step-by-step instructions and numbered the pattern pieces in the order of their use. All of the guide sheets had pictures and diagrams.

Deciding how to work

However, before actual work on constructing the garments began, it seemed wise to study the matter further. The students soon learned that garments are customarily put together in units. That is, smaller pieces and parts of a garment are completed as far as possible before joining them to larger ones. For example, general procedures for assembling a skirt, blouse, dress, and sport shirt would be as follows:

A SKIRT: Front and back assembled separately before being joined at side seams; side opening completed before belt is attached

A BLOUSE: Front and back assembled separately before being joined at shoulder and side seams; sleeves assembled, and then set into blouse

SKIRT	BLOUSE	DRESS

SKIRT

Front assembled

Back assembled

*Front and back joined
Zipper in*

Waistband assembled

Waistband attached

Finished skirt

BLOUSE

Front and back assembled

Front and back joined

*Facings joined and
neck finished*

*Sleeves assembled
and set in*

*Cuffs assembled
and set on*

Finished blouse

DRESS

Waist assembled

Skirt assembled

*Waist and skirt joined
Zipper set in*

*Collar
assembled*   *Collar set on*

*Sleeves
assembled*

Sleeves set in   *Finished dress*

UNITS IN ASSEMBLING GARMENTS

A DRESS: Waist and skirt assembled separately before being joined together; underarm zipper put in; sleeves assembled, and set in waist

A SPORT SHIRT: Front and back attached to yoke; sleeves set in flat; garment joined together by continuous underarm and side seams

The girls, especially, realized that time for fitting needed to be scheduled between basting and stitching, and before working on some of the garment parts. In making skirts and blouses last year, three fittings had been allowed. They also knew that advance preparations for a fitting are important. Time can be saved if those being fitted have equipment ready, and if they come to school wearing shoes and undergarments that will be worn when the garments are completed. (See Book 1, page 411 for other advance preparations.)

Soon the students were ready to start making construction plans. They decided to divide into groups according to the kind of garments being made. Each group would consult references — including the pattern guide — and work out general plans for assembling the various garments. Miss Dennison would assist whenever her guidance was needed. When the plans were completed, each student could begin to carry out the plan set up for his or her garment.

Assembling a dress

1. On the front and back pieces of the waist, baste darts and tucks if used. Baste the shoulder seams together unless there is to be a slash opening at the neck. In this case leave one of the shoulder seams open for fitting. Baste the waist front and back together at the side seams, keeping the underarm darts turned down as you baste. Leave space open on the left side for the placket — about ⅓ of the length of the zipper.

2. On the front and back pieces of the skirt, baste darts, and pleats or gores if used. Baste the side seams together, leaving space open on the upper left side for the placket — about ⅔ of the length of the zipper.

3. Turn under the seam allowance at the top of the skirt. Press lightly. Lay the top of the skirt on the seam line at the bottom of the waist, right sides out. Match the center fronts, center backs, and side seams. Baste, keeping the darts at the waistline turned toward the center back and front.

4. Try on the dress right side out for the *first fitting*. Turn in the seam allowance at the placket opening, and pin the opening together. If one of the shoulder seams was left open, pin it together. Put on a belt, or tie a tape measure around your waist. Check the following, and alter if necessary.

a. Do the shoulder seams run parallel with and about ¼ to ½ of an inch back of the shoulders? Will the armseye line fall where it should on the arms?

b. Is the neckline the shape and size you wish? Remember it will be a seam deeper if faced, or if a collar is attached.

c. Is the garment as loose through the bust as is desirable?

d. Do the darts at the shoulders or underarms match and point to the fullest part of the bust? Do the darts at the waist match, and are they at right angles to the waistline?

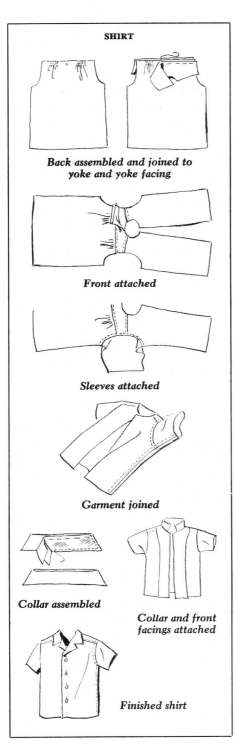

SHIRT

*Back assembled and joined to
yoke and yoke facing*

Front attached

Sleeves attached

Garment joined

Collar assembled

*Collar and front
facings attached*

Finished shirt

e. Is the length of the waist satisfactory? Does it appear to be the same length in front and back?

f. Are the darts in the skirt smooth and straight?

g. Does the skirt fit without the seams drawing, causing wrinkles between the hip line and the waistline, cupping up under the seat, or hiking up in front and poking out in back?

h. If there are gathers at the waistline, are they distributed as you wish?

i. Is the waistline snug enough to stay where it feels most comfortable?

j. Do the side seams run straight from the center of the armpit to the bottom of the skirt in a line perpendicular to the floor?

k. If used, are the pattern markings for bound buttonholes or set-in pockets satisfactorily located?

5. Rip the basted seams enough to stitch the waist and skirt darts. Stitch the tucks, pleats, or gores if used. Remove bastings, and press. If bound buttonholes or set-in pockets are used, make them at this time. Press.

6. Rip the basted waistline seam at the sides. Replace shoulder and side seam bastings in the waist where they were opened to stitch darts. Stitch side seams and shoulder seams of the waist and side seams of the skirt. Remove bastings, and press.

7. Rebaste the waistline seam. Stitch the seam on the right side, along the skirt edge where it laps onto the waist. Remove bastings, and press. Baste and stitch zipper in left side opening. (See Book 1, page 438.)

8. Bind or face the neck, or make the collar and stitch it in place. Remove bastings, and press. From this point on, keep the dress on a hanger when you are not working on it.

9. Assemble the sleeve, and baste it into the armseye.

10. Try on the dress for a *second fitting.* Check the following and alter if necessary.

a. Does the underarm zipper placket fit correctly and lie flat and smooth?

b. Does the neck finish fit the shape intended? If used, is the collar sharply turned? Does it lie flat or roll attractively according to its type?

c. Is the position of buttons or other fasteners correctly marked?

d. Does the lengthwise grain of the sleeve fall perpendicularly to the floor from the highest point of the sleeve? Does the crosswise grain fall horizontally to the floor? Does the armseye seamline run smooth and straight around the hole? Is the sleeve length suitable and even all around?

11. Stitch the sleeves to the blouse. Remove bastings, and press. Finish the bottom of the sleeve.

12. Make the belt.

13. Sew on any buttons or other fasteners needed.

14. Have someone measure and mark the hem. Baste it in place.

15. Try on the dress for a *third fitting.* Check the following and alter if necessary.

a. Do the sleeves feel comfortable and look well? Is the finish at the bottom of the sleeves satisfactory?

b. Is the belt pleasing in width, length, and placement?

c. Are the fasteners, if additional ones are used, suitably placed?

d. Is the length even all around? Is the hem the same width all around?

16. Finish the hem; press it.

17. Give the dress a final pressing.

Assembling a sport shirt, short sleeved

The front and back of the shirt may be put together by basting, and the shirt slipped on to check the fit of the neckline and shoulder length. In checking these lines, seam allowances for attaching the collar and the sleeves need to be taken into account. The neckline will be deeper and the shoulder line shorter when the collar and sleeves are attached.

1. *Attaching the yoke to the back.* Gather or tuck the top of the back as indicated in the pattern. Put the right side of the yoke against the right side of the shirt, and the right side of the yoke facing against the inside of the shirt. Baste all three thicknesses together along the seam line, and stitch. Remove basting. Turn the yoke and yoke facing together up over the seam. Baste, press, and stitch along the edge of the yoke on the right side. See the illustration on page 411. Remove bastings, and press.

2. *Attaching shirt fronts.* Match the shirt fronts to the yoke facing along the seam line, making an outside seam. Baste, and stitch. Remove bastings, and press seams toward the yoke facing. Turn under seam allowance on bottom edge of front yoke. Baste over the seams joining shirt fronts to facing. Stitch, remove bastings, and press. Baste yoke and facing together at the armholes and neck edges.

3. *Sewing the sleeve to the armhole.* Baste and then stitch the armhole of the sleeve to the armhole of the shirt, making a flat-fell seam which turns toward the sleeve. Press.

4. *Underarm and side seams.* Make a flat-fell seam, starting at the bottom of the sleeve and continuing to the

bottom of the shirt, with the seam turned to the front. Press.

5. *Bottom of sleeve.* Make a hem of the desired width in the bottom of the sleeve. Stitch, and press.

6. *Pocket.* If used, make and stitch in place a patch pocket or pockets.

7. *Collar and front facings.* For a tailored effect, a sport shirt collar is interfaced. The interfacing is cut by the same pattern as the under collar. Attach it to the wrong side of the under collar as indicated on the guide sheet. Then make and turn the interfaced double collar. If desired, make a trimming stitch around the collar ¼ inch from the edge. Extensions cut onto the shirt fronts turn back to face the fronts. Hem to the wrong side the cut edges of these extensions — except along those edges facing the neck. Attach the collar to the neck and front facings as a convertible collar is attached. If desired, make a trimming stitch ¼ inch from edge on both front openings.

8. *Lower shirt edge.* Make a hem the desired width at the lower edge of the shirt. Catch in the bottom edge of each front facing.

9. *Front fastenings.* Make worked buttonholes by hand or by machine in the left center front. Sew buttons on the right front to correspond to the buttonholes.

Assembling a wool skirt

See Book 1, page 412 for the directions for making a fitted skirt. Since wool is elastic, baste seams securely and firmly. Be sure that the machine is well regulated to the thickness of the fabric. Steam-press each seam carefully. (See directions for pressing wool, steps 5–7, page 406.) Consider

with your teacher the best seam finish for your particular wool fabric. (See Book 1, pages 441–442.) Shrink in full-

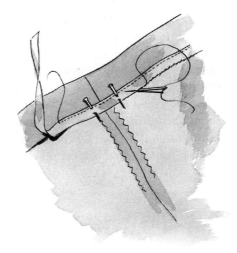

One edge of the seam tape is stitched to the hem. A slant hemming stitch (Book 1, pages 433–434) is used to finish the hem.

ness at the top of the hem. Use seam tape to finish the hem for a flat, inconspicuous finish. See the illustration on this page.

Assembling a blouse

Step-by-step directions for assembling a blouse are not given here, since adequate information is provided elsewhere for students who select this type of garment. See Book 1, page 414 for making a fitted blouse without sleeves and a collar. For new techniques, such as bound buttonholes or bound pockets, a collar, and set-in sleeves, see the listings in *Construction Processes for Intermediates*, pages 419 to 420. Also refer to the steps in assembling a dress, pages 410 to 412, that have bearing on the new processes included.

EVALUATING THE CLASSWORK IN CLOTHING

ONE day when the classwork on "A Four-Point Plan for My Wardrobe" was nearing completion, the students had a lively discussion. The problem was how to evaluate the work they had done toward being suitably and attractively dressed — their four-point wardrobe plan.

The students realized that some of the things they had learned could not be wholly evaluated at this time. For example, they knew quite a lot about buying certain garments. But the ability to buy wisely and to one's satisfaction takes time and experience. Repairing, remodeling, and making garments at school are fine achievements. But the value of learning these techniques lies in being ready to use them at home whenever they are needed.

Name _Walter Brennan_

MY PROGRESS TOWARD BEING SUITABLY AND ATTRACTIVELY DRESSED

Outer wearing apparel	What I have done
Topcoat—one button missing; lining ripped	Matched and sewed on button
	Restitched broken seams
Suit—no longer adequate for dress-up occasions; trousers getting too short	Purchased a new suit. Careful to examine fabric, fit, and workmanship. Selected a color that goes well with my topcoat. Am keeping hanger cover over suit
	Lengthened old trousers by eliminating the cuffs
School trousers—large hole in inside pocket; mud stains on trouser legs	Replaced old pocket with new commercial one
	Removed stains and pressed trousers. Careful to hang them on hanger to avoid wrinkling
Jacket—worn area on elbow	Applied a decorative leather patch.
White dress shirt—collar worn	Reversed collar
Socks—need more	Purchased two pairs—one to go with my new suit, the other for school

Name *Sue Armstrong*

MY PROGRESS TOWARD BEING SUITABLY AND
ATTRACTIVELY DRESSED

Outer wearing apparel	What I have done
Wool skirt—too short; small hole	Lengthened skirt by using a facing
	Repaired small hole, and pressed skirt
Coat—no longer suitable for dress-up occasions, but can be worn to school when minor repairs are made	Purchased a new coat in a basic color that will go with the rest of my wardrobe. Selected material that will wear for several years, but the cost was more than I had planned for.
	Sewed on loose buttons on old coat; restitched part of lining with broken seams; had coat dry-cleaned
Dresses—I have a rayon print in which the material is still good, but the neckline is too small, and the waistline too high	Altered neckline at school, but was not experienced enough to change the waistline. My mother did this, but I helped with the fitting and pressing.
Need another dress for date occasions. Had hoped to buy a new one, but may make one instead, because of extra money spent on coat	Bought pattern and material, and made dress at school. Selected a color that goes well with the new coat I purchased
Blouses—will need at least one in the near future	Am looking around for a pattern and material I like

These considerations led to a general agreement that all they could do now was to present an over-all picture of what they had accomplished to date. Each student would make out a brief report showing how the work in class had been applied to his or her personal wardrobe plan. The reports were to be ready for class discussion by the time the fourth objective was completed.

Space does not permit a detailed account of each student's accomplishments. But two reports are given as examples of the progress that was made toward carrying out a personal clothing plan. A boy's report is reproduced on page 414; a girl's, on page 415.

A boy's report is reproduced on page 414; a girl's, on page 415.

CLASS MEMO:
How will you and members of your group evaluate the classwork you have done toward being suitably and attractively dressed?

MAKING PLANS FOR YOUR CLASSWORK IN CLOTHING

You have read how Miss Dennison's homemaking class set up and carried out four goals for being suitably and attractively dressed. It seemed important to them to do this in terms of individual needs and interests. Each student took an inventory of outer garments and then made a tentative wardrobe plan. The plan was based on the garments they found in good condition, those in need of repair or alteration, and those to be bought or made. Directions were set up for various types of repair work and remodeling. The classwork on buying centered around clothing fabrics and guides for purchasing the various articles in their clothing plans. The students who were to make garments selected patterns and materials, worked out construc-

Holding a store display m... be a desirable means ... learning how to be suitab... and attractively dressed.

tion plans for assembling the garments, and then made them. All in all, it was a very helpful experience.

When you plan your classwork in clothing, you may want to center it around the same goals which Miss Dennison's students set up. Or you may find it more desirable to limit the work to fewer problems and to cover more ground on each one. Then again, you may want to use an entirely different approach.

SUGGESTED EXPERIENCES

THE problem of being suitably and attractively dressed at all times calls for a variety of experiences. Your class may find it worth while to carry out some of the following suggestions, or to adapt them to your personal needs and interests.

1. Perhaps members of your group are planning to take inventories of the clothing they have on hand. If so, they may find it desirable to follow the same procedures used by Miss Dennison's group, along with any suggested improvements. Or a new inventory technique may be worked out.

2. Your class may want to set up general over-all plans for a boy's and a girl's wardrobe. Using the plan as a guide, the boys can work out suggestions for possible garment and accessory combinations, while the girls do the same for their wardrobe. These suggestions may be very helpful when each boy and girl plans his or her individual wardrobe.

3. A "Consultation Service" with the assistance of your teacher and one or two mothers experienced in sewing may be a useful project. Arrangements can be made to bring to class on a certain day garments in need of repair or alteration. Small groups of three or four students can work out

recommendations for the kind of repairs and alterations that might be made. These suggestions can be evaluated by the teacher and the mothers, and any improvements made. When the plans are completed, the class can hold an "It *Will* Be Better" parade. Each student in the parade can explain what is to be done to the garment he or she is demonstrating. Later, after the repairs and alterations have been carried out, another parade "It *Does* Look Better" can be held. This can include a discussion of problems that were not encountered by Miss Dennison's class.

4. In groups of three or four students, you can arrange to visit stores in your community where fabrics are sold. Well-thought-out questions can be prepared in advance. After the visits, the class can discuss the information acquired. If samples of fabrics are available, an exhibit may be arranged. The exhibit could also include labeling, and if possible, recent research findings on some of the newer kinds of fabrics and finishes.

5. Your class may want to assemble more information about buying certain articles of clothing than Miss Dennison's group did. Small groups of three or four students can each select a garment and find out as much as possible about

buying it wisely. Every available source of information can be utilized, such as labels, salespersons' information, and literature from Consumers Union and Consumers' Research. The most useful and interesting findings can serve as a basis for an exhibit in the showcase at school.

6. A series of short skits dramatizing situations encountered when buying various garments and accessories would be interesting to everyone in the class. For example, one skit might include a customer saying "No" to a high-pressure salesperson. The clerk is attempting to sell the customer something he or she does not need and has decided not to buy.

7. Each student can bring to class examples of labels taken from garments recently purchased by themselves, members of their family, or their friends. These labels may then be evaluated in class, on the basis of the points which Miss Dennison's group set up for a good label. The class can decide what additional information, if any, is needed for a particular garment. Volunteers can then write specifications for information needed on some of the labels. Those that are especially good may be sent to the manufacturer as an example of what information the purchaser would like to have on the label.

8. Some of the students in your class who are especially interested in buying clothes may enjoy analyzing clothing advertisements to determine what is "trade puff" and what is useful information. Reports of their findings can be given to the class.

9. Your group may find it a worth-while project to work out arrangements for a "Consultation Service" for the benefit of other students your age in the school. How to buy suits, coats, and dresses can be featured. Suitable fabrics and hidden qualities that one needs to look for can be stressed.

10. One of your class meetings may include brief comments by various students on the values they hold in buying clothes. Any comparisons between their buying experiences and their expressed values may prove to be very interesting.

11. Your group may want to make definite plans for ways in which each member can start to improve buying practices.

12. At the stores where you shop, find out the trade names of chlorine and perborate bleaches used in garment care. Then refer to the chart on pages 372 to 373 to see how you can use the bleaches for taking care of the garments in your wardrobe.

13. For drip-drying a dress, blouse, or shirt, get permission from your mother to use the over-the-tub plan. Work out one or two convenient arrangements to keep the bathroom floor free from puddles.

14. Individually or in groups, collect or work out general guides for articles of clothing you may plan to make in school.

15. A fashion show for a school assembly program may be an interesting way to complete your classwork in clothing. The show could be given in three parts. The first could include clothes that have been repaired and altered. The second part can deal with buying clothes, and the third with clothes that have been made.

Construction Processes
for
Intermediates

CONTENTS

BUTTONHOLES

Bound or piped

A bound or piped buttonhole gives a tailored, decorative effect in medium- or heavier-weight fabrics. A buttonhole of this type needs to be made in the garment before the hem or facing is attached. This means that the location of the buttonholes is checked at the first fitting. Between the first and second fittings, the buttonholes can be made and faced.

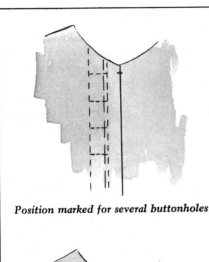

Position marked for several buttonholes

Piping matched for several buttonholes

1. Mark the length of the buttonhole. Its length should be the diameter of the button plus its thickness. When a number of buttonholes are to be used on a front or back closing, mark the length with two parallel lines. See the illustration. Be sure that the length and location markings are straight with the grain.

2. Cut piping on the bias or straight of the material 2 inches wide and 1 inch longer than the buttonhole. For a series of buttonholes, cut one strip 1 inch wider than the buttonholes and long enough to extend 1 inch beyond the two end buttonholes. See the illustration.

3. Mark the center line of the piping for a buttonhole on the wrong side of the material. Be sure to have the marking exactly the same length as the marking on the garment. Then place the right side of the piping to the right side of the garment, being careful to match the markings. Baste a rectangle around the buttonhole marking ⅛ inch or less from each side of the marking, and exactly as long as the marking.

4. Stitch on the rectangle marking, beginning near the center of a side. Use short stitches. Turn sharp corners, being careful to make the same number of stitches across each end. Retrace stitching at starting point. Remove basting, and press.

5. Cut buttonhole through the center to within ¼ inch from the end. Then cut diagonally to the corners, up to the stitching. This leaves a triangle at each end.

6. Turn the piping to the under side. With your fingers, crease back the triangles and the seam exactly on the edges of the triangle. Baste and press. Remove basting.

7. Fold the piping back to the center of the opening to form two folds of equal width. Keep the triangles and the

seams turned away from the slit. Baste along each side of the buttonhole but not along the ends. Use diagonal bastings on the right side to hold the folded edges together along the center of the buttonhole.

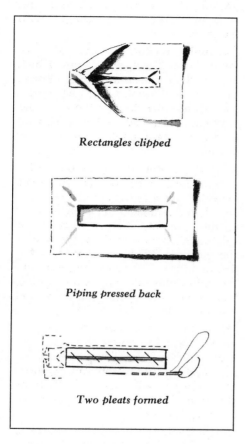

Rectangles clipped

Piping pressed back

Two pleats formed

8. On the under side, make a box pleat at each end to cover the triangle. Press. Then stitch the pleat across each triangle, but not through to the outside of the garment. Use machine stitching or the backstitch, but do not let the stitches show on the right side of the buttonhole.

9. Remove the bastings along each side of the buttonhole, but not the diagonal basting, which is left in until the gar-

ment is almost completed. Press carefully. Trim off piping material all around to ¼ to ½ inch of the stitched rectangle.

10. The buttonholes can now be cut through the attached facing or hem for the closing. Fit the facing or hem to the garment carefully, and pin it in place over the buttonholes. Cut the facing or hem through the center of each buttonhole, leaving a triangle at each end as before. Turn the raw edge under. Hem it by hand to the seam of the buttonhole, being careful that no stitches show on the right side.

Handmade worked

An advantage of this type of buttonhole is that it can be made after the closing is hemmed or faced and the garment is almost completed. But learning to make the buttonhole may require considerable practice before the result is satisfying. Practice on tightly woven material which does not fray easily.

1. Check the placement of the buttonholes. Use pattern markings for spacing, or if necessary, plan your own. If there is little or no strain, the length of the hole may be marked parallel to the edge of the garment. But if there is likely to be considerable strain, it is better to mark at right angles to the edge. The diameter of the button used plus its thickness will determine the length of the buttonhole. Mark the buttonholes with a basting, being sure the markings are straight with the grain.

2. Machine stitching to strengthen the buttonhole before it is cut makes the process easier for beginners. Stitch a rectangle around the marking for the slit, as illustrated on page 423. Note that the ends of the rectangle come exactly to the ends of the slit, while the

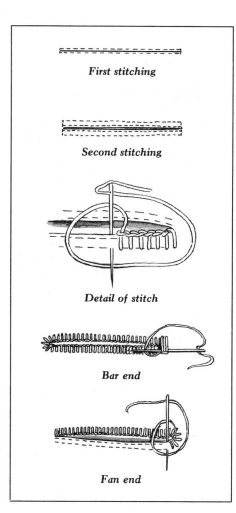

First stitching

Second stitching

Detail of stitch

Bar end

Fan end

sides are close to the sides of the slit. Stitch a second rectangle around the first rectangle. See the illustration. The depth is determined by how deep you plan to make the buttonhole stitch, usually about $\frac{1}{16}$ of an inch.

3. Cut the slit inside the smaller rectangle along the marking and on a thread of the material. Use small sharp-pointed scissors. Do not fold the buttonhole in half to cut the slit. If you do so, the edges of the slit may be cut unevenly. Or you may cut the machine stitching used as reinforcement.

4. To work the buttonhole, use relatively coarse thread, usually 40. Have the thread long enough to finish working the entire buttonhole. Do not knot the thread, but leave a long end at the first stitch. This can be cut off later. Work from right to left on the outside of the garment. Bring the needle through the fabric to the outside of the buttonhole, using the second rectangle stitching as a guide for depth. Throw the thread slightly toward the right. Then pull it under the needle and upward, forming a loop around the needle. See the illustration. Pull the needle through the loop to make a knot or purl on the raw edge of the buttonhole. Continue making stitches even in depth and close enough together to touch each other, but not to overlap. Try to draw each knot or purl with the same tension — neither too tight nor too loose.

a. *For a buttonhole that lies parallel to the edge of the garment,* begin buttonhole stitches at either end. Finish both ends with a bar — extra stitches which hold the ends together. Do this by placing three straight stitches across each end exactly at the tip of the buttonhole. The stitches need to be twice the width of the regular buttonhole stitches. Over these straight stitches, make five buttonhole stitches. Catch under the bar threads for all the stitches except the center stitch. Catch this stitch through the material.

b. *For a buttonhole that lies at a right angle to the garment edge,* begin buttonhole stitches at the end of the slit farthest from the garment edge. This is where there is the least strain on the buttonhole. Just before reaching the opposite end, let the stitches spread out like a fan as shown in the illustration. Five to seven stitches are needed to make a durable, well-spaced fan. Finish the end opposite the fan with a bar, as described for a vertical hole.

COLLARS

Making a double collar

Collars are generally constructed as a unit, leaving the neck edges free. Then the neck edges are attached to the garment. Before commencing the collar, the neckline needs to have been fitted, and the shoulder seams and any other neckline seams finished. Some collars are folded double along the outer edge and seamed only at the ends. However, most collars — with or without an interfacing — are cut out of two layers of fabric. These are usually exactly alike as to size and grain. To prevent the outer edge of the under collar from showing when the garment is finished, ⅛ inch may be removed on all raw edges except those at the neckline. The strain on the material of having the under collar slightly smaller will pull the seam to the under side.

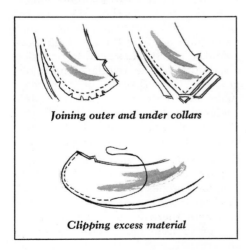

Joining outer and under collars

Clipping excess material

1. Pin the outer collar and the under collar right sides together, matching raw edges at centers, ends, and corners. Baste along seam line of outer collar. Stitch.

2. Remove basting. Trim seam to ¼ inch or less. Cut points away even closer. Clip excess material at rounded corners. See the illustration.

3. Turn the collar right side out. Crease open the seam.

4. Pinch and crease the edges of the collar so that the seam falls just under the outer edge. Baste about ⅛ inch from the edge. Press from the outer edge toward the neckline. Remove bastings, and press to remove marks.

Attaching a shaped collar

A shaped collar may lie flat or may sometimes roll. It is usually attached with a 1-inch bias facing.

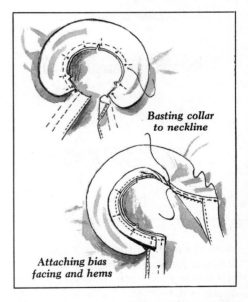

Basting collar to neckline

Attaching bias facing and hems

1. Place under side of the collar to the right side of the garment. Match and pin the neck edges at the centers and notches. Usually the ends of the collar meet at the center front of the garment. Baste the seam carefully with small stitches.

2. Try on the garment to see whether the collar looks as you wish, and adjust if necessary.

a. Is the width and shape of the collar becoming?

b. Does the collar fit the neckline?

c. Does it give the effect desired?

3. *If the neckline has no opening,* start the 1-inch bias facing a little in front of one shoulder seam. Pin the facing right side down over the basted collar and neckline. Hold the inside edge of the facing a little full, so that the finished facing will fit around an outward curve. Baste. Stitch together the ends of the bias facing with a ⅜-inch seam. Trim seam to ¼ of an inch and press open. *If the garment has a hem or facing,* turn this to the right side over the basted collar and neckline. Pin the bias facing to the collar, letting the bias facing overlap the hem or facing about ½ inch. Hold the inside edge a little full. Baste.

4. Stitch the garment, collar, bias facing, and hem or facing if used together along the seam line. Remove bastings. Trim the seam to ¼ inch, and clip curve and corners.

5. Crease open the seam, and turn the bias facing, and the hem or facing if used to the wrong side of the garment. Pull the collar out firmly, and see that the bias facing lies flat and smooth against the garment. In a garment with an opening, the extended ends of the bias facing will be under the hem or facing. Baste through the bias facing and the garment — but not the collar — close to the seam line. Press.

6. Hem the lower edge of the bias facing to the garment. This may be done by hand. Or the hem edge may be stitched and then tacked to the garment.

Attaching a convertible collar

A collar of this type may be worn open or buttoned. It is straight or almost straight and rolls considerably when buttoned. For this rea-son, it is attached differently from a shaped collar. A convertible collar may have its ends continuous with the openings of the garment. Or the collar may be shorter than the openings, thus forming notched lapels. There are different ways of attaching a convertible collar. However, the following method is suitable for medium-weight and light-weight materials. (See the illustrations on page 426.)

1. Place the right side of the under collar against the right side of the garment. Match exactly center backs, notches, and seam edges. Pin and baste the back of the under collar to the back of the neck. Clip the collar at the shoulders. Then pin and baste both thicknesses of the collar to the front neck edges.

2. Finish the inner free edge of front hems or facings by turning under the raw edge and stitching near the fold. *If hems are used,* turn them back on the right side of the garment over the collar. See the illustrations on page 426. Pin and baste. *If facings are used,* match them to the openings, lapels, and collar, right sides together. Pin and baste.

3. On each side, stitch from the edge of the hem or the bottom of the facing to the shoulder seams. Then stitch the basted under collar to the back of the neck.

4. Remove bastings. Trim seams to ¼ inch, and clip corners. Turn hems or facings back to the wrong side. Clip the neckline seams at the shoulder seams. Crease and press the seam, turning the back of the neck seam toward the collar.

5. Turn the raw edge of the outer collar under to meet the machine stitching of the back neckline seam. Hem the collar to the machine stitching.

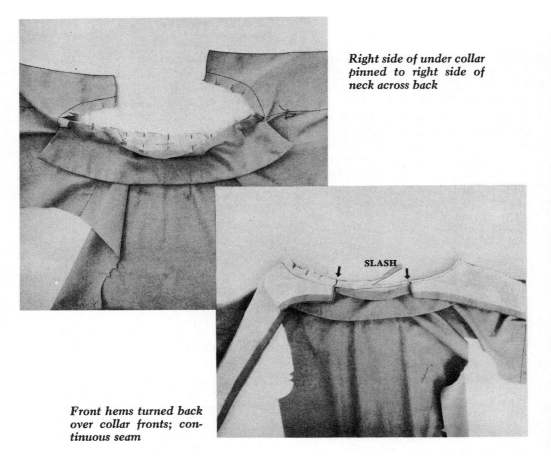

Right side of under collar pinned to right side of neck across back

SLASH

Front hems turned back over collar fronts; continuous seam

Making and applying a detachable collar

A detachable collar is generally used on garments where the collar needs to be laundered more often than the garment itself. Or it may be used when a variety of collars is worn with one garment. This type of collar is easily removable.

1 to 4. Follow steps 1 through 4 for making a double collar.

5. To the neckline of the collar, apply bias binding. Hold the binding a little full, so that it will fit the neck of the garment.

6. Slip the binding inside the neckline. Match center fronts and center backs of garment and collar, and baste the binding to the neckline.

CUFFS

Making cuffs

A cuff, like a collar, is assembled as a unit and then attached to an otherwise finished sleeve. Cuffs with open ends are assembled flat — also like collars. A shaped circular cuff has the under-cuff ends joined, the upper-cuff ends joined, and then the outside edges seamed in a circle.

Both open-end and circular cuffs may be attached to a short sleeve. However, a long sleeve that fits snugly at the wrist requires a placket opening. Sometimes a faced slash opening, such as is used to finish a neckline (see Book 1, page 435), will be satisfactory. Or if the placket falls in a seam line, a simple placket similar to the one used in a gathered skirt (see Book 1, page 437) may be used. Or the slash or seam may be bound with a straight — rather than a bias — binding. The kind used depends upon the type of sleeve and pattern-guide directions.

Attaching shaped cuffs

Shaped cuffs — either circular or open-end — may be attached with a bias facing like a shaped collar. See the illustration. For an open-end cuff on a long fitted sleeve, follow guide-sheet directions for placement of binding over placket openings.

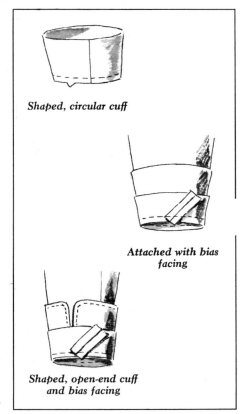

Shaped, circular cuff

Attached with bias facing

Shaped, open-end cuff and bias facing

Attaching a straight open-end band

This type of cuff or band may be used when a close fit at the wrist is desired in a gathered sleeve. Before the ends of the band are seamed and the band turned and pressed, it should have been fitted to the wrist. Put gathering lines in the bottom of the sleeve (see Book 1, page 431).

1. Place the right side of the band to the right side of the sleeve, matching notches and distributing gathers carefully. Match the ends of the band exactly flush with the placket overlap and underlap. Pin, and then baste.

2. Stitch with the gathered side up. Remove basting, and trim seam to ¼ inch. Press, turning seam toward cuff.

3. Turn under the seam allowance of the under band, and pin it to the machine stitching on the wrong side. Hem to the stitching by hand, so that the finish is invisible on the right side.

Straight, open-end band with faced slash opening

Straight, open-end band with bound lapped opening

Making detachable cuffs

Detachable cuffs are used for the same reason as a detachable collar. Usually the addition of a bias binding on the inner edge of the cuff is not needed to attach the cuff to the sleeve. With right sides together the upper and under cuffs are seamed around all their cut edges, except to leave just enough room near the center of the inner edge to turn the cuff. This opening is slip-stitched together after the cuff is turned. The inner edge of the cuff is then basted inside the sleeve, and the cuff is turned up on the right side.

POCKET, *Set-in*

A set-in pocket looks much like a long, piped buttonhole and is made similarly. The pipings are usually wider than those in a buttonhole, since the pocket is longer. The weight of the fabric and the desired effect help to determine the width of the pipings. Directions are given here for pipings approximately ¼ to ⅜ inches wide.

1. Cut a piece of material for the pocket in a rectangle about 10 inches long and the desired width plus 2 inches. Cut on the straight of the material.

2. Check the location and length of the pocket, and mark it with a basting on the right side of the garment. On the wrong side of the pocket piece, mark the location of the pocket opening, also with a basting. Place the marking ¼ inch below the crosswise center of the pocket piece and 1 inch from each side of the piece. See the illustration.

3. Place the right side of the pocket piece to the right side of the garment, matching their marks for the pocket, and aligning grain accurately. Baste the two markings together. Baste a rec-

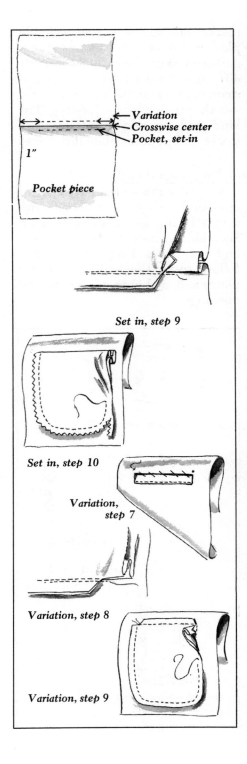

Variation
Crosswise center
Pocket, set-in

1"

Pocket piece

Set in, step 9

Set in, step 10

Variation, step 7

Variation, step 8

Variation, step 9

tangle around the pocket marking of the desired width and exactly the length of the marking.

4 to 8. Follow steps 4 through 8 for making a piped buttonhole, pages 421 to 422.

9. Remove the bastings along each side of the pipings, but not the diagonal basting holding the folded edges together. Press carefully. The bottom piping needs to be reinforced to keep it from pulling out of place when the pocket is in use. But for the best appearance, no stitching should show on the right side of the garment. To prevent this, fold the garment back to expose the narrow seam allowances which extend below the lower piping. Stitch these to the pocket piece beneath them, stitching as nearly as possible on top of the original rectangle stitching. See the illustration.

10. Fold the upper pocket piece down to coincide with the lower part of the pocket. Baste and stitch the edges together, making a curve at the bottom if desired. Press, trim edges, and finish as desired. Pinked or overcast edges are generally satisfactory.

Variation in a set-in pocket

1 to 6. Follow steps 1 through 6 for a set-in pocket. However, this time mark the pocket opening on the pocket piece ¼ inch above the center on the top — rather than on the bottom — part of the pocket piece.

7. Use the lower end of the pocket piece to form one piping or welt the width of the stitched rectangle. See the illustration. Keep the triangles and the seams turned away from the slit. Baste along the bottom of the piping. Use diagonal basting to hold the fold of the piping to the upper edge of the pocket opening. Press carefully. Remove the basting along the bottom of the piping.

8. Reinforce the bottom of the piping on the wrong side. To do this, turn the garment back, and baste and stitch the piping to the pocket piece along the original rectangle stitching. See the illustration.

9. Fold the upper pocket piece down to coincide with the lower part of the pocket. Shape the bottom in a curve if desired. Baste and stitch the edges together, catching the ends of the piping to the triangles at both sides of the pocket. Remove basting, and press. Trim edges, and finish as desired.

SEAMS

Fell seam

The fell seam is a sturdy seam for washable tailored garments. It lies flat and smooth on the outside of the garment, showing two rows of stitching.

1. Baste the wrong sides of the material together on the seam allowance.

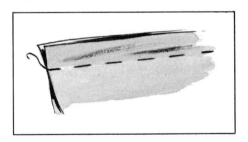

2. Decide what way you want the seam to turn. Stitch on the seam line on the side which will lie on top. Remove bastings. Press the seam open and perfectly flat. Then turn the two edges together, and press with the stitched edge exposed.

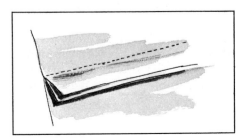

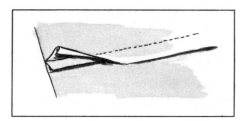

3. Trim the upper edge of the seam, so that it is ⅜ of an inch wide. Trim the under edge to ⅛ of an inch in width.

4. Open out the garment, and lay the seam flat against it with the upper edge on top.

5. Fold the upper edge of the seam to make it ¼ of an inch wide. Baste it in place over the under edge.

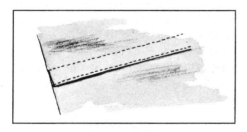

6. Stitch very near the folded edge, keeping the fold to the right as you stitch.

7. Remove bastings, and press.

SLEEVES, *Set-in*

Making the sleeves

Even though the two sleeves of a garment are cut by the same pattern, they must be exact opposites rather than duplicates of each other. An easy way to be sure they are exact opposites is to cut them both at once on a fold of material.

The shoulder seams and the underarm seams of a garment are finished and pressed before the sleeve is begun. The sleeve itself is fairly well assembled before it is set into

the armhole. To make the sleeve proceed as follows.

1. If the sleeves come below the elbow, baste in place any darts or pleats, or put in gathers. These are located on the back of the sleeve near the elbow. Darts or pleats are generally made on the wrong side of the material. Be sure that these are basted on the wrong side of each sleeve.

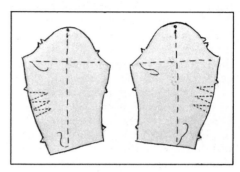

2. Fold the sleeves together as a pair — not alike — with the right sides of the material to the inside of the sleeves. Lay the sleeves on a table, as shown in the illustration. The deepest armhole curve, or the front of the sleeve, should be lying on the top. Baste the underarm seams.

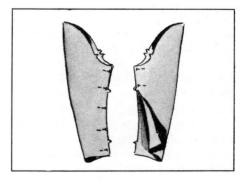

3. Try on the sleeves. Check the following, and alter if necessary.

a. Are the sleeves loose enough to be comfortable but tight enough to look well?

b. If the sleeves come below the elbows, does the fullness come exactly at the elbows?

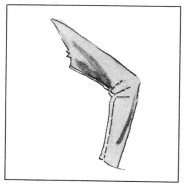

4. Rip the basted underarm seams enough to stitch darts or pleats. Remove bastings, and press. Rebaste, and stitch the underarm seams.

5. Remove bastings, and press open the seams. Finish the edges as desired.

Setting the sleeves into the armhole

The upper edge or cap of a set-in sleeve is cut larger than the armhole. It needs to be larger to fit over the rounded top of the arm. However, in a plain sleeve, no fullness shows.

1. To ease in the fullness and to prevent stretching, put in two rows of stitching for gathers around the sleeve cap — from single notch to double notches. Use a long machine stitch or a running stitch. Put in one row on the seam line, and the other ¼ inch in toward the raw edge of the seam allowance.

2. Decide what sleeve belongs to each armhole. Remember that the deepest curve is on the front of the sleeve.

3. Turn the garment wrong side out. Draw the sleeves turned right side out into each armhole. Hold the inside of

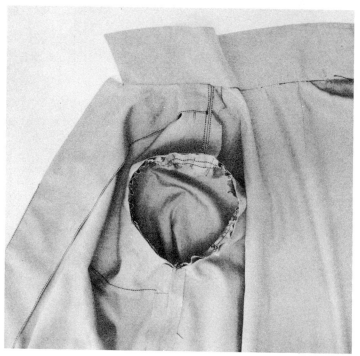

Gathers in sleeve cap; sleeve pinned to armhole

the sleeve so that you can look into it and work on it.

4. Pin the seam of the sleeve to the under-arm seam. Pin the highest point on the sleeve cap to the highest point of the armhole. Match and pin the notches together. Draw up the gathers just enough to ease the fullness into the armhole. Pin at ½-inch intervals. Baste firmly.

5. Try on the garment. Check the fit of both sleeves, and alter if necessary.

a. Do the sleeves hang straight from the tip of the shoulders to the elbows?

b. Do the armholes feel comfortable when the arms are in a natural position? Do the sleeves allow moderate movement of the arms without pulling?

c. Are the sleeves the length desired? Are they even in length?

Finishing the sleeves

1. Stitch the armhole seams with the sleeves next to the presser foot, starting at the underarm. Remove the gathering and basting threads. Press the seam allowance toward the sleeve. Trim and overcast or pink the seams.

2. Finish the bottom of the sleeves with a binding, facing, or cuffs.

6

Enjoying Young Children

Guiding young children at play

*Helping children to enjoy eating foods
that are good for them*

ONE DAY in late winter as the students in Miss Reed's class entered the homemaking room, they were surprised to see a visitor. After the closing bell had rung, Miss Reed introduced Mrs. Clark — a former homemaking teacher — saying that she had a very interesting matter to present to the class. The students settled back in pleasant anticipation of what was to follow.

Mrs. Clark said that she was representing the preschool group of the Parent-Teacher Association. The mothers of this group were anxious to sponsor a play school for their small children. It had been suggested that the students in Miss Reed's class might want to cooperate in making a project of this sort possible. Mrs. Clark went on to say that she understood the students had previously had classwork in child care and were planning to do more. From what Miss Reed had said, she believed that they were well prepared to participate in a play group. In fact, if the students were interested in this idea, they could plan and carry out whatever activities would fit into their regular classwork.

HEARING MORE ABOUT THE PLAY SCHOOL

MRS. CLARK paused to let the students think about her suggestion. Then she continued. "Before you make a decision," she said, "you may want to know something about a play school. I'll do my best to answer any questions you may have."

Several of the students immediately responded. "I'd like to know why the mothers are interested in having a play group," said Dean.

"That's a good question," replied Mrs. Clark, "and one that the mothers themselves have already discussed. I'll give you their conclusions briefly.

• A play school provides companionship for a child in a small group of children of about the same age.

• It offers a child opportunities

1. To share group experiences

2. To experiment with varied play materials and equipment, some of which may not be available at home

3. To enjoy music suited to his development

4. To enjoy books and stories appropriate to his interests

5. To express himself creatively through the use of various materials

6. To promote physical growth and muscular coordination

7. To increase independence by learning to help himself

8. To develop his ability to handle his emotions constructively

9. To increase his liking for others and to understand their needs

• It provides an intermediate step between regular school and home.

"What age children will be in the group?" asked Lucile.

"Children whose age range is between the third and fifth birthday," replied Mrs. Clark. "We realize, of course, that age in terms of years is not an accurate indication of a child's development. Some children at two and a half years may be ahead of others at three and a half. But since we can accommodate only a certain number of children, we have to draw the line somewhere."

"When and where will the play school be held?" asked Juliet.

"It will be held in the morning — from 9:00 to 11:30 — since many of the children take afternoon naps," said Mrs. Clark. "Mr. Chapman, the principal, has given us the use of a room on the first floor in the east wing of the school building. It has its own outside entrance and is near the playground. The school will be in operation twelve weeks."

"Who will be in charge of the play school?" asked Miriam.

"Mrs. Rawlins, who has had considerable experience with preschool children, will be the leader of the group," said Mrs. Clark. "She will be assisted by several of the mothers, and we hope members of your group. Miss Smith, the school nurse, will do the health inspection."

"Where will we get the toys and other things needed? How will the children get to school?" asked Marshall.

"The Parent-Teacher Association has set aside funds for whatever equipment and materials are needed," replied Mrs. Clark. "The school will furnish basic equipment, such as chairs and tables. Mrs. Rawlins will decide what children will attend, and the parents of the children will handle the problem of transportation."

At this point, Miss Reed spoke up. "In your previous classwork you learned about young children through baby-sitting experiences. This was a more helpful approach than just reading and discussing the subject. A play school offers an added opportunity to study children firsthand and to observe their personality development. Some classes organize and conduct their own play schools. Some play schools or nursery schools include lunch and naps. But no matter what the program, a play school offers realistic examples of material that is presented through read-

Participation in a p school helps in und standing and enjoy young children.

ing and discussion in your classwork. As you participate in storytelling, musical enjoyment, and play activities, you improve your ability to understand and enjoy young children."

There was a pause. Everyone seemed to be thinking deeply about the possibility of such a project. Finally Dwight spoke up. "I, for one, think we should cooperate with the Parent-Teacher Association in the play school. It will be a very practical way of getting firsthand experience for our classwork on child care. What about taking a vote on the matter right now? All those who are interested can raise their hands."

The students responded enthusiastically. Both Miss Reed and Mrs. Clark smiled as hands were raised throughout the room. Mrs. Clark then expressed her appreciation and said that after the students had made plans for their classwork, they could meet with Mrs. Rawlins and work out further details.

SETTING UP GOALS

A SHORT time later, the students completed the classwork which they were carrying out when Mrs. Clark brought up the subject of a play school. Now they were ready and eager to discuss and plan goals on child care. Many of the students had already consulted available reference materials and were prepared for active participation in the class discussion.

When the discussion opened, Miss Reed suggested that it might be a good idea to review briefly what they had learned previously about caring for young children. This would give them a background for determining what they would like to study this year.

The review indicated that they had learned a considerable amount about handling preschool children. Problems that might be expected to occur during baby-sitting hours had been discussed. Suggestions for dealing with various kinds of behavior resulting from these problems had been offered by experienced people in the field of child care. Reports of actual baby-sitting experiences had been given. (See Book 1, pages 446–486.) The classwork this year for the play school would be a continuation of what had been learned about children of from three to five years of age. But it would deal with children in a play-school group instead of in a home environment where the care of one child was the usual situation.

It did not take long for the students to decide that their first goal would be *guiding young children at play*. This would include learning to help the children make the most of the opportunities which Mrs. Clark had mentioned in her talk to the students. (See page 435.)

"But what about food for children?" asked Sylvia. "Sometimes getting them to eat food that makes them strong and healthy is a problem. I know it is in my home."

"Yes, that's important," said Miss Reed. "However, the play school will not be serving any food except midmorning fruit juice. But of course we could divide up the available time. Part of it could be spent with the play school and the rest on other aspects of child care."

This suggestion appealed to the students, and they set up a second goal — *helping children to enjoy eating foods that are good for them.*

Miss Reed then said that the two goals which the class had set up would be very helpful, and that they could probably be carried out in the time available. The students would devote as much classtime as possible to the play school. However, the play-school mothers would be on hand to assist Mrs. Rawlins when it came time for the students to take up the goal on food for children.

"What shall we call our classwork?" asked Stanley, who had been busy with paper and pencil. "I noticed that Miss Reed used the word 'enjoy' when she was telling us how a play school might help us. We could call the two goals 'Enjoying Young Children.' That would take in the play school as well as what else we do."

"Fine." "Right to the point," and other responses of approval were heard throughout the room.

ASSISTING WITH PRELIMINARY ARRANGEMENTS FOR THE PLAY SCHOOL

Now that plans for the classwork had been made, the next step was to meet with Mrs. Rawlins to find out what preliminary arrangements needed to be made for the play school. A committee was appointed to begin getting this information over the week end that was coming up.

When the class met again, Dwight, acting as chairman of the committee, said that preliminary planning for a play school is very important. The success of such a project depends largely upon three things: (1) having adequate space and facilities, (2) selecting and assembling suitable equipment and materials, and (3) setting up a workable program. He then said that members of the committee would give an over-all picture of some of the arrangements that were being made.

Determining Space Needed

Lucile, the first one to report, announced that she would comment on having adequate space and facilities. The group working out plans for this aspect of the play school had decided that an adequate setup needed to meet the following conditions.

1. *Sufficient space for the activities to be carried on.* This means enough room to use some equipment on wheels, such as a wagon, a small tricycle, and a doll carriage. These can be left at one end of the room when not in use. Space is also needed for blockbuilding, for playing house, for using sand, and for carpentry. Low tables where children can use creative materials, such as crayons or scissors and paper, easels for painting, and a record player, will also take up room.

2. *Storage space for toys and materials.* Low shelves where play materials are easily available and can be put away by the children themselves are necessary.

3. *Storage space for outdoor wraps.* A place for low hooks where children can hang their coats and sweaters is also needed.

4. *A place to wash hands and to get a drink of water.* It is considered more satisfactory when these facilities are within the room itself and are so arranged that the children can use them without assistance.

5. *Accessible toilet facilities.* These also need to be low enough for independent use. A wooden step can be added if they are too high.

6. *Safe floor conditions.* Floor surfaces need to be well finished, easily cleaned, nonslippery, and free from splinters and dampness.

7. *Pleasing decorations for the room.* Attractive, cheerful colors and designs

Sufficient space for activities includes room for easels and painting.

are suitable in a room where children are to play.

Lucile added that on the basis of these considerations the room for the play school could accommodate about twenty children. Arrangements were already underway for building storage shelves and taking care of other facilities.

Selecting Suitable Equipment and Materials

Dean was the next speaker. He said that Mrs. Rawlins had brought out the point that equipment and materials are the means used to encourage mental, physical, social, and emotional development. But how the children use them in a group situation is the important point. She had then suggested that the students make a list of the equipment and materials for indoor activities at the play school. A survey of available playground equipment could also be made and additional items suggested if advisable.

The students responded enthusiastically to this suggestion. They immediately began to discuss sources of information that would be helpful. It was finally decided that some of the students would use the material on the reference shelves, while others consulted the school and public libraries. A small group was to interview the director of a local nursery school for working mothers.

Characteristics desirable

When it came time for a class discussion, everyone was prepared to offer suggestions on all kinds of equipment. It soon became evident that there were unlimited possibilities. This made it seem advisable to outline certain characteristics which would guide them in setting up their list. Even though these characteristics were similar to those given last year for selecting play equipment (see Book 1, pages 459–460), there were certain differences. For instance, with so many children using the equipment, durability and ease of care were even more important. The characteristics selected for play-school equipment and materials follow:

- *Give personal satisfaction* by offering acceptable ways in which children can express their thoughts and feelings
- *Have educational value* by encouraging all phases of development — mental, physical, emotional, and social
- *Are safe* — no sharp edges; will not splinter

- *Are flexible in use* — in a variety of ways and for different abilities
- *Are adequate for the size of the children using them* — not too heavy to manage, not too small to cause cramped positions, and not too difficult to use successfully
- *Are well constructed and durable* — will not crack or break, will not fall apart
- *Can be repaired and cleaned easily*
- *Require little, if any, adult supervision*
- *Offer additional interests to what most children have at home*

Suggested indoor items and their value to children

While setting up the list of indoor equipment and materials, the students indicated how the various items might contribute toward the children's development. Of course some of the items, such as the wagon or tricycle and the sandbox materials, could serve both indoor and outdoor play needs. But since they would be used indoors some of the time, the students decided to include them in the list. The chart on page 442 shows how the students assembled the material for Mrs. Rawlins and for their own use.

Appraising the school playground equipment

In accordance with Mrs. Rawlins' suggestion, the students studied the playground equipment. There was a swing, a slide, a teeter-totter, horizontal bars, and a sandbox. All of this equipment would be available to the play school except during the recess periods of the kindergarten and grade school children.

After some discussion, the students decided that the playground equipment and the items that could be used either indoors or outdoors might well be supplemented. Soft rubber balls or beanbags, a jumping rope, and perhaps another wagon or a small-size wheelbarrow were suggestions made. However, these smaller items could be added as the play school progressed, and as Mrs. Rawlins believed they were needed.

Assembling the Equipment and Materials

The suggestions for equipment and materials which the class had made proved to be very satisfactory to Mrs. Rawlins. She complimented the students on the way they had presented the material, saying that the selections for both active and quiet play were well represented.

Arrangements were then made for a committee of students and parents to assemble the various items and to determine how many of each type were necessary. Mrs. Rawlins cautioned the group against providing more than are desirable. She stressed the point that effective learning in a play school needs to be largely in favor of group situations. Having too many articles of any one type encourages individual rather than group play. It also hinders learning to share things with other children.

These students are checking, repairing if needed, and putting away equipment at the close of a play school.

INDOOR PLAY-SCHOOL EQUIPMENT

AND MATERIALS FOR THREE-TO FIVE-YEAR-OLDS

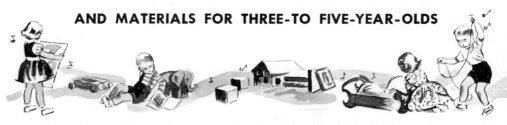

TYPE	DEVELOPMENTAL VALUE
Wagon, tricycle, kiddie kar, preferably with rubber tires	Develops motor skills — the ability to coordinate the movements of arms and legs and to maintain body balance
Blocks of various shapes and sizes	Develops an awareness of size, shape, weight, and proportion; teaches balance and organization of materials; encourages group participation
Workbench with a small vise; broadheaded hammer; short, wide saw; assortment of nails with large flat heads; scraps of wood soft enough to saw easily	Develops arm muscles and eye accuracy; provides an outlet for pent-up feelings
Toys, such as trucks, automobiles, trains, airplanes, and standup human figures and animals	Stimulates imaginative play especially when used with blockbuilding and sand play
Dolls with clothing, bed, carriage, and other accessories; equipment, such as a telephone, cooking utensils, dishes, table, and the like, for housekeeping	Leads to an enjoyment of homemaking activities; encourages group participation; stimulates role playing
Sandbox with spoons, pans, strainers, and the like for pouring, molding, and digging	Handling sand gives a feeling satisfaction; stimulates dramatic and social play
Clay, crayons, paints, and easels	Develops creative and imaginative skills; provides an emotional outlet for getting rid of hostile feelings
Jigsaw puzzles, books	Stimulates mental activity
Record player, records	Develops musical enjoyment
Drum, gong, triangle, rattles, blocks to clap together	Satisfies desire for rhythmic experience; develops a knowledge of pitch and tone qualities

The actual number of the different items assembled for the twenty children is not given. Play schools often differ in the amount and kind of equipment they use. The number of items vary according to the emphasis to be placed on certain kinds of activity. For example, one play school stressing blockbuilding may decide that elaborate commercial sets of blocks are desirable. Another may want a wide range of creative experiences. Mrs. Rawlins planned to provide a variety of activities without stressing any particular one.

The matter of expense was also taken into consideration in assembling the supplies. Although the Parent-Teacher Association was willing to finance the project, it was believed there were various ways of keeping expenditures down. And yet adequate equipment and materials would be available. This is how the matter was worked out.

Here a child is allowed to blockbuild to the limit of his ability.

What the parents did

Two of the fathers made the sandbox and the workbench, using scrap lumber. They were able to borrow a small vise and other equipment for the children's workbench. Several other fathers cut and assembled the blocks, making them in different sizes and shapes. The materials were obtained from a lumberyard. Many of the pieces of lumber were taken from a scrap pile, which decreased the over-all cost. All of the blocks were sanded down to a smooth finish.

One group of mothers was responsible for getting the toys, such as trucks, trains, airplanes, and the larger items with rubber wheels. Another group assembled the equipment for playing house and using sand. In both cases, some of the articles were donated or loaned for the duration of the play school.

One of the mothers also secured the loan of a record player and various records. The records included marches and rhythmic music; some classical selections written for children by Brahms, Schumann, and Tchaikovsky; and several folk songs. Others would be added from time to time if it seemed desirable.

What the students did

The homemaking students contributed in various ways. Several made a supply of chef's aprons to be worn by the children when they were using paints or clay. A pattern similar to the one they had in their classwork the previous year was used. (See Book 1, pages 372–373.)

Some of the students made several simple jigsaw puzzles. This was done by pasting interesting pictures on plywood, and then cutting the plywood into different shapes and sizes. The school shop jig saw was used for the cutting. Some puzzles were cut into six pieces, others into eight or ten.

Another group of students made arrangements with the library for the books to be used by the children. The selection of the books was based on the following characteristics previously decided on by the class.

1. The stories need to include a wide variety of realistic subjects:
a. Familiar activities of the family and community
b. Action, such as boys and girls at work or at play; animal experiences of all kinds; boats, engines, and cars on the go
c. True situations that show sympathy and understanding of how people feel
2. There needs to be humor or rhythm and repetition in some of the stories.
3. The stories need to be simply and clearly written, and well illustrated.

Setting Up a Workable Program

The third point which Dwight had mentioned in connection with preliminary arrangements was setting up a workable program. Audrey gave the first half of the report. She prefaced her remarks by saying that the key to a workable program for a play school is to have it meet the needs of those who are participating. Then she went on to explain how this could be done.

Scheduling the day's activities

It is important to have a basic plan for the various activities connected with the play school. When certain routines, such as health inspection, toileting, rest, juice serving, and cleaning up, come at about the same time each day, the children acquire a feeling of regularity. There can still be uninterrupted time for self-chosen activities. And opportunities for listening to stories, for music enjoyment, and for creative experiences can be introduced into the schedule as desired.

Audrey then referred the class to the blackboard where a schedule had been set up.

9:00– 9:15   Arrival, removal of wraps, and health inspection

9:15– 9:45   Self-chosen activities with physically active play to be encouraged. Activities may be indoors or outdoors, depending upon the weather and each child's interest at the time.

9:45–10:00   Toileting and wash-up time

10:00–10:20   Juice and rest, with relaxing music on records

10:20–11:15   Earlier activities may be continued and new ones introduced, such as storytelling, rhythm experiences, and the use of creative materials. Toward the end of the morning, quiet activities need to be encouraged.

11:15–11:30 Cleanup time, putting on wraps, and departure

Audrey went on to say that a schedule for small children cannot operate strictly by the clock. It must be flexible enough to allow extra time for unexpected conditions. A rainy morning may mean additional wraps, which will require more time for taking off and putting on. There may be a day when most of the children want only active play, changing from one vigorous activity to another. On such a day they will have little or no interest in listening to stories or looking at picture books. It might then be advisable, weather permitting, to include more outdoor than indoor play. Children also show peaks of interest, carrying on one type of activity for several days. It may be a burst of interest in painting, in working with clay, or in playing house. As long as the phase lasts, there may not be much interest in other activities. Those who are guiding the children will need to be ready to cooperate with them in every way to make the learning experiences as worth while as possible.

Taking and using written records

Leo then continued the report by commenting on the subject of written records, which he said are con-

This boy is checking the attendance record at a play school.

sidered a necessary part of program planning. However, he brought out the point that only records which will help in understanding the children were to be kept. Two types had been agreed on.

IDENTIFYING INFORMATION: This kind of record is obtained from the home before the child enters the play school. It includes general information, such as name, address, date of birth, number of children and adults in the family, and whom to call in case of emergency. The record also gives some personal information about special habits and outstanding personality traits of the child. Leo added that the students will be expected to become familiar to some extent with these records. They need to be able to find quickly and easily whom to call in case of an emergency. And the information on a child's habits or outstanding personality traits might prove helpful in understanding any unusual behavior he might display.

THE DEVELOPMENTAL RECORDS: These are records of each child kept by the personnel of the play school. They may include such information as the child's attitude toward other children, his play interests, his ability to do things for himself, and any unusual behavior. In fact, a record of this kind will generally reveal behavior patterns over a period of time. This will be of great value in deciding whether desirable development has been made, and if not, what special guidance may need to be given. Leo said that later on the students could decide what their contribution would be toward these records.

CARRYING OUT THE GOAL — GUIDING YOUNG CHILDREN AT PLAY

THE preliminary arrangements for the play school seemed to be getting well under way. Some of the students were helping to assemble equipment and materials and to set up the room. Others were assisting Mrs. Rawlins in getting the identifying records ready. With the opening of the play school close at hand, the students now decided to make plans for the procedures they would study and carry out in learning to guide young children at play.

Organizing Student Activities

After studying the daily schedule, the students believed that it would meet their needs very well. The regular homemaking period coincided with the latter part of the schedule. During this time, the mothers who were acting as Mrs. Rawlins' assistants had agreed to turn over the guidance to the students. This would make the room less crowded than if both groups were participating at the same time.

The class also decided to spend only the first four days of the week in the play school. The fifth day would be set aside for discussing experiences and learning more about handling children.

Of course everyone realized that it would not be possible for the whole class to participate actively in guiding the children every day. Having too many people around not only confuses children, but tends to inhibit free play. Under the circumstances, it seemed best to set up three group activities for the first four days of the week. One group of about five students would be actively engaged in guiding the children. The same number of students would act as observers, watching what is going on in the play school. The remaining students would be at work in the classroom preparing for their turns with the children. These group activities were to be rotated regularly from time to time so that everyone in the class would get experience in all three.

Some of the students said they would like to put more time in the play school than the regular class period. They thought this could be done by obtaining permission to be excused from the study hall. Miss Reed gave her approval to this plan with the understanding that the students inform Mrs. Rawlins when they expected to be in the play school.

Looking in at the Students as They Prepare for Participation

Now that the group activities were organized, everyone was eager to get started on the class-work that involved the children. But here again, it seemed necessary to make further plans. The question now was: what information is needed to help the students guide the children? Let's look in on the students as they discuss the questions and see what they decide.

Several members of the class have offered suggestions. Now Miss Reed is talking. She points out that the play school offers many learning situations for the children. For example, in the coatroom children develop self-confidence by learning to take off and put on their wraps. During the rest period, they learn to relax. From the equipment and materials they use, they learn to share, to take turns, and to respect the rights and feelings of other persons. The role of the students is to help the children make the most of these and other learning situations.

Miss Reed's remarks give the students a lead as to the approach they can take. They realize that in the few weeks of play-school experience it will not be possible to learn all they would like to know about guiding children at play. Therefore, they decide to assemble information on certain learning situations. These situations can be based on the daily routine activities and those that will be self-chosen by the children, resulting from equipment and materials in the play school. The students will increase their knowledge of several techniques needed for making the learning situations more effective. Lined up on the blackboard, the subjects to be studied are as follows:

Special Techniques
Having a satisfactory appearance and attitude
Giving directions and suggestions to produce the desired results
Preventing conflicts
Handling undesirable behavior

Routine Activities
Removing and putting on wraps
Health inspection
Toileting
Resting
Serving juice
Putting away equipment and materials

Self-chosen Activities
Using a tricycle and wagon
Blockbuilding
Carpentry
Playing house
Music enjoyment
Listening to stories
Painting and drawing
Using clay

Now you can see that the students are beginning to consult ma-

A child learns inde-pendence by hanging up his own wraps.

terials on the reference shelf. The members of the two activity groups who will be the first to take turns in guiding and observing the children are especially busy. They need immediate preparation in order to help with quiet activities, cleanup time, putting on wraps, and departure. Then actual participation in the play school can begin. In the meantime, the third activity group will study the whole schedule more thoroughly. Soon there will be guiding, observing, and studying going on four days of the week, with evaluation on the fifth day.

Seeing the Play School in Action

The days in which there was active participation in the play school proved to be very stimulating and at times quite challenging to the students. It meant being on the alert from the time they entered the room until they left. There wasn't a dull moment, for the children never seemed to react the same way two days in succession. Something new or different was always coming up to keep the students on their toes and, as Dean often said, one jump ahead of the children. Let's drop in on one of the daily sessions after the students have had some experience, and see what's going on.

The students are set for participation

As you watch the students go into action, you can see that they are following certain techniques to make the learning situations for the children as effective as possible.

IN APPEARANCE: The students wear sturdy, washable clothing that permits freedom of movement. Their shoes are comfortable. The girls wear low or medium heels, since higher heels are noisy and make the wearer less steady on her feet.

IN ATTITUDE: The students are cheerful, friendly, and able to call each child by name. There is no babying, or undue display of attention or affection. Instead they try to cultivate a combination of personal interest and a detached attitude. They avoid showing annoyance, disapproval, or favoritism, since children are sensitive to such attitudes.

IN SPEECH: The voices of the students are kept pleasant and well modulated with a natural pitch and range. It is sometimes necessary to speak firmly, but it is never necessary to raise one's voice. Talking slowly is more effective than raising the pitch of the voice. The students do not call or shout across the play area indoors or out, but move nearer the person to whom they are speaking.

IN ACTION: Everyone is alert at all times to the health and safety of the children. This means watching out for hazards that are present when a group of children play together. If loud or excited voices come from an area, the students move quietly near the group.

The children arrive and remove their wraps

Shortly before nine o'clock there is much laughter and talking in the east wing of the school building. As the children arrive, they head toward the coatroom and remove their own wraps. When the play school started, many of them needed assistance. But now they have learned to unbutton or zip down their outside wraps and to hang them on the hooks within easy reach.

What the children wear is very important, because clothes help or hinder play. You will notice that all of them are wearing comfortable, washable outfits in which they can play freely. Suitable clothes are not damaged by dirt, can stand considerable laundering, and are not difficult to iron. They are also as easy for the children to manage as possible. Each child is dressed differently but sufficiently like the others so that he does not feel conspicuous.

Then comes health inspection

For each child the morning starts with health inspection by the school nurse before he is permitted to play with the other children. While the transportation facilities stand by, the child's throat, his nose, and the condition of his skin are checked. If there is a runny nose, an inflamed throat, or other symptoms of illness, the child will return home. This is to protect the others against possible infection, since young children are especially susceptible to communicable disease. After each inspection a drink of water is suggested. Children need plenty of liquids but are often unaware of the meaning of thirst. During the morning session, each attendant is expected to be on the alert to catch any sign that a child is becoming overtired or not feeling up to par. Steps are then to be taken to give him the care he needs.

Now the children select their own playthings

You will notice that the room is set up so that interesting play is suggested. There is ample space for vigorous activity with a wagon, a tricycle, or a doll carriage. On one side of the room are the blocks, and not far away there are toys, such as trucks, automobiles, and trains. The workbench is provided with a hammer, some boards, a saw, and some nails. The sandbox has all sorts of interesting equipment for pouring and digging sand. Over there in one corner of the room is the area for house play with dolls, cooking utensils, dishes, and the like. There are also low chairs and tables containing picture books and jigsaw puzzles, as well as easels for painting and drawing. Supplies are on nearby shelves. Each child chooses the equipment and materials he wishes to use.

These youngsters choose the sandbox and a doll carriage.

Physically active play with a tricycle and a wagon

Marshall, one of several students excused from study hall, is watching some boys using a tricycle and a wagon, which are popular activities early in the morning. Only a limited amount of this equipment is supplied, so that the children can learn to share with others. But here is where guidance is often needed. Three learning situations soon appear, and this is how Marshall handles them.

SITUATION 1: *Learning about possessions* — Dick is riding the tricycle, which is his favorite activity. However, after a while he decides that he wants to build blocks. He parks the tricycle nearby and starts to collect some blocks. Pres-

ently Jim comes up and indicates that he wants to ride the tricycle. "You can't," says Dick, grabbing it quickly and pushing Jim away. "It's mine."

Marshall then explains to Dick that the tricycle is for all the children. But it belongs for the time being to the person who is riding it. Since Dick doesn't want to use the tricycle any longer, he cannot claim it as his. Dick accepts this explanation but relinquishes his hold on the handlebars reluctantly. It is important for him to learn that the other children have an equal right to use the equipment in the play school.

SITUATION 2: *Learning to take turns —* Tommy is sitting in the wagon pushing it around in a wide circle with his left foot. Lester is watching him, anxious to do the same thing. But Tommy does not show any signs of giving up the wagon.

After a while, Marshall tells Tommy that it is time for Lester to have his turn. However, he makes it clear to both boys that Tommy can expect to get the wagon back again later on if he so desires. Marshall says, "Tommy, after you ride around the circle once, Lester can have a turn." Or he might have said, "Tommy, first you ride around the circle and then Lester." Either of these suggestions is better than, "Tommy, you must take turns with Lester."

SITUATION 3: *Learning to share —* While Lester is riding around the circle, George comes up and puts his foot in front of the wagon causing it to stop suddenly. Lester hits George, and then George hits Lester. Marshall moves quietly into the scene and says in a calm voice, "Lester, I guess George wants to use the wagon too." George

nods, and arrangements are made for him to join the group. Now Tommy, Lester, and George are sharing the wagon without any argument. Had Marshall reproved George for interfering with Lester and tried to direct George's attention elsewhere, friendly play between Lester and George might not have developed. The situation showed that Marshall understood the motive underlying George's behavior. He then made it possible for George to meet the need expressed in the undesirable behavior.

At the carpenter's bench

Another activity that interests children in the early part of the morning is carpentry. Over there in the corner of the room, Stanley is supervising two of the older boys at the workbench. For safety reasons, it is important for Stanley to keep a close watch on what the boys are doing. Two children are all that he can manage at one time. One boy has a hammer, some nails, and several pieces of soft scrap lumber. Stanley has shown him how to hold the hammer and how to start the nails. The other boy is sawing a piece of wood. Stanley showed him how to make a straight line with a ruler and a pencil to guide the sawing, and then how to put the wood tightly in the vise. He also demonstrated how to hold the saw properly, so that the teeth will cut on the forward motion and slip back into place on the backward motion.

Stanley also knows that the two boys he is supervising work well together. This is important for safety reasons. The boys understand that they are to remain at the bench and not carry the tools around the room. They seem very happy and are using up a lot of energy in a worth-while experience.

Increasing musical enjoyment

Sylvia is over in one corner of the room with a small group of children who are anxious to listen to some music. At the moment she is asking them what records they would like to hear. They may indicate their preferences by some characteristic of a record which has impressed them, such as "the one that laughs" or "the one with the birds singing." But before Sylvia plays a record, she will mention the title of the selection. In this way, the children learn to associate the name with the music. You will notice that there is

Singing is a form of self-expression— rather than a skill—at this time.

no compulsion about listening. The children feel free to leave or to join the group at any time.

Singing has long been one of the pleasant things in Sylvia's life. In the play school she has tried to share this enjoyment with others by humming and singing spontaneously as she participates in various activities. She knows a number of songs that have repetition or rhythm that the children can imitate. In fact, when the atmosphere in the play school is relaxed and the children are happy, you can hear them singing or humming the tunes as they play.

Sometimes short singing periods are planned. Children occasionally enjoy the group experience of singing together. However, there is no attempt to stress perfection in words or voice control. The children are made to feel that singing is fun whether they can carry a tune or not. Sylvia knows that it is a form of self-expression rather than a skill at the present time.

The children also find enjoyment in walking, running, skipping, and dancing. They are encouraged to set their own tempo and rhythm as they move about. Sylvia will try to fit the music to whatever a child is trying to express, such as playing or singing a lively selection when he is running or skipping. But she will not say that a particular record or song is running or skipping music. In fact, she will not tell a child what responses to make to the music. She knows that any attempt

Building a garage for the trucks is a popular form of group play.

to show a child how to keep time or how to establish a certain rhythm, interferes with self-expression.

Playing in the band is also another musical experience that many of the children enjoy. Using drums, bells, triangles, gongs, and blocks or piepans to clap together is a desirable way of drawing off surplus energy as well as a worth-while group experience.

All of these musical activities do not just simply happen. Sylvia has spent considerable time in learning how to encourage creative expression in music. But because she has some musical background, a pleasant singing voice, and a real love for music, she has been able to develop skill in helping the children increase their enjoyment in music.

Play with blocks

You can see by the activity going on over there where the blocks are that a number of children are engaged in a popular group experience. But play with blocks often requires guidance, which is why Dean is on hand. When the play school first started, the younger children began piling up some blocks and then knocking down their own or another child's construction. Often the blocks were sent flying in all directions. However, they soon learned that blocks are for building, not throwing, and that many interesting things can be done with them. Dean has never shown them *what* to build. But he may need to point out *where* to build.

It may also be necessary for Dean to offer suggestions for safety. Right now he is showing three-year-old Teddy how to move the larger blocks without trying to lift them. He demonstrates by getting down on the floor beside Teddy instead of stooping over from a standing position. This tends to make Teddy feel freer to ask questions.

More about group play

Dean is also watching several children who still have difficulty getting along in a group. Gordon has a tendency to monopolize the trucks, and not to share them with others who may also want them. Frank, a timid child, has not been able to stand up for his own rights. He has let other children take things away from him without protest. When this has occurred, his reaction generally has been a hurt, unhappy expression with no further efforts at play for the time being. Recently Billy, a more aggressive boy, has taken Frank under his wing, calling him his new friend. This morning they are building a garage together, and Dean is quite sure that no child is going to take anything away from Frank without Frank's permission. Dean believes that this friendship will give Frank the confidence and assurance that comes from having a special friend.

Avoiding trouble at the sandbox

Although he is watching the block play, Dean is also alert to what is going on at the sandbox, which is nearby. Suddenly he notices that Irma is about to toss a spoonful of sand in Billy's direction at the garage. Quietly Dean moves between the children building blocks and those at the sandbox to prevent one group from interfering with the other. As he watches Irma, he decides that she is tired of playing with the sand, and does not know what to do with herself. In order to forestall trouble, he makes arrangements with Billy and Frank for Irma to help them build the garage. He then suggests to Irma that she might enjoy helping the two boys. The plan works, and everyone seems happy.

The midmorning break

It is midmorning, and the children know from previous experience that about this time they stop their play. They attend to toileting and wash-up needs, and get ready for drinking juice. But since many of them are so engrossed in what they are doing, Ethel will need to remind them. She approaches a group holding a tea party and singles out Betty who is likely to accept the suggestion. Ethel knows that some children respond more readily than others. Success with one child will generally increase the chance of success with others, since children tend to follow the example of other children.

Before Ethel says anything, she gets Betty's attention. She faces her and speaks directly to her saying, "Betty, it's toilet time. You can

A child enjoys physically active play. Through it he learns to coordinate the movements of arms and legs and maintain body balance.

On the next page some children are enjoying a game of musical chairs. Besides the fun of the game, music experience and physical activity are provided.

Instead of having midmorning fruit juice, this child seems to be anticipating with pleasure an easily digested between-meal snack of well-ripened, peeled apple.

The parents in the family shown on the next page apparently are succeeding in helping their children to enjoy eating foods that are good for them and in making mealtime a happy time. (See pages 474–489.)

leave the tea table just as it is and come back later on." You will notice that Ethel does not repeat the suggestion, because she realizes that it is important for a child to learn to respond to one direction given only once. However, if a single suggestion is not enough, it can be reinforced by offering a different suggestion that will help to carry out the first one. Ethel could also say, "Before you go, you might like to spread a cloth over the dishes."

As Betty leaves the table, the other children in the group follow her. Ethel does everything she can to make the children relaxed and comfortable. She comments about an interesting incident that happened that morning. There is no attempt to hurry any of the children. Most of them are suitably dressed, so that they can be independent about their clothing. If a child has an accident at any time or splashes water on the floor or on his clothes, the incident is passed over as lightly as possible. The wet spot is wiped up immediately, and dry clothing is provided.

A set schedule for toileting does not always meet individual needs, although most of these needs are likely to follow a similar pattern once a routine is developed. However, a period set aside for the purpose prior to juice serving is a logical time for interruption and may insure a more comfortable rest period. Then too the children are learning that hand-washing after toileting and before eating is necessary. Ethel sees that each child wipes his hands on a fresh paper towel and then deposits it in the waste container.

Serving juice and resting

Juice time is usually a pleasant occasion. Several pitchers of juice and a supply of paper cups are placed on one of the low tables. Many children enjoy pouring their own juice, although at first some of it may be spilled. Then another learning situation is presented. No child is criticized for spilling anything. But Ethel may demonstrate that by being careful and not pouring too quickly, better control of the hands and arms can be developed. Ethel also provides toweling for the children to wipe up what they spill.

The children may drink the juice sitting down at the table or standing nearby. No child is urged to take the juice if he does not wish to. But most of the children do after they see that others enjoy it.

Now that the juice has been served, it is time for a short rest period. Ethel knows that helping children to relax is not as easy as it sounds. Some people seem to have more skill in this technique than others. Each child has a blanket of his own which he spreads on the floor to lie on. Ethel's voice is low and quiet as she shows several children who have been very active how to straighten out their arms and legs. She smiles, giving a reassuring pat here and there. Soft, relaxing music is played on the record player, and the children are encouraged not to talk to one another. Everyone is learning to understand that this is a quiet time for the whole room.

Listening to stories

Now that the rest period is over, the children have become active again. Marie and Frances are asking Beatrice to read them a story. In fact they have selected one they are particularly fond of hearing. As Beatrice and the children sit down, several others join them.

You can see that the first thing Beatrice does is to show the group how to open the book — with the cover flat, never bent back. She holds the book so that the children can see the pictures, sometimes passing it around for them to get an even better look. When it's time to turn a page, she does so very carefully and slowly, making sure that everyone in the group is ready to go on.

Beatrice reads distinctly in a pleasant, soft voice, and slowly enough for the children to get the meaning. Occasionally her voice takes on a dramatic quality, but she avoids making any incident in the story overdramatic. The children listen intently, now and then asking a question. Beatrice has learned that too many interruptions cause a loss of interest. Therefore she will try to avoid any discussion until the end of the story.

No child is forced to remain in the group if he desires to leave and to take up another activity. The reading period is never long, and when it is finished, Beatrice will see that the children return the books to the shelf or table where they belong. She has long since made the children understand that books are not put on the floor.

Skill in reading stories gives pleasure to the reader as well as to the children.

Through the classwork, Beatrice has learned that there are four ways in which children enjoy books.

1. To have an adult read word for word while they look at the pictures

2. To look at the pictures while an adult tells the stories

3. To discuss with an adult the pictures and information given in the books

4. To look at the pictures or "read" by themselves

In the play school there are low tables and chairs where the children can sit and look at the books. Nearby are low shelves, but every morning several books are placed on a table to encourage the children's interest.

Drawing and painting

Over there near the windows Walter is watching several children who are drawing and painting. Two three-year-olds have spread large sheets of wrapping paper—eighteen inches by twenty-four inches — on the floor and are using crayons. Some of the older children are painting with finger paints or water colors at the easels. Their clothes are protected with aprons, and the floor with newspapers spread generously around.

The paints were mixed in advance by Walter who used the following recipes.

FINGER PAINT
1¾ cups laundry starch
1 cup cold water
6 cups boiling water
1 cup soap flakes
vegetable colors

Blend the starch with the cold water.
Add the boiling water, and bring to a boil.
Remove from heat. Add soap flakes, and beat to blend.
Separate into several portions, and color as desired.
Place in jars wide enough at the mouth for easy use.

WATER COLORS
½ cup warm water
3 tablespoons colored powdered paint
Mix in quantity desired.
Place in jars heavy enough not to tip, and tall enough for a long-handled brush.

The jars containing the finger paint and the water colors, and a jar of rinse water were placed on the easel troughs, along with brushes and soft cloths. When a child first starts using water colors, he is shown how to hold the brush, so that he can work easily. He is also shown how to wash the brush before using a different color. After that, only a quiet interest is shown in a painting activity. Walter stands by ready to listen to a child who may want to talk about his painting. But he will not question the child or expect him to talk. He will supply a child with fresh paper, and will help him wipe up any paint that is spilled. He will also see about hand-washing at the end of the painting activity.

When a painting is finished, Walter will write the child's name and the date in one corner. He will also record any spontaneous comment about the painting as nearly word for word as possible. Then he will hang the sheet up to dry. Later

When the weather permits, painting and using clay out of doors are fun.

the paintings will go into a portfolio where they will be kept until the end of the play school. This will give the students and parents some indication of whether progress has been made.

Using clay

Not too far away from the easels, Wendy is watching several children who are using clay. Their clothes are also protected by aprons, and the table is covered with a piece of linoleum.

Wendy knows from past experience that there are certain stages of development in working with clay. At first a child pounds, pats, squeezes, or rolls it. As he does this he may see a chance resemblance to something, and then he names it. After a child has used clay several times, he decides in advance what he is going to make.

Although Wendy sits at the table with the children, she does not give any suggestions on what to make. If a child asks her to make something, Wendy will suggest that he show her how to make it. She will avoid asking a child what he is making, but will wait for him to tell her.

There are other things that Wendy also knows are important.

1. It is up to her to see that a child uses clay at the clay table only.

2. She will be sure that each child has his own clay and that he does not take any from another child.

3. She will see that the clay is manipulated with the hands and without the use of molds. It will also be understood that toys are not allowed at the clay table.

4. She will help a child in some cases. For example, when a child is making figures, she can show him that pulling the clay into arms and legs is more

satisfactory than attaching them after the main part of the body is made.

5. She will pick up any clay that drops on the floor, saying, "Keep the clay on the table," not "Don't drop the clay on the floor."

6. She will help the children put the clay away, leave the table and floor tidy, and see that their hands are washed.

Family play

Several children including two girls and a boy have decided to play house. Lucile walks quietly over to where the homemaking equipment is assembled. The children seem unaware of her presence as they plan what to do.

Four-year-old Ellen, who likes to tell other children what to do, announces that she is the mother and Eric the father. "You can go to work now, but come home for dinner," she says to Eric. Ellen then tells three-and-a-half-year-old Kathy that she can be her helper.

"But I don't want to be your helper," Kathy replies. "You'll make me do all the work, and I won't have any fun. That's the way you did the last time we played house."

Lucile notes that Kathy is angry and excited; so she intervenes saying, "Maybe Kathy would like to be the grandmother. There are lots of interesting things a grandmother can do, such as baking cookies or watching the children while the mother goes marketing." Lucile smiles at Kathy who hesitates a moment and then nods in agreement.

The play is resumed. Lucile moves into the background but within hearing distance. The situation will bear careful watching.

Presently she hears Kathy say, "Now I'm going to make some cookies, and we can have tea."

"That's silly," replies Ellen. "You don't have tea in the morning."

"Then we'll have the cookies for lunch," says Kathy.

Ellen concedes this point, but adds, "First we've got to bathe all the children, and then I'm going shopping."

Lucile watches to see how Kathy takes this announcement. Apparently she agrees to it. And so the

These youngsters are enjoying a tea party.

family play continues with some give-and-take between Ellen and Kathy. Lucile will not intervene unless Ellen monopolizes the situation. It is important that Kathy stand up for her own rights. And it is equally necessary for Ellen to learn that she cannot mold an activity into what she alone wants.

Now it is cleanup time

The morning is rapidly coming to an end, and soon the children will be leaving. They already know that part of getting ready to go home is to help put away neatly and quickly the things they have been using. This is another learning situation which is a scheduled routine. The children will acquire a feeling of the importance of putting away their things after they have finished playing with them.

The students know that good housekeeping in a play school includes orderliness at the beginning and end of the day. Since the play school is like a workshop, emphasis is not placed on a clean, tidy room while the various activities are going on. However, when disorder hampers play, then the children are expected to help with a certain amount of picking up. When mishaps, such as spilling liquids on the floor, occur, they are wiped up at once.

You will notice that most of the children appear to know where various articles go. There are low shelves for the toys, and for the sandbox and homemaking equipment. The blocks, with the assist-

ance of some of the students, are stacked up according to size and shape on one side of the room. Aprons are hung on low hooks. Small brooms and dustpans are available for sweeping the floor. In no time at all the room is in order.

Then they put on their wraps

Now you can see that most of the children are hurrying toward the coatroom, chatting gaily to one another. But there are a few who linger, hesitant about leaving behind the toys and materials they have been enjoying. These are the children who generally take longer to become self-dependent with their clothing. And even after they learn to button a coat or to put on rubbers, they are apt to dawdle and to keep the others waiting. The students try to give these children special attention in the coatroom. They will praise a child's efforts to help himself. They will smile and reassure him for trying. Their attitude will convey feelings of warmth and friendliness, which in turn will help the child build up confidence in himself as a person.

The wraps are now on, and the children are saying good-by. For most of them it has been a happy experience — something to talk about at home and something to look forward to tomorrow.

Taking a Look at the Student Observers

Another interesting student activity in connection with the play school is observing the children. As observers, the students are learning to watch the way a child behaves without feeling a necessity for changing his behavior. This is somewhat different from the role they take when they are actively guiding the children. Then they not only observe behavior, but try to direct it in ways that lead to effective learning on the part of the child. Both activities are important parts of the play-school experience and call for the same basic knowledge of children. But let's take a look at the observers and see what they are doing.

How the observers cooperate

The first thing you will notice is that the observers are silent and do not talk. They know that adult conversation will disturb the children. If a child asks a question, a student will smile and answer briefly.

You can also see that the observers do not move around unnecessarily or group together. In fact they remain in the background as much as possible, although they are free to walk about in following a child's activity.

Another point which they are careful to follow is to refrain from displaying any emotion. They avoid showing amusement or concern over anything a child may say or do.

Procedures for observation

The students consider the observation activity a means by which certain aspects of a child's development can be recognized and evaluated. They know that everything a child does or says gives clues to how he feels. And how he feels indicates to a great extent how he is developing. Through reference sources, the students understand that effective observation depends upon two important factors.

1. The observations need to be made systematically and repeatedly, instead of casually and irregularly. Nothing is learned from one experience, and very little from scattered observations.

2. The observations need to be immediately and accurately recorded. An observation held in mind becomes increasingly vague as time elapses.

Each of the five student observers is following one child. The children are of different age levels, and were selected for observation by Mrs. Rawlins. Time does not permit a detailed observation of every child in the play school. Therefore it seems best to concentrate on the five of Mrs. Rawlins' choice.

Each observer checks the same child throughout the four-day observation period. When these students have completed their observation activity, another group of observers will check the same children. Eventually considerable information about the progress of the five children will be accumulated. Toward the end of the play-school experience, the check listings on the children as recorded by the students will be summarized. From the summary, it will be possible to see whether there is agreement among the students on the development of these particular children.

The check sheet used by the observers

The check sheet the observers are using is based on aspects of development considered important in a play-school setup. These include ways in which the child expresses his feelings and emotions, evidences of motor coordination, and his ability to help himself and to get along with others.

The points in the check sheet were determined after the students had consulted and discussed many references. The various items show what the child's behavior indicates. The sheet is easy to check, and space is given for questions that may arise, which can be discussed on Fridays. There is an ample supply of mimeographed copies — enough to carry through the observation activity period. Audrey and Albert, who volunteered to look after the sheets, file them each day under the name of the child and in chronological order. This will make it easier to tabulate the summaries.

Those of you who are taking a look at the student observers, will find a reproduction of the check sheet — as it was developed with Miss Reed's guidance — on the next two pages.

One of the students is using the check sheet during her observation period.

OBSERVING A CHILD'S DEVELOPMENT THROUGH HIS BEHAVIOR

Name of child_____ Name of observer_____

Date observed_____ Directions: Check (√) for each behavior observed.

BEHAVIOR INDICATIONS

Feelings of insecurity

_____Prefers to play alone

_____Seldom talks to other children or adults

_____Disrupts other children at play

_____Attacks anyone who interferes with his play

_____Constantly wants to be the center of attention

_____Unwilling to accept suggestions

_____Timid; will not try a new activity without adult help

_____Stutters or stammers

_____Sucks thumb or finger, or has other nervous mannerisms

_____Seldom smiles or laughs

_____Displays no enthusiasm about any of the activities

Feelings of security

_____Joins group activities

_____Talks to other children and adults

_____Does not bother other children at play

_____Accepts other children who want to play with him

_____Does not demand constant attention

_____Willing to accept suggestions

_____Unafraid to try a new activity by himself

_____Speaks easily and naturally

_____Has no nervous mannerisms

_____Smiles or laughs frequently

_____Claps hands when a new activity is suggested; hums or sings spontaneously

Poor emotional control

_____When angry, resorts to destructive behavior, such as throwing or breaking things, hitting or biting people, tearing his clothes

_____Becomes very much upset when he fails to achieve something he tries to do; gives up after one effort

_____Cries, whines, or sulks when crossed

_____Tense; unable to relax at rest period or during play

Developing emotional control

_____When angry, may stamp feet or cry a little, or call object of his anger names

_____Not easily discouraged; willing to make several trials to achieve something he wants to do

_____Does not become upset when he cannot have his own way

_____Able to relax during rest period; plays easily and naturally

Poor motor performance

_____Awkward about maneuvering tricycle or wagon; bumps into objects or persons

_____Cannot pour juice from pitcher into cup without spilling

_____Holds paintbrush or crayons awkwardly

_____Unable to drive a nail straight, or to saw on a line

_____Cannot button or unbutton coat

Developing motor coordination

_____Able to ride around room on tricycle or wagon with ease, and to gauge distance

_____Can pour juice into cup with little or no spilling

_____Holds paintbrush or crayons as directed

_____Able to drive a nail straight, and to saw on a line

_____Can button and unbutton coat easily

Poorly developed self-reliance and independence

_____Has to be reminded when to go to the toilet and to wash hands

_____Depends on someone to help him select activities

_____Needs assistance in taking off and putting on wraps

_____Leaves equipment and materials where he last played with them

Increasing self-reliance and independence

_____Goes to the toilet and washes hands when necessary

_____Plans his own activities

_____Takes off and puts on own wraps

_____Helps put away equipment and materials without being urged

Poorly established cooperation with others

_____Does not share without being urged

_____Resents taking turns

_____Tries to take anything he wants from another child

_____Has not learned to compromise

Improving cooperation with others

_____Shares on his own accord

_____Takes turns freely

_____Recognizes the property rights of others

_____Willing to compromise

Questions: _____

_____

_____

_____

Extending Learning Experiences Beyond the Play School

If you had looked in on the play school another day, you might have found the students engaged in a different type of activity than those already described. They would be taking the children on a trip somewhere.

Shortly after the play school opened, Mrs. Rawlins suggested that the students might want to extend the children's experiences into the community. This could be done by arranging excursions to various places of interest.

The idea made an instant appeal to everyone. Right away the activity group working in the classroom lost no time looking up helpful material for this learning situation. It wasn't long before they presented the following procedures that would need to be carried out to secure satisfactory results for excursion experiences.

1. Arrange some excursions that introduce new ideas and some that add to the knowledge already possessed.

2. Plan the excursions on the basis of the children's abilities to take part. Remember that younger children may tire more easily and lose interest more quickly than older ones.

3. Form small groups of children who enjoy the same things and who get along well together.

4. Be sure there are at least two adults for each group, with each adult responsible for certain children.

5. Determine the distance to be covered and the approximate time needed for the excursion. If the trip is not within easy walking distance, make arrangements with some of the parents for transportation.

6. Watch for signs of fear or anxiety that may arise when a child sees unfamiliar things. New experiences need to be handled carefully and sometimes slowly. Reassure a child by holding his hand and quietly explaining the situation to him. If he continues to show fear, take him aside and call his attention to something he is more familiar with.

7. Avoid expressing your own ideas or attitudes about the things that the children see. Stand by ready to answer questions. But let the children absorb in their own way what interests them most.

Some time later various excursions were arranged. Several groups went to the zoo. While this was not a new experience to most of the children, they learned about several animals they had not seen before. Another group visited a pet shop where there was a batch of little chicks and several new puppies. Some of the older children who had made a fire station with blocks and trucks went to a real fire station.

The students were especially interested in watching the children's responses to these trips when the play school was resumed. Some of the children painted what they had seen. Others engaged in dramatic play using blocks and toys to express various situations. Those who visited the fire station talked at great length about the way a fireman slid down the slippery pole

An Easter-egg hunt is an experience that is enjoyed by young children.

and about the helmet he wore. Then there was one child who remained silent about the trip he took, although his eyes sparkled when he heard the others talking about it.

The trips showed the students all too clearly that each child has his own way of learning and using what he sees. But there was a general agreement that visiting places of interest is a valuable way for children to explore and to learn about what is going on in the world around them.

Looking in on the Friday Discussions

The discussions held on the fifth day of the week when there was no participation in the play school were very interesting. Although the students were gaining experience in handling children, there seemed to be something new constantly

coming up. Dwight said he thought the students asked more questions than the three-year-olds. "The only difference," he added, "is that the children do not always wait for their questions to be answered, and we do."

Guiding the children at play offered a real situation where information and how to apply it were essential. Merely knowing the answer to a question did not always suffice. How to put the knowledge into practical use required experience. And how the various situations that arose with the children were handled called for continual evaluation.

Most of the questions seemed to center around two subjects: (1) how to give directions and suggestions to produce effective results; and (2) how to handle various problem situations. Let's look in on some of the Friday sessions and see what is going on.

Giving directions and suggestions

The students have just finished finding the answers to some questions on giving effective directions and suggestions. Walter is summarizing the information in the following manner.

• I get the child's attention before I begin to talk. It helps to stand in front of him, and look directly at him if possible.

• I make my suggestions "do's" rather than "don'ts," stating a direction clearly and simply just once. I avoid the tendency to repeat it several times. However, if a single direction is not enough, I offer another that will carry out the first one.

- I avoid talking down to a child. To do so would make him feel inferior and might raise a barrier between us. I also use words that will assure him I am friendly and understanding, although I know he may have acted childishly.

- Once I have given a direction, I follow through to see that it is done. Neglecting to do so may cause the child to disregard the direction if he is more interested in doing something else.

The chart on page 468 shows how the students used the information which Dwight had summarized. To make the points as effective as possible, both desirable and undesirable ways of handling the same situation were given.

Handling problem situations

There were various situations in the play school which the students labeled as problems, principally because they, themselves, did not know what to do about them. Some of these same situations had also occurred in the homes of the students where there were small children. This gave the class an added incentive to find out how to handle these problems.

The information was assembled and applied in much the same way as shown for giving directions and suggestions. Progress in working out various situations at home and in the play school was regularly evaluated. However, since the application of much of the informa-

tion is given in the section "Seeing the Play School in Action," and since home situations vary, only the summaries are given here. For other behavior problems encountered previously by Miss Reed's group, see Book 1, pages 471 to 474.

DISCIPLINE AND OBEDIENCE

- Discipline for a child is largely a matter of accepting limits or restrictions. The adult's role is to set these limits for the child's behavior in situations where he cannot judge the consequences of his action. These include such situations as the use of equipment and materials, health, safety, and the rights of other people.

- It is easier for a child to accept limits if he understands what he can and cannot do, and in some cases why. He can learn that he needs to put away his toys, so that they will not be stepped on and broken. He may even understand that he or others may fall over them, and get hurt.

- A child needs to have confidence in the person who is setting the restrictions. If a child dislikes a person, he tends to take a negative attitude toward things he may be asked to do. Such a person will need to build confidence and establish friendly realtionships with the child before cooperation can be expected.

PUNISHMENT

- To be effective, punishment needs to: (1) be prompt — not hasty — especially with a very young child; (2) be adapted to the individual child; (3) cause the child to be thoughtful about what he has done; and (4) be of such a nature that the child still feels he is loved and accepted.

GIVING CHILDREN DIRECTIONS AND SUGGESTIONS

Situation	This	Rather than This
John is trying to pile the heavy blocks one on top of the other.	"John, leave the heavy blocks on the floor."	"Don't try to put the heavy blocks on top of each other, John."
The children know they are expected to wash their hands after toileting before juice time. Emily has not done so, but starts playing with one of the dolls.	"Emily, it's time to wash your hands. The juice is ready." (No response . . . .) "After you've washed your hands, you can play with the doll again." (Still no response . . . . I wait for Emily to put down the doll. When she still hesitates, I place the doll bed within her reach. I make no comment, but by looking at her, I make it clear that the doll can go to bed. Then I hold out my hand, indicating that we'll both go together for the hand-washing.)	"Wash your hands now, Emily, or you can't have any juice. Didn't you hear me, Emily? I said, 'Wash your hands.' If you don't hurry up, there won't be any juice left. And you know how much you like to pour your own juice." (I walk away, trusting that Emily will do as I suggested about washing her hands.)
Jimmy, one of the smaller younger boys, is bidding for praise and attention. He boasts, "I'm making the best garage you ever saw." Presently Henry, much larger and older, passes by and deliberately knocks down the blocks. Jimmy starts to cry.	*To Jimmy:* "Look, Jimmy. Let's see if we can't work this thing out. Maybe Henry will help you rebuild the garage. I know that the two of you can make something pretty fine." *To Henry:* "Henry, I'm sure you didn't mean to knock down Jimmy's garage. It must have been an accident. You could help him with the heavy blocks, because you are bigger and stronger. How about it, Henry?"	*To Jimmy:* "There's nothing to cry about, Jimmy. No one hurt you. You'll just have to start all over again." *To Henry:* "Can't you be more careful? You know you shouldn't tease someone younger than you are. Now run along and leave Jimmy alone."

- Several methods of punishment have been found to be effective with some children:

1. *Disapproval* if not overdone, and if directed at the deed, not at the child.

2. *Deprivation* of something a child enjoys. If a child is careless or deliberately breaks a toy, doing without it or not having it replaced immediately usually helps him to be more careful with toys.

3. *Isolation* for a short period, especially when a child is emotionally disturbed. If a child hits another child, going without companionship for a while may be effective. Since the desire for companionship is strong, most children will learn to avoid behavior that is undesirable to the group they are with. However, it is not necessary that the child refrain from play while isolated. In fact, getting interested in a new activity may serve as an outlet for the strong emotions he has displayed.

4. *Natural consequences* where danger or health is not involved. A small child who feels pain from touching a radiator may learn to keep away from it. However, the child should not be allowed to burn himself simply to learn that the radiator is hot. If a child runs outdoors without rubbers and gets his feet wet, having to remain in the house until his shoes dry may teach him to put on his rubbers. But the wet shoes should be replaced by dry ones while he is waiting.

RUNNING WILDLY AROUND

- The adult needs to understand why a child is acting as he does.

- If the running around is after a period of rest or quiet activity, there is probably a need for physical exercise. The adult's role is to find some acceptable way of meeting this need.

- On the other hand, if there has already been considerable activity, the wild behavior may be due to fatigue brought on by overstimulation. In this case, a quiet activity needs to be encouraged, especially something which the child particularly enjoys.

STRIKING OR BITING

- When one child takes something away from another, the child deprived may strike or bite the other child's hand. He may also do this to an adult when he does not want to do what the adult suggests. This is his way of meeting the problem.

- The first thing to do is to stop the hitting or biting, at the same time remaining calm and casual. Then it may help the situation to turn the child's attention elsewhere to something he can hit or bite without doing any harm. A substitute response often serves as an outlet for these strong emotions until a child has learned more acceptable ways of expressing himself.

SHOWING OFF

- Some children make a bid for attention by showing off and seeking to be in the center of the stage in a group activity. This behavior may have been learned when a child heard adults comment, "How cute," or "How bright." These remarks indicated that their attention was directed toward him rather than to what he was doing.

- A satisfactory way to handle a show-off is to let him make his contribution to the group. Thank him, and say that what he did was interesting or something equally appropriate. Then let him take his place as part of the group and watch what someone else does. A child bidding for attention needs to learn to be a listener as well as a performer.

TELLING LIES

- It takes time for a young child to learn to distinguish between what is the truth and what is make-believe. The adult's role is to understand what statements arise from imagination and what are made intentionally to deceive.

- It has been shown that children do not become truthful or untruthful at any given age, but usually tell falsehoods under certain conditions. Many children tell lies because they fear punishment. But fear of disapproval, of what others think, or of being ridiculed are also contributing factors. Sometimes a desire for praise or sympathy prompts lying.

- Severe punishment for deceitful lying does not generally produce satisfactory results. It tends to develop a fear of the person making the punishment. This, in turn, encourages a child to be more successful in lying another time.

- A wise procedure is to find the cause of untruthfulness and to direct efforts toward eliminating any need for lying. But it takes time for a child to learn that lying is not a way of avoiding or getting out of trouble. However, you can make it clear that you dislike untruthful statements. You can explain that one way of living together happily is to trust and depend upon one another. More important still is to set a good example of truthfulness yourself.

STEALING

- Learning to distinguish between what is mine and what is thine is a part of a child's development. But knowing that a thing belongs to somebody else is not the same as knowing when it's wrong to take that thing.

- When a child takes a toy or something else just because it appeals to him, you will need to see that he returns it. At the same time, you will also need to give him something else to play with as attractive as what he has taken. This is not rewarding undesirable behavior, because the child has not yet learned what stealing is. However, you can explain that people do not like a person who takes things which are not his own.

DAMAGING PROPERTY

- Much of the damage done by preschool children is done thoughtlessly rather than deliberately. A child learning to use his muscles and his mind seeks ways of developing them without considering the damage he may be doing.

- The only way to be sure that children of four years or under do not damage property is to keep them away from temptation or to watch them. Punishment for damaging one thing will generally not prevent damage to another. A child needs suitable materials on which he can exercise his muscles and his mind. By five years of age, children begin to know what they can and cannot do about damaging things.

USING UNDESIRABLE LANGUAGE

- When children are learning to talk, they repeat what they hear. They often experiment with words without paying attention to their meaning. Children three to four years of age are much interested in sounds, and often use terms which are new to them and seem to entertain them. On the other hand, a child may use undesirable words as a way of showing off or to gain attention.

Or he may call a person whom he dislikes for the moment by a word he knows is undesirable.

- In most cases for children under six years of age, it is best to ignore what they say. If you laugh at what a child says, he is sure to repeat it again and again. Directing his attention to some enjoyable activity will generally result in the use of terms relating to that activity. However, if a child persists in using undesirable language, he can be taken aside and told in a friendly way that these words are not acceptable. The best course for the family members is to set a good example themselves.

STUTTERING OR STAMMERING

- A certain amount of stuttering is not unusual in a child two, three, or four years old. It sometimes occurs when a child is angry or otherwise emotionally upset. Feeling insecure may also be a contributing factor.

- The wisest procedure is not to interfere when a child stutters.

1. Do not ask him to speak more slowly or to try harder.

2. Do not help him along when he repeats or hesitates.

3. Do not bribe him.

4. Do not show anxiety or concern.

5. Do not discuss the stuttering in his presence.

- Try to get the child interested in something he enjoys and can do well. Praise, friendliness, and understanding will contribute toward overcoming the difficulty.

Evaluating a Child's Development in Terms of Behavior Changes

Eventually the class time the students could spend in the play school approached its end. The mothers of the children would carry on without the students. But of course the class would keep in touch with what went on.

However, the time had come to summarize and to evaluate the check-sheet information on the five children whose behavior the students had observed. A tabulation of the number of times an item had been checked was made on the blackboard. The checks were tabulated chronologically, and then studied for indications of possible changes in behavior over the period in which the observations were made.

On the whole, the results were gratifying to the students. In most instances there was agreement on the amount of progress made by each child. Even though some of the children showed better development than others, each of the five showed improvement in one way or another.

After the results had been discussed and evaluated, the class divided into five groups. Each group wrote up a report on one of the children who had been observed. These reports were then turned over to Mrs. Rawlins for the developmental records she was keeping.

Space is not available for giving all of the reports. But the report on Judy is a good example of how the students evaluated her development.

Judy's developmental report

During the first two weeks of observation, Judy seemed very insecure. She was timid and preferred to play alone. She sucked her thumb, stuttered at times, and showed other indications of insecurity. But during the last week of observation, she joined group activities, talked to other children and adults, and was not afraid to try a new activity by herself. She still sucks her thumb, but stutters less.

Judy's emotional control seemed to indicate improvement. At first she cried and whined when crossed, and was unable to relax. But as time went on, the crying and whining decreased, and she was able to relax to some extent, but not wholly.

Her motor performance also improved a little. She gradually held the paintbrush or crayons less awkwardly, and she learned to ride a tricycle. This latter achievement gave her great satisfaction.

There seemed to be some indication that she was becoming a little more self-dependent. By the end of the last week of observation, she was going to the toilet and washing her hands without being reminded to do so. But she is still hesitant about putting on her wraps, and putting away her play materials.

Her cooperation with others is also better. She seems more willing to share on her own accord and to take turns freely. Although she has not learned to compromise to any great extent, she has done so on several occasions.

Understanding the meaning of development

The reports which the students made on the five children led to a discussion of what could be predicted by the information given. Would a child who had begun to show indications of desirable behavior continue to improve as time went on?

Naturally the students hoped that the answer to this question would be yes. There was no doubt in their minds that the play school was doing for the children all that Mrs. Clark said it would when she told the students about the project. (See page 435.)

Miss Reed said that guiding children at play seemed to be an excellent way to encourage desirable behavior. Children learn largely through the satisfaction they get from their activities. And if these activities are carefully planned so that they contribute toward all phases of development, then good habits are more easily acquired.

Of course, the speed and ease with which children acquire acceptable behavior differs with each child. He progresses at his own rate of speed. Some learn more rapidly than others and retain this learning. Others may forget and need to relearn certain things. For example, a timid child who has learned to be friendly and to enjoy group activities will want companions after the play school has ended. If this need is supplied, he will probably continue to practice the behavior he has developed at the play school. For he knows that in order to have friends he will need to share with them, to be willing to compromise, and to recognize their property rights. On the other hand, if companionship is not supplied, there will be no opportunity for him to practice the desirable behavior he has learned. And in time he will tend to forget it. The chances are that when children are given opportunities to carry on their play-school activities under satisfying conditions, the desirable behavior they have developed will become established habits. Then too, most children feel more sure of themselves after play-school experiences. And this tends to contribute toward better development as time goes on.

How the Students Evaluated Their Own Experiences

Before their classwork with the play school ended, the students began to discuss what they had gained through their experiences with the children. When Dean suggested that this evaluation be in terms of what each student had gained personally, the others agreed.

"Let's write a paragraph on 'What the Play School Meant to Me,'" said Lucile. Then she turned toward Miss Reed to see her reaction to the suggestion.

Miss Reed thought the idea a good one, and the room became unusually quiet as each student concentrated on what to say. Before long the rustling of papers indicated that the students had finished. Let's select several, and see what was said.

What Marshall wrote
"The play school meant a great deal to me, because it gave me a greater understanding of myself. At first I didn't like the procedure used when one child hit another child. I was always spanked when I hit my brother. And I don't have to think very far back to remember when. No one ever tried to find out why I hit him. But I was sure I had a good reason. There were other children in the family, and my mother was busy. She probably didn't have time to help my brother and me settle our difficulties together in a friendly way. If we had learned to get along together when we were younger, we might be more friendly now. I can see how important it is to understand why children behave as they do, and to learn the best ways of guiding them."

What Sylvia said
"The experiences that meant the most to me were those that showed me how to handle children. Giving

directions only once, and making them do's rather than don'ts has paid off with my little sister. It's my responsibility to look after her quite often. We get along now much better than we used to. I'm sure it's the tone of my voice and the way I talk to her that make her more willing to accept my suggestions."

How Audrey felt

"The play school meant a great deal to me, because I learned to feel at ease with young children and — I think — to understand them to some extent. I have no brothers or sisters. And I have not done much baby-sitting, because I didn't feel at ease with children. As I really got to know some of the children, I began to see myself in a different light. When I saw a child pout and whine because he was

```
CLASS MEMO:
  If your class is to
  participate in a play
  school, what procedures
  will you use?
  What opportunities
  other than a play school
  can you suggest for
  learning about preschool
  children?
```

crossed, I knew that I had acted the same way when I was young. In fact even now I have a tendency to sulk when I can't have what I want. And then I look at myself and say, 'What! At your age! Haven't you developed better emotional control than that? Why, some of those youngsters in the play school don't know what sulking is.' I guess you can learn a lot by observing children. But sometimes I think they learn a lot faster than we older folks."

HELPING CHILDREN TO ENJOY EATING FOODS THAT ARE GOOD FOR THEM

THE students were now ready to consider their second goal — *helping children to enjoy eating foods that are good for them*. This objective seemed to offer one more step toward developing a better understanding of young children. The students recalled that the classwork the previous year in child care had shown that baby-sitters frequently encountered eating problems when

they served food. (See Book 1, pages 462–464.) In instances where there were young brothers and sisters at home, experience showed that eating was sometimes a problem. Furthermore, some of the mothers of the play-school children also indicated that they had encountered difficulty along this line.

"My three-year-old sister had a good appetite until a few weeks ago," remarked Albert. "Then she seemed to lose it. We haven't yet been able to figure out why."

"Our problem is much the same," added Julia. "My little brother loses interest in food at times and doesn't want to eat anything except desserts. We realize that isn't a good idea, but getting him to eat other things isn't easy."

"Mrs. Hansen told me that Judy dawdles over her food the way she delays putting on her wraps at the play school," said Leo. "She says she sometimes has to feed Judy in order to get her to eat enough food."

These and other comments indicated that the eating habits of some children are far from satisfactory. Everyone agreed that knowing more about why this is true would help in understanding and enjoying young children.

Making Plans for the Classwork

At this point Miss Reed made an interesting comment. "Most people — and that includes children too — enjoy eating because it fulfills a basic need," she said. "To be hungry and then to eat is a gratifying experience, especially when your hunger is satisfied in a way that leaves you happy and content. Problems arise when something interferes with the urge to satisfy hunger. You know from your previous experience that children from two to six are growing and developing rapidly. It's easy for all kinds of behavior difficulties to develop.

Of course, not all children have eating problems. But when they occur, they are generally connected with unpleasant associations at mealtime."

"Then I think we need to concentrate on how to make mealtime pleasant for young children," said Marshall thoughtfully. "We know from our work in the play school that pleasant surroundings tend to help children overcome difficulties. And if children are happy, they don't seem to have problems."

"That's right," added Lucile. "We also need to know how to tempt their appetites with foods that are good for them. Of course we know about a well-balanced diet. But my little sister will accept some new things more readily than others. And I know too from what my mother says that some foods are better for her than others."

There were nods of agreement throughout the room, and other remarks followed. Before long, plans for helping children enjoy foods that are good for them began to take shape. The general idea centered around making mealtime as pleasant as possible. This would include learning what foods are best for children, and finding ways of getting children to accept these foods. Applying this knowledge would tend to prevent eating problems from arising, and would help in cases where difficulties had already developed. Experiences would be carried out by the students at home and at school.

Miss Reed said that there was considerable material on the reference shelves. In addition, everyone agreed to be on the lookout for helpful newspaper and magazine articles. The students also realized that Mrs. Rawlins or some other person with training and experience in guiding children would be an excellent source of help.

Making Mealtime a Happy Time

The students soon learned that there are various factors which contribute toward making mealtime pleasant. Being sure that a child is comfortable at the table, and in so far as possible having him in a happy, relaxed frame of mind were considered especially important.

In some homes additional equipment was bought or improvised to increase a particular child's comfort while eating. And as in the play-school experience, certain techniques used at mealtime helped various children to enjoy eating foods that are good for them.

However, the students' experiences with children are not given at this time. But summaries of the information they assembled and used follow:

Making a child comfortable at the table

Whether or not a child sits at a small table of his own or at the dining table with the family, it is important for him to have equipment that fits his size. It is also important to have eating equipment that is easy to handle. When children are comfortable, they are more willing to remain at the table until an adequate meal is consumed.

A CHAIR OF THE RIGHT SIZE: The chair needs to be of a height so that the child's arms can rest comfortably on top of the table. If a regular dining-table chair is used, it can be made higher by adding a box, a hard cushion, or a thick book. At a small table, the child's feet need to rest on the floor. But a footstool made from a wooden box can be used at the dining table.

A child enjoys mealtime when she — or he — is comfortable and happy.

EASY-TO-HANDLE   EATING   EQUIPMENT:
Some small children find it more convenient to use only a spoon — perhaps
one with a short, straight handle that is
easy to grasp. It is best to let them use
this until they wish to change to a
regular spoon.

A fork is difficult to manage until a
child has acquired considerable manip-
ulative skill. By that time he can handle
a salad fork, which is usually smaller
than a regular fork and has tines which
are more blunt.

It takes longer to learn to use a knife
than it does a fork. But in the meantime, if a child wants to pretend he is
cutting something, he can be given a
butter knife.

Some children enjoy having plates
and cups of their own. A divided plate
with sections that have rims makes it
easy to take up a portion of food without pushing it around on the plate. In
fact any dish with a rim also prevents
food from sliding out of bounds. The
cup needs to have straight sides, a firm
base, and be easy to grasp. As the child
grows older his milk can be put in a
pitcher, so that he can pour it out as he
wishes. This often acts as an incentive
when more milk is needed in the diet.

Helping a child to enjoy mealtime

Emotional disturbances, as well as
an approaching illness or being overly
tired, can affect a child's appetite.
Fear, anxiety, anger, uncertainty, and
insecurity are some of the emotions
that interfere with the desire to satisfy
hunger. Trying to make a child eat
when he is upset generally does a great
deal of harm. In the long run, it may
cause him to have a strong dislike for
certain foods. Finding ways of preventing some of these emotions from
occurring at mealtime is important.

1. Be sure, in so far as possible, that the
child comes to a meal feeling happy
and relaxed. If he has been engaged in
vigorous play and activity, a short rest
before the meal begins may be very
helpful. Let him sit quietly with a
book or listen to some music. If for any
reason he has been crying, give him
time to get over the effects of his emotional distress. If he has been disobedi-
ent so that discipline is necessary,
administer it and get it over with before mealtime. Postponing it and telling him that he will be punished after
he eats will cause fear, and make the
meal very distasteful to him. It may
even keep him from eating at all.

2. Serve small portions of food with the
understanding that second helpings
are available. An overloaded plate may
prove so discouraging that a child will
give up before he starts. The portions
need to be easy to manage.

3. Let the child be the judge of the
amount to be eaten. All young children
do not have the same appetite. Some
have smaller capacities than others.
Urging a child to eat more of this or
that if he does not want it will make
him unhappy. It may also develop a
stubbornness that might otherwise not
appear.

4. Allow the child to set his own pace of
eating. Children differ in the rate of
speed in which they do things. The
family needs to take this into account
at mealtime and let a child eat at his
normal rate, even though he takes
longer than the others. Once this rate
is recognized, it is easy to tell whether
or not he is deliberately stalling or is
naturally a slow eater.

5. Make it easy for a child to develop acceptable table behavior. Until a child can handle a spoon and fork skillfully, some spilling onto the table or the surrounding floor is to be expected. Placing a mat of linoleum under his chair, a waterproof cover at his place, and a large bib around his neck will decrease the seriousness of spilling the food — both for the child and for the family. Scolding or showing displeasure upsets a child and may cause him to lose interest in trying to do better. Quiet suggestions about taking small spoonfuls, not talking with his mouth full, and using his bib as a napkin will produce more effective results. This is especially true when a word of praise for any improvement made is given.

6. Try to create an atmosphere of cheerful friendliness in which the food is enjoyed. Limit the conversation to pleasant topics, and avoid airing pet peeves or discussing money troubles and other worries. It is also important not to make unpleasant remarks about the food. Children are quick to copy the same attitudes as adults. Enthusiasm over a meal also may be imitated.

7. Make a child feel that he is a person in his own right. This does not mean letting him become the center of attention or watching every spoonful of food that he eats. On the other hand, no child likes to be ignored during a meal. There is always a happy medium in which the older members can carry on a conversation of their own with occasional remarks to the child to make him feel that he is one of the family group.

8. Avoid offering a child a taste of food that he is not allowed to have. He might like it and want more. Then not giving it to him may make him angry or upset. Most children do not display interest in foods that are strange to them unless their interest is deliberately aroused. However, if a child does show curiosity, it can be explained that these foods are for big people and that he can have them when be grows up.

9. Keep to a regular mealtime schedule. Most people feel hungry at regular intervals and like to have their meals on scheduled time. This is particularly true with a small child. If he does not get a meal when his stomach is ready for it, interest in food begins to lag. By the time the meal is served, his appetite may be gone. When this occurs too frequently, a child will seldom be hungry at mealtime and may develop into a problem eater.

10. Serve a meal occasionally in a different location — in the yard, on the porch, or in front of the fireplace while listening to music. These occasions make mealtime a pleasant memory.

Providing Suitable Foods

As the students planned and carried out various experiences in helping children enjoy foods that are good for them, information was assembled and used regarding suitable foods for children. During a class discussion, Dwight suggested a novel way for making the summaries. "Since eating is so important and such a personal matter to a child, why don't we set up the summaries in the way children might say it themselves," he said.

Dwight's suggestion appealed to the group, and here is the way the idea worked out.

What we really like

- We like to have our food not too hot and not too cold.

- Red is our favorite color. Maybe that's why we enjoy tomato soup. And red and pink gelatin taste so much better than white.

- We like our soups thin enough to drink from a cup. Or if they are thickened, we like them thick enough to spoon up easily.

- Mildly sweet fruits are very good, especially when they are cut in small pieces with the tough portions removed.

- We like a variety in the same meal of this thing called "texture." Crispy foods, such as celery and carrot sticks or zwieback and crisp toast, make a delightful crunching sound in our mouths. Of course we enjoy some chewy foods too, such as meat, string beans, broccoli, or bread crusts — but not too much of each. And then we like some foods that are soft and smooth. Cooked cereal, applesauce, mashed potatoes, or a creamy pudding are easy for us to manage.

- We like to feel independent and to be able to do things for ourselves at mealtime. Getting up and down at the table without help, putting on our bibs, and clearing away our dishes give us confidence in ourselves.

How to stimulate our appetites

Sometimes we simply don't feel like eating certain things. Why, we don't always know. Perhaps we get tired having some of the same foods over and over again in the same way. Maybe we aren't getting the personal attention we seem to need. Then again, some foods are just distasteful. What can be done about all this? Well, here are some suggestions that might help us enjoy eating the food we need.

- Add a touch of color to the foods in which we seem to lose interest. For example, put a cube of red jelly on top of the cereal, a sprig of parsley — which we won't eat — in the center of the mashed potato, or a slice of tomato on a creamed dish. A red cherry at the bottom of a glass of milk might encourage some of us to empty the glass to get the fruit. Perhaps a supply of variously colored plastic spoons with a different color from time to time might arouse our interest in eating.

- Offer us an occasional choice of how we would like to have a certain kind of food served — potatoes, baked or mashed; eggs, scrambled or poached; meat, broiled or roasted.

- Serve us only one new vegetable at a time and for several days in succession. This will give us an opportunity to learn to like it before we try something else.

- When we show a strong dislike for certain cooked vegetables, substitute others in the same food group. Or if we sometimes lose interest in cooked carrots, serve them raw — grated or cut in pieces. And please, don't give us any leftover reheated vegetables. But if you use them in soups or in other ways, we'll probably enjoy them.

- Why not take us on occasional trips to the grocery store? Letting us choose between beans or spinach, carrots or squash, apples or pears, and make other choices would be lots of fun. And it might give us a new interest in eating the food we select.

- Some of us would enjoy setting our places at the table. We might work up a good appetite if our mothers told us what was going to be served.

Foods that are not good for us

We've heard grownups say that some foods aren't good for young children. It seems that there are two classes — those that do us harm, and those that do us little if any good. Let's see what they are.

- *Foods containing a great deal of fat.* Fat meats, greasy gravies, doughnuts, pastries, mayonnaise, and desserts made with rich cream are foods which digest slowly. They put a burden on our digestion which is all out of proportion to their nutritional value.

- *Foods that are very sweet.* Candies, rich frosted cakes, rich cookies, and bottled drinks are some of the foods that satisfy hunger temporarily. But they tend to make us lose interest in other foods that are better for us. Why make us crave these foods?

- *Highly seasoned foods.* These are undesirable not only because they tend to diminish our liking for natural food flavors, but because an excess of spice may be irritating to the digestive system. If our families desire seasonings, such as mustard, cayenne pepper, chili and curry powder, or horse-radish, they can remove our portions before they season theirs. But wait — a little cinnamon or nutmeg, vanilla or lemon extract may be added to cooked fruits and desserts when flavoring is desirable.

- *Fruit which is either underripe or overripe, skins and seeds of fruits and berries.* These things may prove irritating to the intestinal tract. But if permitted, they should be given to us in small amounts.

- *Olives.* These are not easy for us to digest.

- *Popcorn, nuts, raisins, and corn.* Sometimes we swallow these without chewing them thoroughly. And then we wonder why we have a stomach-ache.

- *Coffee and tea and to a lesser extent cocoa and chocolate.* These foods are considered too stimulating to our nervous systems.

Handling Mealtime Problems

When the class came to the subject of mealtime problems, several questions arose which seemed to call for answers based on considerable personal experience in handling children. Arrangements were made to have Mrs. Packard, a child specialist with several children of her own, meet with the class. The plans also included an invitation to the students' mothers and the play-school mothers to attend the meeting. By this time the play-school children were so familiar with their routine that Mrs. Rawlins could manage with very little assistance.

Presenting some case studies

Mrs. Packard began her work with the class by presenting some case studies. She said that knowing how other people had handled eating problems would be helpful in understanding why they occur. Since other classes may be interested, some of the information given follows:

BETWEEN-MEAL SNACKS

THE SITUATION: The mother of three-year-old Alice was afraid that her daughter was not getting enough to eat. Her older children had always been hearty eaters and never needed any prodding to finish their meals. But Alice became so finicky that her mother let her indulge in snacks at any hour of the day just to get her to eat something. The result was that Alice ate less and less at mealtime, finally refusing to eat anything then at all. The question was: what could be done to establish regular eating habits?

HOW THE PROBLEM WAS MET: A checkup with the doctor showed that Alice was in good physical condition. However, since her eating capacity had always been small, Alice's mother was advised to serve her small portions and not expect her to eat as much as the other children had eaten at the same age. There was to be no prodding or urging to eat. After a reasonable length of time — 20 to 25 minutes — the food not eaten was to be removed and Alice excused from the table. If Alice asked for a snack between meals, she was to be given something that could be quickly digested. Such foods as fruit, fruit juice, an unsweetened cracker, or a small piece of bread spread with a thin coating of margarine or butter were recommended. Any of these would quiet the pangs of hunger but would not decrease the appetite for the next meal. Rich cookies, cakes, and other sweets were to be strictly avoided.

THE RESULTS: Alice's mother followed the suggestions offered, even though at first Alice ate very little or nothing at mealtime. However, the family did not worry or show any concern. At the same time, Alice was given plenty of opportunity to play out of doors. The exercise and the light snacks gradually increased Alice's appetite at mealtime. Before too long, she was eating her regular meals. The portions were small and often needed to be supplemented with something between meals. But there was no further eating problem.

NEATNESS AT THE TABLE

THE SITUATION: At three years of age, Mark was still being fed by his mother, because she did not want him to get the habit of being messy. She believed that when he was older — possibly by the time he was ready for school — he would naturally be able to feed himself, without spilling any food. But recently he began knocking the spoon out of her hand every time she started to feed him. On several occasions when she forced the food into his mouth, he spit it out onto the floor. After Mark was punished for this, he submitted to being fed again, but only for a few meals at a time. The mother then began to wonder what to do.

HOW THE PROBLEM WAS MET: Mark's mother learned that being messy is a normal stage that all children need to go through. How long the period lasts depends to some extent upon the child's ability to handle a spoon or fork. But every child needs practice in using these tools to develop this ability. Skill does not merely appear at a certain age. And even after it has been acquired, many children like to handle a new food. They not only want to touch and feel it, but to eat it with their fingers. Later when they decide that they like it, they will usually return to the spoon or fork.

THE RESULTS: Mark was permitted to feed himself, although he was awkward and did considerable spilling. However, he was so pleased at being allowed to use a spoon that he tried to be careful, even though no pressure to do so was used. The other members of the family made no comments on his failures, and in fact agreed to pay little attention to him while he was learning.

ATTENTION-GETTING BEHAVIOR

THE SITUATION: Four-year-old Susan had been so slow about eating her meals that her mother had resorted to bribing her with desserts to get her to finish the main course. Sometimes she even fed her to speed up the process. Susan's unusual behavior seemed to coincide with the arrival of a new baby brother.

Susan is a healthy child and her appetite is good. However, this mealtime situation began to disturb the other members of the family so much that it became the chief topic of conversation at the meal. Then when Susan's mother began to be irritated at Susan's behavior, she felt that it was time to do something about the situation.

HOW THE PROBLEM WAS MET: Susan's mother was told that many children feel a need for being the center of attention at mealtime. And they often enjoy the excitement caused by exasperated members of the family. Dawdling, refusing to eat unless coaxed or urged, or unless fed by the mother, and accepting bribes are some of the unfailing ways to get attention and create excitement. For this particular situation, the following suggestions were offered.

1. Avoid feeding Susan or urging or coaxing her to hurry, or bribing her with desserts. If she has not finished at the end of 20 to 25 minutes, remove the unfinished portions without comment, and withhold all food until the next meal. Setting an alarm to go off at a certain time might prevent too much dawdling.

2. Have an understanding with the family that they will not comment on Susan's behavior. Urge them to take a casual, matter-of-fact attitude toward anything she may do at mealtime.

3. Avoid having the family pay too much attention to the new baby when Susan is around.

4. Build up Susan's security by making her feel that she is an important member of the family. Praise her from time to time for something that she does well. If Susan's mother can set aside a brief period each day just for Susan, it may fulfill the need for attention she seems to be demanding at mealtime.

THE RESULTS: The suggestions were followed. For the first day or so, Susan ate very little. But since she was a healthy child with a good appetite, she soon began to eat regularly. There was some dawdling for a while, but it decreased when the family began to praise her efforts to finish on time. Susan and her mother are now enjoying a happy relationship.

THE MILK PROBLEM

THE SITUATION: Jane and Randall are members of the same family, but with different eating habits. Randall is very fond of milk and has been allowed to have all that he wanted. On the other hand, Jane began to refuse milk when she was about two and a half years old. But her brother's fondness for it was constantly held up to her as an example which she should learn to follow. This situation really alarmed the parents when Randall began to lose his appetite. He seemed to want more and more milk and less solid food. The parents had long since given up any hope of getting Jane to drink milk at all. It was just one of those things they couldn't do much about without some help.

HOW THE PROBLEM WAS MET: The parents learned that when a child drinks too much milk, he is apt to lose interest in other foods. Although a certain amount of milk — three to four cups a day — is considered necessary for young children, other foods are equally important. The following procedures were then recommended.

1. Avoid any discussion of milk in the presence of Jane and Randall.
2. Withhold Randall's milk until after he has eaten the other foods in the meal. If he is accustomed to drinking milk between meals, substitute fruit juices for the milk. This may increase his appetite at mealtime.

3. See that Jane has some foods that are made with milk, such as custards and puddings. If she is accustomed to a between-meal snack, have one of her friends who enjoys milk, come over for afternoon tea. Serve pink milk — made by adding a few drops of red vegetable coloring to the milk — or a small banana milk shake, or any other disguised milk drink. Include a few animal crackers or a favorite cookie, but not much of anything to spoil the appetite for the evening meal. Be sure not to substitute any other drink in the place of milk if Jane refuses it. Try this plan several times before you decide that it won't work.

THE RESULTS: The suggestions were followed with good results. Randall is now drinking less milk and eating more solid food. At first Jane would not drink anything at the afternoon teas. Then one day at her friend's home she surprised them all by drinking a colorful milk shake. After that she took small amounts at home but seldom at mealtime. However, she gets her daily quota in cereals that are cooked with milk and in drinks or desserts made with milk.

A colorful milk shake tempted Jane's appetite.

Answering questions

After the case studies had been presented, Mrs. Packard said that she would be glad to answer any questions. Space does not permit a full account of all the questions that were asked. However, some of the topics brought up by various mothers follow:

EATING WITH THE FAMILY

Q. . . . Mrs. Hansen: "What do you think about a young child — not a baby — eating with the family at the evening meal?"

A. . . . Mrs. Packard: "This is a matter of personal preference. But many families like to have their young children eat with them as soon as they can feed themselves without too much assistance. There is little evidence to indicate that young children may not safely be allowed to share the evening meal with the family. But the meal hour needs to be sufficiently early to enable everyone to finish before the child's bedtime. Children not only enjoy companionship when they eat, but the evening may be the only meal at which the whole family can be together. In extremely hot weather, it is also better for a young child to eat his main meal in the cool of the evening when his appetite is likely to be better than at noon."

Q. . . . Mrs. Dawson: "Should a young child be allowed to eat with the family when guests are present?"

A. . . . Mrs. Packard: "There is likely to be too much excitement before bedtime if a child has his evening meal with the guests. It is better for him to eat ahead of time. This arrangement also leaves the mother free to enjoy the guests. However, the child may come in and say good night to the company before going to bed."

TABLE BEHAVIOR

Q. . . . Mrs. Maynard: "How soon can a child be expected to learn good table manners?"

A. . . . Mrs. Packard: "There are some things that a child can learn very early. For example, teaching a child to come to the table with his hands and face washed and his hair combed are points that can be stressed as soon as he is able to sit at the table. Encouraging him to take small spoonfuls, to chew his food thoroughly, and not to talk with his mouth full are others. These things are more easily learned if the adult members of a family set a good example. When 'please' and 'thank you' and other courtesies are a natural part of a meal, children usually develop good table manners of their own accord. However, spilling food may occur until the child's muscular coordination has been developed."

Q. . . . Mrs. McCarthy: "Is it advisable to allow a child to leave the table before the older members have finished the meal?"

A. . . . Mrs. Packard: "It is generally agreed that it is desirable for a child to remain at the table until he has finished eating. After that it becomes a matter for the parents themselves to decide when he is to leave. In families where the adults enjoy a leisurely meal, it is often difficult for a child to sit still for so long a time. The muscles of his legs become cramped, and he is apt to squirm and fidget around. If he is expected to remain until the adults have finished, it is a good idea to let him stretch his legs by carrying his dishes to the kitchen and then return. If he is permitted to leave and not return, he can learn to say, 'Mother, may I please be excused?' or make some equally courteous request, and then take his leave."

APPETITE

Q. . . . MRS. BRITTON: "When my little girl was twenty months old, she ate more than she does now at three. We have had her checked by the doctor, and there is nothing physically wrong with her. Why does she eat less now than when she was younger?"

A. . . . MRS. PACKARD: "Between the second, third, and fourth years, children tend to decrease the amount of food eaten. After gaining fifteen to twenty pounds in weight the first year, the growth rate decreases, and a child puts on four or five pounds for each of the next few years. This slowing down carries with it a reduced need for food, and this is reflected in a waning of the appetite. It is quite normal for a preschool child to eat less than his baby brother or sister."

MENUS

Q. . . . MRS. WARREN: "When a child begins to eat with the family, how do you advise handling the matter of foods that are not good for him?"

A. . . . MRS. PACKARD: "Of course there is no reason why small children and adults cannot eat the same foods if these foods are simply prepared and are part of a well-balanced diet. If adults desire highly seasoned food, a child's portion can be prepared separately or set aside before the seasoning is added. When pastry is served, such as custard pie, the child can eat the

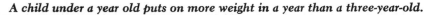

A child under a year old puts on more weight in a year than a three-year-old.

custard and not the crust. Or a separate dish of custard may be made for him when the filling for the pie is being prepared. On occasions when adults are served a menu that is not suitable for children, it is best not to call attention to the matter. But a casual explanation can be given if the child asks any questions as to why he is being served something different."

Concluding remarks

Toward the end of her work with the group, Mrs. Packard brought out three important points. She said that a family's responsibilities toward a child at mealtime consist of the following.

1. Providing him with a well-balanced diet

2. Guiding his progress in learning to eat foods that are good for him

3. Making it easy for him to establish his own satisfying eating habits

Presenting Some of the Experiences with Children

The students' experiences in helping children enjoy foods that are good for them varied. Not everyone in the class had a brother or sister from two to six years of age. But by including the play-school children, all of the students were able to get some experience in helping young children enjoy foods that are good for them.

Mrs. Rawlins and Mrs. Packard were very helpful in working out the situations at home where an eating problem had developed. In these experiences and in others that involved the prevention of eating problems, the cooperation of the whole family was enlisted. In a number of instances, very satisfying results were eventually reported. However, space does not permit a full account of all the home — and school — experiences of Miss Reed's class.

Helping a young sister

The one example of a home experience given here shows how Lucile planned to help her little sister make an adjustment. Lucile's report is not included. But the child was able to make the adjustment satisfactorily, and no eating problem developed.

LUCILE'S PLAN

THE SITUATION: My three-year-old sister, Joan, is going to begin having her evening meal with the family.

What I can do to be helpful

1. I can try to have Joan come to the table feeling happy and relaxed. Since she plays hard, this will probably mean allowing plenty of time for washing, tidying up, and resting before mealtime. We can look at pictures or listen to music on records.

2. I can see that Joan is comfortable at the table.
a. That her chair is the right height
b. That her feet rest on something hard, such as a footstool
c. That she has equipment which is easy to manage
d. That she has a large bib to protect her clothing

e. That there is something under her chair and at her place in case she spills some of the food

3. I can help Joan to enjoy foods that are good for her.

a. By helping my mother plan well-balanced meals

b. By arranging with my mother to have some foods each meal that Joan likes; by not having too many foods at a meal that are not good for Joan; and by taking out for Joan portions of foods that are to be too highly seasoned for her to eat

c. By arranging with my father, who does the serving, to give Joan small portions. He can explain that she may have more if she wants it.

d. By asking the family to agree not to comment on *what* or *how* Joan eats, and by letting her set her own pace at eating

e. By suggesting to the family that they avoid expressing personal food dislikes

4. I can do my part to make the meal a pleasant occasion.

a. By showing that I enjoy the food that is being served

b. By bringing up only pleasant topics of conversation

c. By setting an example of good table manners

5. We can ask for advice and assistance if any special eating problems arise.

Serving lunch at the play school

While the students were working out plans for helping young children at mealtime, Wendy had offered a suggestion that appealed to everyone.

"Let's serve a luncheon to the children in the play school," she said. "Since our regular class period comes just before noontime, it will be especially easy for us to get things ready."

"That's a wonderful idea," said Marshall. "It will give us excellent experience in guiding children at mealtime as well as in selecting foods to tempt them."

"There is an advantage too in having children who feel at ease when we are around," added Beatrice. "It will make the meal more homelike than it would be with another group of children who don't know us so well."

"Oh, do you suppose we can do it?" "Will the mothers let the children stay?" These and other comments indicated much interest in the idea. When Miss Reed said she thought arrangements could be worked out, the students happily set about to find ways of doing so. Eventually plans were made and carried out for using this experience as the final part of the classwork on the second goal.

The menu which the students planned and served was as follows:

Cream of Tomato Soup
(Book 1, page 191)
Assorted Finger Sandwiches
(Book 1, pages 211–212)
Carrot Sticks
(Book 1, page 197)
Baked Custard
(Book 1, pages 198–199)
Mock Sponge Cupcakes
(Book 2, page 197)
Milk

Serving a luncheon to play-school children is a worth-while experience.

Several students volunteered to make out the market order and to arrange with Miss Reed for purchasing the necessary supplies. In working out the preparation schedule, the class divided into five groups. One group was responsible for preparing the soup and the carrot sticks. Another group made the sandwiches and arranged for serving the milk. Two other groups baked the custards and the small sponge cakes. The fifth group set the tables, using those in the play-school room where the luncheon was served.

For the serving schedule, two students sat with the children at each of the four tables. Then four other students served, one at each table. The remaining students observed and were in charge of the cleanup details. The selections for this schedule were made on a voluntary basis, each student selecting the activity in which experience was most needed.

At the next meeting of the class after the luncheon, the various groups reported on the activities in which they had participated. Some of the high lights of the luncheon were as follows:

- The children said the tomato soup was yummy. There was scarcely a spoonful left in any dish.

- The size and shape of the finger sandwiches made a big appeal. It didn't seem to matter what the filling was. This pleased the students, who had put considerable thought into choosing the fillings. The carrot sticks were delightfully crunchy.

- The red cherry on top of the custard and the colored crinkled-paper containers in which the cupcakes were baked certainly gave the meal a party atmosphere.

- Although the children were excited, they ate fairly well. At first Frank pushed aside his custard and milk. But when he noticed how much his friend Billy was enjoying his dessert, he ate all of the custard and finished his milk with gusto. Several others ate so many sandwiches that they did not have room for the cupcakes. This made them sad until Mrs. Rawlins suggested to the students who were serving that the cakes be wrapped in paper napkins so that the children could take them home. Judy enjoyed her soup but did not want very much more. Instead she spent most of her time crumbling her sandwich rather than eating it. After the luncheon was over, Dwight brought the small broom and dustpan to Judy. He didn't need to say a word about cleaning up. Judy knew what she was expected to do.

• The serving was skillfully done, quietly and efficiently, without any fuss or confusion. Even though the group doing the serving had been in and out of the room, they were able to observe a number of points about the children's behavior.

• Miss Reed complimented the group doing the cleanup at the end of the luncheon. Not only had they done a good job then, but they had quietly observed what was going on during the luncheon. And they had made themselves helpful here and there.

CLASS MEMO:
What are some of the problems you have observed in getting young children to enjoy foods that are good for them? How will you handle these situations?

PLANNING YOUR CLASSWORK IN UNDERSTANDING CHILDREN

THE two goals which Miss Reed's group carried out in learning to enjoy young children proved to be very gratifying. The experiences in the play school gave the students an understanding of children which would have been difficult to acquire simply by reading and discussing books or other source materials. In fact, their experiences in handling children in the play school served as a good background for the goal on helping children enjoy foods that are good for them. It seemed to give the students a better idea of children's needs and desires, and why they behave as they do.

Of course, there are various ways of learning to understand and to enjoy young children. Instead of a play school, you might arrange to work with children at such places as a playground, a church nursery school for small children whose parents are attending the church service, or a neighborhood play project where mothers take turns looking after young children. These and other ways are certain to yield valuable experiences.

In helping children learn to eat foods that are good for them, you may want to use a different approach from the one Miss Reed's students followed. It really does not matter how you approach your work so long as you achieve the goal you have set up.

SUGGESTED EXPERIENCES

ANY goal can be worked out in a number of ways, depending upon the personal needs and interests of members of your group. But it is sometimes helpful to have suggestions that will point out possible ways of making the classwork stimulating and helpful. With this idea in mind, your class may be able to use some of the following experiences.

1. In making plans for your classwork, several committees might be appointed to find out possible ways in which group experience with young children could be obtained. These possibilities could then be discussed by the class from various angles. For example, how much time and expense it would take for advance preparations, and whether transportation would be a problem are some of the points that would need to be considered. If a choice is made of one of these ways, detailed plans can then be set up and carried out.

2. Your class may want to make an observation sheet for use over a period of time in gaining a better understanding of small children. You may want to make an adaptation of the one used by Miss Reed's group shown on pages 463 to 464, or work out a different plan.

3. It may be very helpful to set up a "Code of Student Behavior" in connection with matters relating to your classwork with children. For example, the code could start out something like this:

• Do not discuss a child in his presence or hearing.

• Refrain from careless criticism and unkind comments about any of the children.

• Avoid any discussion outside the classroom of individual children and their behavior. If a parent asks for a report about a child you are working with, refer the parent to your teacher.

4. Members of the class might like to discuss group-play situations which they have observed. Such points as who was the leader, what role the other children took, what feelings the children seemed to be expressing, and what satisfactions resulted could be brought out. It might also be helpful to know the answers to the following questions. Were the children dependent in any way upon adults in this particular play situation? If certain kinds of behavior occurred, such as anger, fear, unusual aggressiveness, or lack of cooperation, how they were handled? How long did group play last? What caused it to end?

5. Your class might want to set up a list of toys and equipment that can be made without cost. For example, vari-

ous size rag dolls can be constructed from scraps of material, and stuffed with clipped rags, curled paper, or sawdust. The features can be embroidered with small pieces of colored yarn. Doll equipment can be made of cardboard, wooden boxes, or fruit crates. Wheels from discarded toys, old window-shade rollers, and broom handles can be used for various parts. The articles can be painted from a leftover can of paint. Common clay can be obtained near streams or where bricks are made. It can be kept moist in a covered earthenware jar or a rust-proof metal container.

6. If you are especially interested in blockbuilding as a learning situation in a play school, you might suggest ways of enriching block play. For example, strips of colored oilcloth could be provided for use as streets, parks, or rivers. Or a discarded bicycle pump, a short length of garden hose, some old wheels, and various other items could be obtained without expense. A mechanically minded child might use them to equip a gas or fire station built out of blocks.

7. Suggesting simple equipment that can be used for a child to release pent-up feelings may be very valuable to the child and to you in your guiding experiences.

8. During one of the discussion periods, it might be helpful to list several ways in which members of the class could help a child feel more secure and self-confident. One area might be in improved muscular coordination, another in getting along with other children. Several ways in which children who tend to play alone can learn to partici-

pate with others might also be suggested. For example, an easel with room for two children would provide for social as well as creative experiences. Or a store setup in which small articles are exchanged for toy money would be another way of encouraging group participation.

9. Members of your class who have had experience with an individual child who needed special attention may be interested in suggesting how to handle the following group situations.

SITUATION 1: Several children have built a garage with blocks. For some time they have been bringing in trucks and cars to be repaired, telling excitedly how they were wrecked. Suddenly one of the children accidentally hits the garage and the blocks begin to fall. Then bedlam takes the place of play.

SITUATION 2: It is a rainy Monday morning after a holiday week end. The children are restless and noisy, going from one activity to another without much satisfaction. Occasionally there is shouting and screaming.

10. Several students may want to make a list of books that would be interesting to a group of preschool children. The list might start with the following:
Anderson, Clarence, *Blaze and the Forest Fire.* New York: The Macmillan Company, 1938
Bemelmans, Ludwig, *Madeline.* New York: Simon and Schuster, Inc., 1939
Flack, Marjorie, *Angus and the Ducks.* New York: Doubleday and Company, Inc., 1930
Gág, Wanda, *Nothing at All.* New York: Coward-McCann, Inc., 1941
Several other students may enjoy making a list of records for the record

player. Such a list might include the following.

Bach, *Air on G String*
Brahms, *Cradle Song*
Mozart, "Turkish March" from *Sonata in A Major*
Tchaikovsky, *Nutcracker Suite*

When the list of books and records is completed, they can be checked by a nursery- or play-school teacher for suitability.

11. Students who enjoy storytelling can write several original stories for children of different ages. The stories can then be evaluated by other members of the class on the basis of interest and understanding. Arrangements can be made to tell the stories at a nursery school, at a play school, or at a kindergarten. Or they may be used at home or when a student is baby-sitting. But before the stories are told by the students, it might be helpful to listen to several children's records by gifted readers and storytellers.

12. Several members of your class may volunteer to listen to a week's programs planned for small children on the radio or television. The students can take notes and report their reactions to the class. Constructive criticisms can be offered, and those that seem particularly helpful may be passed on to the broadcasting stations.

13. Compiling a list of suggestions for clothing that is easy for a preschool child to manage may be very worth while. The information may be obtained from the students' personal experiences with children, from consulting various references, from visiting stores, and from pattern magazines. The list could also include suggestions for ease of care. Enough copies could be made for the parents of the children you are working with, or for distribution to the mothers of a Parent-Teacher Association group. The list might include such items as the following.

- A decorative motif on the front of each garment makes it easy for a child to tell front from back.

- Front fastenings on garments are easy for a child to handle.

- A single large button — or a few large ones conveniently placed — is easier than a row of tiny ones.

- Clothing that is large and roomy — but not clumsy — permits more freedom of action than tight-fitting garments. Raglan sleeves permit long reaches and allow for growth.

- Simple step-in panties with elastic — not too tight — at the waist are easy to manage. So are those with a front yoke and elastic across the back. A simple one-piece combination garment with a front closing and a slide-loop belt to hold a drop seat in place is also easy to manage. (See the illustration below.)

Notice how the slide loop-belt allows the seat to drop.

- Simple one-piece styles that open out flat are not only more comfortable, but are also easier to iron.

14. Members of your class may want to do further work on recreation for a young child who is ill. Using the suggestions on pages 236 to 237, other reference sources, and your knowledge of young children, you might work out various plans that can be used in your own home or in a neighbor's home. The class might make summaries on activities for a child who must remain in bed, and for a child who is able to be up and about the house. Whether or not various activities proved to be more popular with boys or with girls might also be of interest.

15. Some members of the class may want to learn more about adapting family dinners to meet the needs and interests of a small brother or sister. These students could set up several dinner menus that are customarily served at home. Then they could indicate the changes that need to be made for the foods to be given to the child. The menus and their changes could be discussed by the class. An example of a menu adapted to meet the needs and interests of a small child might be as follows:

Menu
Swiss Steak
Baked Potato   Broccoli
Tossed Salad
Muffins   Butter
Baked Custard   Cookies
Milk   Coffee

Adaptations for the child
Small serving of meat
Potato mashed without skin
Only flowerets of broccoli
Carrot sticks instead of salad
Toast with butter
Dessert as desired
Milk

16. Holding a "How Would You Handle the Situation?" session may prove very interesting. You might start off with the following situations, and add others of your own choosing.

SITUATION 1: One day four-year-old Nancy refused to eat her supper. She deliberately poured some of her milk on the floor. Then she began to play with the meat and vegetables on her plate.

SITUATION 2: Five-year-old Dennis has been losing his appetite at mealtime. His parents believe this may be due to eating too much candy between meals. They want to curb his candy-eating habit. But they want to do so in a way which will upset him least.

17. Planning special ways to encourage children's interest in eating foods that are good for them may be a worthwhile class experience. For example, one student showed ingenuity by playing "restaurant" with her seven-year-old sister, Mary. The student cut colored pictures of foods in a balanced diet from magazines and put them in the restaurant kitchen, ready to serve. She used a sheet of paper for the menu, printing the names of the different foods to be served and a price for each. Paper money was cut from cardboard, and a cigar box served as a cash register. A large box was used for a table and smaller boxes for chairs. A cloth was spread on the table, and a centerpiece of flowers was added. The student showed Mary to her seat, poured a glass of water, and handed her the menu. As Mary called off different foods, the student wrote them down on a slip of paper. Then she took the slip to the kitchen and brought back pictures of the food on a tray. When

the meal was over, the student added up the amount, and Mary paid the bill, leaving a tip. When a day's meals had been ordered, they were checked according to "The Health Chain of Good Eating." (See pages 84–85.) Needless to say, Mary's interest in eating foods that were good for her was decidedly increased at mealtime.

18. Several members of your class may want to make arrangements to observe meals chosen by school-age children in a school cafeteria. Any evidence of poor eating habits may indicate the need for an improvement campaign. Various posters depicting a balanced diet, and the use of "The Health Chain of Good Eating" (see pages 84–85) may help to improve the situation.

INDEX

Index